Black flags and social movements

Manchester University Press

CONTEMPORARY ANARCHIST STUDIES

A series edited by
Laurence Davis, *University College Cork, Ireland*
Uri Gordon, *Loughborough University, UK*
Nathan Jun, *Midwestern State University, USA*
Alex Prichard, *Exeter University, UK*

Contemporary Anarchist Studies promotes the study of anarchism as a framework for understanding and acting on the most pressing problems of our times. The series publishes cutting-edge, socially engaged scholarship from around the world – bridging theory and practice, academic rigor and the insights of contemporary activism.

The topical scope of the series encompasses anarchist history and theory broadly construed; individual anarchist thinkers; anarchist informed analysis of current issues and institutions; and anarchist or anarchist-inspired movements and practices. Contributions informed by anti-capitalist, feminist, ecological, indigenous and non-Western or global South anarchist perspectives are particularly welcome. So, too, are manuscripts that promise to illuminate the relationships between the personal and the political aspects of transformative social change, local and global problems, and anarchism and other movements and ideologies. Above all, we wish to publish books that will help activist scholars and scholar activists think about how to challenge and build real alternatives to existing structures of oppression and injustice.

International Editorial Advisory Board:
Martha Ackelsberg, *Smith College*
John Clark, *Loyola University*
Jesse Cohn, *Purdue University*
Ronald Creagh, *Université Paul Valéry*
Marianne Enckell, *Centre International de Recherches sur l'Anarchisme*
Benjamin Franks, *University of Glasgow*
Judy Greenway, *Independent Scholar*
Ruth Kina, *Loughborough University*
Todd May, *Clemson University*
Salvo Vaccaro, *Università di Palermo*
Lucian van der Walt, *Rhodes University*
Charles Weigl, *AK Press*

Black flags and social movements

A sociological analysis of movement anarchism

Dana M. Williams

Manchester University Press

Copyright © Dana M. Williams 2017

The right of Dana M. Williams to be identified as the author of this work has been asserted by him in accordance with the Copyright, Designs and Patents Act 1988.

Published by Manchester University Press
Altrincham Street, Manchester M1 7JA
www.manchesteruniversitypress.co.uk

British Library Cataloguing-in-Publication Data

A catalogue record for this book is available from the British Library

ISBN 978 1 5261 0554 7 hardback
ISBN 978 1 5261 0555 4 paperback

First published 2017

First reprinted 2018

This work is licensed under the Creative Commons Attribution-Non-Commercial-ShareAlike 2.0 England and Wales License. Permission for reproduction is granted by the editors and the publishers free of charge for voluntary, campaign and community groups. Reproduction of the text for commercial purposes, or by universities or other formal teaching institutions is prohibited without the express permission of the publishers.

The publisher has no responsibility for the persistence or accuracy of URLs for any external or third-party internet websites referred to in this book, and does not guarantee that any content on such websites is, or will remain, accurate or appropriate.

Typeset
by Toppan Best-set Premedia Limited
Printed in Great Britain
by CPI Group (UK) Ltd, Croydon CR0 4YY

CONTENTS

FIGURES

TABLES

PREFACE: WHERE DOES ANARCHY BEGIN?

Black is negation, is anger, is outrage, is mourning, is beauty, is hope, is the fostering and sheltering of new forms of human life and relationship on and with the earth. The black flag means all of these things. We are proud to carry it, sorry we have to, and look forward to the day when such a symbol will no longer be necessary. (Howard J. Ehrlich)

The misperceived movement that doesn't exist?

This book aims to destroy many of the assumptions and stereotypes about anarchism, anarchists, and anarchist movements.[1] There is ample obscuring fog surrounding anarchism to disorient anyone in a web of unhelpful false assumptions, double-think, and libel. Those who wish to truly understand anarchism must labor to discard much of the popular "common sense" knowledge that many self-anointed experts (e.g., law enforcement officials and hostile journalists) possess and profligate. I argue that we are best served by maneuvering around and out-flanking such assumptions. Herein, an array of sociological tools – theories, methodologies, and analyses – are brought to bear on a movement that has possessed the worst possible reputation, since even before that movement existed in its modern form.

While many popular assumptions about anarchism are simply wrong (as demonstrated here), movement scholars – Americans in particular – seem wholly oblivious to the existence of anarchist movements. Only rarely are anarchists mentioned in American sociological studies of social movements and always in an indirect reference to their main subject matter. Indeed, even when contemplating highly anarchistic movements – such as the anti-capitalist wing of the global justice movement – many academic observers seem incapable of connecting the very obvious dots.

This intellectual deficit can be seen most clearly by surveying the premier English language academic journal dedicated to the study of social movements, called *Mobilization*. First published in 1997 to create a peer-reviewed journal within sociology and political science for the scholarly study of movements (where no such publishing venue existed before), *Mobilization* has attracted the subfield's biggest names and heaviest hitters. While the incestuous nature of the social movement subfield is itself a worthy topic for critical discussion, it is enough to note the preeminence of *Mobilization*. Thus, a movement that rejuvenated itself in the 1990s, and evolved in numerous ways, would presumably present a fascinating subject matter for the astute movement scholars of *Mobilization*. But, astonishingly, not a single article (of over 1,000 separate pieces) in the history of the journal – nearly two decades' worth and counting – focused on anarchism,[2] although dozens focused on small, locally specific movements.[3] The same paucity can be observed in the leading edited books of the subfield, whose chapters are written by the same prestigious scholars.[4]

Despite their willful avoidance of anarchist movements, these scholarly attempts to better understand social movements are important in many ways. First, they are cracking open the very difficult to understand – let alone predict – phenomena of social movements. Second, they respect and acknowledge the need for numerous methodological strategies; they use both qualitative and quantitative methods, ethnographic, content analysis, and statistical analysis of survey data. And many of the scholars are themselves dedicated to many progressive movements. Yet their approach has been to distance themselves in value-neutral language from their subjects. They study certain movements because those movements provide excellent examples of the specific abstract movement dynamics they wish to write about – not because those movements are themselves important for readers to know about. I suspect – but cannot prove – that this desire to be *objective*, to be *scholarly*, and to be *respectable*, is also what has kept their analytical focus away from one of the most unrespectable of movements: anarchism (that, and the reformist interests of these scholars, generally).[5]

It could be that movement scholars view anarchism as something other than a movement – perhaps a revolutionary tendency. But even the dynamics of contention theories (discussed in greater depth in Chapter 4), which incorporate revolutions into the study of movements, forgo the potential of analyzing anti-state movements. Scholars of revolution have themselves avoided opportunities to analyze anarchism, even in regards to some of the most widely studied revolutions, like the Spanish Revolution of the late-1930s, the Russian revolutions of 1905 and 1917, the Mexican Revolution, and others. The participation of anarchists within these revolutions – and most surprisingly, their anarchistic qualities – are simply skipped over and omitted. Even the prestigious studies by Barrington Moore (1972), Theda Skocpol (1979), and Pitirim Sorokin (1967) typically pass on critically analyzing anarchism. Moore (1972) dismisses anarchists in the Russian Revolution using the same argument of Marx and Engels (apparently missing Mikhail Bakunin's observations that rejected their now-falsifiable claims). And Sorokin's (1967) deep familiarity with anarchism during his own time in Russia is all the more puzzling given its absence in his work (see Jaworski 1993; Williams 2014). These scholarly blind-spots regarding anarchist participation in revolutions as diverse as the Russian, Spanish, and Chinese revolutions is curious, especially given the ample evidence of crucial anarchist contributions in each instance (e.g., Avrich 1967; Dirlik 1993; Peirats 2011).[6]

What should we conclude from the eerie absence of anarchism within the scholarly study of movements? A few possibilities – some of them just plain silly – exist: anarchist movements don't really exist or simply aren't movements, per se. Anarchist movements may be of only marginal significance and impact, and thus not worthy of mention. Or, anarchism may be consciously kept off academics' radar – movement scholars' radar, especially – owing to some sort of malevolent intent, discriminatory or ideological bias, inability to study, or intellectual lack of curiosity. Some of these reasons are less likely, while others are almost assured. Lacking actual evidence for the reasons for this absence of research, I can only speculate here on these possibilities.

Some scholars may assume that anarchist movements simply don't exist – any discussion of them is as circumstantial and absurd as discussing mythical creatures. Thus, if anarchist movements are *not real*, why study them? Even if anarchists themselves *are* real, they surely can't be part of movements – given their chaotic natures – and especially a wholly anarchist movement! To those with a strong belief in hierarchy, why not discount the sanity of anyone who chooses to resist hierarchy? Or, if individuals seem to be using anarchist slogans or symbology in the context of a movement (e.g., at a political march), the scholars may have concluded that we're not really seeing an anarchist movement, just other legitimate movements (such as squatters, radical queers, or revolutionary syndicalists) who have adopted anarchist symbols.

Other scholars may have decided that anarchist movements aren't movements. Since anarchists are widely assumed to be ultra-individualists, then large numbers of anarchists are just that – a random collection of individuals. They are not "social," they do not "move" together (and thus do not exist in movements), and the thought of organized anarchists is akin to imagining flying pigs. Thus, "anarchist movements" are nothing like other movements, so we ought to just think about groupings of anarchists as something else altogether.

Some movement students believe that only major movements are worthy of study. Anarchist movements seem to be of such marginal significance in the world – participants almost seem to be deliberately self-marginalizing. And, since anarchist movements lack broad visibility, they must be small in size. So, why study small, marginal movements? Why care about movements that also have almost no practical policy demands (assuming the slogan "abolish the state!" refers to an action-able policy)? Why consider movements that have so little policy impact on the world? Since policy is a major preoccupation of social scientists, why study something that is openly hostile toward state-based policy?

Scholarly avoidance may be linked to a general dislike of anarchism. Presumably, people with advanced degrees have been thoroughly socialized into dominant systems and within hierarchical institutions (like universities), thus making it difficult to appreciate anti-authoritarian movements. Most movements studied by scholars are reformist-oriented; the revolutionary aspirations of anarchism could be a potent turn-off. Likewise, anarchists may have annoyed these scholars in some way (e.g., criticized or thwarted movements they do like, been obstinate students in their classes, etc.), causing them to spurn the study of those radical movements. Anarchists also appear to most people to be too violent and chaotic to be a social movement worthy of study. For example, the movements most lionized in the USA – like the civil rights movement – are usually considered liberal, reform-oriented, and strictly nonviolent (incidentally, all of these widely believed stereotypes about the civil rights movement are, in various instances, easily disprovable).

The ability of scholars to study anarchism may be limited. In order to conduct interviews, gather surveys, or make observations, a scholar has to know some of their subjects or at least where they can be found. Even if anarchists were easy to locate, most scholars do not know any. Consequently, anarchists – who are legitimately concerned with spies and provocateurs (having been victims of them throughout their history) – may not trust those they don't know, especially people claiming to be "scholars" wanting to study them. Such intrusive people are apt to appear to anarchists as little different than an undercover cop intent upon tricking activists to commit thought-crimes. In order to properly study and understand anarchists, one has to be able to understand the guiding logic of anarchism, which is at odds with how most movements are organized – with charismatic leaders, lobbying directed at politicians, and reformist, system-preserving ideologies.

Finally, scholars may simply not care about anarchists. Other movements may appear – for personal, political, or professional reasons – to be more interesting and valuable. If a scholar lacks intellectual curiosity about a group of people, they are unlikely to study them in greater detail. If anarchists seem too oddball-ish or strange to understand, many observers may cease trying.

Whatever the reason for the scholarly silence, *Black flags and social movements* serves as a counter to the staggering silence from social movement researchers. In other words, this book thoroughly and conclusively disproves the above claims. Even though they are more ideologically diverse

than most comparable movements, I argue that it is still appropriate to refer
to "anarchist movements." This book attempts to gather together the scholarship that does exist, combine it with activist accounts of their movements,
and present new data and analysis that can help advance a realistic, interesting, and useful sociological accounting of anarchist movements.

So, why study anarchist movements? Many possible reasons exist. For
example, anarchism has become a key topic of discussion in the mass media
(while less so in academia), which has led to much intrigue. It has been,
and continues to be, feared by governments and policing agencies – or they
at least pretend to fear anarchism (see Borum & Tilby 2005 for a more
intellectual manifestation of these fears). Many young people have come to
be influenced by anarchism, arguably more than Marxism, the "Occupy"
movement being the best current example in the USA (Bray 2013: Schneider
2013: Williams 2011a). Finally, anarchism is having a noticeable impact on
contemporary politics, often via anarchists' participation in broader social
struggles.

The uses of sociology in the study of anarchist movements

In academic disciplines beyond sociology and the field of social movements,
"anarchism" and "anarchy" usually refer to conceptions that are entirely
theoretical, thus uncoupling anarchist movements from their historical and
contemporary context, and ignoring the use of the term "anarchism" by the
very activists who call themselves anarchists. Since this is a sociology book,
a case should be made for using sociology to study something like anarchism and anarchist social movements. First, sociology represents an established tradition, which has for decades (in Europe, North America, and
elsewhere) honed its sights upon social movements. In the process, multinational strands of sociology have generated a diverse and occasionally
contradictory set of analytical tools for the study of the phenomena, so
robust that some elders of the discipline, like Alain Touraine (1981) (con-
troversially) refer to as the core subject matter of sociology.[7] Successive
waves of theorizing have occurred, each either building on or demolishing
the old, or augmenting a previously incomplete picture. The methodological
strategies for generating these theories are equally diverse, involving numerous approaches. The diversity represented in sociology's study of social
movements represents – in microcosm – the poly-theoretical, poly-
epistemological, and poly-topical focus of the broader discipline itself. As
Michael Burawoy (2005) wrote in his scathing analysis of the discipline's
trajectory, sociology is analogous to (ironically, for this book's focus)

anarcho-syndicalism. By this, Burawoy meant that incredible decentralization, tolerance of difference, and autonomy exists in the discipline; the
different subject areas, paradigms, and types of scholars need not toe any
"party-line." Instead, sociologists can pursue their own interests and contribute to the overall whole as they see fit.[8] Sociology's diverse approaches
make it flexible and able to study topics as controversial and diverse as
anarchism.

Additionally, the sociological study of anarchist social movements makes
sense, as it has been sociology's historical mission to study all forms of social
organization. And, whatever one may think about anarchism, it is undeniable that anarchist's social organization is unique and worthy of a sociological eye. Needless to say, mainstream jokes about anarchist disorder or lack
of order are poorly informed, stereotype-dependent jokes. In fact, there is
substantial evidence that sociology and anarchism have far more in common
that many may assume (Williams 2014). The cross-over between early
sociologists and anarchists, and their frequently parsimonious focus upon
society suggest that sociologists may be the best breed of academically
trained scholars to study anarchist movements.

The compatibility between sociology and anarchism does not imply that
anarchists are unable to eruditely observe their own movements. Thus,
anarchists also may make solid arguments cautioning against entrusting the
study of their movements to professional sociologists. In fairness, there is
great merit in these concerns: sociology has often shown itself to be either
liberal in orientation or flagrantly in favor of status quo. Regardless of the
specific ideological orientations that sociologists adopt,[9] it is likely uncon-
troversial to state that most sociologists – especially American sociologists,
with whom I am most familiar – adopt anti-radical positions. Unsurprisingly (for anyone with a modicum of familiarity with political history),
Marxist sociologists are often the most hostile to anarchism, even though
they may superficially appear to have the most in common (among sociologists) with anarchists.

Others may note that sociology is still a *discipline*, which means it is
premised upon a limiting and bounding of knowledge, analysis, and interests. Martin (1998a) charges that the hierarchical nature of disciplines
themselves pose a threat to freedom within the academy – surely a substantial threat when studying a freedom-prioritizing movement like anarchism.
Disciplines – which have links to interest groups, value specialization, and
engage in internal and external power struggles – typically translate their
subject matter into objects for the purpose of study. While the entire purpose
of *Black flags and social movements* is to study anarchist movements, we
should be conscious of concerns that reducing such movements to mere
objects of study can also reduce – rather than enhance – their revolutionary
potential. As an author with deeply held sympathies with the anarchist

tradition – and on my good days, I'd call myself an anarchist – I should
express my personal concern that getting lost in the ivory tower of an academic discipline may mute a movement that I believe (and hope) has the
potential to radically transform a deeply troubled planet.

Compared to many other scholarly topics, work on anarchism has been
relatively scarce and academics have only recently increased their focus on
modern-day anarchism. Consequently, a research program that aspires to
achieve stronger ontological conclusions of, and greater practicality for,
anarchist movements has not been attempted with a sociological lens. So
far, most anarchist movement studies have been histories of particular
organizations (e.g., Direct Action, Angry Brigade, Iron Column, or Earth
First!), campaigns or episodes (e.g., anti-poll tax campaign, Spanish Revolution, or a specific series of protests), individuals (Gustav Landauer, Voltairine de Cleyre, Rudolf Rocker, or Ricardo Flores Magón), or focused in one
specific geographical space (e.g., the USA, Argentina, Britain, China, Spain,
or France). This book, however, focuses its analysis on anarchist social
movements generally.

Some academic studies have considered radical movements (especially
radical organizations – e.g., squatters, Weather Underground, the Black
Panther Party, Marxists guerrillas, etc.), but few have broadened their
analyses to include movements that transcended national borders. Many
comparative studies exist (e.g., comparing radical student movements in the
USA and Germany), but few try to consider global movements (although
this is changing with analyses on global justice movements – but most focus
remains on the reform/moderate tendencies within that movement).The
closest efforts made by academics in recent years (since the early 2000s) to
focus on anarchist movements seem to focus on the global justice movement
and the strong anarchist influence on its more radical (read: non-NGO-
based) sectors. Many studies have remarked on the anarchistic nature of
this movement (Epstein 2001; Graeber 2009; Juris 2008; Notes From
Nowhere 2003), but few have written about anarchism as an independent
dimension both within and outside of that movement (this is a relative
observation, not an absolute one).

An international community of anarchist scholars has grown since the
1990s, leading to the founding of the British peer-reviewed journal *Anarchist Studies*, a grant-giving foundation for anarchist research called the
Institute for Anarchist Studies, occasional theoretical conferences like
Renewing the Anarchist Tradition, various online forums for anarchist
academics, and other projects (including the Anarchist Studies Network in
the UK and the North American Anarchist Studies Network). The ASN and
NAASN have held semi-regular conferences, which gather participants from
across dozens of countries, with varied scholarly and activist backgrounds.
Yet, the English-speaking academy has rarely studied the anarchist movement itself as a social movement. Further, even more so than qualitative

analyses, quantitative research – that involving numerical estimation – on the current anarchist movement's composition, beliefs, and current political activities, has been almost non-existent.

What is anarchism?

This is not a book about the social, economic, and political philosophy of anarchism, per se. Instead, *Black flags and social movements* focuses on anarchist movements. Our subject here is the organized expressions of anarchism. But since the entire book is about anarchist movements, a few initial words about anarchism will help.

The word "anarchism" is typically used to refer to stateless societies. Thus, to be an anarchist means to oppose the existence of the state. However, anarchism entails so much more than this myopic, dictionary definition.[10] Anarchists generally critique many things beyond just the state, in fact, anything with "rulers." Most anarchists consider "anarchism" to be an opposition to rulers, not all of existent social order – although "anti-civilization" anarchists exist, too. Earlier in the nineteenth century, anarchist opposition centered on the newly solidifying nation-states of Europe, but also on industrial capitalism and organized religion. These three dominant institutions wielded enormous political, economic, and cultural power over Europe at the time. Anarchism existed as a counter-hegemonic reference point and ideology, adopted by single individuals often, until it grew into an active movement. The influence of the Russian Mikhail Bakunin was crucial in this, helping to unite various Proudhonian, collectivist, and anti-authoritarian factions within the First International (Graham 2015). Anarchism grew as an ideological competitor to classical liberalism – which also sought greater freedoms – but which was more preoccupied with the independence of the bourgeoisie class, and thus did not care as much about the accompanying economic inequality created by capitalism.

Marxism and social democracy were also ideological competitors to anarchism; while they agreed about capitalism's injustice and the need to create a more equal, socialist society, Marxists and anarchists disagreed about the role of the state. Marxists and social democrats wished to *use* the state to create socialism (and communism), while the anarchists thought that impossible, since political elites (whether capitalist or pro-socialist) would not like to give up their power. Bakunin assessed this confluence of political anti-authoritarianism and economic Leftism – and captured the essence of anarchist thought – when he famously, and succinctly, stated: "liberty without socialism is privilege, injustice; and [...] socialism without liberty is slavery and brutality" (Maximoff 1953: 297).[11] This interpretation has been echoed by many others who have tried to categorize the major

Table 0.1   Ideologies of the twentieth century

	High equality		
Low state power	Anarchism	Communism	High state power
	Libertarianism	Fascism	
	Low equality		

Adapted from Chirot (1986: 145).

ideologies of the nineteenth and twentieth centuries, including sociologist
Daniel Chirot. As shown in Table 0.1, Chirot (1986) classified anarchism
– in contrast to communism, fascism, and libertarianism – as valuing low
state power, but high equality.[12]

Anarchists (and Bakunin) were kicked out of the First International by
Marx's supporters (who then cynically moved the organization to the USA
to distance it from the influence of European anarchists – a move that
effectively killed the International). But, from this point on, the anarchism
encountered by most people (regardless of country) was within the context
of the revolutionary labor movement. Anarchism became deeply embedded
in the working class's intellectual analysis of capitalism and its strategies
for combating capitalism (direct action). It is difficult to differentiate most
anarchists of this "classic period" from other members of the revolutionary
labor movement.[13] After leaving the International, anarchism goes international. While heavily concentrated in Europe, it also appealed to workers
in many poorer countries, including Mexico, Argentina, China, and Ukraine.

Anarchist philosophy is often identified at the intersection of its ends
and means. Anarchists generally oppose hierarchy, competition, and domination, and instead support efforts of horizontalism, cooperation, and self-
management. These goals can be viewed as dialectical. But the means
through which this opposition and support are pursued must be consistent
with the ends. Thus, the methods utilized to pursue a society free of hierarchy, competition, and domination ought to be just, empowering, potentially collaborative (not top-down), and democratic. It would be illogical
(and philosophically inconsistent) to have bosses within anarchist organizations. Anarchists' opposition to Marxist strategies stem from Marxism's
misalignment of ends and means; it is inappropriate to create a world free
of oppressive authority figures by using the state – a major institution of
oppressive power – to eradicate oppressive authority.

Anarchism is very social – and thus, as Jeff Shantz and I have argued
(Williams & Shantz 2011), highly compatible with sociological analysis –
since it considers the problems (and alternatives) that humans face to be
rooted in social structures and institutions. For example, inequality does
not result from the random behavior of individuals, nor does violence occur

just because of a few "bad people." Most modern societies are organized – deliberately, consciously, and for the benefit of some – with hierarchy, competition, and domination as their core. For example, George W. Bush (or Barack Obama or Donald Trump) are not the problems (by themselves), as they are mere representatives of an unjust, violent, and undemocratic American state. This does not mean that anarchists let Bush or Obama personally "off the hook," since it is "the system" that is ultimately responsible for inequality and violence. Instead, anarchists advocate for looking to the individual instances of "bad things," but also remembering that they are not isolated anecdotes. Consequently, it should perhaps not surprise people that C. Wright Mills, who coined the term "the sociological imagination" to help people connect their personal troubles to social issues, was himself strongly sympathetic to anarchism.[14]

Early notes of caution for anarchist subject matter

It is crucial to acknowledge a triumvirate of misperceptions about anarchism: chaos, violence, and fantasy. Allow me to explore each of these three misperceptions in greater detail below.

First, anarchism is associated with chaos. As any dictionary can confirm, the word "anarchy" is routinely used as a synonym for disorder, confusion, and anti-logic. This assumption is likely why many people are surprised to discover that an *organized* and self-conscious anarchist movement exists (see how often people ask, "How could there be anarchist organizations if anarchists are against order?"). This is perhaps the oldest and most cynical misperception about anarchism. The framing of anarchism as chaotic stems from: (1) the belief that a social order lacking hierarchical leadership is no order at all, and (2) the observation that anarchists (as radicals opposed to the existing order) would stop at nothing to up-end that order and replace it with something else.

Since the anarchist alternative was usually open-ended, the anarchist future looked chaotic to many observers. To believe this misperception requires us to ignore numerous, central characteristics of anarchist movements. By avoiding these facts, the chaos misperception is allowed to persist. First, anarchist movements *do* possess order. Anarchists belong to organizations (despite jokes to the contrary)[15] and these memberships are not oxymoronic. Second, anarchists make decisions. Although it may appear that anarchists are always spontaneous actors, doing whatever emotions move them to do at any given moment, most anarchist actions are premeditated, and decided upon, or prepared for, in some kind of collectivity. Thus, third, anarchists are deliberate. They do not act without reason or purpose. Even things that appear to be senseless (smashing the window of a chain store, graffiting a wall, or blocking the traffic on a busy road), are in fact saturated with meaning, intent, and rationality. Finally, although the chaos frame suggests otherwise, anarchists are highly conscious. Not only do anarchists tend to be thoughtful, engaged, and (in many cases) well-read, they also are highly aware of their surroundings and the ramifications of their actions (as this book continually demonstrates). Anyone who has witnessed internal anarchist movement debate over things of concern to anarchist values (e.g., veganism, property destruction, decision-making rules, the role of vanguards, etc.), know well the degree to which anarchists regularly engage with their individual and collective consciousnesses.

By ignoring the contradictions and omissions of evidence with the chaos misperception, a fear of anarchists is generated. Much of this fear is abstract, and portrays anarchists as "crazy," incapable of rational thought or predictability. Critics who encounter anarchists who say they have formed an organization are likely to scoff at this claim and dismiss them as deluded. All of this will imply that people who wish to act collectively in the world must either place their faith in authoritarian leaders, or at the least form organizations whose leaders who will help to steer change.

Second, to many, the word "anarchy" implies violence (Monaghan & Walby 2012).[16] Consequently, anarchists are perceived as dangerous, aggressive, and possibly terrorists. ("How could you honestly trust someone who *calls themselves* an anarchist?") Allegedly, the dog-eat-dog approach of anarchism throws every individual against each other in a crazed fight for bloody domination. To believe that anarchists are inherently violent requires either great confusion or self-delusion. Begin with radical feminists' assertion that governments are the most dangerous gangs of violent men. Consequently, all those who have directed states throughout history, whether they identified as democrats or Democrats, republicans or Republicans, fascists or Marxists, social democrats or autocrats, have all relied upon violence. Sociologists in particular cannot forget Weber's key observation that the state holds the monopoly on violence; the evidence can be witnessed in murderous wars, incarceration of citizens, and symbolic and actual violence against people. Thus, to associate "anarchist" with "violence" misses the most obvious of contradictions: when the state uses violence, it is simply *being the state*; but when others, especially anarchists, use force (not even violence), they are acting criminally. This contradiction thus ignores the regularly stated goals of peace and justice sought by anarchists (note that these two are joined-requisites, one must accompany the other – thus the chant "No justice? No peace!"). The anarchist opposition to state violence (e.g., anti-imperialism) clearly shows its opposition to the most extreme and destructive forms of violence. Then, the violence that is associated with anarchists in the past was the isolated act of *attentats* against rulers[17] or today of self-defense against police. Even if such acts *are* violent, they are

of a different caliber than hierarchical forms of violence. Except for pacifists, few today would argue that to kill Hitler and avert the genocide and
madness of World War II (granted, with considerable hindsight) would not
have been a sensible act of *anti*-violence.

By propagating the misperception of anarchist violence – mainly by
refusing to compare the violence used by the powerful and the out-of-power
– police violence against protesters is justified. Media can show images of
unarmed protesters "fighting" riot police who have large arsenals of
weapons, but also plainly claim "protester violence" caused police *response*,
even when the opposite is usually true. This all reinforces the perceived
"need" for the state to intervene in society's madness – which it contributes
to and manages – and "protect" citizens from each other. Thus, the claim
that we need police and their violence to prevent us from killing and robbing
each other.

And third, even though many may appreciate anarchist ideas, it is often
dismissed as fantasy ("yes, a world without bosses does sound nice, but be
realistic!"). Consequently, to identify as an anarchist is to be naive, utopian,
to have one's head in the clouds, and to be foolishly ignorant of "human
nature." This may be the most serious misperception (although it appears
to be the most benign), since it means anarchism is rejected as being child-
ish, poorly thought-out, or absurd. Consequently, this misperception is
incredibly devastating to anarchist movements in the long run. Chaos and
violence myths prevent short-term goals from being achieved and others
from joining the movement.

But the notion of anarchist fantasy permanently stalls the potential for
anarchism altogether. Those who believe in another world, one without
hierarchy, are clearly delusional, according to this misperception. However,
this myth ignores a number of key realities to anarchist movements. First,
anarchism is notoriously practical, going so far as to provide for the most
essential provisions. Consider Food Not Bombs' catering protest events; this
is not fantastical, but a practical acknowledgement that people get hungry,
and that movements ought to and *can* provide for themselves and others.
Second, anarchists are actually prefiguring the world they would like to live
in through their actions. In other words, they do not simply make lofty
statements about what kind of world should exist in the future or what
they should do, but instead try to do it right now in the present. If they can
make it work on a small-scale basis, it demonstrates the potential for entire
societies to be organized differently. Third, these conscious projects and
actions convey a reasonableness that is alleged to be absent from anarchist
movements. Finally, it is rather obvious that change *does* occur and that
most past changes have been considered ludicrous to many people before
those changes happened. Consider the fall of American slavery. Of course,
the systems of racial dictatorships and domination were slow to be completely dismantled (and they still persist in impressive ways), but slavery

was *officially* ended. How many Americans in the late 1850s (even within the Abolitionist movement) actually thought that possible? Yet, it happened. Or consider the Russian Revolution of 1917 or the worldwide revolutionary movements of 1968. Who could have expected that these uprisings would occur when and where they did?

The ultimate consequence of the fantasy misperception is that is dismisses, out of hand, anarchist values. While these values may sound attractive to many people – most publicly or secretly crave and favor the ideas of freedom, solidarity, and self-management – they also appear naive and absurdly optimistic. Thus, the core of anarchist ideology is presented as contrary to "human nature," which is itself proposed as selfish, individualistic, and aggressive. Of course, these expressions of human behavior are also part of our nature, but they are not the only potential expression of our humanness. Most of our lives are lived via norms of solidarity with others (especially our families and friends). Anarchism acknowledges the Janus-faced qualities of human nature, thus encouraging skepticism of those in power, but encouraging optimism towards all others (this is the essential observation made at the end of Chapter 7). Anarchism is inherently pragmatic and cognizant of human nature, which is why it prioritizes an array of values that might appear internally contradictory (e.g., solidarity with others *and* self-management).

This triumvirate – chaos, violence, and fantasy – or at least one element of it, is usually present whenever anarchist subjects – whether topical or personified – are discussed.[18] These misperceptions find their way into media, history books, and the mouths of everyday people who repeat the same narrative everyone else has told them.[19] This book goes beyond such "common knowledge" to explore the values, beliefs, actions, and goals of anarchists. It quickly becomes clear that the triumvirate is a sophisticated smokescreen that makes understanding anarchist movements almost impossible and undoubtedly makes people unlikely to support and join them. Like all propagandistic distortions, these misperceptions ignore key facts that would refute their claims. And the repetition of these misperceptions throughout societies cause very specific consequences that adversely affect anarchist movements' opportunities for increased success.

However, as the saying goes, even stereotypes often contain kernels of truth. Anarchists do embrace decentralization and what often looks like "chaos," even inviting a healthy measure of unpredictability, spontaneity, and catharsis. Also, many anarchists advocate "self-defense," which, in societies enamored by "mythos" of nonviolent social movements, sounds almost like a call to war. Even more, other anarchists advocate or at least defend positions of armed struggle or civil war. (Of course, few who might hear such advocacy will be able to comprehend its meaning without seriously considering the arguments that these anarchists will surely provide.) And finally, some anarchists are utopians (although usually practical ones, too), and most are "dreamers" who wish to see a better world. This does not make them unrealistic, although the world they envision and try to create might *sound crazy* to others.

In the interests of fairness, we should ask whether other movements or systems of thought are also linked to these same stereotyped outcomes – chaos, violence, fantasy. Would representative-democrats really be honest enough to admit that their system requires massive violence, through police, prisons, and armies? (And comparatively, whose violence is more widespread, indiscriminate, and vicious – the *behaviors* of nation-states or that which activists are alleged to *argue for*?)[20] Would capitalists admit the sheer fantasy inherent in a "self-regulating market"? Or would they be willing to acknowledge the indiscernible chaos it causes internationally or the violence necessary to enforce these "markets"? In other words, if incriminating accusations are going to be made, following the lead of Zinn (1997), is it not worth asking: when the most powerful institutions in modern society – militaries, multinational corporations, and states – call anarchists chaotic, violent, and naive, is this merely an example of the pot calling the kettle black?

Authorship and readership

I'm a sociologist and I study social movements. I teach classes on social movements. But, just as importantly, I've participated in social movements. And for all the movements I have participated in (both deeply and superficially), many have inspired me. Towards the top of that list is one of the more challenging to define, complicated to interpret, and one that wears a scarlet letter: anarchism.

I wanted to know how I could better understand the anarchist movement, a movement I value and want to succeed more often. Thus, I have a large stake in the humble results of this book. This doesn't mean I write as a propagandist who will twist facts to glorify anarchism. I do not think it serves the movement to overlook its shortcomings and its blemishes. If we care about someone or something, we don't mislead others about it, but we speak honestly. More personally, I have been involved in some of the activities described here. Most academics and writers would admit as much in their more honest moments: we often write about that which is most dear and within our own experience.

Like many sociologists receiving their PhDs after the 1960s, I and numerous others of my generation were influenced by the radical social movements that we participated in. Marxists, feminists, anti-imperialists, and other radicals started their "long march through the institutions" (consciously or not), including American higher education, earning the highest

degrees available to them in various social science and humanities disciplines, including sociology. It was almost a foregone conclusion that
the movements that were having such a dramatic impact upon American
politics, culture (and subcultures), and daily life, would eventually trickle
into the academy. For me and other young scholars, the radical movements
of the 1990s and early 2000s were a source of political and intellectual
engagement.

Of course, we and many others take inspiration from the exciting and
dramatic events around us, the movements we helped to create and participated in. For us, the highly educated – and some might say (not necessarily
incorrectly) the over-educated – we have taken that inspiration into our
classrooms and graduate programs. Some have made these movements the
topics of their term papers, their classroom discussions, even their theses
and dissertations. All this activity augments – but in no way substitutes –
the activities that take place in the streets, the meetings, community campaigns and project, and informal conversations of movements.

Exactly which audiences could benefit from this analysis? I see two
primary audiences: sociologists and anarchists. Sociologists could benefit
from a critical analysis of these unique and under-studied movements.
Beyond the subject matter itself, sociologists will also likely have their theoretical perspectives challenged by a radical movement that does not conform
to typical expectations and goals. Liberal and reform movements – the
subject of most scholarly research on movements – do not follow trajectories that are similar to anarchist movements. Some sociology instructors
may see value in using this text within a social movements course, while
most will hopefully find scholarly interest in it.

Anarchists are another obvious audience for this book. Radical activists
have done far more critical exploration of their own movements than scholars, owing to their intense stake in movement outcomes. Still, this book
offers a unique analysis, very different from those typically generated by
anarchist movements. I offer an explicitly sociological viewpoint; while
many anarchists are implicitly sociological in their analysis, fewer have
training in the epistemological tools of social inquiry or familiarity with
sociological concepts that could inform their political work. Many anarchists have a seemingly intuitive sociological sensibility (perhaps due to
schooling or movement activity), but this sensibility is usually not self-
conscious or reflexive. For example, most anarchists are probably unfamil-
iar with sociological social movement theories, which could provide strategic
assistance. This book attempts to emphasize and re-characterize discussions
of anarchist movements as sociological.

I think many anarchists who have an interest in engaging in sociological
social movement theories will happily take on the task of reading a work
that appears to address a mainly university audience. I think this is in line
with much of the writing being produced under the label or rubric of

"anarchist studies" today – generated largely by academics and written for college audiences (including students), but meant to be accessible to wider groups of readers, including movement activists.

I would like this book to be a provocation. By thinking of issues outside the usual frames of reference, we can grow – or at least be challenged to grow. Activists rarely engage with social science scholarship. Its topical selection seem irrelevant, its theories esoteric, and its analysis unhelpful. Sociologists often believe that they can operate in academia's bubble, not worry about the consequences of their scholarship, and study that which amuses them but whose impact is indeterminate. Instead, I think we can actively participate in studying, articulating, *and* participating in actions that will create a more just, equal, and liberatory world.

I hope both anarchists and sociologists read this book. As my co-author Jeff Shantz and I wrote in our introductory chapter in *Anarchy & Society*, these two parties can learn from each other. They don't have to become best friends – and they probably won't – but they can develop a mutual appreciation for things of shared importance, which may contribute to the construction of anarchist-sociology – or, better still, the construction of a better world.

About this book's methodology

The book includes a broad, multifaceted analysis. Data is collected from multiple levels, involving many units of analysis, using and testing many theoretical perspectives, and interrogating a smörgåsbord of topical subjects pertinent to anarchist movements. I use data gathered from quite a few unexamined movement sources (multiple surveys of anarchists and other activists, movement news stories, the Anarchist Yellow Pages directory and International Blacklist), as well as providing a re-analysis of existing movement documents and interviews. The analysis involves a wide array of quantitative and qualitative techniques, including content analysis, historical analysis, means testing, associational statistics, and geographic mapping. While each chapter uses one or two of the above, they are orchestrated to mutually reinforce each other and to triangulate across chapters. We can thus interrogate the anarchist movement from many vantage points (especially macro- and meso-analyses), in both longitudinal and cross-sectional contexts. Consequently, *Black flags and social movements* can be characterized as having a mixed-approach design (Brannen 2005). All the characteristics of a mixed-methods study are present here, while a partisan drive propels along the practical conclusions. A mixed-methods orientation necessitates continual reappraisal, testing interpretations and conclusions with new methods and data.[21]

I refer to "triangulation" to suggest that there is not one way of viewing the world and that a better understanding comes with considering multiple perspectives. Here, I argue that utilizing multiple data sources and analytical techniques is a good strategy. We should be wary of conclusions drawn from simply one data collection method or source. If we were to simply trust the first story we heard about anarchists (likely from mass media), many would not take it serious, nor seek out second or third opinions.

Black flags and social movements differs from most all mainstream sociological studies of social movements in its focus on a radical, anti-state movement, conceptualized as a movement that exists in a global context. While some scholars deal with the latter (global movements), hardly any have addressed the former (anti-state movements – at least as movements, per se). Although I engage with sociological social movement theory throughout, my objective is somewhat divergent from most of my peers (especially those who work in the North American tradition) – I am a bit less interested in simply refining theoretical explanations, and instead prefer to richly describe a unique, particular movement.

The book also differs from most that have been authored by anarchist movement participants (or their sympathizers), in that it does not rely upon "militant ethnography" (i.e., inductive, radical participant observation). There is nothing bad about this approach – it generates a rich, provocative, and satisfying depiction of its subject matter. But, by itself, it may be too unduly influenced by the limited experiences one is able to have and possibly the researcher's own particular biases. I have been a participant in anarchist activities and projects, yet I do not rely upon my own observations, conversations, or ethno-methodological conclusions here.[22] (My experiences, of course, do influence the choices I make in respect to focus and in providing me with certain initial insights.) While it is pointless to discard my own experiences and perceptions, I look beyond them, seeking additional evidence, especially that which is broader than what I can individually experience. Also, while participation is sometimes helpful for analysis, it can also distract from general patterns. I wish to construct a bigger picture of anarchist movements than ethnographic strategies can alone provide. Some of the following chapters focus on the subjective interpretations of anarchists, while other chapters seek independent verification and identify macro-level phenomenon which impact anarchist movements. Many chapters are focused upon critiquing empirical evidence to substantiate claims made by anarchist movement participants. All involve efforts to gather data and references independent of my own experiences, in order to answer research questions. This allows me to address the big, gaping deficits in the field (such as sociologists' general allergy to investigating anarchist movements or themes). I begin the task of describing anarchist movements from the vantage point of a sociologist, emphasizing sociological concerns and utilizing sociological theories.

In 2013, Jeff Shantz and I argued that the study of anarchist movements was a tricky proposition. After defining exactly *who* is an anarchist and *what* constitutes a movement, other challenges remain. To name just a few: do we study anarchism as practice or anarchism as a movement, do we focus on individuals or their organizations, are overt anarchists more important than the covert ones, and exactly what qualifies as supportive evidence? Answers that are "correct" 100 percent of the time ought to be viewed with extreme skepticism. But, the inverse of this conclusion is also significant: there are things we can still say with incomplete data and all data offer at least some insight into their content matter. See the Appendix for a longer digression on error-making with movement analysis.

Finally, a necessary disclaimer: while anarchism is assuredly internationalist, this book will not satisfy the reasonable standards this requires. While I am versed on a variety of anarchist movements throughout the world, and while Chapters 2 and 5 are deliberately international and cross-national analyses, this work is unfortunately Euro-centric (for reasons that are described later). I have tried to compensate for this, but most of my experience and insights have been generated as an American and most accessible data available is in English and from the Global North, so the book mainly uses examples from the USA. Thus, while I hope *Black flags and social movements* works towards a broadly helpful analysis of anarchist movements, I realize – and readers should be aware – that it is likely most illuminating of a Western context generally and an American one specifically. I encourage others to attempt comparable sociological analyses that widen the scope of inquiry, and consequently, shrink the world a bit more.

Key questions

This book attempts to answer some basic, exploratory questions about anarchist movements, from a sociological perspective. Unlike other analyses that are more concerned with anarchist philosophy, history, or culture, this study emphasizes and focuses on social movements as the primary – but not exclusive – unit of analysis. These four broad sets of questions include: (1) Are anarchist "movements" really social movements? More specifically, do individual anarchists participate in a social phenomenon identified as a movement, as per sociologist's definitions? This is the main focus of Chapter 1, where I situate anarchist movements within the broader ecosystem of movements, explore the various components that constitute anarchist movements, and consider how the study of these movements is a unique task. (2) Who are anarchists and where are they? Since anarchists *do* exist, what kinds of people are they and what do they believe? I answer these questions in Chapter 2, via the use of surveys of individual anarchists. Chapter 3 addresses the questions, Where do anarchists tend to be located and what do they do there? via an analysis of anarchist organizations throughout the world. These micro and meso analyses, respectively, are complemented by macro analyses in subsequent chapters. (3) What explains the prevalence and activities of anarchist movements? How can we better – via the use of social movement theory – understand the micro- and macro-level dynamics of anarchist movements? Specifically, what explains their rise and fall in certain societies and are they different than in the past? What strengthens anarchist movement bonds? Chapter 4 gives a general overview of sociological social movement theories and uses some popular theories to incompletely, but convincingly, interpret anarchist movements. I focus on political opportunity and new social movement theories in Chapters 5 and 6 (respectively) as more robust, but still contentious, frameworks. Given the radical and disadvantaged positions of anarchists, I argue that social capital theory is also of primary importance for anarchist movements, a contention I explore in Chapter 7. Finally, (4) what is the relationship of anarchist movements to other social movements? Chapter 8 investigates how anarchist ideas and practices are continuously borrowed and recycled by activists for organizations that are not often explicitly anarchist. Do anarchists participate with other non-anarchists on the basis of shared values or shared organizing strategies?

Dana Williams
Chico, California

Notes

1   I refer to "anarchy" exclusively in regard to ideas, not movements. Instead, the organized efforts of individuals within movements who are motivated by the ideas of anarchy, I call "anarchists" and "anarchist movements." There are numerous, sensible reasons for making this deliberate distinction. First, it is easier – and maybe more helpful – to describe movements in terms of their members and actions as opposed to their ideas. Second, as Russian-American anarchist Alexander Berkman once wrote to Emma Goldman, distinguishing between a social arrangement and a philosophy: "None of us are ready for anarchy, though many are for anarchism" (12 March 1904).

2   Determined by an EBSCO database search of the journal, using "anarchist" and "anarchism" as terms in article titles and abstracts; searched up to the year 2016.

3   In fairness, one article did discuss black bloc tactics (Wood 2007).

4   The UK-based journal *Social Movement Studies* is less tied to American-style theory-bashing and has featured more work on anarchist movements (e.g., Atton 2003; Karamichas 2009; Pallister-Wilkins 2009; Rosie & Gorringe 2009; Starr 2006; St. John 2008).

5   While it may be inappropriate to over-psychoanalyze these scholars –
    especially given my lack of training in such an endeavor or any hard,
    explanatory evidence – I think another observation about this conundrum is
    warranted. There seems to be an assumption – that I sometimes find myself
    persuaded by – that if we scholars know more about movements, this
    knowledge could be translated into an advantage for the movements we
    sympathize with. Of course, most sociologists lean left (see Zipp & Fenwick
    2007), and this is probably particularly true for those who study movements.
    However, there is a strangely liberal (and dare I say naive) assumption that
    even if conclusive knowledge could be ascertained, this could somehow be
    used strategically by movements and not by the forces that aim to repress
    movements (counter-movements as they will be called shortly). I wonder if it
    would not be a better use of our time – and better for the movements we
    care about – if we spent less time writing about them and more time
    organizing within them, furthering their goals?
6   Sanderson (2005) also describes the Cuban and Nicaraguan revolutions,
    without noting the substantial anarchist movement that pre-dated, as well as
    collaborated early on with, Castro's 26 July movement's overthrow of Batista
    (Fernández 2001), nor how the namesake of the Sandinistas, Augusto
    Sandino, himself identified as an anarcho-syndicalist (Hodges 1986, 1992)
    – thus the red and black colored flag of the Sandinistas.
7   Additionally, Touraine (1984) has argued that social situations are the result
    of the conflict of social movements.
8   Burawoy (1982) is a Marxist sociologist and does not seem to suggest
    anything about the study of anarchism, nor its relationship to the discipline
    of sociology. As a side note, Burawoy associated – undoubtedly with his
    tongue planted firmly in his cheek – the field of economics with state
    Communism: there is only one tolerated dogma (Friedmanian, free-market
    ideology), from which no deviance is tolerated. Say what you will about
    Burawoy and public sociology, but he was really on to something here!
9   Lofland (1988) associates functionalism and conflict theory with both right
    and statist-left ideologies.
10 As Gordon (2006) points out, the varied meanings – both slanderously
    negative and supportively positive – date all the way back to the original,
    classic Greek usages.
11 Bakunin made this argument in an address to the League for Peace and
    Freedom in 1867.
12 A popular adaptation of this sort of typology can be found in the "political
    compass" found on the Internet.
13 Similarly, anarchism became a large, prominent part of the radical
    second-wave feminist movement in the West in the 1970s, so much so that
    some observers (Farrow 2012) have argued that radical feminism and
    anarchism were virtually inseparable.
14 See Mills's own correspondence, in which he wrote "way down deep and
    systematically I'm a goddamned anarchist" (cited in Mills & Mills 2001:
    217–218).
15 The joking, tongue-in-cheek faux-Marx-inspired slogan is an old standard:
    "Anarchists of the world, unite!"

16 The irony is that rarely is there an actual identifiable act of "violence"
    associated with anarchists when that label is applied. On further
    investigation, most instances of "violence" turn out to actually be property
    destruction, self-defense, or hostile rhetoric – and *not* violence.

17 *Attentats* were usually small or singular conspiracies, although most
    attackers were active participants in anarchist movements.

18 The principal medium that delivers this triumvirate to people throughout the
    world is the mass media. Television news, newspapers, movies, and other
    corporate popular culture disproportionately presents anarchists as crazy,
    untrustworthy, and malevolent. While media is the key propaganda
    institution perpetuating and propagating the triumvirate, others are at work,
    too, such as most societies' educational systems. Even when schools do not
    directly engage with anarchism, they provide orthodox narratives that intend
    to negate anarchist arguments and evidence (the "democratic" natures of
    many polities, the meritocratic quality of economic labor markets, and the
    necessity to engage in war-making on behalf of national (read: corporate)
    interests.

19 These notions are widely present, so much so that otherwise
    anarchist-sympathetic organizations are susceptible to replicating these
    misperceptions. For example, while working with Food Not Bombs (FNB),
    we encountered resistance from a local Catholic Worker collective (the CW
    is itself often anarchistic) *due to* FNB's loose ideological affiliation with
    anarchism.

20 Although we ought to reject Asal and Rethemeyer's (2008) characterization
    of anarchists as "terrorists," their empirical conclusions are noteworthy:
    "Anarchists are the least likely to kill of ideological types that we could test
    probabilistically" (2008: 257). The other ideologies evaluated included
    leftists, religious, ethnonationalist, and ethno-religious.

21 Detailed information about all data sources can be found in the chapters
    which utilize each source. The chapters that follow not only analyze these
    data, but also reflexively critique that data sources themselves.

22 This book is not opposed to ethnographic research or writing. Nothing could
    be further from the truth! I highly value these approaches and respect the
    contributions of ethnographic research conducted thus far on anarchist
    movements. My multi-methods orientation values the continual appraisal of
    ideas from multiple vantage points, testing interpretations and conclusions
    gathered via one method with other methods and data sources. I think this is
    a fair and appropriate way to do social science, but I also think it is a
    politically critical way to engage in self-appraisal in movements, too, where
    we judge the multiple perspectives/vantage points, experiences, and concerns
    brought to the table to arrive at the best possible, collective course of action.
    My own activist experiences are anecdotal (by definition) and specific to the
    time and place where I have participated. So, the ideas I have developed
    about the anarchist movement are not completely wrong, but they are
    limited. Even after many conversations with a wide array of anarchists, my
    ideas are still confined to whom I have had the chance to dialogue with. This
    should not suggest that I believe in positivist objectivity, but simply that it's
    possible to improve upon past research, theory, conclusions.

ACKNOWLEDGEMENTS

Anarchists know that a long period of education must precede any great fundamental change in society, hence they do not believe in vote begging, nor political campaigns, but rather in the development of self-thinking individuals. (Lucy Parsons, *The Principles of Anarchism*)

There are two reasons why making this book felt like an anarchist project. First, it was a labor of love, which means it took a ridiculous amount of effort to keep it alive and to eventually see value in it. Second, lots of people supported the book at key moments, contributing in major and minor ways. Without their participation, this book would have been stillborn, incomplete, or simply not very good.

I would like to extend my earnest gratitude to the editors of the Contemporary Anarchist Studies book series: Laurence Davis, Uri Gordon, Nathan Jun, and Alex Prichard. Each are not only helpful and wise editors, but also exceptional activist-scholars. The academy could use more like them, as could many anarchist scenes. I appreciate their support for this book and their patience with its slow production. Alex, in particular, offered detailed, critical feedback that was crucial for adjusting the manuscript's precision and concision. The anonymous reviewers of the book proposal and manuscript provided an invigorating mix of encouraging support, constructive criticism, informed skepticism, and pragmatism. This book is much better, owing to their contributions. I hope this book lives up to the high standards they all demanded.

Others offered helpful thoughts and critiques with prior drafts of certain chapters or fragments (some dating back well over a decade), including Andy Cornell, David Meyer, Matthew Lee, Suzanne Slusser, Ben Stabler, Spencer Sunshine, Sam Tylicki, and Jake Wilson – and a few others who wish to remain anonymous. I would like to express my sincere appreciation to the editors and anonymous reviewers of *Humanity & Society* and *Comparative Sociology*, in which earlier drafts of some of these chapters appeared. In particular, I would like to thank Immanuel Ness who solicited my participation as a co-editor for a special issue on anarchism and labor movements in his *Working USA: The Journal of Labor & Society* (in which parts of Chapter 2 first emerged). Portions of this book were also presented at three different sessions at North Central Sociological Association conferences, as well as meetings for the Midwest Sociological Society, Sociologists Without Borders, and the Mid-South Sociological Association. Clarence Lo and Richard Simon, in particular, went out of their way to support anarchist titled sessions at some of these conferences. Thanks are owed to PJ Lilley for expert indexing.

A special thanks goes to my collaborator Matthew Lee, who originally co-authored parts of Chapters 3 and 5, and generously supported their adaptation and expansion here. I appreciate the learning space created many moons ago in Becky Erickson's Contemporary Sociological Theory class in regards to a portion of Chapter 7 and André Christie-Mizell's Secondary Data Analysis course for parts of Chapter 2. Barbara Gray provided some research advice, helpful for Chapter 8. Rudy Fenwick deserves praise and credit for never discouraging my preoccupation with anarchist themes in classes, or worrying that such work distracted me from my dissertation (which it did).

Members of the North American Anarchist Studies Network (NAASN) gave helpful advice, cautions, and promising leads. The NAASN routinely demonstrates the anarchist adage that people do not need hierarchy or compulsion in order to collaborate, as does the European-based Anarchist Studies Network (wherein Jonathan Purkis, Jamie Heckert, and Alex Prichard have previously been enormously helpful comrades). These two networks combine the best of the scholarly and activist worlds, as they provided considerable mutual aid for my repeated requests and inquiries – regarding subjects as diverse as Chinese autonomy movements in the late 1980s, theoretical concepts derivable from classic age anarchists, the sociological imagination, public sociology, punk rock, the 1985 British miners' strike, anti-Polish sentiments in the USA, Zapatista governance structures, an Errico Malatesta reference, and numerous other things – as well as other food for thought that has greatly influenced the thinking in this book. Wayne Price, Spencer Sunshine, Christopher Hobson, Jon Bekken, and others helped provide insight into recent US anarchist history (particularly the Social Revolutionary Anarchist Federation and Love & Rage).

Some data or materials were provided (or midwived) by Felix Frost, Chuck Munson, Denise Montgomery, and Steve Aby. The patient interlibrary loan staff at the University of Akron, Valdosta State University, and California State University, Chico all deserve praise for finding all sorts of rare, inaccessible treasures (like the International Blacklist, *Earth First! Journal* directories, and many other finds). Allan Antliff (with the Anarchist Archive at the University of Victoria) and Candace Falk (at the Emma Goldman Papers at the University of California, Berkeley) were helpful archivists who scrounged old articles and citations. Activists Greg

Coleridge, Jerry Gordon, Justin Hons, Nina McLellan, Sam Tylicki, Burning River Collective members, and many others were willing to be interviewed and probed for information. Special thanks to my Sociological Theory and Social Movements classes at Valdosta State University for the opportunity to explore, present, and critique some of the theoretical ideas explored here. Jessica Bostick helped with the work on horizontal and hierarchical trust. Certain elements in Chapter 7, in particular, received thorough attention from a number of faculty writing circles (of whom I should most importantly thank Julie Holland, Kathe Lowney, and David McCoy). I am appreciative of my former colleagues at Valdosta State University who supported or talked research with me, especially Mark George, Carl Hand, Thomas Hochschild, Kathleen Lowney, and Anne Price. I also appreciate the kind support of my current colleagues at California State University, Chico while the final draft of this manuscript was prepared, especially as I acclimatized to a new department and environment.

Credit must be given to the many anarchist (or anarcho-tolerant) organizations that I participated with over the years, for experience, insight, and inspiration, including (but not limited to) Food Not Bombs, Indymedia, Critical Mass, Students Taking Action for a New Democracy, the Northeast Ohio Radical Action Network, the Mary Turner Project, the Earthworm Collective, and the American Friends Service Committee – as well as a variety of radical reading groups, affinity groups, and many other fly-by-night projects that I have had the joy and privilege of participating with.

Finally, none of this would have been possible nor coherent were it not for the expertise, thoughtfulness, solace, dedication, tolerance, affection, and love of Suzanne Slusser. She is a more consistent and principled anarchist than I, though she rarely adopts the label. She is my partner, my Roslyn, my best-friend, and the love of my life.

Thank you.

ABBREVIATIONS

AFA	Anti-Fascist Action
AFO	anarchistic franchise organization
ALF	Animal Liberation Front
APOC	Anarchist People of Color
ARA	Anti-Racist Action
ASN	Anarchist Studies Network
ATTAC	Association pour la Taxation des Transactions financières et pour l'Action Citoyenne
AYP	Anarchist Yellow Pages
BAS	"Big Anarchist Survey"
BBB	Biotic Baking Brigade
CIRCA	Clandestine Insurgent Rebel Clown Army
CM	critical mass
CNT	Confederación Nacional del Trabajo
CW	Catholic Worker
DIY	do it yourself
EF!	Earth First!
ELF	Earth Liberation Front
FAI	Federación Anarquista Ibérica
FBI	Federal Bureau of Investigation
FNB	Food Not Bombs
G8	Group of 8
HDI	Human Development Index
HNJ	Homes Not Jails
IBL	International Blacklist
IMC	Independent Media Center
IMF	International Monetary Fund
IWA	International Workers' Association
IWPA	International Working People's Association
IWW	Industrial Workers of the World
NAACP	National Association for the Advancement of Colored People

NAASN	North American Anarchist Studies Network
NEFAC	Northeastern Federation of Anarchist Communists
NGO	non-governmental organization
NSM	new social movement
NYT	*New York Times*
PO	political opportunity
POUM	Partido Obrero de Unificación Marxista
RABL	Revolutionary Anarchist Bowling League
RMT	resource mobilization theory
SM	social movement
SMO	social movement organization
WOMBLES	White Overalls Movement Building Libertarian Effective Struggles
WS	world-system
WUNC	worthiness, unity, numbers, commitment
WVS	World Values Survey

Part I
Movement overview

1
Introduction to social movements: anarchism as a unique example

The purpose of my life all has been focused on: helping everyone to have a spring, so that everyone's heart will be bright, everyone will have a happy life, and everyone will have the freedom to develop in any way they want. (李尧棠 [Ba Jin])[1]

Today's anarchist movements are not brand new, neither are they simple replicas or resurrections of old anarchist movements. They are reasonable – if not always predictable – descendants of previous anarchist movement iterations. While new in many of their foci, rhetoric, and tactics, today's anarchist movements also have remarkable consistency over time and a solid connection to past anarchist movements, both in outsider aesthetic, radicalism, and vision. There has also been regular overflow between anarchist movements and other movements in the same local environment. Anarchists routinely cross over into other movements, and in doing so they labor to blur boundaries between those acting as anarchists and those who self-identify as anarchists. In most times and places, conscious anarchists have likely been in the minority of the non-anarchist movements they participate in, although they may often be some of the most active partisans driving forward campaigns and struggles in those very movements.

This chapter introduces the central issues relevant to the sociological study of anarchist movements, especially Mario Diani's (1992) well-known definition of a social movement: networks of individuals and organizations, united by some shared identity, that engage in extra-institutional action with the interest of changing society. This definition is used as the starting place for understanding how anarchist movements are similar to, and different from, other movements (in terms of leadership, representation, and autonomy), and the chapter presents an overview of certain attributes of anarchism that continue across the next two chapters. Perhaps surprising to some critics, anarchism does indeed satisfy all the requisite criteria for being a social movement. The chapter ends by modeling the anti-anarchist counter-network (corporations, governments, and media), considering the various levels of analysis of anarchism that could be investigated, and describing the helpful comparisons worth making to better understand anarchist movements. Where relevant, I note future chapters which include further exploration of a topic.

First steps toward understanding anarchist movements

The Preface presented some anarchist history and a summary of major anarchist ideas. But we should consider what the term "anarchism" can refer to. Owing to the slanderous triumvirate of chaos, violence, and fantasy, it is possible to confuse the subject of focus. There is an anarchist *identity*, which is a way of describing, or labeling oneself. Along with anarchist identity, there is a lifestyle to adopt and imitate, as well as cultural codes to employ around other anarchists. While relevant, these anarchist identities are not themselves the sole subject of this book. There is also an anarchist *ideology*. This ideology can be viewed as a radical impulse that influences adherents' behaviors. It is a historically derived set of strategies, attitudes, and practices, linked to anarchist theories, concepts, and values (such as anti-authoritarianism, self-management, and mutual aid). In practice, anarchist ideology serves as a cognitive and moral system of guiding beliefs which help to ensure that the codes used by those identifying as anarchists are employed appropriately and correspond with expectations. Of course, there are many ideological subvariants, which may share similar strands of agreement, but also vary significantly. Although ideology is part of this book's story, it is not the central focus. Finally, there is an anarchist *movement*. Anarchism is a movement independent of other movements, but also one that has much interaction and overlap with many compatible movements. Consequently, much of this book seeks to explore where movement "boundaries" exist, and where we can find blurry, unsuccessful attempts to distinguish anarchism from other movements.

Anarchism is and can be all of the above, but I am most interested in it as a movement, and thus anarchist movements are the subject of this book. I chose a plural identifier for anarchism, since it is inaccurate to claim there is *an* anarchist movement, let alone *an* anarchist identity or *an* anarchist ideology. There are actually multiple variations of each, sometimes incredibly varied and even at odds with each other. There is a joke that hints at this diversity: "Ask three anarchists to describe anarchism and you will get four, maybe five different definitions." For example, anarcho-syndicalists (a.k.a., "workerist" anarchists) and green anarchists (a.k.a., "anti-civilization" anarchists) find themselves at great odds with each other, and some might even argue that their versions of anarchism are incompatible (see Williams 2009b). A primary way to identify this movement diversity is in the focus on different anarchist movements throughout the world, noting that anarchist movements differ by country, and even by city and region. Consequently, I refer to *anarchist movements* from hereafter, as opposed to, presumptively, *the* anarchist movement. It is inappropriate and inaccurate to assert that all anarchists see themselves as part of the same movement, or that they are even capable of being part of a singular movement.[2]

Of course, some – including some anarchists, most notably, so-called "philosophical anarchists" – have been indifferent or hostile to associating anarchism with social movements. While none of these arguments hold much weight for me, I present five such idealized arguments that are worthy of brief consideration – in order to be formally rejected.[3] These arguments are sometimes vague assertions from critics as well as general claims that flow from the misperception triumvirate. First, there may not be "enough" participants in an anarchist movement – thus, its membership is too small to warrant the label "movement." This presumes that movements must contain a large, if unspecified, number of participants to qualify. Over the course of this book it will become clear that there are surely hundreds of thousands, likely millions of conscious anarchists throughout the world. If far smaller groupings can be designated as "movements," then so can anarchism.

Second, anarchism is too unorganized (recall the "chaos" misrepresentation already described); since movements are organized and anarchism is supposedly disorganized, then anarchism is not a movement (QED). Many movements also lack centralized coordination bodies and seem unpredictable, yet no one thinks to challenge their status as movements. Even if other movements were not similar to anarchism in this regard, this assumption ignores the obvious reality that anarchists have *always* formed – and continue to form – organizations (see Chapter 3 for ample evidence of this fact), dating back to the founding of the International Working People's Association in 1881. Anarchists' preference for decentralization and networked organizing styles actually make them definitive, quintessential movement organizers.

Third, and relatedly, anarchists may be too individualistic or anti-social to be able to work with others and thus form a *social* movement. While some brands of anarchism are ultra-individualist, there are still structures of coordination for collaboration. Since anarchists believe in the sanctity of free will among individuals, critics assume it is impossible for anarchists to collaborate. But this cynical view of individual free will seem just as poorly suited to explaining most of human intercourse and community, not just anarchist movements. The logical extension of this argument would presume that sociability is only possible under hierarchical structures and in coercive conditions. Among social anarchists, there is endless evidence of a collectivist spirit, as borne out by numerous examples of joint endeavors throughout this book, including across movements.

Fourth, if movements are phenomenon that only target governments and demand reforms, then anarchism would not fit the bill. Were this proposition correct, then, yes, anarchism would not be a movement. However, this would also discount all types of revolutionary movements, including some movements of national liberation and anti-colonialism that were, and are, indifferent to state concessions. This severe definitional constraint would also exclude portions of many other movements that seek extra-institutional or revolutionary outcomes, including sizable factions of feminist, anti-racist, labor, and other movements, or movements whose main targets are economic or cultural elites rather than political elites. Thus, while movements surely act outside of the established halls of power – anarchism more exclusively than most other movements – this does not mean that their extra-institutional efforts are, or ought to be, focused on merely changing the state.

Finally, there is no anarchist *movement*, per se, just self-identified anarchists who work in *other* movements; thus, allegedly, no independent anarchist movement exists that is autonomous from other social movements. While anarchists may be found throughout all sorts of organizations (see Chapters 8 and 9), this does not preclude their concurrent involvement in explicitly anarchist organizations and movements, too. Individuals who identify as anarchists often belong to many other movements, and their anarchist identity and ideology neither negates that participation, nor does it preclude their participation in anarchist-only environs. Indeed, if organizations, events, and other mediums are occupied by anarchists alone, then it must be possible for purely anarchist movements to be defined, separate from other movements.

To be true, these objections may possess a certain limited, superficial reasonableness, even a face validity of sorts. However, throughout this book, the reader should note copious evidence that refutes each of these objections, illustrated through examples and logical argument that anarchist movements exist. In other words, there is a reasonable rationale for pursuing the study of anarchism as a social movement, a definitional task which I turn to next and focus on for the remainder of this introductory chapter.

Anarchist versus anarchistic versus archist

A core prerequisite to studying anarchist movements is to distinguish between that which is actually anarchist and that which isn't, as well as between what identifies as anarchist and that which doesn't. In other words, to study anarchist movements, we must appreciate both movement participants' intentions as well as their self-awareness. The differences between anarchist movements, anarchistic movements, and non-anarchist movements are important, meaningful distinctions, but these terms can also sometimes blur together.

Three criteria can be used to assess anarchism (beyond simple, stated claims). First, the *values* that people profess; second, the *structures* created and adhered to in movement activity; and, third, the type of additional *actions* chosen to pursue movement goals. While there is a fair amount of overlap or congruence here, these criteria still constitute separate elements of an anarchist whole. Values are the things that people prioritize. For anarchists, values ought to be compatible with long-held priorities such as anti-domination, liberation, self-management, and mutual aid (Ward 1996). Activists and social movement organizations – indeed, any individuals – may state an adherence to these values without specifying such values as "anarchist." Structure refers to the ways in which people create social relationships – especially organization – that is of practical use for movements. For example, anarchists choose to organize without charismatic or permanent leaders, and utilize collaborative, participatory processes. Everyone's input, desires, and efforts are valued in these structures, as is the autonomy of the individual to participate or not (Ehrlich 1996; Graeber 2009). Finally, the actions chosen by movements channel collective energies toward certain outcomes. Anarchists are apt to use direct action to manifest change, as opposed to using indirect efforts. Actions that lobby or vote for policy options, appeal to representatives or elites for them to change, are at odds with the anarchist style of creating the world they would choose to live in and doing so without speaking through proxies (Gordon 2008; Milstein 2010). These criteria are all interlinked, of course. Values drive not only the structures anarchists create, but also the actions they choose to take (i.e., means are as important as the ends arrived at).

Some people and organizations openly embrace these criteria, while others don't. Some of the former (and a few of the latter), further identify as anarchists. But, since anarchist movements lack any credentialing agency – a hypothetical body that would grant official permission to identify as Anarchist or legal standing as a member of The Anarchist Movement – there are bound to be gradations of anarchists and non-anarchists. I divide this continuum by the possession of the aforementioned anarchist criteria and formalized identification with anarchism. The four ideal type (c.f., Weber 2011) categories I describe are explicitly anarchist, improperly anarchist, implicitly anarchist, and non-anarchist (see Table 1.1).

First, *explicitly anarchist* movement participants and organizations are the most easily identified, and they are the primary (but not exclusive) topic of this book. Without debate, explicit anarchists reside and participate within an anarchist movement. They identify themselves as "anarchists" and appropriately embody the three above criteria. They prioritize anarchist values, they create anarchist structures, and they act as anarchists.

Table 1.1 Typology of claimed anarchist identity and possession of anarchist qualities

	Claim anarchist label	Do not claim anarchist label
Qualities		
Possess anarchist qualities	Explicitly anarchist	Implicitly anarchist
Possess anti-anarchist qualities	Improperly "anarchist"	Non-anarchist

Organizations like the Anarchist Black Cross and the International of Anarchist Federations would fall within this category, as they are explicitly anarchist and achieve the requisite criteria.

Second, and somewhat surprisingly, *improperly anarchist* people claim to be "anarchist," but some (or all) of their values, structure, or actions cannot be reconciled with contemporary anarchist criteria. In other words, something is fundamentally amiss between their claimed identity and lived "anarchist persona." Based on the general consensus of what constitutes anarchism at any given time, people who are starkly at odds with the current interpretation of anarchism are anarchist more in name than in fact. For example, they may be sexist or opposed to worker-control, they may have a "leader," or vote and run candidates in elections. So-called "national anarchists" have cryptically racist or fascist views, although they have attempted to claim the anarchist moniker (Schlembach 2013; Sunshine 2008). The same is true for so-called "anarcho-capitalists" (who seem concentrated in unusual numbers in the USA), whose critique of domination is limited to state domination, but see no problem with capitalist exploitation of workers, and sometimes white supremacy, patriarchy, or the like (McKay 2008). For the purposes of this book, I argue that we should reject the usurpation of anarchist identity by the "improperly anarchist," not because such people lack sincerity, but because their identities are irreconcilable with anarchist history, culture, values, and practice (i.e., over a million anarchists were part of the resistance to European fascism during the 1930s and 1940s), and all leading anarchist figures during earlier periods (even individualist-anarchists) were *anti*-capitalists. It is fair to say that the claims of people in this category offend anarchists of the first category (explicit anarchists) the most, as they are seen to tarnish anarchist reputation and contaminate anarchism with highly repugnant qualities and can thus be classified as "archists."

Third, the *implicitly anarchist* may be the most interesting category. A case may be made that they are part of an anarchist movement, although they do not pretend or attempt to be. Implicit anarchists possess some combination of anarchist values, structure, or action, but do not consciously identify themselves as "anarchist." Even though they do not self-identify as such, their values and practices place them in close proximity and sympathy to the explicitly anarchist, with whom they often can easily collaborate. Many social movement organizations can be categorized as implicitly anarchist, such as Food Not Bombs (FNB) – an anti-war, food-sharing organization – which rarely officially identifies as anarchist (although anarchists often work within FNB), but its values, structure, and actions are highly anarchist in nature and spirit. The same could be said for other organizations (some of which I later label in Chapter 8 as anarchistic franchise organizations), like Earth First! (EF!), Anti-Fascist Action (AFA), and others.[4] Squatted social centers throughout Europe have a strong anarchist quality to them, although they do not always identify as anarchist (many identify with autonomism, which is highly compatible with anarchist philosophy). Some implicit anarchists possess some anarchist criteria, but not other criteria; others, like Peoples' Global Action, possess all three criteria, all while still eschewing an anarchist label (de Marcellus 2000; Wood 2005). Since the value-based consistency of someone's actions is more important to anarchists than the labels they cling to, implicit anarchists are more compatible with explicit anarchists than improperly anarchists. Throughout this book, I also refer to implicit anarchism as "anarchistic," as it constitutes anarchist values, structure, and action, albeit without the self-conscious identity, culture, and history of explicit anarchism.

Finally, the non-anarchists are also "archists" and, without debate, are not part of an anarchist movement. These movement actors do not claim the label of "anarchist," nor do they embody the expected anarchist criteria mentioned. They do not prioritize anarchist values (perhaps emphasizing civil rights or access, instead of liberation), possess anarchist structures (have steering committees, boards of directors, paid staff, and nominally representative decision making), or act as anarchists (sign petitions, attend rallies led by famous speakers, or have telephone lobby campaigns to elected politicians). Numerous movement actors are non-anarchist, including many political parties (like the Communist Party), large non-governmental organizations (the National Association for the Advancement of Colored People [NAACP], Association pour la Taxation des Transactions financières et pour l'Action Citoyenne [ATTAC], or mainstream unions), and liberal, pro-status quo community groups. Non-anarchists can be radicals or reformers, Left or Right (or neither), and electorally focused or not. *Black flags and social movements* explores how anarchist movements collaborate – but also find themselves at odds – with non-anarchist movement elements.

To be fair, this typology is not without flaw. I have attempted to untangle the application of anarchism in various contexts, but details are often messy in reality. Consequently, this should be seen more as an *ideal type* classification (*à la* Weber 2011), rather than a strongly coherent categorization system where we can easily place individuals and organizations. For example, the border between explicitly and implicitly anarchist is likely porous in many cases, because people may identify as anarchists in some situations but not others, or their commitment to anarchism fluctuates over time. Also, numerous people who explicitly identify as anarchists and vocally reject some systems of domination, may happen to be homophobic, racist, or sexist. Historically, this was very likely; for example, male anarchists during the Spanish Revolution were often no less misogynist than the rest of non-anarchist Spanish society (Ackelsberg 1991), while numerous anarchist organizations have had racial blind-spots to their white privilege (e.g., Ferguson 2011 discusses Emma Goldman's general avoidance of race in the US). Over time, it has become less legitimate, although still possible, for self-identified anarchists to promote such beliefs or contradictory practices. This messiness illustrates the problems with using the above typology as a rigid measurement tool, without negating its analytical utility for contrasting real individuals and organizations against idealized types.

Social movements and their networks defined

What exactly *is* a social movement? There are numerous definitions, but the one I like best comes from Diani (1992). He suggests multiple criteria and necessary conditions that need to be satisfied in order to characterize something as a "social movement." Phenomena that possess some, but lack other criteria, should more appropriately go by other labels, such as political parties, crowds, activists, mobs, policy and policy-makers. I demonstrate in the following, that anarchism fulfills every aspect of Diani's definition, thus indicating satisfactory grounds for identifying anarchism as a social movement.

First, movements are deliberate formations, composed of conscious individuals who recognize they are part of a movement. Contrary to popular belief, movement participants generally know what they are doing – or, at least, trying to do. And even the "spontaneity" that many successful movements involve often necessitates much planning. But, crowds are not movements, random people who bump into others on the street are not movements, and unreflective resistance (such as within certain uprisings) do not independently constitute a movement. So, do anarchists deliberately create movement? Well, if people are creating and joining organizations with the word "anarchist" in the name (e.g., Anarchists Against the Wall, Grupo Anarquista Libertad, or Jakarta Anarchist Resistance) or consciously attending events that are widely advertised as anarchist (e.g., anarchist book fairs, continent-wide anarchist federation conferences, or anarchist-sponsored protests), it would seem that there exists deliberate, conscious action on the part of anarchists. Even the willingness to identify as an anarchist is a deliberate act that suggests intent to form or participate in a movement.

Movements engage in extra-institutional action. They cannot be part of a government or be composed of elites who use their positions of power to orchestrate changes. People who are voting are not involved in movement activity, although movements may sometimes organize electoral campaigns. Politicians and government agencies are not movements, corporations are not movements, ideas are not movements, and behavior which exclusively lobbies behind the closed office doors of government bureaucrats does not constitute a movement. Obviously, these criteria are satisfied most strongly in the case with anarchists: they are extra-institutional by practice and ideology. Anarchists do not attempt to lobby political elites for newer or better laws (let alone to abolish their own authority). No anarchist parties run for public office. All anarchist activity happens outside of the halls of power.[5] Anarchist movement activity is not only extra-institutional, but also counter-institutional; in other words, the movement not only operates outside dominant, hierarchical, and elite institutions, but also opposes those institutions' very existence and seeks to replace them with a more horizontal, self-managing social order. (See the discussion in Chapter 5 for more on how anarchist movements' anti-statism poses problems for political opportunity theory.)

Movements are engaged in conflictual struggles with other social entities – often governments, other dominant institutions (e.g., corporations, white supremacy, patriarchy), or even other movements (e.g., fascism, Leninism). This conflict delineates boundaries of the movement: who is on one side and who is on (or leaning towards) another side. Consequently, movements are also interested in changing society. They reject some element (and often large parts) of the status quo. They aim to change society through a transformation of individuals and/or social systems. Change is always key. Movements intend to redirect society and thus do not aspire to remain in the present moment where status quo arrangements rule. Unsurprisingly, anarchists participate in much conflict, although conflict can range from the dramatic to the mundane, aggressive to the calm. The pre-figurative orientation of anarchist activity is by definition oppositional in respect to dominant, hierarchical institutions. Much of this conflict today is directed at anarchism's historic foes: state and capitalism (and, to a lesser degree, organized religion). The practical, daily conflict may be with specific institutional actors and components: governmental agencies, individual politicians, military recruiters or specific corporations, polluting industries, wealthy people, banks, or influential trade associations. While these (state and capitalism) may be the two most regular institutions that anarchists enter into conflict with, they are not the only ones. Other conflictual action may target anti-choice activists, fascists, bigots, media agencies, public celebrities or intellectuals, or large non-profit entities (e.g., universities, hospitals, think-tanks, liberal NGOs, etc.) Yet, conflict is not the only descriptor of anarchist action, as most anarchist activity is also thoroughly cooperative.

Movement participants are united by shared identities. A common affiliation, reference, or label is accepted by participants. Sometimes the labels change a little or are not exactly the same, but movement participants understand the complexities of the differences in such variant labels and can determine the significance of those differences. For example, people who use terms such as "anarchist," "anti-authoritarian," "radical," "autonomist," or "libertarian socialist," are likely to have a great deal in common, will see each other as allies, and will work together within the context of a movement. Even though such people identify differently and may even reject all labels, they will be able to recognize their kinship as centered on key values, and the aesthetic and execution of their politics.[6]

Finally, movements are – in a structural sense – social networks of individuals and organizations. This complicated and often unmappable set of relationships involves all sorts of people, some who are unaffiliated and others who are active members of formal and informal groups. The complex and multifaceted connections between these individuals and organizations creates the movement's structure. For anarchist movements, these networks will be somewhat distinct from other movements, given anarchism's far greater emphasis on decentralization, but anarchism resembles other movements in its complexity and the ambiguity of collaboration. Not everyone knows everyone else, nor does the same things, and the network can organically reconfigure itself in response to changing external conditions or evolving internal understandings. Figure 1.1 depicts an attempt to visualize such networks (focused on North American anarchist movements during the 1990s and 2000s).

Networks are often too complicated to understand immediately. They not only require sufficient time to discover and appraise all the constituent parts, but also to situate the network in relations to other broader networked systems. Anarchist movements are similarly complex. To use North American anarchist movements during the 1990s and 2000s as a case study, we find a combination of organizations, super-organizational structures, coordinating structures, individuals, and quasi-external supporting actors. Numerous organizations of varied design exist, including simple anarchist collectives (organizations founded for individuals who wish to pursue certain goals together) and other organizations that have adopted specifically replicate-able styles, which I identify in Chapter 8, as anarchistic franchise organizations (AFOs). These AFOs include groups such as Anti-Racist Action, Earth First!, Food Not Bombs, and others. The anarchist press is itself a complex mini-network of magazines, newspapers, radio programs, book publishers, and websites, all of whom may share information, circulate communication, create forums for debate, and propagate

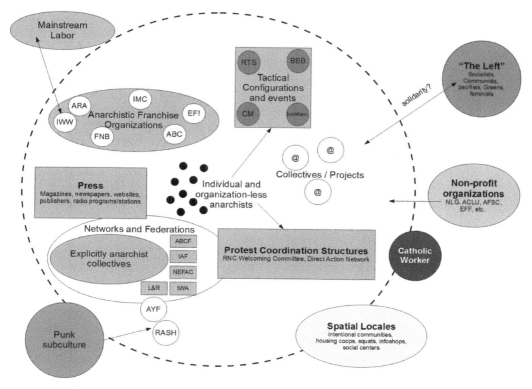

1.1 The 1990s and 2000s North American anarchist movement (as a network)

anarchist ideas to non-anarchists. Super-organizational structures such as networks and federations (e.g., Anarchist Black Cross Federation, Northeast Federation of Anarchist Communists, and International Workers' Association) help to facilitate the interaction of numerous individual organizations, while also maintaining these organizations' autonomy.

Many North American anarchists are also fond of creating planning and communication structures that, while refraining from creating formalized organizations, still coordinate anarchist activities for individuals and in affinity groups on a temporary or ad hoc basis. Here, protest coordination structures like the Direct Action Network or the RNC (Republican National Committee) Welcoming Committee may be the best known. These structures may create additional, physical infrastructures, such as "convergence spaces," that allow for anarchist interaction and planning of direct action (see Lacey 2005; Routledge 2003). In addition, anarchists have created modular, tactical configurations and events which can be replicated and temporarily established within any given community, for particular purposes, such as Critical Mass, Reclaim the Streets, the Biotic Baking Brigade, or anarchist book fairs. Finally, individual anarchists who belong to none of the these organizations may themselves participate in coordinating anarchist activities from time to time, or may not be involved in any of the above listed activities. All of the above are also open to anarchistic individuals' participation, but they usually exclude improperly anarchist individuals.

Technically outside of the explicitly anarchist movement network are numerous supporting actors, organizations, and fellow movements. These will often (but not always) provide resources, solace, solidarity, and cross-fertilization of ideas and activists with the anarchist movement. For example, the labor movement's more radical sectors interact with the anarcho-syndicalist-influenced Industrial Workers of the World, just as the punk movement regularly introduces music fans to anarchist themes, projects, and scenes – the Red and Anarchist Skin Heads and Anarchist Youth Federation have been two organized examples of this anarcho-punk relationship, although punk's influence has been even broader (see Cogan 2007; O'Connor 2003b). A variety of small spaces give anarchists places to live, work, and interact, including many intentional communities, housing cooperatives, unofficial squats, infoshops (similar to, but also different from, European social centers), and anarchist bookstores. Likewise, many (but definitely not all) Catholic Worker communities have strong anarchist orientations, serving as places for sympathetic individuals to live, organize, and meet each other. Finally, the USA's diverse, but diffused liberal Left sometimes supports the anarchist movement (although often ignoring it and other times working against it). The Left – including socialists, communists, pacifists, greens, feminists, and others – sometimes attend or support anarchist-sponsored events, and anarchists regularly return such gestures. This solidarity, while not guaranteed, occurs regularly at local levels where individual anarchists and Leftists know each other, and may fraternize and organize side by side. Other liberal-oriented non-profit groups have provided resources (even if sometimes only indirectly) to the anarchist movement; the National Lawyers Guild will help as legal observers at protests, the American Civil Liberties Union supports the rights of anarchists to dissent and may defend them in court, or the Electric Frontier Foundation will defend the online rights of anarchists who may be digitally spied upon or have their webservers seized.

While this description of recent iterations of North American anarchist movements is both idealized and simplified, it does present a society's movement as a complex interaction between varied components and constituencies, generally working together for their shared goals. This network is manifested when people converge at events, "gather" ephemerally on the internet, or communicate via the anarchist press.

There are a few consequences to emphasize that result from Diani's definition. Many of these following points are strictly about the meaning of terms. Uprisings are distinct from anarchist movements (although anarchists may participate in uprisings). Simple campaigns are not themselves anarchists movements, even though they may have anarchistic goals. To be a movement, something would have to last longer than a campaign and involve more than just a single campaigning organization. And, of course, political parties, single organizations, or projects are not anarchist movements. No part of Diani's definition implies the size necessary for a movement, or pretends that a movement must be successful in its ultimate goals to be called such, neither does it have any bearing on the character of the movement (it could be insurrectionist, anarcho-syndicalist, green anarchist, anarcho-communist, anarcha-feminist, or all the above).

However, a purely structural and organizational analysis of anarchist movements would paint an incomplete picture. Much can also be learned via a social constructionist perspective. For example, anarchists create narratives (i.e., stories) about their movements and exchange meaningful frames (i.e., deliberate representations) within different social and geographic spaces. The variety of these narratives and frames range from formal to informal, long-lasting to short-lived, anonymous to intimate, generalizing to idiosyncratic. Exchange of narratives and frames reinforces identity, encourages intellectual growth, expands knowledge and experience, changes perspectives and goals, and creates a sense of belonging to a larger community of like-minded, sympathetic, affiliated individuals. The different spaces and venues for these exchanges all serve to accomplish key goals in respect to anarchist identity. These spaces include face-to-face gatherings like meetings where people can dialog directly to discuss, debate, and decide (see Atkinson 2009 regarding a North American gathering). Or, at events where social "performance" is involved, like at a Food Not Bombs food sharing, a musical concert at a squatted social center, a direct action "lockdown," or an unpermitted protest march.

Or, these spaces could be virtual or digital, with dialog or performance taking place via simulation, on message boards, email listserves, movement news websites, blogs, or email conversations (Owens & Palmer 2003). The anarchist press can be traced far back in anarchist history; while today this includes electronic mediums, it also includes more traditional venues like magazines and newspapers, all of which can be read widely and circulated (Atton 1999). People read and debate polemical articles, digest reports of past events, and consider acting on proposed future activities. Then there are all the informal gatherings; people socialize at parties or at local hangouts (a bar, park, or street corner). Within these gatherings, people share collective experiences, but also socialize on an individual basis. More intimate, personal encounters can be just as transformative, as people are able to interact more deeply and intensely with a single person, learning specific things quickly, gaining insight, seeing new perspectives, and becoming inspired.

Of course, narratives and frames are also indirectly circulated and processed through mass media presentations, but these fall outside the control of anarchists (unless an anarchist reporter is making the presentation).[7] The typical construction of anarchists in the mass media – as already indicated – is highly distorted and caricatured.

A unique movement?

While it is now a bit clearer what anarchist movements *are*, it may still be unclear why they matter and how they differ from the countless other social movements found throughout the world. All movements are different, but in what ways is anarchism uniquely and fundamentally distinct from other movements?

First, anarchist movements exclusively use direct action. Those who act as anarchists do not choose the route of representation via bureaucrats, elected officials, or spokespersons. Anarchists do not wish the state (or other hierarchical institutions) to act on their behalf. Anarchists do not target the state, demand that it change, implore it to get better, or even to change other people. Anarchists are resolutely anti-state. According to David Graeber, "Direct Action is a matter of acting as if you were already free" (Graeber 2011b). The movement that comes closest to the anarchist rejection of representation and instead places an emphasis on anti-statist action might be the autonomist movement. From the vantage point of many, autonomist Marxists may be a few shades away from anarchists themselves. This autonomist movement seeks separateness from the state and a collectivist path towards social revolution as opposed to a statist path (see Katsiaficas 1997). Although modern "Libertarians" (at least the self-declared American variety)[8] may claim they want to shrink the state, they are actually a rather poor example of anti-statists, since they seek to use the state to enact this end, even running presidential candidates who would, paradoxically, act to undercut their own authority once they acquire it. Of course, these "Libertarians" really just want to empower capitalists, a goal that places them distant from anarchist movements that see capitalism as one of society's major hierarchical institutions in need of elimination.

Second, anarchist movements internally organize themselves without leadership or authority figures. This prohibition includes undeclared leaders or people of great influence; anarchists typically expend considerable effort to create structures and practices that limit the influence of one person or a small group of people, in order to regulate the potential power of any self-appointed or unintentional leaders. Organizations that could acquire resources and thus allow certain members to wield power, are kept as horizontal and decentralized as possible. Contrast this with many guerrilla movements. These may, perhaps, be equally revolutionary in their aims, but utilize leadership structures that are often highly authoritarian (see Gambone's 1997 essay on the iconic Che Guevara) with varying degrees of transparency. Compare this to popular insurrections and uprisings, to the extent they are unplanned events, which usually lack leaders and may reflect anarchist values. Still, these dramatic events often may involve martyrs or popular figures with undue influence (see Katsiaficas 2013).[9]

Third, anarchist movements involve multi-issue foci. Instead of concentrating on one or a small number of social problems, hierarchies, or issues, anarchists focus on hierarchy itself as a source of domination and inequality in society. As such, any social issue that other movements may focus on, most likely involves the wielding of hierarchical power, and thus may be a target of anarchist movements (Williams 2012). Many movements today have become intersectional and have branched out of a rigid single-issue orientation towards their key targets. For example, the feminist movement has broadened to include a variety of interests and other issues that intersect its concern with female empowerment, including people of color, immigrants, youth, and so on. But, such movements do not evenly weigh all actions and struggles that involve a key issue are still generally prioritized (e.g., gender issues). Likewise, socialist movements have often prioritized class-struggle issues over gender parity and feminist concerns.

Fourth, anarchist movements advocate and act for eternal vigilance against hierarchy. Anarchists tend to believe there is unlikely to be a final, total "victory" in this struggle. Just as Patricia Hill Collins (among many others) argued that "Democracy is never finished" (Collins 2009: 182), so anarchists believe that hierarchy always has the potential to re-emerge within social communities, even in societies that may resemble utopias. This belief is perhaps presented most elegantly in Ursula Le Guin's (1975) anarchist science fiction novel, *The Dispossessed*, in which the lead character Shevek, criticized his home planet Anarchos, which, although it was the result of a successful anarchist revolution, had become stagnant, stifling, and had veered away from anarchism. Or, consider a real world, strategic example: it wasn't good enough for some Spanish anarchists that the Confederación Nacional del Trabajo (CNT) identified as anarcho-syndicalist and had approximately one million members in the 1930s – thus, the Iberian Anarchist Federation (FAI) formed to keep the CNT on its revolutionary anarchist path (Christie 2008). Most other movements believe it is possible to ultimately achieve their goals, which are often seen as the successful passage of favorable legislation or the eventual end of a particular form of discrimination. Reformist organizations like the Women's International League for Peace and Freedom, Egyptian Organization for Human Rights, and the Environmental Foundation for Africa, presume that satisfactory gains can be made, short of revolutionary transformation. For many revolutionary political parties (i.e., Marxist-Leninist), a seizure of the state's machinery signifies the end goal; yet anarchists like Bakunin presciently argued that a "red bureaucracy" just as terrible as the capitalist bureaucracy would ensue in such conditions (Guérin 1970).

If these four characteristics – direct action, internal anti-authoritarianism, intersectional focus on hierarchy, and endless struggle – describe anarchist movements' uniqueness, then exactly what problems do these characteristics cause for standard social movement analyses and theories? I believe three problems due to anarchism's uniqueness ultimately stymie the pursuit of greater comprehension and wisdom. First, it is hard to compare the outcomes of anarchist movements to those of other movements (such as those that pursue reform to laws). If anarchism's goals are seemingly insurmountable – even ephemeral ("the end to all structures of domination") – then how can we really compare the various attributes of anarchism to, say, immigrant rights movements demanding specific policy changes? Vagueness or radicalism can prevent a complete assessment of anarchist movements. Second, it is difficult to gauge the influence wielded by anarchist movement network actors. Exactly who or what occupies the important nodes in movement networks if no one is "in charge"? This is crucial, since many movement frameworks focus on the roles and contributions of key movement actors (whether individuals or organizations). Even though organizations and movements can adopt an anarchistic approach (or even be populated by self-identified anarchists), from the outside such movements do not register as being anarchist movements.[10] And, third, we cannot expect anarchist movements to only emphasize certain things or to be active in limited areas, since everything is in the anarchist's crosshairs and every situation is a field of potential resistance. How can the emergence of anarchist movements or the appearance of individual anarchists be explained if almost anything could be a cause for anarchist action – from a dictatorship to a liberal democracy, to a single instance of sexual violence or an imperialist war, to differential influence in activist organizations or systemic inequality throughout society? Since the causes of anarchist action are not all the same, how can we predict such action if nearly anything could serve as that cause?

Counter-networks

By viewing anarchist movements as networks it is possible to account for their flexibility, distribution, overlap, and fluidity. But another way to situate an anarchist movement network would be to compare it against its adversaries and enemies, in individual and institutional terms. Smith (2008) has argued for viewing movements as networks that also rival *other networks* (e.g., counter-movements). For example, she focuses on the global justice movement as an international network, but also describes a counter-network that is neo-liberal in character and opposes this movement. This raises the question of who would belong to the rival, anti-anarchist network? Conceivably, the anti-anarchist network could include any institution that has a vested interest in maintaining the hierarchical status quo, but also any other unintentional, non-elite supporters.

Let us refer to this rival, anti-anarchist network as the domination network. Most societies (unless they are revolutionary societies) that have anarchist movements will also have accompanying domination networks. These networks will probably look rather similar, at least in terms of values and intent, although their form and constitution may differ. Presumably, every domination network will include all key components of the state. Central to state nodes of the domination network are politicians or state officials who make decisions, create laws, and have a strong interest in restricting anarchists and their ideas from greater social influence. Any and all elements of the state's law enforcement and social control sectors belong to domination networks. This part of the network will include intelligence agencies whose purpose is to gather information on dissidents, and any police who monitor and arrest the population (and usually have a special interest in suppressing anti-state radicals).[11]

Also, a likely part of domination networks will be very wealthy individuals, prominent corporations, and their advocates (trade associations, public relations agencies, chambers of commerce, union-busting law firms, and others). These parties are concerned with anarchist opposition to capitalism and, thus, pro-capitalists regularly spy on their critics (including anarchists), entrap them, and sometimes physically have goon squads attack and murder them. These domination network nodes are surely affiliated to a greater or lesser degree with the statist nodes of the network.[12]

Finally, domination networks include all institutions responsible for shaping public opinion. Mass media is actively involved in dissuading people from sympathizing with anarchism by churning out crude caricatures of anarchists, libelous news coverage, and fear-mongering.[13] This helps to create a general distrust and opposition to professed anarchists, and will discourage people from identifying with those that the media associates with the aforementioned triumvirate (chaotic, violent, naive people). These messages are also transmitted through formal education. While not necessarily involved in direct anti-anarchists propaganda (although it may do this in many places), educational institutions still indoctrinate youth with national myths, status quo values, favorable histories about elites, and platitudes about dominant institutions (especially the state and capitalism). One reaction to pro-domination history has been alternative histories, such as "peoples' histories," told from the perspectives of disadvantaged groups (see Zinn 1995). Religious institutions that foster individuals' blind obedience to authority, encourage a culture of subservience within hierarchical institutions, and oppose solidarity among dominated groups are also key components of domination networks.

The domination network includes people who are both conscious and unconscious of their participation in an anti-anarchist network. Participants may be actively involved in suppression, or may only act indirectly to accomplish goals that parallel or support direct suppression.[14] Regardless of people's awareness or commitment, members of the domination network do work against anarchist movements. For example, even though not every police officer or history teacher may despise anarchist ideas – and want to reduce anarchist liberties to speak and organize – they are still willing agents within systems that accomplish these ends. Their acquiescence, while seemingly better than the teacher who lies in order to indoctrinate or the belligerent cop who pepper sprays protesters, still facilitates the domination network's mission to successfully defeat anarchist movements.

Who is the subject?

For practical reasons, a politicized identification and public "outing" of an individual or group of anarchists is rather unwise, especially in places where fewer respected freedoms of association and speech exist. But, for strictly intellectual purposes, let's say we want to identify an anarchist. And then, presume we'd like to describe that anarchist. How would we do this? What criteria should we use? This was a major question that Jeff Shantz and I addressed in our book *Anarchy & Society* (Shantz & Williams 2013).

We could use verbal claims by people ("Yeah, I'm an anarchist"). But, should we accept at face value someone's claim that they *are* an anarchist? Should there be any minimum knowledge of anarchist principles or history for their assertion to be believed or in order to qualify?[15] We could look for passive indications, like someone sporting a "circle-A" symbol, maybe on a button or T-shirt. If we just trust symbolic representations, is it possible that these are simply stylistic performances, without (again) a recognition or acceptance of the political significance of the symbols? For example, many punk bands utilize circle-A symbols in their names and artwork, but does this make them anarchists? More importantly, does the presence of anarchist symbology imply that the musical fans who wear the band's merchandise are anarchists? Do fans that sport Rage Against the Machine paraphernalia do so because they appreciate the band's far-Left, anti-authoritarian political message or because they enjoy its hard rock musical riffs?

We could hypothesize that this person wearing black clothing who is in the vicinity of a radically themed protest is an anarchist. But, it's possible someone could just incidentally be wearing a combination of black clothing and stumble upon a protest. What explains people who just happen to like wearing black?[16] Mainstream media and politicians regularly insinuate that people wearing black clothing and covering their faces with bandannas at protests are anarchists. A critical inquiry should judge such claims as an impressive leap of logic to make such an assumption, to imply that one's political beliefs are conclusively discernible by one's clothing or presence. Many other groups, subcultures, and individuals favor the color black, and surely not all of them are anarchists.

Does the average media reporter know enough about radical protest tactics to be able to make key distinctions? For example, many reporters seem unaware that a "black bloc" is not an organization, but in fact a protest tactic. An individual does not need to sign a membership pledge ("Yes, I hereby swear that I am anarchist, under penalty of law …") in order to participate in a black bloc. Witness the scores of undercover police and fascists who "joined" the huge black bloc formations at the Genoa anti-G8 protests in 2001 – note that those individuals did so for the purposes of subversion, libel, and violence on protesters (see One Off 2001). Consider this rhetorical question: does a reporter witnessing a black-clad individual smashing a bank window, in the midst of a rowdy black bloc formation, ever bother to approach the individual in question to quiz them about their politics? "So, where do you stand on the insurrection versus organization debate? What do you think about The Platform? Can you name three famous nineteenth-century anarchists? Would you, in fact, identify as an autonomist, libertarian socialist, anti-authoritarian, or anarchist?" Of course, such questions are not asked. Why shouldn't time-tested, journalistic verification be the watermark when the media makes claims about individuals' politics? It's easy to carry out such verification with people who are enrolled political party members, but what about an ideology that has no membership requirements, and very little or no canon or dogma to uphold (or to blasphemy)? Thus, we ought to view such "reporting" as speculation, guesswork, hyperbole, or assumption. For social movement scholars, the bar must be set even higher. Such high standards are more serious, yet difficult to achieve when analyzing anarchist movements, given their unique qualities.

Some of this confusion is surely generated by mass media claims about those who identify as anarchists. Media regularly feel compelled to contextualize these identifications as questionable assertions. These contextualizations suggest that the individuals claiming to be anarchists are deliberately trying to deceive the media. All the inaccurate, but hegemonic, framings that media propagate (i.e., chaos, violence, fantasy), are likely reasons why reporters find it inconceivable that people would identify as anarchists. Witness the predictable weasel-language on TV news broadcasts or even the most prestigious newspapers "of record." An anarchist's identity is modified and questioned by placing the words "self-described," "self-proclaimed," or "self-styled" in front of it. Or, the word anarchist itself is placed in quotes – "anarchist" – as if to suggest that such people are something other than what they claim. Curiously, individuals of other political orientations are not subject to similar challenge and skepticism, for example, "self-proclaimed liberal," "self-described Christian Democrat," or "self-styled Republican."

This media presentation results in contradictory and paradoxical conclusions. People are assumed to be anarchists for the most superficial reasons (style of dress, symbols, behaviors), but then incredulously disbelieved when people actually claim the anarchist label. This seems to indicate something significant about the tension between mass media's desire to control the discourse and the sympathetic representation of anarchists' agency. Especially in the USA, mass media wishes to ascribe anarchist identity or membership only when convenient (often to propagate the triumvirate), or to downplay association when that identity might appear more attractive due to the positive and likable activities of the anarchists involved.[17]

While self-identified anarchists participating in anarchist movements are the subject of this book, it is sensible to acknowledge other populations of interest: non-movement anarchists and anarchistic individuals. Consequently, a strict emphasis on anarchist movements results in a severe undercounting of anarchists and activity level of anarchism in most societies. This is one of the many troubling issues of subject identification with social movement research, which has unavoidable consequences.

There are undoubtedly many people who identify as anarchists, but who do not actively participate in anarchist movements (although they may participate in non-anarchist movements). There is no way to conclusively determine how many such individuals exist in a given society, but it is likely that they consist of some former anarchist movement participants who still identify as anarchists and anarchists who have never (for whatever reason) participated in anarchist movements. Sometimes their lack of active participation is due to a disinterest in politics or geographic isolation, while for others it is due to competing time demands, responsibilities, and preferences. While this population is an important indicator of the state of anarchism, these individuals typically fall outside the bounds of this book's mission. Such individuals indicate the potential for bringing anarchist socio-political ideas into non-anarchist settings.

The second population of anarchistic individuals is even more challenging to interpret. These people do not identify as anarchists, but they or others are able to interpret either their beliefs or actions as being compatible with anarchism. In other words, anarchistic folk (the implicitly anarchist, described here) are akin to anarchists, but still reject the anarchist label, consciously or not. Numerous examples of such individuals can be found, just as anarchistic organizations are common in progressive movements. I focus upon a variety of anarchistic organizations that collaborate with anarchist movements or coexist within the same political milieux as anarchists, in Chapter 8 of this book. Here, I consider various anarchistic organizations or projects in North America. None are considered to be 100 percent anarchist and all include at least some non-anarchist-identified individuals, but their organizational structures and their practices are highly compatible with anarchist structures and practices.

Next, I consider the scope in which we can analyze explicitly anarchist movements.

Multi-level analysis

Social scientists are keen to describe the unit and level of analysis that their research focuses on. For most studies, this signifies the limiting of research scope. But I do not wish to limit the scope of this book to one particular level of analysis or subject. Thus, many different types of observations and data sources are included in the pages that follow. At the micro-level, analysis can focus on individual anarchists – famous or not, alive or deceased, old or young, activists or inactive, and so forth. Chapter 2 presents an analysis of some anarchists, as individuals, and describes some of their key traits, such as their political ideology, socio-demographic characteristics, behaviors, and opinions. This is a crucial element to a study of anarchists, who tend to prioritize individual autonomy. We could also engage in a meso-level analysis, where the organized (and less-than-organized) configurations created by anarchists are the unit of analysis. Here the formal and informal anarchist organizations, groups, and projects can be interrogated. Everything from affinity groups, anarchist soccer clubs, or reading groups to syndicalist unions, federations, or collectives are not simply subjects warranting study, but are also the lived expressions of anarchist movements. Chapter 3 provides an incomplete snapshot of the global anarchist organizational field. At a slightly more scaled-up unit of analysis, we could focus on anarchist events, protests, or other actions. Perhaps anything organized by anarchists, attended by anarchists, or even anarchistic in design or execution could be of interest. Finally, a larger focus is possible, which can be characterized as macro-level. Here the structure of society (whether anarchist or far-less-than-anarchist) or entire movements can be analyzed in all their grandness and complexity. Chapters 5 and 6, which focus on political opportunity and new social movement theories, respectively, embrace this sort of macro analysis, due to their concerns with political, economic, and cultural institutions.

There are pitfalls, regardless of the unit of analysis we choose to study. Methodologists warn against committing "logical fallacies," two principal ones being the ecological fallacy and reductionist fallacy (Babbie 2010). The fallacies occur for inappropriately drawn conclusions for the data available. Thus, we have to consider what the data "says" for the unit of analysis we have, and what conclusions we can honestly and legitimately make. For example, to avoid the ecological fallacy, we should remember that even though many anarchist organizations exist in a country that does not mean that, proportionately, there are a lot of individual anarchists; there could just be one or two members (or the same people) in each organization. In other words, the anarchist movement may have many organizations, but few participating individuals. Or, to commit the reductionist fallacy, we could inappropriately assume that the presence of certain types of anarchists implies particular types of organizations that exist or what kinds of actions will occur. Maybe the organizations that exist are very unrepresentative of the actual orientations of individual anarchists.

Thus, although we can appraise information of any unit of analysis, translating one set of information about anarchists to a different unit of analysis is unwise. Just because we can find (or even gather together in a room) a few dozen anarchists and some organizations in a city, does not mean there is any kind of a coherent movement, let alone one that coordinates or contains individuals who like each other. Or, similarly, we cannot assume that every anarchist living in a city is, in practice, a member of that city's anarchist movement (even if it were a very active movement). A dramatic protest even does not imply a large movement – those involved may simply be influenced by Saul Alinsky's (1971) "rule" about making a lot of noise when activist numbers are small. Just because anarchists attend or even organize an event that supports striking workers, doesn't mean that the anarchists in attendance identify as anarcho-syndicalists. Or, finally, when an anarchist protest or action involves property destruction, we cannot assume that any anarchist at the event (or anarchists in general, including those who did not attend) supports any particular act of property destruction (or vice versa). Nor should we assume that those anarchists would themselves commit that property destruction given the chance.

Important comparisons worth making

Like all social scientists, movement scholars operate by making comparisons (Klandermans & Smith 2002) between various subjects – the intent and ideal result is greater illumination.[18] Comparison helps to explicate what is different and what is similar – and directly or indirectly also indicate potential causes. We can make a variety of comparisons regarding anarchists and social movements, thus bringing the nature and specific details of anarchist movements into clearer focus (see Table 1.2). For example, we can compare those parts of anarchist movements which are explicitly and

Table 1.2 Understanding anarchism via comparative approaches

Subject of comparison	Case 1	Case 2
Movements	Anarchist movement	Non-anarchist movement
Individuals	Anarchist individuals	Non-anarchist individuals
Organizations	Anarchist organization 1	Anarchist organization 2
Faction/subvariants	Movement faction/ subvariant 1	Movement faction/ subvariant 2
Locations	Location 1	Location 2
Time periods	Time period 1	Time period 2

overtly anarchist against those who are anarchistic (i.e., reject the label "anarchist," but act in accordance with key anarchist values). Or, anarchist movements may be understood by contrasting them to other "like movements" or "unlike movements," such as liberals, Marxists, or parliamentarians. These inter-movement comparisons delineate salient lines of separation between movements, so certain qualities of anarchist movements will appear distinct from those of other movements. Other potential comparisons include specific comparisons of anarchists to non-anarchists, anarchist organizations to non-anarchist organizations, and so on.

We could also make intra-movement comparisons: contrast those of differing ideological subvariants within an anarchist movement. For example, how do anarcho-communists differ from anarcho-syndicalists? There are strong differences, but perhaps many of these differences would lessen if they were compared to individualists, primitivists, insurrectionists, or anarcho-punks. Or, what kinds of activities do anarchist collectives and affinity groups engage in, and how are they different? What effect does organizational structure have on their activities? Chapter 8 compares a variety of anarchistic organizations, such as Earth First! and Food Not Bombs.

Comparisons across space would result in other enlightening matches. For example, how do anarchist movements in North America differ from South America, Europe, Africa, or Asia? These continental comparisons might be proxies for wealthy versus poor countries, or even comparisons within the world-system. How about comparisons between anarchist movements within dictatorships and democracies? Within a single country, we could further compare anarchists within certain areas. In the USA, such comparisons could highlight differences between West coast and East coast (Williams 2009b), or rural versus urban, small town versus big city. Chapter 3 utilizes data from the Anarchist Yellow Pages (AYP), showing the variations across space and organizational type.

Finally, we could make comparisons across time. A variety of students of anarchist movement history have noted various waves of mobilization and activity (Cornell 2016; Sunshine 2013; and Schmidt 2013 to name a few). For example, to understand the nature of anarchist movements at certain moments, we can compare their conditions, composition, and strategies to other times. How do movements vary during anarchism's "golden age," after World War I, after the Spanish Revolution in the late 1930s, during the 1960s, and at the current time? To be more specific, contrasts could consider making explicit comparisons, such as between the contemporary period and golden age, or the contemporary period and the 1960s. Analyses may have to be somewhat ad hoc, but we can be assisted by certain data, comparing, say, the 1983 International Blacklist and the 1997 AYP to the 2005 AYP (see Chapter 3 for an analysis of this example). Chapter 5 uses the A-Infos newswire to illustrate the longitudinal changes in numerous local anarchist movements, and looks for patterns and dissimilarities across these movements. This comparison could show which countries have changed the number of anarchist organizations, what kind of organizations, and what has been the overall change throughout the world during those years.

Levels of analysis considered temporally

In addition to comparing time periods, we can also use time constructs to reflect on anarchist practice and goals. We can use a temporal model that considers past examples, current examples, and future examples based on utopian design or anarchist ideology. As with participants in many other movements, anarchists wish to preserve past anarchist movement history, to continue anarchist activity in the present, and to aspire to an anarchist vision for the future. And to make for an even richer exploration of anarchist movement by time, let us add a social scale dimension. As indicated earlier, sociologists regularly measure social phenomenon at a variety of levels of analysis, specifically the micro- (individual, interactional or situational), meso- (organizational), or macro- (institutional) levels. When we combine these levels with different time periods – both of which have three categories – we generate a three-by-three grid, or a typology with nine potential categories. By viewing anarchist movements with a chronological dimension we can better understand where they have previously been, where they are now, and where they would like to go (in line with their ideological aspirations). The second dimension of social scale helps to consider the magnitude of these efforts in a societal context. Let us explore how time interacts with scale (see Table 1.3).

Past micro examples could include amazing, influential personalities or relationships. Here, we could select Emma Goldman as such an exemplar

Table 1.3 Anarchist movements understood via time and level of analysis

Level of analysis	Past (previous successes)	Present (current examples)	Future (ideologically suggested)
Micro (small: individual, event)	Amazing, influential personalities EX. Emma Goldman	Real-existing mutual aid EX. gift-giving	Future interaction EX. intuitive individual-social balance
Meso (middle: group, organization)	Successful models, organizations EX. CNT, IWW	Current organizations EX. Food Not Bombs	Future organizations EX. revolutionary general assemblies
Macro (large: institutions, societal)	Revolutionary societies EX. Barcelona 1936, Paris 1968	Current societies EX. Zapatista-controlled Chiapas	Grand models EX. ParEcon, anarcho-communism (platform)

individual and her incredible relationships with fellow anarchists, such as Johann Most, Ben Reitman, Voltairine de Cleyre, Rudolf Rocker, Peter Kropotkin, and most importantly Alexander Berkman (Goldman 1970). We could also investigate the individual characteristics of past anarchists, such as their social class. If we looked to past organizational models, we could focus on the Confederacion de Nacional Trabajando (CNT), which was the major trade union in revolutionary Spain in the 1930s. The organization represented approximately one and a half million Spanish workers and had an anarcho-syndicalist ideology. The Iberian Anarchist Federation (FAI) formed with regards to the CNT to emphasize revolutionary anarchist strategy, so today many people often refer to the CNT-FAI (see Garner 2016). Or, in the Anglo world and elsewhere, the Industrial Workers of the World was a syndicalist (not necessarily anarcho-syndicalist) union that represented many unskilled laborers in the USA (van der Walt & Schmidt 2009). Then, past macro-level analyses could emphasize the experiences of revolutionary Spain, especially in 1936 Barcelona, or other revolutionary societies, such as Mexico in 1910 or Russia in 1917 (see Marshall 2010; Schmidt 2013, among others). In each case, everyday people created their own democratic institutions that directly made decisions, expropriated (or tried to expropriate) the means of industrial production, and advocated for wide social changes.

When focusing on the current period, our micro-level focus might look for examples of really existing mutual aid. The prevalence of gift-giving within anarchist movements would meet this criteria, as would the occasional Really Really Free Markets that operate like open-air "free stores," where no money is used and no products are traded – everything is available for anyone to take. At the meso-level, we could note current organizations such as Food Not Bombs, Crimethinc, the Zabalaza Anarcho-Communist Federation, or the International of Anarchist Federations. These present-day organizations put anarchism into practice on a daily basis in their organizing. Lastly, a present-day example of a macro-level phenomenon might be harder to ascertain, but we could point toward Zapatista-controlled Chiapas, Mexico, where local communities administer their territories via popular assemblies. (Note: the Zapatistas do *not* generally identify as anarchists, but many autonomist-oriented and communal-indigenous movements have strong anarchistic tendencies.)

Finally, forecasting anarchist movements is more challenging. What exactly would qualify as a future anarchist interaction at the micro-level? Perhaps the ability of all individuals to instinctively understand how to pursue their own interests and desires, but also knowing how the rights of others and the collective good places restraints on individuals' actions. We could predict future organizations at the meso-level, like revolutionary general assemblies (perhaps akin to, although also expanded from, the wave of popular, directly democratic uprisings during 2010–13, such as those in Egypt, Spain, Puerto Rico, the USA [Occupy], and many other places). Finally, many grand models exist within the anarchist tradition that suggests the ways in which macro-level institutions would be constituted. Some of these include anarcho-communism, in particular the Platform, which illustrates a future libertarian communist society (Skirda 2002). Or the highly detailed participatory economics (ParEcon) model developed by Michael Albert and Robin Hahnel (1991) suggests the ways in which production, distribution, and consumption could be structured to occur in line with anarchist values (e.g., diversity, worker self-management, equity, solidarity, and efficiency).[19]

Drawing primitive, tentative conclusions

This chapter has introduced the essential characteristics of social movements and their sociological study. The principal example I have used are contemporary anarchist movements. Based on this discussion, it is possible to draw a number of rudimentary conclusions. These may seem obvious to many movement participants or students of social movements, but they are still crucial points to emphasize: movements are real, complicated, and analyzable.

First, social movements are real. This phenomenological approach assumes that real things have a physical, real-world form that we can observe and study. Although academic movement research prefers to focus on successful reform-oriented movements, anarchist movements are also legitimate and worthwhile subjects. Although movements have objective realities – for example, anarchists do stage protests, congregate at real book fairs, and belong to collective organizations – they can also have subjective realities. Anarchist movement participants do not view their movement or their own involvement via the mainstream triumvirate. To truly understand anarchism, we should consider the objective conditions of anarchist movements, as well as the subjective vision and interpretation of anarchism by movement participants. Such movement behavior makes the most sense when viewed through anarchist *verstehen*. Further, the lack of largesse or successful acquisition of long-term goals (i.e., revolution) does not negate a movement's existence. Movements exist because self-aware people identify their own collective participation – in other words, movements exist because people say so and act accordingly.

Second, social movements are complicated. It is difficult for outsiders to truly understand the experience of movement insiders. Likewise, it is often challenging for movement participants to fully articulate the breadth of movement experience, behavior, and goals to non-participants. A diverse, multifaceted approach is necessary to understand a movement's complexity. Unlike the crude caricatures offered in mainstream media, propagandistic dismissals offered by politicians, or even the "talking points" offered by many social movements' spokespeople, movements are neither simple nor without contradiction. In the case of anarchist movements, this complication begins with deliberate obfuscation (recall the anti-anarchist network's activities), but also involves varied ideologies, strategic priorities, and organizational methods (recall the figure depicting the American anarchist movement network above).

Third, social movements can be explained and modeled (although never to everyone's satisfaction). These ends are the purpose of theory. Numerous larger theoretical frameworks have emerged (not quite "grand theories," but definitely focused on the big picture), as well as smaller theories that have applicability in certain limited contexts. The diversity of movement theories – indeed, the contradictory nature of many of these theories – suggests a post-modernist approach to theories' utility from situation to situation, movement to movement. Consequently, no movement theory seems to work perfectly, in all instances. And nor should it. Chapter 4 begins the critique of movement theories, which is continued into Chapters 5, 6, and 7.

Next, I delve deeper into the multi-level approach presented in Table 1.2, by analyzing contemporary anarchist movements from both micro- and meso-perspectives (Chapters 2 and 3, respectively).

Notes

1   Ba Jin. 1932. *The Autumn in the Spring*, pp. 8–9.
2   There is another semantical meaning to "movement" that I wish to mention. Some have argued – Black feminist bell hooks (2000) being my favorite example – for conceptualizing movements in literal, temporal terms. Thus, anarchist movement, like feminist movement, is a trajectory that people follow. People move in movements. Things are changing and people are brought along with these changes. While I do not use the word "movement" in this sense here, I do want to acknowledge its conceptual value.
3   These arguments may appear to some readers as strawmen, but I have personally heard each objection, even though no scholarly reference can be given to prove a claim's existence.
4   However, some AFA, EF!, and FNB collectives *do* identify as anarchist organizations, while many others do not.
5   To say that someone is "an anarchist in government" is to grossly misunderstand the meaning of anarchism. Dennis Kucinich take note!
6   Collective agreement of what constitutes anarchism allows for out-grouping improperly anarchists like "anarcho-capitalists."
7   For more on "frames," see Chapter 4's discussion of the frame alignment theory of social movements.
8   "Libertarian" in most non-North American countries is simply a synonym for left-wing anarchist, especially when the label is appended (as it often is) with a "-socialist" or "-communist" suffix. The American proto-capitalist "libertarian" Murray Rothbard (2007) bragged of his "side" finally "captur[ing]" the term "libertarian" from his "enemy," whom he identified as "anti-private property anarchists, either of the communist or syndicalist variety" (2007: 83).
9   A remarkable consequence of this anti-authoritarianism is best seen in contrast to the many varieties of socialism named for authoritarian leaders (e.g., Leninism, Stalinism, Castroism, Trotskyism, and Maoism). Preceding all such varieties is Marxism which, as Grubacic & Graeber (2004) note, is the only political philosophy named after an individual with a PhD. Yet, no such patterns exist within anarchism: there is no Malatestaism, Landauerism, or Kropotkinism.
10   Consider the British anti-poll tax movement (Burns 1992), the Indian decolonization movement (Ramnath 2011), or numerous examples discussed in Lynd and Grubacic (2008), where anarchist were important players, but were not alone.
11   The American manifestation of these has been "red squads" and "anti-terrorism units," who attempt to enforce authoritarian legislation such as the Sedition Act, Smith Act, "criminal syndication laws," and so on. Even the European agency Interpol has origins in monitoring and suppressing anarchists (Jensen 1981).
12   There may be affinities here with organized or individual fascists, who are also part of the domination network, who often act violently toward anarchists, albeit without legitimate authority to do so.

13 Whether in the past (Cobb-Reiley 1988; Hong 1992) or in the present (McLeod & Detenber 1999; McLeod & Hertog), media distortion has been a consistent dynamic during the entire history of anarchism (and other radical social movements).

14 Note here the similarities between the domination network and the institutions that Boykoff (2007) describes as instrumental in the suppression of dissent (specifically the state and private media).

15 Recall the above bewildering claims of groups in the USA as diverse as Libertarian Party members, the Unabomber, or "national anarchists" to the anarchist moniker. Unfortunately, most media uncritically report these claims of identity (probably because in doing so "anarchists" are negatively libeled), as opposed to properly characterizing these people as ultra-capitalists, terrorists, or racists, respectively.

16 Note that this assumption also leads to the implication that people might cease to be anarchists when no longer wearing black. But, anarchists do not simply engage in black-bloc type events, but a wide variety of activities, most of which do not require "masking up."

17 There are a few notable exceptions, especially local media who are a bit naive to the issue.

18 Émile Durkheim famously argued that the core analytical approach of sociology is comparison.

19 Like many future-oriented systems, ParEcon has been criticized, including by a number of anarchists. For example, class-struggle anarchist critiques may be found at www.nefac.net/parecon

2

Anarchists as individuals: a micro-structural analysis

How can a rational being be ennobled by anything that is not obtained by its own exertions? (Mary Wollstonecraft)[1]

Anarchists are people – but what *kinds* of people?

Social movements must be composed of individuals. But what kinds of individuals? Anarchist movements are so called not only *because* of who they involve, but also *in spite of* those individuals' characteristics. Key concerns for movement scholars are how participants identify socially and politically, what the movements' class composition are, and whether anarchists belong to labor unions and worker organizations like those from "golden age" anarchist movements. Many observers, pundits, law enforcement agents, intellectuals, and others claim to know the answers to these questions, but their self-proclaimed "knowledge" is often speculative, myopic, anecdotal, or just fallacious.

This chapter attempts to provide new insights into individual participants in anarchist movements by investigating two related questions. First, what are the micro-level characteristics of contemporary anarchists? Second, how do these characteristics differ from those of anarchists in past movements? To address the former question, I explore the socio-demographics, identities, and behaviors, actions, and experiences of today's anarchists. To make these characterizations, I rely on two large, convenience sample-based internet surveys, the 2002 Infoshop.org user survey and the 2010 "Big Anarchist Survey." While the quantitative analysis that follows is not generalizable, per se, many meaningful observations can be made to help understand *who* populates today's anarchist movements.

To address the latter question, I provide a brief overview of past anarchist movements, which were strongly rooted in working-class and intellectual communities, prioritized a certain political focus (anti-capitalist, anti-state, and anti-clerical), and worked through a variety of organizations (especially worker organizations). This preliminary analysis, albeit incomplete and imperfect, helps us to understand in what ways today's anarchists are different from those of the past. While some prominent changes and developments have occurred, there are also striking points of overlap that caution us against the notion of a complete transformation or discontinuity of anarchist movements of the past and present.

Those from the domination (i.e., anti-anarchist) network – especially mass media and law enforcement – warn their respective publics that today's dangerous anarchists[2] are young, privileged men (and in Global North countries, white men). In other words, rebellious anarchists are claimed to be, paradoxically, individuals who society has thoroughly rewarded. The implication is that anarchists are ungrateful individuals who do not appreciate all that the system has provided them. For example, a redacted document from the Federal Bureau of Investigation – a key actor in the American domination network – claims that anarchist movements are "made up of younger, educated, middle to upper class individuals" (FBI 2011). While not citing any thorough analysis or data source, the FBI seems to claim that (American) anarchists come from backgrounds of relative privilege. Additionally, anarchists are "not dedicated to a particular cause," are "criminals seeking an ideology to justify their activities," and are "generally unorganized and reactive." Each of these claims can easily be interrogated with the right data. It is clear that the FBI wishes to denigrate current anarchists – libeling them as either privileged cry-babies, muddle-heads, criminals, or chaoticians. Notice how these claims closely reflect the three misperceptions described in Chapter 1: they are criminals (and, the FBI goes on to allege, violent), disorganized malcontents, and overly educated kids who have pie-in-the-sky ideas (which aren't well thought out). Curiously, the document's negative intonation of current anarchists contrasts with the FBI's more benign and almost positive description of "past" anarchist movements, who were "highly dedicated," "individuals turning to criminal activity [only?] out of frustration" (instead of being criminals from the start), and were "fairly well-organized and proactive" (see these two FBI slides in Figures 2.1a and 2.1b).

So, are anarchists today "just kids"? Do they all come from privileged backgrounds? Do they possess scattered political ideologies? Do they not really *do* the things they claim to do, with principle? These are crucial questions, whose answers are not as simple or as supportive of FBI claims as one might expect from the confident propaganda of the domination network.

Anarchists of the past

In order to determine how modern anarchism differs from the past, we must briefly consider what anarchism has previously been like. Anarchism has

Anarchist Extremism Overview

- Past Characteristics of the Anarchist Movement
  - Highly dedicated to a specific cause / ideology
  - Individuals turning to criminal activity out of frustration
  - Fairly well-organized and proactive
  - Made up of educated individuals from various backgrounds, often students

UNCLASSIFIED/LES

Anarchist Extremism Overview

- Current Characteristics of the Movement
  - Not dedicated to a particular cause
  - Criminals seeking an ideology to justify their activities
  - Generally unorganized and reactive
  - Made up of younger, educated, middle to upper class individuals

UNCLASSIFIED/LES

2.1 Characteristics of the anarchist movement from Federal Bureau of Investigation slideshow "Anarchist extremism"

changed depending on who anarchists are and on their evolving analysis of the world, but it is also due to changes in the rest of the world. The impact of external changes upon anarchist movements are worthy of reflection, as these changes have influenced both the anarchists as well as the issues that they have deemed worthy of focus. The maturation and extension of capitalism is surely one of the crucial factors since the origins of anarchism's early years in the mid-1800s. One development that has had a definitive impact on most societies, especially the wealthy countries of the West, has been the growth of the middle classes and expansion of white-collar jobs. In addition, the Global South has been influenced by decolonization and independence movements, as well as the imposition of neo-colonialism under the tutelage/boot of free-market economics, the International Monetary Fund and World Bank, and through integration into the world-system. Finally, due to the de-industrialization of Western economies (and the subsequent shift of production to semi-periphery and periphery countries) private-sector unions have weakened (particularly in North America, but also elsewhere). Consequently, anarchists have had to change their strategies as they face new struggles and perceive new enemies.

Historically, anarchism was deeply embedded within labor movements (Schmidt & van der Walt 2009), which include, but are not the same as trade unions, per se. Of course, there have been many manifestations of anarchism and many anarchists unconnected to labor struggles, but since anarchism's origins overlap with the beginnings of the Industrial Revolution, it is not surprising that anarchist movements focused so heavily on the plight of laborers throughout the world, as laborers were the principal participants in those movements. Thus, the centrality of organizations like the International Working Peoples' Association and other such organizations in the resistance to growing industrial capitalism and rapacious colonial empires. Many anarchist movements also saw the active participation of peasants – not only in Mexico, Korea, Bolivia, and the Ukraine, but also in Spain (Hirsch & van der Walt 2010).

To definitively compare participants in historical anarchism movements to today's versions is tricky, as little effort was made to systematically record information on the social constitution (i.e., the socio-demographic characteristics of individuals) of earlier waves of anarchist activity. Numerous studies exist that purport to show anecdotal patterns in previous anarchists, but to provide a general overview of such characteristics – particularly when individuals may come and go, or when they choose to express their participation in such movements without organizational membership – would seem to necessitate having access to historically gathered survey instruments. Anarchist journalists and authors recorded some of this history, as do some of the records of the members and activists involved in anarchist projects and organizations (the records of which were recorded by both movement participants and the state). But, such documentation is either ad hoc, or horrendously incomplete and partial. Still, each year numerous new projects continue to fill in the gaps in various society's historical records.

While there have always been egoist or individualist-identified anarchists, who eschewed the class-struggle models of syndicalists and anarcho-communists (as well as so-called "lifestylism," focused on things like nudism or vegetarianism), almost all past anarchists or "libertarians" were anti-capitalists who rejected the Marxist and social democrat strategy of using the state to liberate the working classes. Instead, anarchists advocated self-liberation, whether through personal autonomy or class struggle.

Some things have not changed between the various waves of anarchist activity. Anarchism remains internationalist in orientation and action – not only is human liberation viewed as a global challenge, but anarchists continue to investigate the struggles taking place elsewhere in the world, share information about other locales, as well as coordinating and providing assistance to other anarchists. Anarchists continue to find themselves in conflict with police and other state authorities. The earliest anarchists found themselves arrested, beaten, imprisoned, blacklisted, deported, repressed, and sometimes murdered just like anarchist movements today.[3] Since anarchists have rarely (although not never) represented a dominant tendency in most societies, they continue to collaborate with various non-anarchist struggles deemed worthy of support. We can use the life of a single anarchist from the past, to illustrate some of these overlaps: Emma Goldman in the USA not only participated in working-class movements, but also supported free speech, birth control, feminist, and pro-gay movements of her era (Ferguson 2011). Finally, anarchists have always and continue to engage in propaganda efforts, designed not only to share anarchist analysis and information with fellow anarchists, but to advocate that other non-anarchists adjust their own thinking to pursue individual and collective liberation.

Anarchists have published hundreds of newspapers and magazines (read by millions), operated publishing presses, and websites and other digital media (e.g., Renz 2005).

There is also considerable evidence that anarchists have been a regular presence in post-1968 Western social movements for decades. In the US anti-nuclear movement, approximately one-quarter of participants at the Seabrook occupation in 1978 identified as anarchists (Katz & List 1981;[4] also confirmed by Epstein 1991). The contentious poll tax rebellion in the UK was initially instigated by Scottish anarchists (Burns 1992; Kanaan 2004). Participants in the squatter movement and social center organizers in mainland Europe often have anarchist identities (Martínez 2007; Mudu 2004). Anarchists continue to be active in various left-wing movements throughout North America and the world (Epstein 2001; Graeber 2002; Shantz 2003b). There has been an increased focus on anarchists in recent years, particularly on participants in global justice, anti-capitalist, and anti-war protests, of which anarchist participation in Occupy Wall Street and other anti-austerity movements are just the most recent examples in the early 2010s (Bray 2013; Schneider 2013; Williams 2011a).

If anarchism today is a "new social movement" – like the environmental, peace, or women's movements – then a large anarchist working-class constituency, or a movement emphasis on class and labor issues, ought to be absent. In particular, a major social movement organization in the past century – the labor union – would presumably be invisible within anarchist movements. Some have claimed that anarchists tend not to participate in unions and labor-oriented campaigns for varied reasons, including differing culture, backgrounds, organizations, and tactics (Sheppard 2002). Is this true? What *would* explain the participation of anarchists in labor unions? Additionally, there is much evidence suggesting that the middle class is the economic class most directly engaged in social and political change activism today (Cohen 1985; Melucci 1989). Is the working class thus invisible in current anarchist movements? In order to explore these assumptions, responses from anarchist-focused surveys are analyzed. In particular, anarchist movements are assessed via their membership in a commonplace organization, the labor union. The analysis uses some theoretical arguments from new social movement (NSM) theories; a more complete analysis of the relationship between NSM theories and anarchist movements is conducted in Chapter 6.

Anarchist surveys

Here I try to empirically gauge how contemporary anarchists differ from both their historical predecessors and from popular depictions of anarchists.

To do this, I utilize an interesting collection of data: surveys gathered by anarchists about themselves. While it is crucial to caution that these survey respondents are not necessarily representative of all anarchists, they do constitute a body of data from which much can be learned. In particular, I conduct an analysis primarily of North American anarchists – since this is where most survey responses came from – and their various characteristics and attitudes, analysis that until now has been severely lacking. More generally, I compare these survey respondents to the abstract perception of contemporary anarchists, especially their identities, class positions, and relationship to labor unions.

This data was extracted from two sources. First, I used a 2002 user survey of the prominent North American anarchist website, the Mid-Atlantic Infoshop (www.infoshop.org [Infoshop]). Previous mass media research has shown that Infoshop is an online nexus for anarchist information (including "counter-propaganda") and it links to other anarchist websites (Owens & Palmer 2003). The full survey includes 968 responses. I also supplemented this survey with the secondary results from another internet survey, administered in 2010, known as "The Big Anarchist Survey." The Big Anarchist Survey (BAS) had more respondents ($N = 2,504$) and included many questions (64 total), some of which are comparable to the Infoshop survey (Knoll & Eloff 2010).

Although some have expressed concern that web surveys do not achieve representative samples comparable to the general population, Koch and Emrey (2001) determined that web surveys *were* a suitable method for surveying marginalized populations, such as gays and lesbians, in their study, due to the difficulty in identifying a suitable sampling frame in a population. Thus, studying another marginalized population like anarchists with an online survey may be appropriate. Yet, in using surveys with unknown response rates, I must re-emphasize that the results only summarize Infoshop users and BAS respondents who took these surveys, not anarchists more generally, although similarities should be expected. The Infoshop survey includes some respondents who are unemployed (the majority of whom are under 18 years of age); these people are removed from some of the upcoming analyses on identity, class, and unions based on the premise that it is unlikely that they will be union members, based on their employment status.

It is important to not commit an ecological fallacy with these surveys by assuming that (for example), because most anarchists in these surveys appear to be males, any particular anarchist scene is therefore itself male-dominated. Or, just because anarchists also appear to be relatively young (under 40), we should resist concluding that many cities do not have large numbers of anarchists over the age of 40. Likewise, we should resist committing a reductionist fallacy where we may assume that because news media propagate images of young anarchists (most of whom *seem* to be male) smashing windows, *all* anarchists are young male insurrectionists. As we will see, there are many female anarchists, older anarchists, and non-insurrectionists (or those who don't participate in black blocs). In other words, these surveys provide guidance for our analysis, but do not provide any definitive *final* analysis.

Also, the Euro-centric nature of these surveys may create the misperception that anarchist movements are exclusively North American and European phenomena. A digital divide exists that prevents many people in poorer countries from participating in online surveys.[5] Language barriers such as mastery of English may also restrict the participation of anarchists whose native language is Arabic, French, Japanese, Russian, Spanish, or some other language. These sorts of issues reduce the likelihood that very different types of anarchists from the Global South participated in these surveys. Consequently, this analysis, while possibly informative about global anarchist movements, is most useful for interpreting Western anarchist movements.

Other factors may have also restricted participation of non-internet users (especially those who are older, poorer, reside in countries of the Global South, or may be illegalists).[6] Luddite tendencies in certain strains of anarchism have also likely filtered out anarchists who have strong oppositions to the use of technology (advanced or otherwise). The inability to include such anarchists weakens conclusions based on this data. Likewise, potential participants may have been deterred by their (reasonable) concerns about the safety of online communications, as they may know their online activities are or could be monitored. Thus, disclosing intimate personal information, even to a trusted partner, may be risky. Also, since it is likely that few survey respondents personally knew the survey designers, many anarchists may have had concerns either about the intentions or identities of the survey designers (i.e., what will this data be used for, how can I guarantee that this survey designer isn't really working for law enforcement, etc.?). While both surveys were widely circulated among anarchists – lending legitimacy and trustworthiness – and were presented by well-known anarchists (especially in the case of Infoshop.org), there were surely some who simply refused to share information about themselves. Some of these safety issues and the efforts of spy agencies are discussed in greater depth in Chapter 9.

I argue that web surveys such as those described here remain a reasonable source of data for small, subcultural populations – like anarchists – regardless of the difficulties of generalizing with the data (see Peytchev *et al.* 2006). These surveys accomplish certain objectives that the data in later chapters (such as Chapter 3) are not able to do. By gathering responses from individual anarchists, we are able to understand more about the anarchist movement's composition beyond the organizations (meso-level) that individuals are involved in. Surveys are therefore desirable as they obtain data on more than just the participants in formal organizations (like the anarchist organizations listed in directories like the Anarchist Yellow Pages), since not all anarchists are members of such organizations. In fact, many anarchists do not belong to these organizations – for a variety of ideological, practical, and incidental reasons. Thus, surveys facilitate an analysis that transcends the far more organized realms of anarchist movements. However, there is nothing wrong with retaining some skepticism about these surveys' generalizability and taking their results with a grain of salt.

I use the Infoshop and Big Anarchist surveys to loosely compare contemporary anarchists to anarchists of the past and to the much-feared anarchist bogeyman of the popular media. (Again, lacking a comparative sample from the past, this discussion is necessarily ad hoc.) To do this comparison, I divide the analysis into three separate inquiries. First, I consider the socio-demographics of anarchists, their ideological orientations, and other identities. Second, I explore the class backgrounds and identifications of anarchists. Finally, I assess anarchist participation within "old" social movement organizations of the past: labor unions.

Anarchists, ideology, and identity

The range of concern for the anarchist movement is now far more diverse than it was during the classical age, when its primary focus was economic; the largest groupings at that time were collectivists and individualists – who concerned themselves with collective and individual freedom, respectively (Nettlau 2001).[7] Contemporary anarchists have ideologically branched out into other issues that were not widely part of social movements in the past (e.g., gender and the environment). There are examples of nearly all of the following contemporary labels in past movements, although they used different language. This diversity can be seen in how anarchists sometimes identify with particular strains or tendencies, often noted in the prefix or suffix applied to their ideology label. People who call themselves "social anarchists" focus on general social injustices and hierarchy (Bookchin 1995; Ehrlich 1996). "Anarcha-feminists" emphasize gender-related issues, such as reproductive choice, domestic violence, and other forms of patriarchal domination (Kornegger 2002). "Eco-anarchists" emphasize a tandem focus on defense against corporate and governmental destruction of the environment (Purchase 1997; Foreman and Bookchin 2001).[8] "Anarcho-communists" emphasize egalitarian, communist values such as producer and consumer cooperatives and collective ownership of all the means of production in society (Berkman 2003). "Anarcho-syndicalists" advocate worker control and ownership over the means of production in the workplace, often practiced in the form of radical unionism (Rocker 1990). Finally, insurrectionist tendencies favor immediate confrontation with the state and capitalism, emphasizing anarchist participation in popular uprisings.

Presumably, if one chooses to claim a specific orientation such as those mentioned above, such self-identification will reflect a tendency towards certain actions. For example, those with an anarcho-syndicalist focus may be more likely to join and organize labor unions. There are also those who identify as "anarchists without adjectives," which signifies an embrace or tolerance for all the various ideological strains (Nettlau 1996; De Cleyre 2004). Although seemingly disparate in nature, all these strains are linked and grounded by a common rejection of hierarchical authority and domination, and the desire to address society's problems in a fashion that allows for self-determination and cooperation (see Jeppesen *et al.* 2014) Thus, contemporary anarchists are imitators of past generations of anarchists who have extended those earlier analyses into new and different contexts (such as race, sexuality, and other areas).

The average age of the Infoshop survey respondents was 25. This result suggests that either anarchists are, on average, younger than the general population or that anarchists who take online surveys are apt to be younger (perhaps due to older anarchists not having internet access or knowing what Infoshop.org is). The respondents appear to be a cohort of only one generation, and a handful of middle-aged and older respondents skew the mean age to appear older than one might expect at first glance. We do not have any strong demographic studies of anarchist movements from previous generations. If we did, it would be possible to compare the average ages.[9] Surely, many past anarchists were also young, but a strong anarchists and radical working-class culture kept alive an interest in anarchism for the entire life course of many individuals. Thus, while young anarchists continue to age, they actively convey movement history and culture to younger generations.

Respondents to the Infoshop survey differ from the general US population in a number of other noteworthy ways – only 20 percent were female and 80 percent identified as white. North Americans constituted 85 percent of respondents, which reflects the orientation of the website and the fact that the survey was asked only in English.[10] The Big Anarchist Survey reflected these general trends, albeit to a more extreme degree. Of those who selected female or male gender, only 14 percent were female – showing that the BAS respondents were more likely to be male than for the Infoshop survey. This could point to a problematic masculinity trend in the anarchist movement or simply be indicative of who was answering surveys during these two different time periods.

The male domination in anarchist movements has often been the subject of commentary by contemporary anarcha-feminists and other anarchist females who have referred to anarchist movements as "boys' clubs" or exclusionary environments (Beallor 2000; Threat n.d.). Of course, there may be simple selection effects that either excluded anarchist females' participation in these surveys or have reduced anarchistic females' formal self-identification with anarchism. Women *are* active participants in radical movements – and often serve as the glue which holds those movements together – while at the same time receiving less credit for doing so, having a marginalized visibility in movements, and rejecting formal definitions (see Hurwitz & Taylor 2012). Also, there exists a great degree of sexual identification variety in the Infoshop and BAS. Many respondents indicate being "genderqueer" and far more identify their sexuality as bisexual and queer than one might expect to find in the general populations of European and North American countries – only 73 percent of BAS respondents identified as heterosexual. This suggests either a willingness to more openly identify beyond simply sexual dualisms or that anarchist movements attract a disproportionate share of LGBTQ individuals.

Even more Big Anarchist Survey respondents identified as white (89 percent); while this indicates the whiteness of anarchist movements, it is also at least partly a result of where the survey was circulated and who lives there (Europe and North America are majority "white").[11] The BAS designers ruefully comment that 48 percent of their survey's respondents were straight white males between the ages of 16 and 45 (Knoll & Eloff 2010). These surveys are representative of the societies in which they were drawn – which are whiter than the rest of the world (e.g., there were fewer respondents from Latin America, and thus a low response rate from self-identified Hispanics or Latinos).

Infoshop respondents who specified an economic anarchist ideology (anarcho-communist or anarcho-syndicalist) accounted for 15 percent of responses. There may be far more who *would* identify or sympathize with these ideologies, but chose to respond simply with the more general answer of "anarchist" or "anarchist without adjective" (overall, 30 percent in the Infoshop survey chose such responses). Over half (54 percent) considered themselves to be part of an anarchist movement and 71 percent identified as activists. It is clear that anarchists in the Infoshop survey are overwhelmingly movement-oriented activists. Respondents to the Big Anarchist Survey selected a variety of ideological orientations, the most popular of which were economic-focused ideologies. A full 13 percent of respondents selected anarchist-communist, 11 percent libertarian-socialist, and 10 percent anarcho-syndicalist. Unlike the Infoshop survey, respondents to the Big Anarchist Survey were allowed to select more than one ideology, so those preceding categories overlap and may include many of the same people. Thus, at least 13 percent – but likely more – selected a red-anarchist orientation, not unlike in the Infoshop survey. Other popular responses were "I don't like labels" and "anarchist without adjectives" (both 9 percent).

While the FBI claims that anarchists are "not dedicated to a particular cause," the Big Anarchist Survey provides considerable counter-evidence for this dismissive claim. For example, when asked what was the most important struggle faced today, 57 percent stated that "all struggles are interlinked," indicating a general resistance to hierarchy and domination, and advocacy of freedom. Thus, the FBI was partially correct: anarchists do not focus on *one* specific cause or issue. But the FBI was incorrect if they meant anarchists have no focus. In addition, there is still a strong opposition to capitalism (unlike the very small minority of so-called "anarcho-capitalists" who found their way into the Big Anarchist Survey),[12] as 25 percent of respondents said that "class struggle" was the *most important* struggle.

New ideologies and varied orientations have arisen or strengthened since early anarchist movements, represented by the presence of contemporary anarchists who identify with green anarchism/anti-civilization,[13] anarcha-feminism, and other anarchist orientations. And other contemporary anarchists are willing to cooperate with non-anarchists, including their oft-political adversaries, Marxists. "Red"-leaning anarchists expressed a greater willingness to work with Marxists ("yes" or "sometimes"), especially anarcho-communists (93 percent), anarcho-syndicalists (93 percent), and Platformists (96 percent).[14] Others were far less amenable to such "red-black" coalitions:[15] individualists and primitivists said "no" to coalitions with Marxists at the highest rates (35 and 27 percent, respectively). Some of this willingness to collaborate with other Leftists may derive from the way some anarchists previously identified. Seventy percent of BAS anarchists stated that they had previously "experimented or been affiliated with other political currents," such as Marxism (42 percent), social democracy (38 percent), liberalism (35 percent), and the Green Party (32 percent).

Other crucial identifiers can be noted from the Big Anarchist Survey, such as the 38 percent who stated that they were also part of a separate subculture. Of the anarchist respondents who were also members of a subculture, 45 percent identified as punks and 10 percent as hippies. Twelve percent of all survey respondents stated that they were active participants in punk subculture – and surely, many other respondents were former punks (or punks not active in punk subculture). Hippie identification is likely a smaller proportion of current anarchist movements, compared to a generation ago, given the apex of hippie subculture during the 1960s and 1970s, and the ascendancy of punk subculture since the 1980s and 1990s. Current hippie practices that converge on anarchism may be best located with the Rainbow movement (Amster 2003; Niman 2011).

Another new development in anarchist identity pertains to religion. Previous anarchist movements actively targeted organized religion (with a few notable exceptions, like Tolstoy, Thoreau, Day, and others), but today anarchists tend to be less anti-religious and more non-religious. Although 66 percent of Big Anarchist Survey respondents described themselves having a religious upbringing, 88 percent did not currently identify as religious (although 32 percent did describe themselves as "spiritual"). These findings are supported by anarchists' statements and actions in defense of religious minorities. Still today, one can find numerous religious individuals in various anarchist movements. While they are often in the minority, Catholic anarchists (especially those affiliated with the Catholic Worker), Muslim anarchists, and Buddhist anarchists were represented in this survey.[16] We lack data for how exclusively the majority of individual anarchists rejected religion in the past. If it was a fairly universal rejection, contemporary anarchists do not appear to strongly oppose religion itself, however much anarchists are in opposition to fundamentalism, and other strains of authoritarian and repressive religion, per se. Fifty-five percent of BAS respondents said it did not matter whether anarchists were religious or not, 18 percent felt religious anarchists should be moderate, while only 27 percent felt that anarchists should be atheists.

Consequently, anarchism today constitutes a "big tent," with much internal diversity.[17] Although movements appear to be far more male than one would expect to randomly find, anarchists include people from very diverse backgrounds, ideologies, and identities. One of the more interesting micro characteristics involves that which typically unified classic anarchist movements: social class.

Anarchists' social class

Social class has always been a central focus of anarchist movements, particularly due to anarchism's concern about the oppression of disadvantaged groups. Early waves of anarchist activity were strongly anchored in revolutionary working-class movements, especially through the late 1800s and early 1900s (Hirsch & van der Walt 2010). Although an anarchist orientation would seem to be antithetical to an owner or ruling-class position, there were a few anarchists who came from such upper classes (Bakunin and Kropotkin themselves were from Russia's aristocracy). However, the mass of anarchists seem derived from working-class or peasant origins, of whom Proudhon and Goldman may be famous examples.

The phrase "working class" is an amorphous one; a loose sociological consensus does exist, although it is a flexible term that can be defined to include or exclude certain populations. To be working class usually requires that one is in a non-professional, non-managerial occupation. Others describe the class in terms of its overall location in the class structure – towards the bottom. Those who identify with this label may be manual laborers, or possibly anyone who works for a living and takes orders from someone else.

To even speak of "class" presumes social and economic inequality, a non-controversial conclusion for anarchists. While not all anarchist may agree with the language used by sociologists to describe class, many anarchists (and socialists) adhere to basic Marxian classifications of workers and capitalists. Some anarchists go a bit beyond this – perhaps in the way that Otis Duncan might define "socio-economic status" – and include the possession of social power in their definitions of power (not unlike Max Weber's inclusion of "party"). Including power concerns into class may not be economic in nature, but it does link economic standing to the ruling interests of the state, particularly the "ruling class."

Unsurprisingly, anarchists strongly identify with the non-privileged classes of their societies. Even for the few who come from, or currently occupy, upper- or ruling-class positions, their presence in this class location is just by happenstance and not a desire to conquer other classes (unlike the motivations of capitalists in those classes). Still, while anarchists are likely to identify as members of the non-owning classes, other anarchists (an admittedly small minority) reject the very notion of class or at least the significance of class itself. These strains of "anti-work" or "post-Left" anarchists fall along a continuum ranging from those who do not think that social class is important or should be a factor to mobilize resistance around, to those who do not even think social class is real. Both extremes along this continuum reject a focus on class and any movement affiliation with "the working class," as well as class-based organizing (whether through unions or otherwise).

Despite media and law enforcement insinuations, nearly one-third of Infoshop respondents claimed their economic background as working class. There may be a tendency for radicals like anarchists to consciously lean more towards a self-identification with the working class, as an oppressed group (but given anarchists' greater class consciousness, I expect they would be more accurate in ascribing their class location). But, even if self-reported class is exaggerated, the survey still reflects substantial levels of working-class participation in anarchist movements. In general, the working class appeared more often in the survey than one would expect from a movement supposedly dominated by middle-class interests (as mass media has been apt to dismissively claim).

The BAS includes a comparable working-class segment, with numbers of middle-class folks equivalent to the Infoshop survey. Indeed, 66 percent (two-thirds) identified as middle-class (upper middle or lower middle), while only 33 percent identified as working-class or poor. (Another 1.5 percent identified as "upper-class").[18] Of course, it is notoriously difficult to get survey respondents to self-identify their class positions (for example, Americans in particular generally pick "middle-class" even if there is little empirical evidence to prove that). While a middle-class movement of anarchists might seem strange, it is not remarkably different from many Marxists organizations in the Global North. Also, since middle-class people are not part of a ruling or owning class, their middle-class identification may just describe their white collar jobs (which are, in Marxian terms, typically "working-class" jobs, too).

Many BAS respondents had university degrees (44 percent) and a full 61 percent had attained "some college." Even though only 39 percent of respondents had only high school educations or less, many BAS respondents were under 25 years of age, which does not provide adequate time to measure an "expected" college attendance. Many respondents were also unemployed (15 percent), thus indicating a precarious class position. However, given that many of such respondents may be students (high school or college), their current unemployment may be very non-indicative of their future class positions. Given the other characteristics of these survey respondents – mostly young, male, and from the Global North – their class positions are not remarkably different from the expected average resident of such countries. Only about one percent identified as upper class (and some of these people may be the oxymoronic "anarcho-capitalist" respondents), thus indicating that most anarchists are overwhelmingly *not* of the ruling or owning class. Thus, the FBI's statement that anarchists are "middle to upper class," is deceptively false – one-third of respondents were neither, and less than one-quarter were upper-middle or upper class.

Using a different measure for class, such as annual income, may provide a different result from the questions used in the Infoshop and Big Anarchist surveys, which asked respondents to determine their own class background. Anarchist respondents may have ideologically aligned themselves with the working class, regardless of the economic background of their parents or their current occupation. In addition, the ability to separate certain sectors of the middle class – non-profit workers, students and academics, and retirees – would aid in testing who in the middle class is supportive of the anarchist movements and in what forms.

Anarchists and labor unions

Anarchist movements of the past were not only largely working-class movements, they also were deeply embedded in labor movements. Do contemporary anarchists still belong to unions? Throughout Europe, anarchists were early contributors to the International Workingmen's Association (or "First International"). After the Marxist expulsion of anarchists at the Hague Conference in 1872, anarchists formed their own "black international" known as International Working People's Association (IWPA). The IWPA had a considerable influence in the USA, where supporters helped draft the Pittsburgh Proclamation in 1883. Many of the central figures of Chicago's labor movement – including Albert Parsons of the Knights of

Labor, who are now remembered as the Haymarket Martyrs for their role in Chicago's eight-hour-day struggle – were IWPA participants, and later founders of the Industrial Workers of the World (notably Albert's widow, Lucy Parsons).

Throughout both the West and the Global South, anarchists were active in labor movements and unions in dozens of countries (Schmidt 2013). In some cases, anarchists created explicitly anarchist unions, while in other cases they merely infused their anarchist orientations into syndicalist unions that were not explicitly anarchist-dominated. The German Freie Arbeiter Union (Free Worker's Union) was an example of the former, while the American Industrial Workers of the World was an example of the latter (Kornbluh 1998). After the increasing anarchist condemnation of Bolshevik actions in Russia, anarcho-syndicalists throughout the world formed a federation in 1922 that linked anarchist working-class organizations together called the International Workers' Association (IWA). This new federation was not only anti-capitalist, but also opposed to the reformism of social democracy and the totalitarianism of the Bolsheviks. The founding organizations of the IWA included anarchist unions from Argentina, Chile, Denmark, France, Germany, Italy, the Netherlands, Portugal, and Sweden (Damier 2009).

Anarchists have had a long-standing, working relationship with labor movements. Famous anarchists like Emma Goldman, Alexander Berkman, Peter Kropotkin, Errico Malatesta, and Rudolf Rocker worked with unions. The Spanish Civil War in the 1930s involved an anarchist union called the Confederación Nacional del Trabajo, under which over a million people organized during that country's tumultuous political and social changes (Alexander 1998; Bookchin 1977). It is safe to say that nearly all of anarchism's "Golden Age" activists and authors saw labor as the major point of societal conflict, although opinions differed on working with various unions (Berkman 2003; Brecher 1997; Goldman 1970; Rocker 1990). Or, put more concretely: "The largest organisations in the broad anarchist tradition were the syndicalist unions" (Hirsch & van der Walt 2010: xlvii).

More generally, from the perspective of contemporary sociology, unions are considered to be a central social movement organization of "old social movements." By definition, unions are composed of individuals from the working classes. People who hold management status within corporations or other work organizations cannot typically be members of a labor union. Because of this, unions have very strong links to the "working class." Although unions have traditionally been composed of people who perform "blue-collar" labor, there has been a shift in recent decades towards more non-industrial union organizing, specifically in service sector jobs and even among professionals. For instance, in the USA's anarchist-sympathetic IWW union, many chapters represent service workers (e.g., recyclers, coffee shop baristas, printers, pizza shop cooks, and public service workers).

The lack of present-day anarchist participation in unions and the labor movement that Sheppard (2002) refers could be symptomatic of larger trends, such as the move towards a more service-based economy and the widespread creation of "McJobs" (Klein 1999; Schlosser 2002). More generally, there has been a steady decline in union membership in the USA and other countries since at least the 1980s (Bureau of Labor Statistics 2004). Anarchists like Sheppard and others (Chomsky 1973; Dolgoff 1977) have advocated a direct engagement with the labor movement, potentially along the lines of anarcho-syndicalism and radical trade unions (like the IWW; Rosemont 2005), revolutionary working-class organizations (Brinton 2004), or participation in wholly worker-owned cooperatives (as detailed in Rothschild-Whitt 1979). There are contemporary anarchists who have organized with class in mind (particularly with the working class), such as the IWW in the USA (and many other countries) and the Class War Federation of Great Britain (Class War Federation 1992).

While most anarchists are very supportive of the working class and other exploited people, they have not been uncritical of certain trade unions. To the extent that a fixed, hierarchical leadership emerged within unions, suppressing their spontaneous and democratic control, anarchists have been critical of the roles unions played in working-class struggles. Unlike other union critics (especially right-wingers), anarchists believe that unions sometimes squelch working-class resistance and solidarity, speak on behalf of the working-class (robbing them of their own voices), are sometimes run like mini-businesses by despotic "leaders," and focus only on reformist goals (more pay, safer conditions for union members only) as opposed to revolutionary goals (the abolition of capitalism). Sociologist and ex-syndicalist Robert Michels (1949) wrote about anarchism as a "prophylactic" against hierarchy in *Political Parties*, where he described the centralizing tendencies of leaders in Left-leaning organizations, such as labor parties and unions. Other critical, anti-authoritarian labor advocates (such as Stanley Aronowitz and Jeremy Brecher) are in sympathy with anarchist critiques in this regards.

Modern anarchists and radical Marxists (Brinton 2004; DeLeon 1996; Meltzer 1996; Pannekoek 2003) have frequently – and cynically – characterized modern trade union leaders as "class traitors," noting leaders' collusion with large corporations against workers' class interests. This analysis is also present in Marxism (Robinson 1988). Aronowitz (1973) has argued that formally recognized unions also act as a pressure valve to release interclass tensions (such as strikes), thus avoiding explosive situations, and exist as a way to regulate conflict via "business unionism." Additionally, unions today are frequently subservient to both capital and major political parties, like the Democratic Party in the USA (Aronowitz 2005). All these critical characterizations are often moderated by the observation that the idea of a union is not itself the problem; the bureaucratic and hierarchical way in which many are run is enough to keep many anarchists at arm's length. If unions are the central social movement organization of "old social movements," do present-day anarchists belong to such organizations? Of course, we do not know how many anarchists in the past belonged to unions, since no such surveys were carried out and because in many countries labor organizations were illegal – but the rate of anarchist participation in unions was surely significant.

In the present period, 24 percent of overall Infoshop respondents stated that they belonged to a union. For the US respondents – the largest subsample overall – only 19 percent were in a union. In contrast to the less than 13 percent of US workers who were union members in 2002 (Mayer 2004), this suggests that anarchists are more likely to be union members than non-anarchists. This is particularly true when considering that the Infoshop sample includes non-employed individuals (e.g., students, retirees); thus the overall percentage of US residents who are union members is likely *far less* than 13 percent. Thus, union members represent a sizable, yet minority, sector of anarchist movements. This unionization level is half that of employed Infoshop respondents from Europe (40 percent). But compared to the height of the anarchist movement in the early 1900s, these contemporary levels of union membership are likely much lower than in the past.

The Big Anarchist Survey also indicates a marginal role for unions in contemporary anarchist movements, at least compared to the past. While 30 percent of BAS respondents – who answered a question about organizations they belonged to – were part of a trade union, 41 percent belonged to a community group. This reflects a common belief among anarchists that there are many struggles worth contributing to, not just labor or workplace ones. Interestingly, nearly 45 percent of respondents thought that "anarchy would be achieved" through a general strike. This considerable minority suggests that many anarchists believe there is an important role for working people within revolutionary struggles. It should be noted that "general strike" was a less frequent response than "building and extending autonomous communities," "by practicing mutual aid," and "revolution of everyday life," which are more culturally oriented and evolutionary strategies, as opposed to the economic and revolutionary strategy of a general strike.

Importantly, despite the vast ideological differences among anarchists and their varied participation in certain organizations like unions, anarchists are fairly unified in their emphasis on movement solidarity. The majority of BAS respondents (84 percent) stated that it was important for different types of anarchists to work together, while less than 3 percent said they were "against working together." Thus, despite clear disagreements in analysis, strategy, and tactics, anarchists are incredibly united in their desire to collaborate and struggle together in movements.

Curiously, only 40 percent of Infoshop respondents said they were part of an anarchist organization or affinity group. Is this a consequence of the anarchist respondents who use the internet, which allows people to participate in a survey even though they do not live somewhere with an active anarchist scene/movement? If so, then the anarchists who are participants in anarchist organizations or projects – but also anarchist movements more broadly – seem to be overlooked by these surveys.

Union and non-union anarchists

How did Infoshop survey respondents in unions and those not in unions differ? Table 2.1 presents mean differences for both groups. Predictably, those who self-identify as working class are significantly more likely to be in unions (41 percent) than non-union members (28 percent). The high working-class response to the Infoshop survey suggests that not all anarchists are middle-class activists, evidence contradicting claims by the media (and the FBI) that anarchists in particular – and sociologist claims that modern movements in general – are primarily populated by the "new middle class." These findings are made all the more curious given that the working class is likely to have had more restricted access to the internet to complete web surveys. However, it is interesting to note that the percentage of working-class union members is *not higher* given the typical nature of unions as a working-class organization. It is conceivable that many anarchist union members are drawn more from the public sector (such as teachers) and who thus may have a higher level of education and thus a more middle-class identity. Perhaps a more representative sample (if it were possible to obtain for a marginalized population like anarchists) would be helpful. A clearer question that distinguishes between self-identified and actual class status, or measures class differently perhaps via a typology like Wright's (1997) could make a better approach. Still, the logic would hold that people who relate more to the working class will act more on its behalf, particularly when that class status is self-identified and coupled with an activist identity.

Neither race nor gender differed significantly for union and non-union respondents, unlike mainstream union membership, which varies by race depending on union type and which tends to be more male than female (particularly in blue-collar, manufacturing work). In the Infoshop survey, there were more non-whites and males in unions, but these levels compared to non-union members were not significantly different ($p > .10$). Thus, female- and male-identified people, and those of various races who

Table 2.1 Differences between union and non-union member anarchists

Variable	Union member	Non-union member
Working class	0.412	0.282**
White	0.779	0.807
Female	0.166	0.214
Age	28.704	24.453***
North American	0.776	0.875**
Economic anarchist	0.265	0.116***
Anarchist movement	0.620	0.510*
Activist	0.771	0.690†

Source: Infoshop 2002 User Survey
Note: All variables except Age are coded 1 = yes and 0 = no. Analyses of mean differences use *t*-tests:
*** p < .001
** p < .01
* p < .05
† p < 10.

took the Infoshop survey were equally likely to belong to labor unions than not.

Union members were older on average than non-union members, at nearly 29 years old for members and 24 for non-members. The Infoshop survey includes many respondents who are young adults who have not perhaps begun "career jobs" which are more likely to have union representation. The standard deviation of respondents to age is roughly eight years (above or below the entire survey's average age of 25), and thus the survey does not capture more than one generation. Young respondents are more likely to work at lower paying jobs and, as mentioned, jobs that are usually not represented by labor unions. This finding may also be partially explained by the need for security that increases with age due to familial obligations, health concerns, and the like. The need for security tends to lead people to find stable work, something provided by labor unions. Still, since these respondents are overwhelmingly anarchists who are not likely to have an interest in becoming part of the corporate or state-world – there may be other explanations. Perhaps age causes an evolution in one's view of how change must occur in society. Youth tend to be more inclined towards impatience and want immediate, perhaps insurrectionary revolution – something unions seem unlikely to provide. Also, there could be attrition within the anarchist movement and those attached to stable organizations like unions (whether anarcho-syndicalist or mainstream) are more likely to remain engaged and continuously supplied with resources, inspiration, and new members. Old anarchists may more strongly identify with anarchism's class struggle tradition.

Fewer union members were North American (78 percent) than non-union members (88 percent). This difference is also statistically significant. Since three-fifths of the non-North Americans in the Infoshop survey are Europeans, this regional difference suggests either variations in anarchist movements' attitudes across the Atlantic Ocean, varying levels of unionization in workforce, or the higher numbers of labor-oriented organizations within European anarchist movements. To give supporting evidence to the latter possibility, the Anarchist Yellow Pages directory of anarchist organizations lists large numbers of class-based organizations (including syndicalist unions, IWW branches, or International Workers Association chapters) in countries like France, Spain, and Sweden – far more per capita than in either the USA or Canada (Williams & Lee 2008). Such organizations are discussed further in Chapter 3.

It is clear that when anarchists identify specifically with an economic ideology they are more likely to belong to labor unions. There is a large and statistically significant difference between the percentage of economic anarchist union members and non-union members. Those who identify as anarcho-communist or anarcho-syndicalist constitute 27 percent of union members, while less than 12 percent of non-unionists do. This finding suggests that one's political ideology – particularly the emphasis upon economics – is related to membership in unions. If an individual actively identifies as an economic anarchist – as opposed to just an "anarchist" – this commitment would seem to lead to acting on that "class struggle" ideology, at least by joining a union. However, there is the question of causal order here: does ideology cause union membership or vice versa? It is possible that someone may take a job at a unionized workplace and begin to identify with an economic anarchist's ideology, just as someone who possesses an ideology that drives them to seek out unionized employment, perhaps with the intention of influencing and radicalizing the union.

But an important caveat here may explain a substantial part of this question. The IWW is the only implicitly anarchist union in the USA. However, not all IWW members are employed at "organized" workplaces. Many general membership branches exist in the USA; thus, it is possible for anyone to be an IWW member without being part of a collective workplace bargaining unit. Some workplaces are organized under the auspices of the IWW, but not all IWW members or chapters are affiliated with workplace unions. This possibility would suggest an even greater tendency (not to mention ease) for anarchists to ideologically affiliate themselves with unions even outside of their own economic interests. If this is the case, IWW members could base their membership on identity. Given the structural inhibitors that prevent workers from joining unions (see a discussion of the American context in Clawson & Clawson 1999), it is amazing to note that a majority of workers would join a union if there was one to join. Perhaps having an ideologically inspired and general membership union has facilitated anarchist involvement in labor struggles.[19]

Also, while anarchists would be most suited to being members of anarcho-syndicalist or anarchist-friendly unions, it is highly possible that many of the union members among the Infoshop and BAS respondents are members of non-radical, mainstream unions. This does not modify the importance of anarchists' economic ideologies, but it does suggest that their beliefs may be more "insurgent" than commonplace in those mainstream unions.[20]

Infoshop respondents who saw themselves as active participants in an anarchist movement were significantly more prevalent in unions (62 percent) than outside unions (51 percent). Additionally, 77 percent of union members identified as "activists" while 70 percent of non-members identified as such, although the difference for activists is only marginally significant (at the $p < 0.10$ level). Self-identified movement members and activists usually see themselves as doing things in social movements and are more likely to be involved in an organization oriented around shared goals.

Of course, unions are not the only working-class or economic-focused organizations that exist, but they are the most prevalent and prominent. Anarchist participation in non-union organizations is likely to be different than membership or participation in labor unions. This possibility would strengthen the confidence that other structures of traditional movement values are still being utilized, even if in new organizational forms with new strategies, not just unions. The extent to which unions may be viewed as "social movement organizations" also needs to be considered, since some unions are remarkably more activist-oriented and radical than others. Clawson (2003) also differentiates between unions and the labor movement – the former being a "circumscribed institution" while the latter is a "fluid formation ... [which] depends on high-risk activism, mass solidarity, and collective experiences" (2003: 24).

Thus, despite the relatively small proportion of union members (to non-unionists) within anarchists movements, there are still innumerable pathways for opposing capitalism outside of the workplace. For example, Robinson (2009), determined that "Centerville" in the USA had an anarchist movement that revolved heavily around class issues and an opposition to capitalism. Indeed, even anarchists whom identify as "post-Leftists," green anarchists, or individualists are still usually anti-capitalist, despite providing less support for union activism or explicitly working-class-centric organizations. Most anarchist collectives specify anti-capitalism as a central value and action-oriented principle, regardless of their other ideological leanings.

Conclusions: knowing and not knowing about anarchists

There are numerous similarities between contemporary anarchists and those of previous generations (a mixture of class backgrounds and some union membership), although it also impossible to confidently prove due to the lack of comparable historical data. However, we can concretely interrogate the claims made by media and law enforcement about anarchists. While there is initial resonance in many stereotypes, the reality is often far more diverse and nuanced than claimed. Although difficult and complicated to quantify, there is much diversity in the anarchist movements. Anarchists are not (simply) hooligans and window-smashers, as media reports often focus upon. Anarchists themselves view their ideological diversity as both a strength and a weakness (for varied reasons, of course). Anarchist socio-demographics appear to be more diverse than often alleged, but still highly male and (at least within Europe and North America) relatively white. The class composition of anarchists and anarchist movements is more complex as is their anti-capitalist activism.

Future research on anarchists may wish to seek a better way to more comprehensively explore connections between the anarchist movements of today and the past. This chapter does not deeply assess anarchist values and attitudes, so a comparison based on these criteria is not possible. It is difficult to answer these larger questions with just two surveys, especially limited ones. Subsequent work on this highly under-analyzed movement should heed these considerations. Anarchism's complex, contentious, and sometimes contradictory advocates and organizations deserve greater study, not least for those movement participants themselves.

Anarchists ought to know that their movements are not monolithic, neither are they as homogeneous as their critics and opponents claim. Such adversaries wish to associate anarchist movements with the kinds of things that anarchists themselves would dislike: homogeneous, non-diverse, privi-leged, anti-old people, and so forth. In fact, anarchists can rest assured that while patterns can be found in anarchist movements, these movements are more diverse than the crude caricature offered up by the domination network. Additionally, much ideological variation exists within anarchist movements, particularly across geographic location (Williams 2009b). One conclusion (and goal) to be drawn by active anarchists, is that there is ample evidence that greater efforts can be made to create space in anarchist move-ments for women and female-identified persons, people of color, and older people.

Crucially, anarchists can also appreciate that their movements have changed over time. Although anarchist movements of the twenty-first century are likely different in certain respects than those of the early 1900s, numerous similarities can still be found with past waves of anarchist movements.[21] Recognizing the connection between past and present encourages a rare connectivity to tradition, and possibly an awareness that contemporary anarchists are active parts of today's movements in ways comparable to the anarchists who created the vibrant history of past movements. Working-class (and middle-class) anarchists remain a central core of anarchist movements, just as union member anarchists constitute a sizable (but maybe shrinking) minority of these movements.

Notes

1 Wollstonecraft (1999).
2 Law enforcement agencies "amplify the threat" of anarchists by uncritically conflating anarchism with criminality (Monaghan & Walby 2012).
3 Some may disbelieve claims that anarchists have been murdered for politically motivated reasons. However, numerous murders of anarchists have occurred in places as diverse as Mexico, Argentina, Italy, Turkey, and Russia.
4 Based on 113 surveys of the many thousands of participants in the 1978 action.
5 This digital divide surely affects older potential respondents, too, especially for the 2002 Infoshop survey.
6 Illegalism refers to an anarchist movement trend that originated in continental Europe, which adopts confrontational and criminal tactics in their attacks on the state and capitalism, including propaganda by the deed, bank robbery, and shoplifting.
7 Numerous other noteworthy anarchist identities existed in the past, including mutualists, nihilists, Makhnovists, and so on. Some of the historical terms overlap with contemporary terms, even though the labels are different. Alex Prichard generously pointed out that the current practice is to use suffixes (e.g., anarcho-X), while previous anarchists used different terms altogether.
8 This category can include a variety of ideological subvariants, some of which are fiercely antagonistic toward each other, such as deep ecology, primitivism, anti-civilization, and social ecology.
9 Perhaps the two best data sources for acquiring age data on previous anarchists, include: (1) membership data for formal organizations, probably labor unions (or other worker associations), and (2) police data documenting those arrested "as anarchists." Neither method is ideal, nor would they guarantee that whatever data could be obtained would actually pertain to self-identified anarchists.
10 Other evidence suggests that anarchist movements are likely larger and thriving in other places, particularly in European countries (as evidenced in Williams & Lee 2008).

11 Consequently, a certain degree of white privileging happens in anarchist movements within Western countries (see Williams 2015 for specific examples).

12 Although so-called "anarcho-capitalists" are not this book's focus, their responses to the BAS are interesting (although also unsurprising). For example, these individuals had a relatively "conservative" upbringing compared to a more "liberal" one among both Platformists and primitivists. This constitutes more evidence that "anarcho-capitalists" are "improperly anarchist," as their values – apparently derived, in large part, from upbringing – are out-of-sync with core anarchist values.

13 While it is important to acknowledge that past anarchists, notably Élisée Reclus, invented and innovated these orientations (such as green anarchism), they were organizationally weaker in the past and have evolved (or "matured"?) to be a more prominent presence in contemporary movements.

14 The "Platform" was a draft document written by Russian anarchists in the post-Bolshevik Revolution era, to prioritize unity about how to organize anarchist organizations to participate in working-class and peasant movements (Skirda 2002).

15 Here, I refer to Marxist (red) and anarchist (black) coalitions. Red is usually meant to refer to philosophies of the socialist tradition, while black represents anarchism.

16 Of the 12 percent of BAS respondents who were religious, 42 percent identified as Christian, 28 percent Buddhist, 18 percent Pagan, 7 percent Jewish, and 4 percent Muslim. Also, see research on Rastafarian-anarchists (Blackstone 2005).

17 This tent can be staked "too widely," though, as seen by Foster's (1987) attempt to identify the Amish as "eco-anarchists," given their direct democracy, civil disobedience, resistance to oppressive outsiders, small-scale community, and voluntary simplicity; despite these connections, they are unconscious anarchists at best (i.e., "implicit anarchist"), since they also adopt incompatible practices, like patriarchy, deity-submission, small-scale capitalism, and so on.

18 Totals are for 100 percent of respondents, without rounding.

19 It is important to note that IWW membership is still rather low, particularly when compared to its heyday in the 1910s. Gordon (2007) observes an IWW membership in 2005 of 1,298, which although potentially representing a considerable minority of the anarchist cadre in the USA, still ranks among the smallest national unions in the USA. Using Gordon's original source, the Department of Labor's Employment Standards Administration (http://erds.dol-esa.gov/query/orgReport.do), shows 922 IWW members during the Infoshop survey year. Of course, these are official "members" – the ranks of IWW supporters is likely sizable as well.

20 For example, few of the anarchists with whom I am acquainted in the USA belong to the IWW, although many belong to mainstream (and non-radical) teacher and professor unions, and others like the

Teamsters. As such, their union membership may be more pragmatic, than ideological.

21   While some, such as Graeber (2002), have argued that today's anarchist movements embody a "new anarchism" patently distinct from the past, the analysis presented in this chapter and subsequent ones provokes my skepticism, as it does for other observers (see Hirsch & van der Walt 2010).

3
Anarchists of the world, unite! A meso-structural analysis

The need for organization in social life – even the symphony between organization and society, I would be tempted to say – is so self-evident that it is mind-boggling that it could ever have been questioned. (Errico Malatesta)

Anarchism in organizations

Despite jokes about "organized anarchists as oxymoronic," anarchists clearly self-organize and belong to organizations. Yet, sociological research has not comprehensively assessed the factors that influence where anarchism thrives and its particular domains of activity. Most studies of anarchist organizations have been theoretical (Day 2004; Shantz 2003b), anecdotal (Graeber 2002; Katz & List 1981), or qualitative and focus on a single anarchistic organization (Blickstein & Hanson 2001; Boehrer 2000, 2003; Ingalsbee 1996; Luke 1994; Maiba 2005; O'Brien 1999; O'Connor 1999; Roy 2003; Shantz 2002b; Shantz & Adam 1999). There is very little organizational uniformity in anarchist organizations, particularly when surveying their distribution across the world. But, few attempts have been made to disaggregate anarchist organizational content across nation-state boundaries. Even less research has sought to account for the appearance of particular types of anarchist organizations in specific social and political contexts. A central problem associated with attempts to understand anarchist organizations is that they are, by their very nature, decentralized, so no master source of information exists. These organizations may focus on local, national, and/or global struggles; address political, cultural, and economic concerns; and target government, corporate, religious, or cultural authorities. Some members of such organizations may perceive their involvement as contributing to a larger anarchist social movement with the explicit goal of achieving fundamental societal transformation; others may have become involved for more prosaic reasons and adhere to anarchist ideology to a lesser degree, if at all. Regardless, anarchist organizations are "everywhere," as a movement slogan claims.

Very little research from the sociology of organizations is directly relevant to anarchist organizations. The closest scholarly works applicable to anarchist organizations focus on *alternative* organizations. For example, Rothschild-Whitt (1979) studied collective-democratic organizations that run counter to nearly every other form of modern organization. Most anarchist organizations are comparable to these collective-democratic characteristics, which include diffused authority, minimal rules, a communal ideal, egalitarianism, and minimal division of labor. Likewise, anarchist organizations also fit well into Fitzgerald and Rodgers' (2000) typology of radical social movement organizations (RSMOs), in contrast to mainstream social movement organizations. RSMOs are anti-hierarchical and participatory, have radical and structural-change orientations, utilize nonviolent direct action, are ignored or misrepresented in mainstream media, tend to have limited successes, and are subject to intense state opposition.[1]

While some of this sociological literature is of relevance, most ignores both anarchist organizational concerns and anarchists themselves. This chapter has two goals, which should be viewed as small steps toward a more quantitative and theory-grounded critique of modern anarchist movements. First, using the Anarchist Yellow Pages (AYP) directory and the International Blacklist (IBL), I offer a systematic description of the types of organizations that comprise the contemporary anarchist movement, as well as its international geographic patterns. I argue here that the best existing resource available to researchers is the AYP, which listed over 2,000 organizations in its 2005 edition.

I provide an initial descriptive and analytical account of the geographic clustering of types of anarchist organizations. Using these data, we can map the spatial distribution of anarchist organizations, view a profile of their topical diversity, and track their changes over time. Although the global anarchist movement is an international phenomenon, it is not evenly distributed through the world. The concentrations of anarchist organizations found in the AYP suggest that the movement tends to be strongly European-centered. In addition, North American anarchists are disproportionately involved in various media organizations; Spain, France, and Sweden have strong syndicalist tendencies; Italy and Germany tend to have a high percentage of physical spaces like social centers and infoshops (Ruggiero 2000).

Anarchist organizations tend to be deliberately small (cooperatives, collectives, and affinity groups being the typical organizations of choice); if there are many members in an organization, it tends to be a federation of smaller groups participating in an equal fashion (Martin 1990). Simpler and smaller structures are desirable because anarchism values direct action as opposed to representative action (Polletta 2002). Whereas many conventional definitions of "organization" include components such as a chain of command and a relatively permanent formal structure, Howard J. Ehrlich (1977: 6) argues that this excludes "virtually all organizational forms that an anarchist would take to be central to community life." Some anarchist organizations have no membership roster or formal procedures because anarchist thought suggests that decision making is more democratic, empowering, and easier with fewer involved constituents, less structure, and minimal standard operating procedures. This aspect does not mean to imply that industrial society – with its dense rules – is incapable of becoming more liberating, but that social relationships must be made as horizontal as possible. Ehrlich (H. J. 1977) also suggests that anarchist preferences for organization are small, impermanent, and anti-follower-oriented.

To my knowledge, no previous study has explored the contours of the distribution of anarchist organizations across countries. This gap in the literature becomes especially problematic when trying to account for the ecological features of countries that might be shaping the births, longevity, and deaths of anarchist organizations in specific environments. Implicitly, this analysis helps to assess the structure of anarchist movements.

Thus, my second goal is to begin to understand this "population ecology" of anarchist organizations at the national level (cf. Hannan & Freeman 1989), as an initial step before assessing anarchism through the lens of political opportunity theory. Additionally, by exploring certain macro-level forces, we can witness some of the phenomena that shape the characteristics of populations of anarchist organizations (cf., Friedland & Alford 1991; Hannan & Freeman 1989). For example, the presence of rights and "democracy" in different countries may, in part, explain where the global anarchist movement is concentrated. I begin by offering a brief description of anarchism and anarchist organizations. In Chapter 5 I utilize additional international data sources that address issues raised by the political opportunities movement theory (McAdam 1982, 1996). I argue that political opportunities theory is particularly relevant for understanding how features of country-specific ecological environments might facilitate or inhibit the development of certain kinds of anarchist organizations.

Because this chapter breaks new ground with its focus on anarchist organizations, and because these data are mostly cross-sectional, I do not wish to push the "natural selection" metaphor of organizational survival too far. But I believe that the patterns uncovered here are highly suggestive with regard to the environmental pressures that shape the preponderance of types of organizations in specific countries.

Before progressing to data on anarchist organizations, a hypothesis may be worthwhile. Of course, generating specific research expectations is difficult given the lack of prior studies on the topic. But given the history of anarchism, we ought to anticipate that the majority (although surely not all) of the world's anarchist organizations will be located in European countries.

Finding data on a decentralized movement

As one might expect, anarchists have never made efforts to file for government-sanctioned "non-profit status" and thus facilitate a "proper" census of their movement.[2] Instead, they have usually taken up the task of recording their own organizational networks and contact information. Perhaps the best contemporary example is the AYP, a major international directory, which has existed since the 1990s, of anarchist organizations and projects. The directory's name is a playful adaptation of a well-known American and British phone book, where one can find telephone numbers for corporations and shopping malls. The AYP lists anarchist collectives and their contact information, and was available in both website and print versions. The AYP is the work of a small number of anarchists who have aspired to compile a thorough, yet stable collection of contact information for anarchist groups and projects throughout the world. The directory's purpose is not scholarly but thoroughly political: to connect anarchists and fellow travelers with each other in order to facilitate the goals of individual groups and the movement as a whole.

The AYP lists the organization's name, address, city, state or province (in the USA and Canada), country, world region, phone, fax, email, webpage, category, and other information about the organization's purpose. I use a version of the AYP completed in 2005 that includes entries for 2,171 organizations worldwide; anarchist organizations exist on every continent (except Antarctica). This version is well over a decade old at the time of writing, which thus indicates a historically dated snapshot of anarchist movements.

It is undeniable – and acknowledged by one maintainer of the AYP (Felix Frost in an email dated October 26, 2005) – that the directory could include many more anarchistic organizations than listed. Organizations such as Anti-Racist Action, Critical Mass, Earth First!, Food Not Bombs, Homes Not Jails, Independent Media Centers, and others could also easily be listed as anarchistic organizations, and are often readily referred to as such. Ironically, the AYP includes at least one of each of these organizations, but does not include the hundreds of others found in various other cities or regions throughout the world.[3] To take a few of these as examples, the AYP lists only four Earth First! (EF!) collectives: EF! Netherlands, EF! UK, Orange County EF!, and the *Earth First! Journal*. However, according to the *Earth First! Journal* itself –which includes a list of international EF! collectives and other contacts in every issue – 28 EF! groups were found in the USA alone in 2005 (across 21 states), along with another 38 American radical, non-officially EF! ecology groups (totaling 66). Not all these EF! and other radical ecology groups may identify as anarchist – or be anarchistic (as the inclusion in the AYP suggests) – but surely more than four of them are. Or, consider the EF! groups in existence almost a decade earlier in 1997, which was during a high point for EF!: 59 EF! US groups were listed by the *Earth First! Journal*, while zero EF! collectives were featured in an earlier AYP edition that same year (this edition is discussed in greater detail in the section "Going back in recent anarchist history").

Or take another example: the Independent Media Center (IMC) movement, which began in 1999. The 2005 AYP identified eight "Indymedia" groups (Belgrade, Hudson-Mohawk, Jakarta, Manila, New Hampshire, Poland, Thunder Bay, and San Francisco), whereas during that same year the Global Indymedia page listed in a whopping 151 separate IMCs across dozens of countries. While not all these IMCs were equally active, and surely not all identified as anarchist, there were undoubtedly more than just eight who would have found sympathetic inclusion in the AYP.

More generally, the classification of some organizations as "anarchist" and not others may introduce certain biases to a straightforward assessment of the AYP. In fact, there is an entire category called "Libertarian Marxist/ Ultra-Left" to accommodate the ambiguity and overlap that some organizations may have with anarchism. One could make the distinction between an organization being explicitly anarchist and being anarchistic, anarchist-inspired, or a non-anarchist organization consisting mainly of anarchist members. The criteria used to differentiate between these formats and constitutions are unknown.

The AYP only includes what ought to be called formal organizations – those groupings that have given themselves a name. Surely there are just as many – perhaps more – groupings that are *informal* in character, meaning they are closed to the rest of the world and/or lack an identifier. Such informal organizations could include everything from group houses, loose networks, or affinity groups (see Dupuis-Déri 2010). The importance of informal organizations in anarchist movements is described in greater detail in Chapter 7, in the context of schmoozers and social bonding capital. To assess the structure of anarchist movements, one must necessarily consider formal organizations. But, the requisite emphasis on formal organizations is limiting. Thus, despite its many benefits, the AYP surely glosses over many, many crucial anarchist organizations, providing a serious under-counting of worldwide organizations.

Even formal organizations are surely under-counted. Problematically, it is unknown just how many organizations are not listed. The only true way to construct knowledge on such organizations would be via surveys of local anarchist movements. By using "ground-truth" (see Pickles 1995) methodologies, a knowledgeable observer could piece together the dense networks of anarchist organizations within a certain geographic locale. My suspicion is that most all such locales have anarchist movements that are severely under-represented by the AYP. This problem might stem from a quick turnover rate in anarchist organizations, which may begin and end faster than non-members are even aware of. Also, knowledge of organizations may be linked to organizational size – something else the AYP does not indicate – as many organizations may be small in membership size. Thus, the organizations described may have only two members, or perhaps thousands. Again, the only way to know is via intimate knowledge of each organization, a noble task that is undertaken by many activists and historians including some mentioned at the opening of this chapter.

Despite such limitations, I believe that there is a great deal of value to using the AYP. First, it is a worldwide directory that contains many of the most prominent anarchist organizations that currently exist, all classified into a useful typology. Second, it is the most comprehensive source of information available. Thus, even though some anarchist organizations are not included in the AYP, under-counting is a problem that plagues virtually all social research. For example, it is widely acknowledged by criminologists who rely on data collected by police agencies that more than half of all crimes that occur in many societies are not even reported to police and remain unknown to them. It is highly probable that these are not randomly missing cases, but are absent in patterned ways that bias the data on which criminologists rely. Such biases are unavoidable, but I suggest that the information that the AYP provides on anarchist organizations allows us to at least establish a baseline for discussion about the larger social forces that shape the distribution of organizational forms in the anarchist movement throughout the world. This approach and data represents a point of departure and certainly not the final word on this topic. So although I cannot provide definitive proof that these findings accurately represent the reality of anarchist organizing, I hope that future research will build on this analysis, further explore the possible biases in the AYP, and draw on other sources of data to develop a more complete picture of the contemporary anarchist movement.[4] The AYP is also be utilized toward the end of Chapter 5.

"Oh my! There are anarchists *here*?"

I wish to address *what* anarchist organizations exist and *where* they are found. Organizations in the AYP are principally classified in twenty different categories. Of these categories, the most prevalent are general "anarchist groups" (330), "infoshops/bookstores" (283), and "community spaces/social centers" (241). The least commonly appearing organizations are "disobedients" (12), "social ecologists" (9), and "situationists" (8). I have

Table 3.1   Categories of organizations in the Anarchist Yellow Pages (N size)

Class-oriented	Physical spaces	Media
Industrial Workers of the World (57)	Community space/social center (241)	Alternative media (109)
International Workers Association (208)	Infoshop/bookstore (283)	Libertarian publication (142)
Syndicalist Union/Group (174)	Archive/library (56)	Publisher/distributor/mail order (100)
Total: 439	*Total: 580*	*Total: 351*

Franchise	Other
Anarchist Black Cross (75)	Disobedients (12)
Anti-Fascist Group (69)	International Anarchist Federation (87)
Food Not Bombs (35)	Libertarian Marxist/ Ultra-Left (25)
	Other (130)
	Radical Environmentalists (21)
	Situationist (8)
	Social Ecologists (9)
Total: 179	*Total: 292*

Note: General anarchist groups N = 330, author's analysis.

collapsed most of these twenty categories into larger groupings based on a category's general purpose (see Table 3.1). Anarchist groups have not been placed into any super-category, since they are general anarchist organizations without an apparent specific purpose or emphasis. The "physical spaces" constitute the largest super-category of anarchist organizations, an interesting fact considering the probability of such organizations being less campaign- or action-oriented in and of themselves, and instead serve as "infrastructure" for the action and goals of anarchist movements.

Class-oriented organizations include those that focus on conflicts regarding class stratification, particularly workplace struggles or labor solidarity. Physical spaces are organizations that have a building in which organizing can happen or where anarchist materials are available. Media organizations attempt to share alternative views on political and social matters, distributed in a wide variety of mediums. "Franchise" organizations refer to organizations that do very similar things and have the same name, yet are not in direct communication with each other. These organizations are akin to "franchise" businesses and include Anarchist Black Cross, Food Not Bombs, and Anti-Racist Action (or Antifa, short for "anti-fascist"). "Other" organizations include those that are neither listed in the previous categories, nor are general "anarchist organizations." This category ranges from various leftists and ecologists to protest formations (like "disobedients") and the broad International Anarchist Federation.

The next question is where organizations are located. Organizations can be found in seven different world regions: Africa, Asia, Europe, Middle East, North America, Oceania, and South America. Some of the AYP's classifications, such as the Middle East and Oceania, surely have debatable geographies – would Asia be more appropriate for some countries in each of these? Similarly, organizations in the Caribbean and Central America are placed in either North or South America. Regardless, it is clear that Europe has over two-thirds of all anarchist organizations. This finding supports the earlier hypothesis that Europe would have the greatest number of anarchist organizations. The second most populous region is North America, with less than one-third as Europe's. Africa has the fewest organizations. (See Table 3.2.)

Two arguments can be suggested to explain the large proportion of European organizations in the AYP. First, European anarchist organizations truly *do* dominate the international anarchist movement. Such a reality could be due to various factors. For example, this large percentage could reflect anarchism's "birthplace" in the European Enlightenment tradition; even this plausible suggestion is premised upon a misperception that anarchism was predominantly a European phenomenon, which was surely not the case (see Hirsch & van der Walt 2010).[5] Or, political opportunities may be afforded to Europeans and are not available elsewhere, a possibility I explore further in Chapter 5. It could be that countries with highly Western cultures and institutions would be more amenable to Western-derived philosophies like anarchism. But, this is also easily disputed.[6] Also unlikely is that there could be a more crucial need for anti-authoritarian movements

Table 3.2 Number of anarchist organizations per region

Region	Organizations	Percent of total
Africa	6	0.3
Asia	44	2.0
Europe	1527	70.3
Middle East	31	1.4
North America	460	21.2
Oceania	41	1.9
South America	62	2.9

in Europe – more so than the rest of the world. Second, the high number of European organizations *may not accurately represent reality*, but may reflect certain methodological biases associated with the AYP. Some reasons for this possibility may include: Europeans and other Westerners have a higher number of computers and Internet access compared to less affluent countries (Kellerman 2004; World Bank 2006), thus restricting the ability of non-Western organizations to be listed in the AYP. As such, the AYP reflects the interest, scope, or contacts of its compilers, who are themselves Westerners. The political climate in non-Western countries may not be conducive to "above-ground" anarchist organizing – including highly public listings in the AYP – in the face of repressive governments.

A look at the countries and cities in the AYP with the greatest number of anarchist organizations also reveals noteworthy findings. Not surprisingly, European and North American countries and the largest Western cities have the greatest number of anarchist organizations. The top ten countries and cities with the largest number of organizations are listed in Table 3.3. Buenos Aires, Argentina – a city not in Europe or North America – barely missed making the top ten (with 14 organizations).

If we know what types of organizations are in the AYP and where the largest aggregations of organizations are located, the next question is: which types of organizations are found where? Even though "physical spaces" and "class-oriented" organizations represent huge numbers of organizations, there is no guarantee that they are proportionately distributed throughout the world. Thus, Table 3.4 shows the types of organizations found in the ten countries listed. A few striking numbers are instantly apparent. An incredibly large proportion of anarchist organizations in Spain, France, and Sweden are class-based.[7] The same is true for physical spaces in Germany,

Table 3.3 Countries and cities with the greatest number of anarchist organizations

Ranking	Countries	Cities
1	USA (360)	Rome (48)
2	Spain (263)	London (40)
3	Germany (237)	Berlin (37)
4	Italy (231)	Milan (30)
5	France (209)	Madrid (28)
6	Great Britain (119)	New York (27)
7	Sweden (83)	Montreal (24)
8	Canada (72)	Paris (22)
9	Poland (64)	Stockholm (18)
10	Netherlands (38)	Copenhagen (15)

Note: Organizational counts listed in parentheses.

Table 3.4 Number of anarchist organization categories in the top 10 most popular countries

Country	Anarchist	Class	Physical	Media	Franchise	Other
United States	64	38	76	80	52	50
Spain	12	156	41	30	7	17
Germany	5	30	138	37	12	15
Italy	22	17	146	19	1	26
France	33	92	20	9	4	51
Great Britain	25	14	20	21	5	34
Sweden	8	27	7	11	12	18
Canada	9	9	10	18	13	13
Poland	23	12	9	9	10	1
Netherlands	7	0	14	9	4	4

Note: "Anarchist" organizations are general organizations not classified in any specific category.

Italy, and to a lesser extent the Netherlands. The USA and Canada have more media organizations than any other grouping. The largest quantity of British organizations fall in "other," while in Poland the most popular are simply anarchist organizations. For more detail, Figure 3.1 provides a map showing the major categories in Europe, the region with the most organizations overall.

Going back in recent anarchist history

Next, I compared the organizations listed in the 1997 AYP to those in the 2005 AYP (Table 3.5).[8] The clearest trend apparent is that nearly every category of anarchist organization increased during this time period. The major exception is anti-fascist organizations (primarily Anti-Fascist Action, Anti-Racist Action, and Red & Anarchist Skinheads), which dropped almost half their number in a span of eight years. Many of the losses from these organizations occurred in Germany (25 to 3 groups), Great Britain (23 to 1), and the USA (51 to 21). Originally, such groups sprang up in Europe in response to the rise of anti-immigrant sentiment following the Iron Curtain's fall in the East and may have been replaced by other types of organizations as the pressing social issues changed over time (Katsiaficas 2006). A smaller organizational type loss came from the "spaces" category. Crucially, the time-span from 1997 to 2005 also represents an intensification of popular attention on anarchism, including high-profile mass protests (e.g., Seattle during 1999 and Genoa during 2001), which anarchists played

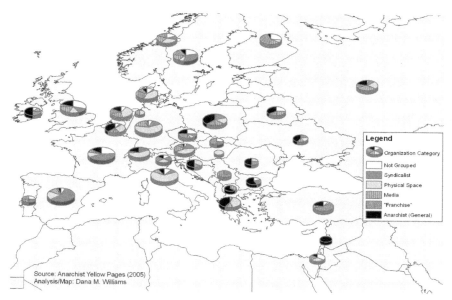

3.1 Categories of European anarchist organizations

Table 3.5 Number of anarchist organizations in the Anarchist Yellow Pages in 1997 and 2005

Organization type	1997	2005	Percent change
IWA	62	208	+235%
ABC	30	75	+150%
Anti-Fascist	125*	69	−45%
IWW	38	57	+50%
Syndicalist	50	174	+248%
Spaces	261	241	−8%
Anarchist groups	243	330	+36%
Total	*809*	*1154*	*+43%*

* *Note*: Anti-fascist organizations in 1997 included only RASH and ARA (the above figure of 125 is their combined total); the 2005 figure includes additional anti-fascist groups.

a prominent role in organizing (Crass 2001; Graeber 2009). As a consequence, anarchist organizations likely benefited from a heightened focus on protest politics.[9] During these eight years, there was a net 43 percent increase (from 809 to 1154) for the International Workers Association, Anarchist Black Cross, anti-fascist, Industrial Workers of the World, other syndicalists, spaces, and general anarchist organizations.

Another international dataset to compare the changes in contemporary anarchist movements – as well as the impact of changing the definitions of who are anarchists and who is included in anarchist movements – predates the 1997 AYP by more than a dozen years. A version of the International Blacklist (IBL) was released in 1983, detailing organizations and prominent individuals who belong to many different anarchist movements, in a way comparable to the AYP. The IBL is a directory of anti-authoritarian, anti-capitalist groups – designations that are largely interchangeable with anarchism.

Across 28 countries, the IBL lists 1,354 total entries. The USA had the largest number of organizations, most of which were media organizations (journals, newspapers, and book publishers). Yugoslavia had only one entry, an individual. Surprisingly, no anarchist organizations were listed in Africa, while very few were in Asia (only Hong Kong and Japan), and a few more were in South America (Brazil, Costa Rica, and Venezuela). The bulk of organizations listed in the IBL were found in Europe and North America, just as with the AYPs. Many physical spaces – at least 75 – were recorded in the IBL. This only accounts for bookshops and documentation centers, not infoshops or social centers, which were not listed in separate categories within the IBL directory. Even more class-struggle organizations existed – at least 122 organizations were listed, although three-quarters were in Spain and the USA alone. Also, an incredibly large number of media organizations were found in the IBL; among newspapers, journals, reviews, publishing houses, and distributors, a total of 455 separate projects existed. As with the AYP, it is very likely that these IBL figures under-estimate the actual number of all of these types of organizations throughout the world in 1983.

There is a limited amount of overlap between the IBL in 1983 and the AYP in 1997, as most organizations in one are not found in the other. For example, Left Bank Books in Seattle, Le Combat Syndicaliste in Paris, and the Advisory Service for Squatters in London were listed in both the IBL and AYP. But, other organizations in the IBL during 1983 – such as Germany's Anarchistische Gruppe, the Netherland's Spartacus, and Canada's Direct Action – were not listed later in 2005. And, still other organizations – such as Poland's Praska Grupa Anarchistyczna, Mexico's Colectivo Deseos de Libertad, and Turkey's Al Jabha Al Taharouria – existed in 2005, but were not listed (and probably did not exist) in 1983. This suggests either the disappearance or appearance of organizations or methodological inconsistencies between the two directories and time periods.[10] Both, I believe are true in various cases.

The growth or contraction of anarchist movements can be ascertained, however incompletely, from numerous comparisons between the IBL and AYP data. One comparison to make is among certain high-frequency countries – this is a safer comparison than low-frequency countries which may be more at risk of methodological issues of under-counting. France, Germany, Italy, Spain, the UK, and the USA are the top-ranking countries in both directories; these first four saw an increase in entries from 1983 to 2005, while the latter two (UK and USA) saw slight decreases.[11] France increased by 137 percent, Germany by 339 percent, Italy by 300 percent, and Spain by 204 percent, while the UK decreased by 39 percent and the USA decreased by 6 percent. These top six countries represented nearly three-quarters of all entries in the IBL, while less than two-thirds in AYP-05. The shrinking share of the top six countries indicates that a greater increase happened *outside* these large, dominant countries. This represents a clear increase in anarchist organizations, especially considering the greater classification stringency for inclusion.

The second possibility, that there are problematic methodological issues resulting in the appearance of an organization in the IBL (or not), is worth further consideration. The IBL's editors clearly state that their list is not exhaustive, and that they include organizations which do not expressly identify as anarchist (just as the AYP did), such as "libertarian socialists," or the IWW and CNT unions (both revolutionary syndicalists, but not necessarily anarchists in the analysis of some). The IBL editors included, with strong reservations on their part, the Catholic Worker organization, which the AYP did not, and the League for Evolutionary Anarchism and Freedom that believed that anarcho-communists can collaborate with so-called anarcho-capitalists. The USA's Libertarian Party is excluded, although it was featured in the 1983 documentary *Anarchism in America* (Fischler & Sucher 2006). Other authoritarian groups that boasted of having anarchist members were also not included (e.g., the Revolutionary Communist Party, New American Movements, Prairie Fire Organizing Committee). The IBL can also be differentiated from the AYP for its inclusion of certain prominent individuals who are unattached to anarchist groups in the directory (e.g., Noam Chomsky). The list overzealously includes organizations or projects that are related to punk rock culture, despite the lack of clear anarchist identification. The IBL also includes an Afterword written by anarcho-primitivist John Zerzan (IBL 1983: 141), criticizing the inclusion of the IWW (who prioritize "self-managed oppression" through unionization), college professors, religious organizations (who subordinate members to a hierarchical deity), and the Wages for Housework organization.

These variables, minor and major objections over inclusion and exclusion, and changes over time clearly illustrate that anarchist movements are profound social constructions. What organizations are seen as "anarchist" depends on the definitional criteria that someone accepts; thus observers may delineate slightly – or radically – different anarchist movements. This suggests that the IBL editors and AYP editors likely created their respective directories based on criteria that expanded or contracted the potential list of anarchist organizations in a given country, and thus, the IBL and AYP are not directly comparable. Even though this is certainly the case, a quantitative analysis shows that some countries experienced a relative growth in the number of organizations, while others showed a decline in number. Some of these changes are certainly congruent with the first possibility noted above: real changes are occurring. Various factors may, therefore, be influencing the ebb of a society's anarchist organizational ecology. Table 3.6 lists the total number of entries for each country, for all three directories (the IBL and the 1997 and 2005 AYPs). The table also notes larger macro phenomena occurring during or around the time period covered, which surely had an influence on this organizational ecology.[12] While an overly stringent analysis is likely to draw inappropriate conclusions, I think the anecdotal evidence is intriguing.

Given the scant overlap between the IBL and AYPs, I propose using each in tandem to assess the overall density of anarchist organizations in the modern era. Despite the shortcomings of each, they compensate adequately for each other. The sum of each directory's total entries per country are illustrated in Figure 3.2. This map shows the concentrations of anarchist organizations across the IBL, AYP-97, and AYP-05. The shading signifies the variation from fewest anarchist organizations per country to greatest, using an equal count shading scheme; thus each degree of shading represents an equal number of countries as does every other shading degree. Unsurprisingly, the USA, Germany, Italy, Spain, and France are best represented – although, when considering the per capita density of organizations, the USA's lead (n = 941) over Spain (n = 415) is far less impressive.

Another key question that these data can address is: how many organizations survived the long generation from 1983 to 2005? As Howard Ehrlich alluded (H. J. 1977), anarchist organizations often have a short-lived existence. Only 74 entries in the 1983 IBL were still listed in the 2005 AYP. Viewed from the vantage point of 1983, only 5.5 percent would survive until 2005; from the vantage point of 2005, only a paltry 3.4 percent organizations had existed during an earlier period.

I initially hypothesized that these "carry-over" organizations would overwhelmingly be syndicalist unions, since the resources and continued purpose of such groups ought to keep them stable. However, were it not for the ten IWW chapters in the USA, syndicalists would have nearly zero carry-over representation between 1983 and 2005.[13] Instead, other organizations seemed to be the mainstay of anarchist movements (see Tables 3.7a and 3.7b): libertarian publications (n = 14), infoshops and bookstores (10),

Table 3.6 Number of anarchist organizations by country in 1983, 1997, and 2005

Country	IBL count (1983)	AYP count (1997)	AYP count (2005)	Carry-over 1983 to 2005	Notes
Africa					
Nigeria		1	1	n/a	
Sierra Leone		1		n/a	
South Africa			5	n/a	a
Asia					
Afghanistan			1	n/a	
Armenia			1	n/a	
Bangladesh		1		n/a	
China			1	n/a	
– Hong Kong	3			n/a	b
India			2	n/a	
Indonesia			9	n/a	
Israel			6	n/a	
Japan	9	2	17	0	
Korea			1	n/a	
Lebanon			3	n/a	
Malaysia			4	n/a	
Philippines			3	n/a	
Turkey			21	n/a	
Europe					
Austria	13	8	21	0	
Belgium	8	5	20	2	
Bulgaria		3	5	n/a	c
Czechoslovakia				n/a	d
– Czech Republic		7	12	n/a	
– Slovakia			4	n/a	d
Denmark	12	4	32	0	
Finland	3	14	30	0	
France	153	38	209	8	
Germany	70	154	237	9	e
Greece	15	7	30	0	f
Hungary		2	2	n/a	
Ireland	4	2	8	0	
Italy	77	118	231	8	
Luxembourg		1	2	n/a	
Netherlands/Holland	40	15	38	1	
Norway	15	11	21	2	
Poland		3	64	n/a	c
Portugal	25	3	4	1	f
Romania			4	n/a	c
Slovenia		1	6	n/a	c
Soviet Union	2			n/a	g
– Belarus			12	n/a	g
– Estonia		2	1	n/a	g

Table 3.6 Number of anarchist organizations by country in 1983, 1997, and 2005 (Continued)

Country	IBL count (1983)	AYP count (1997)	AYP count (2005)	Carry-over 1983 to 2005	Notes
– Kazakhstan			1	n/a	g
– Latvia			1	n/a	g
– Lithuania			1	n/a	g
– Russia		4	27	0	g
– Ukraine		1	5	n/a	g
Spain	129	23	263	3	f
Sweden	32	34	83	2	
Switzerland	20	8	27	1	
United Kingdom					
– England	160			12	
– Great Britain		81	119	n/a	
– Northern Ireland	4			0	
– Scotland	18			0	
– Wales	12			1	
Yugoslavia	1			n/a	
– Croatia			6	n/a	h
– Serbia-Montenegro			4	n/a	h
– Macedonia			3	n/a	h
Latin America					
Argentina		1	17	n/a	f
Bolivia		1	4	n/a	
Brazil	9	3	14	0	f
Chile		4	6	n/a	f
Colombia		2	4	n/a	
Costa Rica	2		5	0	
Guatemala			1	n/a	
Peru			6	n/a	
Uruguay			8	n/a	
Venezuela	2		3	0	
North America					
Canada	71	28	72	4	
Mexico	9	4	20	0	
Puerto Rico		1	2	n/a	
United States	384	197	360	18	
Oceania					
Australia	43	13	29	2	
New Zealand	9		12	0	
Totals	*1354*	*808*	*2171*	*74*	

Notes on major political regime transformations: a. End of racial apartheid (1994); b. Absorption into China (1997); c. End of East Bloc (1989–92); d. Czechoslovakia split (1993); e. Unification of East and West Germany (1990); f. Fall of fascist or military government (1975: Greece, Portugal, Spain; 1983: Argentina; 1985: Brazil; 1990: Chile); g. USSR disintegration (1990–91); h. Yugoslavia disintegration (1991–2008)

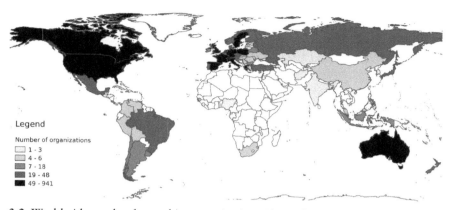

3.2 Worldwide totals of anarchist organizations (from the IBL, AYP97, and AYP05)

Table 3.7a Organizational carry-overs from 1983 to 2005

AYP 2005 organizational classification	Count	Category
Alternative media	1	Media
Anarchist group	5	
Archive/library	6	Physical spaces
Community space/social center	2	Physical spaces
Industrial Workers of the World	11	Class-oriented
Infoshop/bookstore	10	Physical spaces
International of Anarchist Federations	7	Other
International Workers Association	2	Class-oriented
Libertarian Marxist/Ultra Left	2	Other
Libertarian publication	14	Media
Other	2	Other
Publisher/distributor/mail order	9	Media
Radical environmentalists	1	Other
Situationist	1	Other
Syndicalist union/group	1	Class-oriented

Table 3.7b   Aggregate and percent organizational carry-over from 1983 to 2005

Category	Total organizations (in 1983 and 2005)	Carry-over (in common)	Percent carry-over
Class-oriented	439	14	3.19
Physical spaces	580	18	3.10
Media	351	24	6.84
Franchise	179	0	0.00
Other	292	13	4.45
Anarchist groups	330	5	1.52

publishers and distributors (9), affiliates of the International of Anarchist Federations (7), and archives and libraries (6) constituted the bulk of overlap. Compared with their new parallel organizations, almost 7 percent of media organizations could be dated back to 1983, whereas only 1.5 percent of anarchist groups could be (incidentally, none of the "franchise organizations" found in the AYP existed in the early 1980s).

This incredibly low rate of carry-over signifies the continual organizational rejuvenation of anarchist movements over time. Yes, most anarchist organizations do not seem to last across the generations (the enduring Freedom Press in Great Britain, founded in 1886, being a rare exception), but few organization members even assume they will. But, even though there is so little carry-over, the correlation between the organizational counts by country between the two time periods (1983 and 2005) is substantial ($r = 0.84$, $p < .001$). This suggests that, while the organizations are themselves not *the same organizations*, countries seem to foster equally active (or inactive) anarchist movements across time. For example, the country with the highest number of entries in 1983 *and* 2005 was the USA. Among the 28 countries that had both 1983 and 2005 entries, there was only slight movement in their count rankings. When ranking the countries from most to fewest anarchist organizations, the average country only moved 3.7 rankings (out of 28) from 1983 to 2005 (or a median of 2 rankings). The most extreme changes in ranking were Finland and Russia, which both moved up 12 places in ranking (gaining 27 and 25 organizations, respectively), and Portugal, which fell down 15 places (losing 21 organizations).

There are a few possibilities for the non-consistency of organizations over time, even while similar levels of organizations exist during both time periods. First, it is possible that the same actual people are involved as members and founders of different organizations during both time periods. This is very probable, especially in large cities, but it does not (and likely cannot) explain all the consistency. Thus, second, it is possible that different people formed the organizations during the different time periods. This more likely possibility suggests two further sources of pattern. Anarchist organizations may keep movement momentum high, even while the individual organizations come and go. Or, favorable (or unfavorable) conditions may exist that facilitate (or discourage) new organization formation, even in the absence of stable anarchist organizations.

The organizational big picture

Thus far, this chapter has explored organizational-level data sources featuring international anarchist organizations. There are no other comparable datasets for anarchist social movements. The erratic inclusion of EF! and IMC in the AYP (far fewer local collectives than other sources note for these two organizations) suggests that scholars who rely on "official" documents – even movement-based ones like the AYP – will almost always run the risk of under-counting the presence of anarchist organizations. In other words, anarchist movements are surely much larger, in terms of organizational number and capacity, than anyone can quantitatively determine, based on empirical records. Although the AYP has flaws and although one can only interpolate the attitudes or actions of individual anarchists from it – let alone the macro-scale goals and strategies of anarchist movements – this analysis offers many original insights.

I began by providing an overview of the geographic distribution of anarchist organizations. General anarchist organizations constitute the largest single category of organizations. Yet, when categories are grouped together, physical spaces outrank both class and media organizations. Organizations tend to be found in North America and Europe, and, unsurprisingly, in major cities of those countries. Germany and Italy are dominated by physical spaces, France and Spain by class organizations, and the USA and Canada by media organizations.

The general pattern of organization types (from 1983 to 2005) is highly suggestive of the nature of modern anarchist movements. The heavy concentration of physical spaces demonstrates the priority given to collective experiences and empowerment that can be gained via meeting in a common location that is radically self-managed by its participants. The frequency of class struggle organizations illustrates the enduring significance of workplace-based conflict and anti-capitalism within anarchist movements. And the large number of media organizations throughout the world – publishing in at least 20 major languages – indicates the continued importance that anarchists place on radical journalism and propaganda; to reach ever wider audiences, anarchists do not strong-arm others to participate, but attract them through new perspectives, revolutionary ideology, and anarchistic assessments of current events. All these organizational forms are part of anarchist movements' infrastructure and are typical components in their activism, outreach, and organizing strategies.

The number of comparable anarchist organizations has also grown since an earlier version of the AYP in 1997, increasing over 40 percent in size. This growth could indicate an evolution of anarchism's social movement politics – that could have long-term consequences – or the growth could be a temporal "protest cycle" (Tarrow 1998) that may presently be peaking and could recede in upcoming years.

Some aspects of population ecology may help to explain changes in anarchist movements (e.g., the founding, growth, and disbanding of organizations). But, one of the central criticisms of the population ecology approach to understanding organizations is that it ignores the power of organizations to shape the environment. For example, one influential critique disputes the notion that the biological theory of natural selection is appropriate for explaining whether certain kinds of organizations are "negatively selected" (killed) or "positively selected" by the environments in which they are located (Perrow 1986: 209). This critique argues that many corporate organizations are so powerful that they actually control and reshape the environment, rather than the other way around. In this view, the population ecology perspective plays a "mystifying" role by "removing much of the power, conflict, disruption, and social class variables from the analysis of social processes" and substituting "vague natural forces," almost implying that "God does the negative and positive selecting" (Perrow 1986: 213). However, the population ecology model would seem well suited in the case of anarchist organizations because none of these organizations have anywhere near the power or resources of a giant corporation like General Motors or British Petroleum. Anarchist organizations are often small by design, prefer decentralized action, and are disconnected from the power structures that corporations use to control their environments (especially the state). The stark variation found across countries (with respect to the relationship between local contexts and the existence of types of anarchist organizations) suggests that anarchist organizations are shaped by ecological constraints in ways that participants may be unaware of.[14] If the anarchist movement is to grow internationally, future efforts at organizing will have to pay more explicit attention to such concerns.

In conclusion, this chapter has offered an initial foundation on which other studies can be built. With the global picture in mind, future researchers may wish to investigate a broader range of ecological conditions in a smaller number of countries to determine how they impact the presence or absence of types of anarchist organizations. Cross-national case studies could reveal the historical development of the movements and provide clues as to particular geographically specific characteristics and emphases. These exploratory findings suggest strategic locations for such research, as well as specific political factors that should be examined.

Despite the ability to categorize organizations by country, anarchists have a distinctly transnational character. In fact, anarchism is explicitly internationalist in orientation, even more so than other radical movements since it opposes nation-state boundaries. An analysis of these movements' transnational coordination is impossible with the data used here, but a bit of its aspirations can be gleaned from the international diversity depicted in the AYP/IBL. For example, the density of potential information channels may provide a potent form of international social capital (see Chapter 7) as well as a method for organizational and tactical diffusion (see Chapter 8).

Organizational implications for anarchists

If they don't already, anarchists ought to consider formal anarchist organizations to be important structures within anarchist movements. Organizations are structural anchors for people who wish to network with anarchists. The searchable directories discussed in this chapter provided an access point for outsiders who sought contact with anarchists as well as fellow anarchists who wished to contact others. The greater the diversity of anarchist organizations' functions and orientations, the more vibrant anarchist movements are. Some countries had highly diversified movements, while others were far more monolithic in nature. But, it would be a mistake to believe that a single anarchist organization constitutes a movement, even if it is a substantial organization. As with biological diversity, organizational diversity is an advantage.

Anarchist movements are more diffuse and decentralized than other political entities (e.g., political parties), as there are few anarchist organizations in most areas of the globe. Many anarchist organizations are relatively small in size and may include only a handful of people (or even just one) who are the most active. Also, given possible overlap between anarchist organizations' personnel, multiple organizations do not necessarily indicate a lot of anarchists. But just because only one organization was listed in the IBL or AYP, does not mean there is no local anarchist movement; while many organizations may not be listed or "above ground," many places *do* have a movement. Probabilistically, anarchist organizations can be found most readily in Europe and North America, but they may also be found in most other countries in the world. Many poorer countries – which are under-represented in the IBL and AYP – undoubtedly have anarchist organizations, but these are are simply not listed in these international directories or above ground (for reasons discussed further in Chapter 5).

Throughout the world, the AYP likely reveals a dramatic under-counting of the social structure of anarchist movements. Recall that individual anarchists do not merely belong to anarchist organizations. Schmidt (2013) emphasizes anarchism's use of the "mass movement strategy,"[15] in which anarchists help create broad organizations for large numbers of participants (not just anarchists), along with smaller, consciously anarchist organizations to keep the former focused on appropriate goals of anarchist revolution. Of course, the AYP/IBL only include the latter group, but overlook anarchist efforts to create the mass organizations, which are anarchistic (implicitly anarchist), while not overtly anarchist.

Finally, it is worth considering what the implications are for the presence of anarchist organizations – does this constitute an anarchist community or even functioning anarchist relationships? As Wright (2003) suggests, anarchist organizations may actually be creating an *imagined community*, "conceiv[ing] of themselves as belonging to a community that represented in idealized form what social life should be like" (2003: 10). The intricacies of anarchist community is considered in greater depth in Chapter 7.

Notes

1   The biggest immediate difference between RSMOs and anarchist organizations is the latter's occasionally tactical rejection of "nonviolence." Even though likely 99 percent of all organized anarchist activities are "nonviolent," many anarchists assume revolutions involve violence, however much it should be avoided in practice.

2   Incidentally, governments and law enforcement agencies around the world are likely keeping track of anarchist organizations (since they represent some of government's severest critics and opponents). Even international policing organizations such as Interpol – ironically founded as a response to an earlier wave of the anarchist movement (Jensen 1981) – could be involved in such data collection. Yet the prospects of gaining access to these documents is highly improbable. Still, state documents would provide an interesting view of anarchist movements.

3   A number of reliable, although often-fluctuating directories for these organizations exist and to add them to the AYP, would greatly augment the size and breadth of that directory.

4   While a full listing of entries would be prohibitive and more than a little boring, a perusal of the AYP directory shows the particular flavor evinced by the organizations founded by anarchists. A full seven organizations bear Emma Goldman's name (often just "Emma") – an honor bestowed on her more often than for any other individual. The color black is prominent in organizational names, too, describing the tint of many things, from cats, roses, mosquitoes, flags, falcons, stars, hoods, doves, sheep, and crosses. Finally, the words "rebel," "resist," and "revolution" are found throughout, as are derivations of "liberty" and "freedom."

5   "Informal internationalism" led to the simultaneous emergence of anarchism across Europe, Latin America, and Africa during the 1860s and 1870s,

connecting movements in many countries in patterns of exchange and sharing with each other (Hirsch & van der Walt 2010: liv).

6 Although anarchism's emergence during the Industrial Revolution is usually connected to Europe, some authors suggest that anarchist ideas and tendencies have existed in non-Western cultures for some time (Bender 1983; Marshall 2010; Mbah & Igariwey 1997). But, even tracking the word "anarchism" to its much earlier etymological roots brings us to Greece, usually considered a birthplace of "Western" culture. Ancient Chinese history, especially the tradition of Taoism, is clearly, in part, sympathetic to anarchism.

7 For research on anarcho-syndicalism as an ideology, see Williams (2009c). Anarchists were significantly more likely to be union members if they possessed an economic ideology and were working class.

8 The year 1997 was chosen because it was the first edition of the AYP available online, in a rudimentary, archived format: www.spunk.org/texts/biblio/sp001653/ayp.html.

9 However, a critic could suggest that the increases in other categories could simply be attributed to better record-keeping and contact networking as easily as it could be attributed to an increase in anarchist organizing.

10 For contrast, another dataset potentially useful for charting organizational birth and death is the organizational directory of Earth First! organizations included in every issue of the *Earth First! Journal*. Some organizations appear in that directory for years, while others exist for a much shorter period.

11 The presence of a small number of individuals in the IBL is an important factor to keep in mind with this comparison.

12 A few immediate difference between the IBL and AYP include: different parts of the UK (England, Wales, Scotland, and Northern Ireland) are separated in the IBL; the centripetal dynamics that located Hong Kong in the IBL, but not the AYP (when it was partially subsumed by China); and the centrifugal forces that caused a few countries that were not in the IBL (e.g., the USSR, Yugoslavia) to no longer exist, while some of their constituent parts are found later in the AYP. The notes on Table 3.6 (a–h) indicate some of these changes, as well as a variety of transformations from military or fascist regimes to (nominally) democratic ones.

13 Another reason here could be the missing entries for many major syndicalist unions and their branches in the IBL.

14 It is plausible that specific anarchist organizations may be so influential upon their own local ecologies (i.e., anarchist movements) that they shape those local environments.

15 A claim echoed in Garner's (2016) work on syndicalist means and anarchist goals.

Part II
Theoretical interpretation

4

The significance of social movement theory to anarchism

Revolutions are brought about by those who think as people of action and act as people of thought. (Emma Goldman)

What is social movement theory?

Even though anarchism is itself a social theory, anarchism has been under-utilized by sociologists developing sociological theories (Williams 2014). Likewise, anarchist movements – themselves the social application and embodiment of anarchist theories – have not been interpreted via sociological social movement theories. Of course, activist theorizing happens within all social movements, but academics have tended to focus almost exclusively on reformist, mainstream movements. There have been impressive contributions by sociological theorists of movements, but activists remain frustrated and indifferent to the poor attempts to theorize about revolutionary or anti-authoritarian movements, such as anarchism. Consequently, I argue that the established theoretical explanations for movements – including relative deprivation, resource mobilization, frame alignment, dynamics of contention, and numerous others – are of mixed relevance to anarchist movements. The key handicaps for most of these theories stem from an unwillingness to commit anarchist movement analyses to these traditions. By avoiding anti-state and revolutionary movement examples, theories have formed to describe some, but not all, of the social movement ecosystem.

The task of this chapter is to explore the usefulness (or lack thereof) of social movement theories for understanding anarchist movements. Various noteworthy theories are applied to anarchist movements in this chapter; some of these theories address crucial concerns, like risks, scale, strategy, and timing of movements. In subsequent chapters I more inten-sively apply social movement theories to anarchist movements, specifically political opportunity, new social movements, and social capital theo-ries (Chapters 5, 6, and 7). An appropriate orientation is taken toward developing "better theories": conserving and improving what is good (of both American and European scholarly origin), and building better theories in response to currently unaddressed concerns. Finally, this chapter explores the utility of social movement theory for anarchist movements themselves.

A social theory can be a variety of things, but, at heart, a theory explains and models. An explanation gives answers to "why?" questions. It helps to transform something confusing into something that makes sense. A model gives answers to "how?" questions. It is an interpretation of how something in society works. Thus, theory provides a framework or guideposts for understanding. Although there are many theoretical traditions within contemporary sociology, some can be in direct conflict with each other (e.g., social constructionism vs. functionalism). In other words, it is entirely possible for a theory to explain an observation contrary to another theory. Or, the model created for how something works could be very different based on the theoretical vantage point assumed. Therefore, the ultimate benefit of a particular theory is likely to be relational.[1]

Sociological theories have had an influence on social movement theories. But, social movements have also had a noticeable impact on social theory itself.[2] Indeed, this latter pattern tends to predate the former. Many classic accountings of movements can be traced to individuals now recognized as central "classical theorists," including Karl Marx, Émile Durkheim, and Max Weber (Buechler 2011; Ruggiero & Montagna 2008).[3] Curiously, much European social theory exists *due to* the efforts of social movements – theory exists in reaction to or because of movements (Cox & Fominaya 2013). This means that sociology is intertwined with and dependent on the study of movements, particularly in Europe. This is less so in North America, where sociological movement theory is heavily biased toward an American interpretation and typological approach.[4]

However, in both European and North American sociology, the study of social movements has inevitably led to the creation of theories that aim to explain the behaviors of movements (their existence, actions, and consequences) and to model the life cycle of movements; this modeling has involved theory elaborations, proliferation, and competition (Wagner & Berger 1985). While revolutionary movements have been part of these analyses and of theory building, reform movements have been a more prevalent subject matter in recent decades. While most social movement research addresses, tests, or builds theory in one way or another, numerous individuals – in particular activists themselves – question the importance of distance-inducing research and advocate for answering pointed questions about movements in ways helpful to those who encounter or participate in them.

Answering questions in lieu of movement theory

While this chapter's principle focus is social movement theory, not all analysis of social movements needs to prioritize the objective of theory building and testing. Social movement theory is a strong concern of sociologists and political scientists, and it seems to be of less use to movement participants. Thus, before focusing on social movement theories, a slight diversion is warranted. John Lofland (1993) has claimed that continual back-and-forth arguments around social movement theory are counterproductive; he argues that "theory-bashing" is far less important than "question answering." Lofland, who is also knowledgeable about anarchism – see his essay in *SSSI Notes* (1988)[5] – has proposed a number of key questions about movements that are more immediate in explanatory power and utility than what the majority of movement theories achieve (Lofland 1996). The problematic fetishization of theory ought to be a concern not only for activists who sometimes see it as an intellectual diversion, but also for scholars for whom theory-building may be a myopic excursion into the minutiae of social conditions.

Lofland (1996) describes seven questions, which he claims are central for social movement students to understand; he focuses specifically on social movement organizations (SMOs) as the unit of analysis. The focus of these questions include beliefs, organization, causes, membership, strategies, reactions, and effects. I will re-state each of Lofland's questions and then provide a general answer for contemporary anarchist movements.

First, what are the beliefs of SMOs? Since, SMOs are organized around some sort of beliefs, morals, and assumptions, what are these for anarchist movements? Surely at the core of anarchism is the belief that the state, capitalism, and other institutions of domination are bad. The related belief that follows is that people and their communities do not need these institutions, and can accomplish goals and provide for their own needs better themselves.

Second, how are SMOs organized? Since movements presume people work and act together, how do such SMOs organize? Anarchists are not always in agreement about whether to have a formal or informal organization. But, anarchist movements are consistent in their opposition to fixed authority figures in organizations and favor having some form of democratic or decentralized decision-making structures, the forms of which may vary. Anarchist organizations appear to be, generally, smaller and few endure for long periods.

Third, what are the causes pursued by SMOs? Since movements organize together, how did such SMOs come about? Anarchists have many causes that extend beyond their opposition to authority, including long-term support for women's reproductive rights, support for striking workers (whether unionized or not), their intent to end imperialist wars and police terrorism, and to protect and empower disadvantaged populations, such as immigrants or queer folks. These "causes" are viewed as fundamental issues, stemming from systems of hierarchy; thus, while most movement participants who struggle for these causes are not anarchists, the general and radical efforts within these struggles are compatible to anarchists' goals.

Fourth, why do people join SMOs? If people act collectively within movements and SMOs, how did they come to be part of them? Surely, the pathways to individual participation in anarchist movements are diverse. Some come into contact with other anarchists through word of mouth, while others come across, or hear stories about, anarchists. Part of the impetus for seeking other anarchists results from one's own personal transformation and curiosity about anarchism. And, of course, it is possible for people to simply encounter anarchists through random coincidence; if this encounter is favorable, the individual may be influenced and inspired to participate more in a given SMO. Anarchists are motivated by a strong opposition to systems of hierarchy and the realization that the struggle against these systems cannot be waged by an individual, but must be collective.

Fifth, what are SMO strategies? Since SMOs – almost by definition – do things, how exactly do they go about them? Anarchists have a varied toolkit, just like many other movements. Most movements, including anarchist movements, need to find ways to reach non-participants. Anarchists accomplish this through educational efforts and propaganda aimed at the masses in a society. Communication is a valued strategy, as it helps to break down mistrust, build consensus, and exchange information, both within the anarchist movement and with its allies. Anarchists also engage in direct action and non-hierarchical campaigns and projects with any interested persons or organizations (at least those who can also adhere to an anarchist ethos). These efforts have the dual purpose of attacking the legitimacy and practical consequences of hierarchy, while also advocating for, and putting into action, an alternative set of social arrangements.

Sixth, what are the reactions to SMOs? Since SMOs are doing things, what do others think about those things? Owing to the pre-existing perceptions most societal members have about anarchism (recall Chapter 1's description of the violence, chaos, and fantasy mythos), anarchists receive a conflicting array of reactions to their actions and strategies. On the negative end, reactions include marginalization and denigration by those within the domination network, as well as attacks by the state. Others, such as ideologues, educators, and other opponents, may dismiss anarchist movements, while "everyday people" may also have an initial, reactionary opposition. And, some extend solidarity and occasional sympathy towards anarchist movements, although this is surely a minority response. A surprising number of people seem to support certain anarchistic assumptions and analyses – especially if de-coupled from direct association with the term "anarchism."

Finally, what are the effects of SMOs? In other words, what are the consequences, results, or benefits of SMO actions? While "revolution" is an oft-stated goal of anarchist movements, this is a very rare achievement (see the mismatch between goals and outcomes in Chapter 5). Instead, anarchist movements often serve to put authoritarians "on notice" or make enemies pay (marginal) costs. This effect can sometimes be achieved by causing a ruckus and attracting attention. Other consequences of anarchist movements include challenging liberals and sectarian socialists – either to call questions to their short-sighted goals or actions, or provoking them to "change their tune" and support more broad-based participation, radical action, and transformative strategies. Much of anarchist movement activism also aims to simply build community, strengthen the ties between individual anarchists and anarchist organizations, and to provide social capital (see Chapter 7) for future campaigns, events, and uprisings. And, of course, some effects experienced by anarchist movement organizations involve simply failure. As with most organizations, anarchist ones have limited "shelf lives" and regularly end before their goals can be achieved.

Recent attempts to analyze anarchist movements do not use established social movement theories. As Shantz argues, "Conventional analyses of social movements continue to overlook the emergence of unconventional manifestations of resistance" (2003b: 90). Consequently, the generalizability of standard movement theories is severely limited. Additionally, the most basic questions typically asked about radical social movements remain largely unanswered. For example: What explains the existence of anarchist movements? Why do these movements do what they do? Who is involved in these movements? I argue that it is both possible and practical to utilize a variety of social movement theories to see if (and how well) they explain anarchist movements. A formal, direct application of movement theories to the movement has yet to be conclusively carried out, although Purkis (2004) has attempted a parallel task in critiquing major movement theories from an anarchist perspective.

Introduction to some social movement theories

Social movement theory is typically anchored in the academic discipline of sociology, as well as political science. Many of the theoretical traditions I describe in this chapter have been around for decades. Some have been very active areas of scholarship with many researchers contributing to them, while others have been the dedicated work of a small number of scholars (and may be somewhat abandoned in other cases). The theoretical lenses described in this chapter are not the subject of intensive focus later in the book (unlike political opportunity, new social movements, and social capital theories that are given full treatment in subsequent chapters). Instead, I set out some brief reflections on significant theories; I focus on describing the potential of each theory for understanding anarchist movements and do not offer the following as original "research." In other words, my descriptions of the strengths and weaknesses in each theory form only tentative conclusions; the possibilities discussed are only hypothetical, but I believe they are reasonable.

These theories are part of different traditions, including collective behavior, critical theory, North American political process, and other paradigms. Here, I focus on structural strain or value-added theory, class or Marxian theories, world-systems analysis, the Eros Effect, relative deprivation and grievances, resource mobilization, frame alignment, Charles Tilly's work, and the dynamics of contention.

Adding value to movement emergence

In the 1960s, Neil Smelser (1963) developed a theory of collective behavior that formed the basis for much early scholarship on social movements, especially the movements of the 1960s. His theory borrowed from the economic theory of "value-adding"; the value of a material good can be increased by adding to it or transforming it in some fashion. Likewise, by "adding" elements or conditions to certain situational contexts, people can be moved further toward collective behavior and movement formation. Smelser's work seems intended to create a grand theory of collective behavior and social movements, attempts which were popular at the time. While sociologists are less enthusiastic about his value-added theory today, there is much to appreciate about it. In fact, Crossley (2002) has argued that Smelser's original criteria and concerns are still present in much modern social movement theory, albeit spread across different contemporary traditions; Smelser consolidated multiple concerns under one umbrella.

Value-added theory argues that six essential steps are necessary for collective behavior to occur. The first, most general condition is one of structural strain. In other words, something must "strain" society – an inequality in the marketplace or unjust treatment by police, for example – that authorities are unwilling to address. Anarchist analyses of modern societies have never lacked subject matter for critique, as there are innumerable ways in which institutions of domination exert control over people. Thus, "strain" is ubiquitous, although not always perceived. Second, there must be structural conduciveness which makes collective behavior conceivable and possible. Anarchist theorists and activists point to already existing networks of mutual aid, sites of community collaboration, and positive orientations towards trust as preconditions for future action. Third, generalized beliefs must exist and continue to spread throughout the social environment. People come to terms with newly changed realities and begin to draw conclusions about those conditions. People may eventually come to see that economic conditions continue to worsen regardless of which political party is in power. Or the generalized belief emerges (as in Latin American and European radical squatting movements) that housing crises are not random or episodic, but systematic in nature – thus a specific policy fix will likely fail as it does not address the underlying causes of crises (e.g., capitalism and private property).

Fourth, once this groundwork has been laid, a precipitating factor occurs that triggers some kind of incident. Such triggers often create the initial elements that will become movements. Thus, a particularly egregious example of police violence – like the failed prosecution of four white Los Angeles police officers in 1992 or the police murder of a 15-year-old Athenian boy in 2008 – may drive people to such outrage that it puts large numbers of people in the same frame of mind and makes them ready to act, which in these cases trigger uprisings. Or, an outrageous statement by someone in power or an impressive act of principle by someone in resistance may attract considerable attention and disrupt "business as usual." Fifth, a period of mobilization begins, where people start acting collectively. Previously alienated and atomized individuals find each other and move together. People may attend the same anti-police demonstration, blockade the same munitions manufacturer's factory, occupy an abandoned building to claim it as a community center, or camp out in a public square. All the previous conditions have culminated and driven people together in joint outrage, where their intentions are to deal with the strains and respond directly to the precipitating factor. However, collective behavior may be short lived if "the system" can handle this mobilization. Thus, the final condition of Smelser's value-added theory is the failure of social control; if authorities do not react quickly enough, adequately, or at all, they miss a key opportunity to absorb the accumulated strain and channel people's collective energy (and anger) back into the system.

These social control efforts can take wildly different forms. On social control's "nice" extreme, politicians may agree with demonstrators, but counsel working within the electoral system for reforms. Or, on the not-so-nice extreme, authorities may send out armed state agents (police or the military) to violently suppress dissidents and/or arrest them. In doing so, the state aims to limit the emerging movement's potential for sustaining their resistance. If authorities can achieve this social control, the mobilization may die. For example, the US state helped coordinate dozens of police raids and crack-downs on large Occupy encampments in major American cities in late 2011. State efforts at social control effectively stopped the gaining momentum of Occupy's mobilization (which in many cities had taken a decidedly anarchist trajectory).

Critics have alleged that Smelser made value-added theory too deterministic, by claiming that all elements had to be present for movements to emerge – even requiring the conditions to occur in the "correct" order. Others have alleged that it was a "grand theory," too hegemonic and myopic in focus, and that it missed many essential elements of movement mobilization. Still, a few factors relevant to anarchist movements can be noted. Specifically, Smelser differentiated between "norm-oriented" and "value-oriented" movements. Norm-oriented movements are interested in changing the practical norms under which people act (such as established rules or expectations of how to behave in a squatted social center or during a black bloc action), while value-oriented movements concern themselves with modifying the underlying values that drive people's actions (prioritizing self-management, heterogeneous/intersectional solidarity, or broad anti-authoritarianism, for example). Here, anarchist movements are both norm- and value-oriented, believing it necessary to change people's practices as well as the values that support and justify such practices (see Williams 2011b). These two categories echo characteristics found in reform and revolutionary movements, respectively. While anarchism is clearly pro-revolution, it also functions on the basis of evolving and reforming norms and values to make broader revolutionary gains possible. Still, value-added theory seems more well-suited to interpreting the conditions that may precipitate anarchistic revolt (riots or uprisings), as opposed to consciously organized anarchist movements, per se.

All in for the class struggle!

Despite usually being referenced as Marxian, class struggle theories of anarchism are not specific to Marx's writings. In fact, many of the theoretical concepts Marx is credited with creating were in fact co-developed by countless participants of the radical, internationalist labor movements of his time, over a period of many decades. Marx made these concepts clearer and his authorship helped to spread the ideas far and wide, beyond the labor movement. As anarchists and those who were later to identify as anarchists were active participants in these movements, then the theory of class struggle often attributed to Marx is, of course, also influenced by anarchism.

During the golden age of anarchism (late nineteenth century, early twentieth century), anarchists were almost indistinguishable from radical labor movements. In fact, anarchists were simply some of the more radical voices within these movements.[6] Class struggle theories presume that movements and their participants are motivated by capitalism's class offensive against workers. Therefore, labor movements are a direct consequence of capitalist exploitation. Clearly, this was in part true. But it does not explain the advocacy of labor movements by non-working-class individuals, including Marx himself. Although he was not a member of the bourgeoisie, Marx was also not a physical laborer in factories. Rather, he was employed throughout his life in occupations that some later neo-Marxists would identify as a "contradictory class positions": journalist and author. The same was true for well-known anarchists, including Proudhon, Bakunin, Kropotkin, and Reclus. While Malatesta worked as an electrician, he also had middle-class origins. To be sure, most rank-and-file anarchists (unknown and unrecorded today) were working class, such as more famous individuals, like Emma Goldman, Nicola Sacco, and others. But it was commonly believed during this period that capitalism was the root cause of the labor and anarchist movements, with the state acting as capitalism's defender. People reach a level of class consciousness when they understand their position as a member of an exploited class (i.e., the proletariat) and that they have shared interests with each other. Thus, movements in general, and anarchism in specific, seek to challenge and overthrow capitalism by fostering consciousness and solidarity.

Yet, problematically, many movements in which early anarchists participated had, and have, far less to do with class, class inequality, or exploitation, such as movements that Goldman also struggled within: the birth control, sexual liberation, or free speech movements. Even for explicitly labor-oriented movements, class consciousness is arguably on the decline today in many countries.[7] Not all exploited workers see the value in rising up against capitalism – although this is dependent on the society in question. In fact, many workers identify *with* capitalism, aspiring to pull themselves out of poverty and become rich themselves (thus are falsely conscious); so many workers are likely to be some of the more reactionary members of many societies.

Anti-systemic movements in the world-system

The internationally integrative social change theory called world-systems (WS) analysis emerged in the 1960s. WS analysis utilized ideas from sociology, political science, economics, and history (Wallerstein 2004), in order to understand the creation of the historic and current international state system. From the beginning, WS analysts saw two types of movements – national and social movements – as central to not only the world-system's evolution, but also its continuing change.[8] The different spheres of the world-system – core, semi-periphery, and periphery – were alleged to foster certain dominant types of movements (Buechler 2000). The wealthy core countries were influenced by reformist social-democratic parties. The semi-periphery countries were often regional powers and were influenced by Marxism. The poor periphery countries were used as a resource and labor base for the core countries, and were consequently dominated by the influence of national liberation movements. While anarchist movements are distinct from each of these movements, they do share some overlapping features. Most of the countries to experience anarchist revolutions during the twentieth century – Mexico, Russia, Manchuria, Spain – are non-core countries, although anarchist movements are largest in the core (recall Chapter 3's analysis on organizational concentrations from the International Blacklist and Anarchist Yellow Pages).

WS analysts have focused on 1968 as a pivotal year in which the world-system changed. The USA lost its hegemonic influence across three power centers – economic, military, and political. It was also a definitive year because movements throughout the world were challenging not only nation-states, capitalism, and colonial empires, but were also challenging supposedly Left regimes. Thus, the anarchistic May/June revolt in Paris was also a rejection of the Communist Party's control over the French Left (see Cohn-Bendit & Cohn-Bendit 2000). The USSR invaded Prague that year, further disrupting international support for capital-C communism, which had previously been threatened by the 1956 events in Hungary and Khrushchev's revelation of Stalin's crimes in Russia.

Immanuel Wallerstein is the best-known proponent of WS analysis, being the author of the *Modern World-System* series (1974, 1980, 1989). In his *Decline of American Power* (2003), he articulated numerous positions sympathetic with anarchism (although he rarely qualifies them as such), while simultaneously overlooking anarchist movements or simply mischaracterizing them. For example, 1968 was not only an uprising against US hegemony, but also centered on the disillusionment with the old Left; center-Left parties were unable to deliver on their revolutionary promises once they gained control of the state in Europe. Wallerstein assumes that "all" movements seek to seize the state and *then* to transform the world (as the social-democrats, Marxists, and nationalists have all done in different zones of the world-system), despite their inability to create just societies.[9] When these movements succeed in coming to state power, but then fail in their transformative goals, a corresponding delegitimization of the state has followed; consequently, he argues that centralism won't work and advocates decentralization, and that anti-systemic movements should oppose hierarchy and privilege. Although Wallerstein channels (but does not cite) the classic Bakunin sentiment that there is no way to separate liberty and equality, he strangely alleges that anarchists only seek "individual transformation" (Wallerstein 2003: 260).

Feeling the Eros effect

George Katsiaficas (1987, 2006), well known for his autonomist interpretations of the 1968 revolutions and subsequent events throughout central Europe and Asia, has developed the "Eros effect" idea. Just like anything erotic, social movements may turn us on, excite us, animate our emotions, and make us long for future moments of thrill. Also, eroticism is infectious and it is spread in rather unpredictable ways from person to person; whoever sees another person turned on can be stimulated to change their own behavior. Innumerable movements, uprisings, and near revolutions throughout the world have had a comparable socio-political impact on people in resistance to capitalism and the state. Each episode unconsciously laid the groundwork for future events, in ways impossible to predict. Thus, the Eros effect is a swirling consciousness that travels around the Earth, inspiring people to act as others before have and to resist that which oppresses them.

Katsiaficas discovered that students and radical workers were the usual initiators of uprisings throughout Asia. Large street demonstrations coalesced and people would gather en masse to attend popular assemblies that further animated the population to become even more militant. During these moments, people refuse party politics and the pre-packaged solutions of politicians, and explode cathartically with a creative and destructive force on society. These episodes are often far shorter than the moments of abeyance between uprisings, but the condensed period of time quickly shifts people's expectations and perceptions of what is possible (Katsiaficas 2013). As attractive as this explanation is for anarchist movements (or anarchistic events), it is more of a theory about uprisings than movements per se. The conscious organization and long-term activism of movements does not play a large role in the Eros effect theories; if anything, movements and their key strategists and activists are often swept aside during explosive episodes, as they become marginal forces compared to the collective actions of the masses. The Eros effect occurs indirectly, with no single factor guiding all the ways in which people influence each other (what Chapter 8 calls non-relational diffusion).

The Eros effect seems compatible with Tarrow's description (1998) of protest waves, in which the frequency of movement mobilization increases dramatically, inspiring the formation of new movements. A protest wave during 2010–12, in which the "spirit" of revolution circulated around the world, infected people with the rebellious energy of others (see CrimethInc 2012a). After the global financial crisis began in 2007/8, many radical movements struggled to figure out how to respond. Ironically, a series of seemingly unrelated events transpired, in some ways traceable to a high-volume data leak from the US military to the WikiLeaks organization. Although some have described WikiLeaks founder Julian Assange as an anarchist, he is more appropriately identified as a hacker and maybe libertarian (putting aside, of course, the dominant influence he has upon WikiLeaks itself). Regardless, the leak of US State Department diplomat cables included all sorts of controversial materials about other countries, which foreign journalists began reporting on. The individual immolation of a Tunisian vendor combined with WikiLeaks information about corruption in the Ben Ali regime led to a countrywide revolt. The discontent spread throughout the Arab world, engulfing Bahrain, Libya, Syria, and most famously Egypt. The Arab Spring picked up on the fervor of Tunisia, and with many anarchistic elements active within Egypt (see Bamyeh 2013) and global solidarity (including support from the anarchistic hacktivist network known as Anonymous), the three-decades-old dictatorship of Hosni Mubarak was overthrown. This Eros spread to the anti-government protests in Wisconsin, where government workers, union members, progressive and radical activists (including anarchists) occupied the Capitol building. Later events fed on the energy of the Arab Spring in Greece and Spain, eventually returning to the USA in the form of the anarchistic Occupy Wall Street movement (which spread throughout the USA and world).

Feeling the pain: relative deprivation, grievances, and strain

It is universally assumed that movements orbit around conclusions that *something is wrong* – whether with a very narrow issue or instance, or with the very foundation of society. Anarchists see innumerable examples of the former, but ascribe ultimate responsibility to the latter. Strain theories, of which Smelser's can be considered one, tend to view some social element to be "out of balance" and that movements emerge to rectify those problems. In some respects, this is a less politicized version of Marxian class struggle explanations of social movements. Strain can imply social disintegration or a breakdown, absolute deprivation, or "quotidian" disruption (see Snow & Soule 2010).

The most compelling theory concerned with movements and their judgment of what is "wrong" is relative deprivation (which takes many forms, including Ted Gurr's famous version). Relative deprivation is a social-psychological phenomenon, a subjective perception more than an objective reality, and is the engine for movement motivation. According to this theory, inequality and riots are linked, just as injustice is linked to movements, and so forth. Deprivation is a regular narrative in nearly all anarchist activism – there is no shortage of hierarchical aspects of society to critique, in whatever society or time period. Gurr (1970) described relative deprivation as a contrast between expectations and capabilities. Thus, people who expect to command their own lives, may find they lack the capability to do so (e.g., workers who seek self-management in their workplace are stymied by their boss's desire and ability to continue giving them orders). Anarchists wish to eliminate not only their own deprivation, but level the playing field for all, along all sorts of axes (including class, gender, race, power, etc.).

From an organizing perspective, anarchists tend to adopt a short-term political goal of making people aware of their deprivations and to mobilize those people to challenge such deprivation. In the long term, anarchists seek the elimination of all structural mechanisms of deprivation (although it is unreasonable and likely impossible to eliminate all grievances, forever). More specifically, "grievances" are claims about deprivation that movement actors assert, often referencing them when talking to others or engaging in protest. Anarchists often frame grievances dualistically. First, in contrast to liberals, anarchists decry the economic inequality of capitalism, claiming that no amount of personal freedom or rights will eliminate economic injustice. Second, in contrast to Leftist statist radicals, anarchists decry the authoritarian "solutions" sought in legislation, political parties, or "revolutionary" states (compare this to Bakunin's famous quote from the Preface).[10]

Quite a few weaknesses have been pointed out in regard to relative deprivation (Gurney & Tierney 1982; Morrison 1971). First, such deprivation is a constant factor of everyday life, ubiquitous for nearly everyone (even the rich claim that they could be comfortable if only they earned a few more million dollars). If everyone experiences deprivation, how can it explain movements? Most people do not join movements. Of course, people who *feel* the deprivation most immediately and personally, and are the most offended by the ubiquity of deprivation (such as many anarchists), are likely to participate in movements more than those who have a passing appreciation of such matters. Second, and relatedly, the theory does not seem to explain why many of the most ardent movement activists are not the most deprived. Artists, students, or the middle classes are regularly found within movements (including anarchist movements), yet they do not necessarily or typically experience the worst excesses of capitalism. This illustrates that one does not have be the most objectively deprived to have the loudest grievances, and thus seek the overthrow of capitalism – here an ideology of justice or liberation, as opposed to hierarchy, seems to drive activism. Finally, relative deprivation is an overly easy explanation of movements; people in power regularly claim that protesters are just a bunch of complainers. But, deprivation on its own does not thoroughly explain the actions of those who participate in movements. The incompleteness of relative deprivation theory has since been supplemented with the additions of other necessary movement ingredients, like resources, opportunities, and framing.

Mobilizing those resources

One of the first efforts by North American sociologists to compensate for these numerous weaknesses in relative deprivation theory came to be known as resource mobilization theory (RMT). Its origins are simple: many new, young sociologists in the 1970s were themselves active in the movements of the 1960s (or at least the "long decade" of the 1960s, which trailed into the 1970s). These young scholars knew that the small successes the movements achieved were due to factors that activists had influence over, and that activists were clearly conscious of this. The sociologists who developed RMT noticed that most movement activity took place in organizations (however broad, unstructured, or open-ended they might be), thus they decided that relative deprivation theory was focused on the wrong level of analysis. Rather than worrying about the micro-level concerns and attitudes of individuals, a more useful focus was the meso-level. Here, individuals participated collectively in various organizational configurations and accumulated resources of varying degrees of value.

One prominent conceptualization of RMT interpreted social movement organizations (SMOs) as roughly analogous to commercial enterprises; activists behaved in entrepreneurial ways and they gathered explicitly economic resources, which they deployed in the marketplace of other organizations. Like small businesses, these SMOs were conscious of their actions, were driven to pursue clearly articulated goals, and were pragmatic and strategic actors coping with finite resources in a challenging field (McCarthy & Zald 1977). Of course, anarchists are anti-capitalists, and thus this analogy will strike many as simply odd if not offensive. But, even for anarchist projects that are anti-profit (such as propaganda-oriented collectives), there is often an element of deliberate planning and allocation of resources in strategic moments. Anarchist structures *do* exist and goals are often articulated, even though they may be rather lofty (e.g., eliminate capitalism, the state, and all forms of domination). But perhaps more problematic with the RMT framework for anarchist movements is the prioritization of *formal* organizations, which include mainstream non-profits that have annual budgets and paid employees. If the strategic use of economic resources by these flexible, yet resource-rich organizations is the pathway to attaining organizational goals (reformist that they are likely to be), what are the chances for informal organizations that are deliberately small with weak (or non-existent) leadership structures? If anarchist groupings lack the infrastructure that other SMOs have, what are their chances for success, especially since their long-term goals require an even more thorough social transformation?

The economic determinist emphasis of RMT was not just an impediment to understanding anarchist organizations, but also to many other organizations that do not have NGO-like characteristics. Thus, a more recent adaptation of RMT broadens how "resources" are conceptualized. Instead of just thinking of resources as physical and material assets (that have economic value), Edwards and McCarthy (2004) classified five possible categories of resources. Now, anarchist projects may be seen to have other valuable forms of resources, including cultural and moral resources, added to the forms discussed earlier (e.g., socio-organizational, material, human).

Anarchist movements involve a variety of socio-organizational resources, including social networks, local "scenes," and other anarchist social milieux. While many of these are highly informal, there are also formal structures, including stable projects, collectives, and federations. This combination indicates infrastructure to support anarchist action, which involves these communities and coalitions of organizations, which may even work to quickly respond to changing situations.

Material resources are also available to anarchist movements – although not in the same kind or quantity as other movements. Access to monetary resources may be acquired through donations or organizational dues, or may be raised via proceeds from benefit shows or even through illegalist methods. Property is a more scarce resource and is rarely possessed as legally and clearly by anarchist movements. While, some spaces may be donated or lent by private individuals to movements, others may be seized private spaces or squatted buildings (see van der Steen *et al.* 2014). These places are likely to be communally and democratically managed (see Polletta's 1999 description of "free spaces"). Office space is harder to come by, as it often involves rent (when not squatted). Sometimes such space may be donated or rented; if the latter, the lowest possible rent is often sought due to limited monetary resources. The Greek social centers and squatted spaces in Athens were valuable for anarchist organizing during the 2008 uprising (Makrygianni & Tsavdaroglou 2011). Of course, anarchists also appropriate public property for movement activity, including parks and public squares.[11] Equipment and other supplies are likely to be donated, reclaimed (possibly "dumpstered"), and communally owned.

Anarchist movements also possess various human resources, such as labor. Human labor is often irregular in anarchist movements – lent whenever people have the free time or interest, as it is neither compulsory nor highly structured – just as in adhocracies. A diversity of experiences are also apparent within anarchist movements; today there are still active anarchists who came of age in the radical movements of the 1960s, while others were politicized in subsequent decades. The lived experience of activists may accumulate over time, resulting in diverse skills and expertise. Finally, leadership resources (as Edwards and McCarthy describe them) is less clear for anarchist movements, as these movements usually involve either a "no leaders" or "we are all leaders" conceptualization. Still, instrumental leaders who may be more charismatic, skilled, courageous, and articulate (and well-written) may be able to accumulate more influence, as well as help direct or inspire collective action within anarchist movements.

Cultural resources have been less widely discussed by movement scholars. For anarchist movements, conceptual tools like anti-authoritarianism may be of particular utility. Specialized knowledge, as diverse as social theory, meeting facilitation, permaculture, or how to prevent injury during protests, may be useful for anarchists. Tactical repertoires developed by anarchists – and their sibling movements – include various protest strategies, like decentralization and protest blocs: black blocs, feeder marches, disobedients, and others. Finally, organizational templates that are conducive to anarchist culture are important, such as leaderless and horizontal organizations, which I call anarchistic franchise organizations (see Chapter 8).

Lastly, moral resources are surely of importance, especially for a movement that is founded upon a principled orientation towards all aspects of daily life. Legitimacy is likely a resource of relevance within a certain limited realm, such as among self-identified rebels in some subcultures, or as a "legitimate threat" in the eyes of authority figures – yet it is unlikely that many mainstream people see anarchism as possessing legitimacy. Resources such as solidarity may exist with other progressive, Leftist, or community-oriented organizations, but solidarity is often something that must be extended first by anarchists in order to be reciprocated later. Thus, other groups can interpret anarchists' principled support as something worthy of returning. Finally, the moral weight of anarchist ideas such as skepticism of authority have popular resonance (according to much survey data, a hint of which is available in Chapter 7), at least when not publicly associated with "anarchism."

Also, the "fungibility" of the resources is finally acknowledged: one need not be in the immediate "possession" of a resource to deploy it, nor is the resource "used up" when it is used once (as in the case of money). Yet, the criticisms raised by Piven and Cloward (1979) still remains: the most disruptive movements are those that lack strongly structured organizations. Since revolutionary anarchism is premised upon social disruption, this suggests that (if Piven and Cloward are correct) organizational capacity and resources (of whatever kind, material or not) may be more of an impediment to revolution than a tool or aid. How is it possible for anarchist movements to utilize their organizational structures to facilitate disruption and revolution? The Spanish Revolution offers a few insights, as it involved highly organized anarchist structures, including the CNT labor union, FAI federation, armed militia units (the Iron Column, Durruti Column), agricultural cooperatives, the Mujeres Libres, and others (see Ackelsberg 1991; Christie 2008; Guillamón 2014; Mintz 2013; Paz 2007, 2011).[12] The key element that connected these disparate projects and organizations together under an anarchist umbrella was that each had a certain degree of autonomy from the other and disrupted a particular element of the old society (and thus the movement's adversaries).

Framing reality, on whose terms?

Movements aim to convey meaning and interpretation; the way they do this is through the use of framing. Frames are deeply embedded within the rhetoric, philosophy, and actions of all movements, including anarchist movements. Movements must accomplish a variety of goals in respect to others, which are accomplished by framing, most importantly to improve a movement's chances by increasing support and decreasing opposition. Therefore, anarchist movements want to inspire disaffected people who wish to see society transformed with radical critiques. These movements also want to rejuvenate inactive anarchists who may formerly have been active. And, just as important, anarchist movements must neutralize their enemies, such as the controlling power of the police or the propaganda of the corporate media.

Anarchist movements – like all others – are perceptional, subjective, conscious, and performative. They socially construct their own existence, and in doing so construct their own interpretation of reality: what is wrong with society and what needs to be changed? Frame alignment theory is indebted to Erving Goffman's (1974) theory of framing, where people construct and present their interpretations of economic, political, and social issues and attempt to convince others of these interpretations. For example, anarchists wish to convince others that "society is broken," "civilization is destructive," "just another new law won't work," or that "the system is the problem." The more people that anarchists can convince of these interpretations, the more likely anarchist movements will be successful. These core messages are called "master frames" – dominant frames of interpretation within a movement. Master frames provide an anchor for their movements and successors, as well as to "turn the heads" of movement participants to see issues in a certain way (Oliver and Johnston 2000)

According to Snow and Benford (1988), there are three central framing tasks that social movement actors use to mobilize others. First, diagnostic frames portray an event or a characteristic of social life as problematic, even intolerable, and in need of alteration. Anarchist movements employ a number of diagnostic frames, including their critiques of hierarchical institutions (capitalism, patriarchy, the state, white supremacy, etc.), the destructive role of authority figures, and the self-neutering consequences of allowing others to represent your interests for you. It is not enough to simply diagnose a problem, since outsiders would interpret the movement as simply being opposed to something, but not in support of something else (in other words, a movement that just "hates," but had no alternatives in mind). Thus, a second task includes prognostic frames. These frames propose a solution to the previously diagnosed problems, thereby suggesting the need to do certain things. Many anarchist movement prognostic frames are expressed in demands and treatises, but also in organizational structures and projects. Anarchists offer prognostic frames that seek egalitarian, horizontal, and cooperative social relationships. Anarchists wish to be in control of their own individual and community decisions, and they want to act to create the world they want rather than asking someone else to do it for them. Creating collectives that operate via consensus decision making, topless federations, and cooperatives and mutual aid projects are all practical prognostic frames.

A final task is necessary to put the diagnostic and prognostic frames into action: a motivational frame. Such frames serve as an inspirational "call to arms" or rationale for engaging in collective action. Of course, anarchist movements use many motivational frames to inspire people to resist the diagnosed conditions and pursue creating the prognosticated conditions. "Smash the state!" "Resist!" "Organize!" "Revolt!" and so forth are simple messages that are meant to move people into action. Successfully practiced and attractive alternatives can also motivate people to emulate the prognosticated practices.

Finally, frames may be "aligned," in order to better resonate and accomplish other goals for movements. Frame alignment is the process of finding and using a frame that successfully reaches and resonates with the right potential population. Four types of frame alignment can be delineated (Snow *et al.* 1986). First, *frame bridging* links together two ideologically congruent, yet separate, frames. Anarchism has actively sought out comparable or useful ideologies, thus linking anarchism with other tendencies such as feminism, humanism, syndicalism, Situationism, socialism, pacifism, environmentalism, and so on. Bridging involves taking the general anti-authoritarian frame of anarchism and combining it with other concerns to create a hybrid perspective. For example, bridging anarchist and environmentalist frames can create joint perspectives like eco-anarchism, social ecology, or primitivism. Thus, the anarchist frame of "the hierarchical system is the problem" can be melded with concern for the protection of the earth, wilderness, or non-human life. Thus, environmentalism is bridged with the anti-authoritarian rejection of electoral politics and bureaucratic SMOs, and the contrary tactical preference for direct action, which can be witnessed by the tree-sitting tactics of Earth First! or the property destruction of the Earth Liberation Front. Another good example of frame bridging is Bookchin's (2005) "social ecology," where he considers hierarchy to be the root of both social *and* environmental problems, thus joining the two by their shared concern.

Second, *frame amplification* clarifies and invigorates an existing frame that relates to a particular problem, issue, or event. Thanks to the relative accessibility enjoyed by Western anarchists, there is active debate, evaluation, and propaganda on the internet. This discourse takes place after major protests, during campaigns, in response to changing current events, or to incorporate new analyses of already acknowledged issues or views. For example, protests against various international organizations, like the G8 (or "Group of 8"), must be fine-tuned for audiences to suggest why the G8 deserves vigorous opposition. The already existing frames of anti-capitalism and anti-imperialism are directed toward the G8 (or the G-20) so anarchists (and others) understand just what the organization's purpose is in coordinating the activities of the richest and most powerful countries in the world. The excessiveness of G8 countries is likely already appreciated by anarchists, but accenting the importance of the anti-capitalist and anti-imperialist frames when a G8 meeting is about to occur nearby is an important spurt of motivation and inspiration. Also, the intricate issues that country leaders debate at G8 meetings must be explained to non-expert anarchist audiences. Webpages, periodicals, meetings, teach-in, protests, and informal conversations help to amplify the importance of opposition to the G8.

Third, *frame extension* incorporates others by expanding the boundaries of the existing frame to include that target group's views, interests, or sentiments. Here, Black anarchists have projected anarchism through the lens of militant Black nationalism, thus extending the active interests of anarchism into "non-White" circles, as well as introducing radical nationalism into anarchist circles. The development of the anarchist people of color (APOC) tendency and project demonstrates this significance (see Williams 2015 for more on the development of Black anarchism). Likewise, CrimethInc (2012b) has called Food Not Bombs a "gateway drug for activism" (2012b: 165), suggesting that something not explicitly anarchist in name could attract others, as FNB has attracted those who have pro-recycling, "do-gooder," or punk orientations.

Fourth, *frame transformation* occurs when a proposed frame does not resonate with individual's own interpretative frames, thus requiring a shift in the frame to something that better secures participants and support. It is always possible that anarchism will cease to provide an appropriate roadmap or strategy for action, thus leading some to reject it in favor of other ideologies; to give a few anecdotal examples: Daniel Cohn-Bendit's shift to the Green Party, John Zerzan's rejection of radical unionism for primitivism, or Murray Bookchin's shift from Stalinism to Trotskyism, then to anarchism and finally a variety of self-created ideologies including "social ecology," "libertarian municipalism," and "communalism." Or, upon the dissolution of the Love and Rage federation – initially founded by both anarchists and Trotskyists – some returned to a "revolutionary socialist" viewpoint, not anarchism.

These shifts, whether in individuals or organizations, require a shift in how the primary frame is presented. The anarchist frame will be presented in terms different than a Stalinist, Trotskyist, or unionist frame. Often, such a shift must be justified, particularly to observers who have been aware of the anarchist frame – the new frame is in part validated by a criticism of the prior (anarchist) frame's shortcomings. Perhaps anarchism does not have a disciplined enough organizational structure, thus Trotskyism is more appropriate. Or, maybe anarchism is rejected since it has not yet created a revolution; thus it must be abandoned for other ideologies that appear to have a more promising strategy. Or, anarchists may transform their more abstract anarchist frame to be more programmatic, as some anarcho-communists have with their adherence to the Organizational Platform of Libertarian Communists of 1926. It could also be argued that frame trans-formation is part of the move among some anarchists to reject all class struggle elements within anarchism – particularly that involved with unions, large federations, or "the Left." Here, a post-left perspective has embedded itself within some strains of anarchism, which rejects pursuing historical currents that were tied to overtly working-class interests and "work" (see Black 1997). Such "old anarchism" is argued to be archaic, ineffectual, and even totalitarian; thus a frame transformation is required to direct anar-chists away from their affiliation with the broad Left.

Tilly's essentials: Campaigns, repertoires, and WUNC displays

As indicated, many analyses of social movements exist. In addition, the ways in which movements are defined is also of theoretical importance. For example, Charles Tilly (Tilly & Wood 2009) argues that social movements consist of campaigns, protest repertoires, and what he self-consciously calls "WUNC displays." Taken in sum, these characteristics indicate not only what qualifies as a movement, but also what movements *do*.

First, campaigns are sustained efforts to engage with specific issues, toward a broader public. For anarchists, campaigns may vary widely, from workplace organizing drives, anti-police/cop-watching projects, or "don't vote" efforts to (political) prisoner support efforts and campaigns to use propaganda for inspiring insurrections. The key element with a campaign is its ongoing, longitudinal nature, and its focus on engaging others. Anar-chists will typically use campaigns to dialogue with non-anarchists, convey anarchist ideas and practices to these audiences, and to spread anarchist orientations of resistance to hierarchy.

Second, movements possess tactical toolboxes of protest "repertoires," which may be deployed at different times (during campaigns or otherwise), to address specific conditions. The more diverse the repertoires a movement possesses in the practical experiences of its members, the more flexible it can be to adapt to changing conditions. Anarchists share many protest repertoires with other movements (particularly on the Left). While anarchists are less apt to hold large rallies and permitted marches, they will use symbolism, parody, guerrilla theater, civil disobedience, monkey-wrenching, targeted property destruction, militant marches, and others. None of these are viewed as universally appropriate for all situations, but are considered better suited for some situations and not others. For example, it may be sensible to use large puppets and other symbolic representations during public gatherings involving non-anarchists (and elderly or children), where there is a low risk of police harassment. In different conditions, where there is a heavy police presence and more dramatic efforts are desired, anarchists may "mask up" and take direct action against corporate property during a fast-paced march. The more versatile and experienced individual participants are in diverse protest repertoires, the stronger anarchist movements likely will be, as they can use the most efficacious tactics to accomplish short-term goals.

Finally, efforts that represent or display what Tilly abbreviates as WUNC will help to establish a movement positively in relation to its allies and foes. The first of these four qualities is worthiness (W), or the degree to which a movement and its goals demand attention and respect from others. For anarchists, it is typically difficult to get many non-anarchists to consider anarchist ideas worthy of attention, let alone respect. Even when anarchist critiques are accepted (e.g., authorities are viewed to be corrupt and not trustworthy), anarchist strategies may alienate potential supporters. Instead, anarchists will discuss specific situations (e.g., manipulating bosses at work, exhaustion from work, a lack of joy with work, poverty wages, etc.) to provide evidence for the general conclusions which seem harder for many to accept (i.e., capitalism is bad for people).

Second, the quality of unity (U) implies that members of a movement are in agreement with each other about their goals and strategies – the greater the unity, the stronger the movement can be with its coordination. Contrary to Tilly's expectation, anarchists often consider there to be strength in diverse opinion and strategy. Of course "solidarity" is important – anarchist ought to support each other – but the multitude of anarchist ideological subvariants and interpretations is visible to anyone willing to observe anarchist movements, and many who have other movements as their reference point, will see anarchists as dis-unified, unorganized, and weak. Thus, a philosophical dualism exists between anarchism's support for mass action (e.g., a general strike or large-scale occupation) and support for the autonomy of individuals and small groups (e.g., feeder marches, affinity groups, autonomous actions).

Third, movements ought to have numbers (N). The more people who identify with a movement, actively support it, or participate in its campaigns, the better the chances that movement will accomplish its goals.

While it is next to impossible to accurately estimate the global number of anarchists (active or otherwise, in movements or not), there are very likely hundreds of thousands, maybe millions (see Chapters 2 and 3 for analysis about anarchist individuals and organizations throughout the world). However, this is a small number relative to the world's total population and the number of anarchists in any given country may be equally small. Yet, the perception of numbers may be as important as raw numbers themselves. Just as with Saul Alinsky's (1971) maxim that movements should make a lot of noise when they are weak, anarchist dramatic actions are intended to reach wide audiences and convey a boldness that most would assume indicates a large base of support. Along with "unity," these "numbers" do not need to be all doing the same things, but can be engaged in a multitude of diverse projects, working among varied populations – all still qualifying as large numbers.

Lastly, commitment (C) is a crucial representation to convey to outside observers, as it will suggest that the movement will not give up easily and will persist until its goals are met. While many observers of anarchist movements (especially those within the anti-anarchist network) may think that anarchists are disorganized and foolish, few will dispute the level of commitment that the most visible anarchists display. For example, the willingness to flaunt laws and social convention (risking arrest and ostracization) suggests a level of commitment that appears uncomfortable to most. Of course, many critics claim that anarchists do not "stick with" movements for very long, either burning out, giving up, or rejecting their former beliefs. While such evidence is anecdotal and lacks proof thus far, these losses to anarchist movements do not different from most movements. Future research may wish to explore the longevity of active anarchist movement participation, the process of radical aging along the life course, and how older and younger anarchist mix in contemporary anarchist movements.

Finding mechanisms to the dynamics of contention

Some of the most well-known American social movement theorists – who were largely responsible for shaping what was known as the political process model (deprivation, resource mobilization, political opportunity, framing) – decided to subvert the presumed clarity of their own model. Doug McAdam, Sidney Tarrow, and Charles Tilly (2001) wrote *The Dynamics of Contention*, which while not rejecting their earlier work, sought to identify the mechanisms and processes that function behind it. They identified mechanisms – such as brokerage, identity shift, radicalization, convergence, signaling (2001: 26–27, 162) – as events that "change relations among specified sets of elements" in various movement situations (2001:

25). Thus, mechanisms are the things that explain how their classical model functioned.

The target of their new work also broadened beyond simple social movements; McAdam, Tarrow, and Tilly intended to unite scholarship from many areas of "contentious politics," looking for similarities across various phenomenon, like movements, revolutions, nationalism, democratization, strike waves, ethnic conflicts, and so on. While the subject most immediately relevant here is social movements, some of these other phenomenon are clearly relevant to anarchism. For example, revolutions constitute the complete overthrow of the existing order (or at least of political elites) and can be anarchistic; but many revolutions end in highly reactionary conditions, as in the case of capitalist, Bolshevik, military, or fascist revolutions. Bookchin (1996), for example, describes how major revolutions in the modern democratic era actually involved multiple revolutions, some more progressive or regressive than others. Democratization is pertinent to anarchist goals insofar as it reduces state strength and other elites' power. In other words, democratization that creates a complex system of competing political parties, or that simply expands the franchise for a few extra social groupings, is not necessarily anarchist. Strike waves can help to impede capitalism – and in some instances, may succeed in temporarily crippling it – but such strikes are not unto themselves anarchist. Indeed, strikes are not even the ultimate objective of anarcho-syndicalism, which prioritizes the achievement of general strikes, as the transformation of working conditions into popular, self-managing councils and workplaces is also a requisite part of its vision. Thus, strikes are part of the anarchist toolkit to monkey-wrench capitalism, but are not the be-all-and-end-all of anarchist activity (even in the classic era). The nationalism and ethnic conflict that McAdam, Tarrow, and Tilly describe is definitively non-anarchist, especially as it refers to state-building and the erosion of egalitarian tendencies in society.

The authors separate contentious politics into contained and transgressive categories (i.e., institutionally based or extra-institutional conflict). While anarchism would presumably be transgressive, the authors still assume that such transgressive contentious involves "claimants" who target a government. This is at odds with anarchist movements, which neither seek to pressure governments to change, nor overthrow a government and put themselves in power (see Chapter 5 for more on this paradox regarding political opportunity theory). Attempts to explain the mechanisms that occur in these various contentious phenomena could hypothetically pertain to multiple anarchist movements, which may have mechanisms and processes in common with the non-anarchist movements that McAdam and his colleagues describe. But the biggest potential incompatibility with the dynamics of contention perspectives is its reliance on states. Anarchist protest or direct action that simply oppose capitalism or try to build communes outside the state are overlooked.[13] In summary, the dynamics of contention has a "faintly authoritative tone" (Stanbridge 2006), which others might also identify as authoritarian, too. Flacks (2003), concludes that the social scientists are wholly uninterested in talking to non-scholarly publics or providing useful theories to social movements themselves, thus limiting the practical potential of the entire framework.

The use of social movement theory

In summary, the social movement theories reviewed here say a lot of things, but what and how much do they say that is *meaningful* for all movements, especially radical movements like anarchism? These theories may describe necessary factors (grievances, framing efforts, organizational resources, etc.) but, by themselves, each is insufficient to guarantee that successful and challenging anarchist movements can emerge. Even with all of the above factors present, we still cannot predict the emergence of anarchist movements or their successes. This lack of predictive power is because we are missing the magic, luck or good fortune, or randomness that is either present (when a movement can emerge, succeed) or is absent.[14] There are some known necessary conditions for movements, but these known things are clearly not sufficient. Let me borrow a statistics analogy: multivariate regression modeling tries to measure the impact of the independent variables upon the dependent variable. Yet, even with a theoretically sound model and good evidence of movement emergence, there is always unexplained variance (or error). The stronger the association between potential movement causes, the less calculated error. Linear regression shows explained variance in the R^2 statistic. However, as most social scientists know, most multivariate models rarely explain even half the variance in their dependent variables (and typically far less). Few movement theories seem to even do this well.

The most basic contribution of sociological movement theory to anarchists may lie in the expansion of vocabulary. The issues, components, and discourse generated by social movement scholars is qualitatively distinct from those of most anarchists. It is reasonable to assume that broadening anarchists' conceptual vocabulary will allow for them to strengthen their self-critique and empower their movements. While jargon alone cannot make a movement vital or successful, the ecumenical incorporation of other perspectives and analytical tools will likely be more helpful than harmful to anarchist movement possibilities.

Presuming there is something of value to be found in sociological social movement theories – well, at least of value to movement participants – how could anarchist movements actually *use* social movement theories? The key is to go beyond the typical endpoint of scholarly published research whose last question is "why does this movement occur/arise/exist," and push on to ask "what makes movements more likely to succeed"? Most North American, scholarly movement researchers stop short of making proscriptions, sometimes even when pointedly asked. Theirs is an intellectual curiosity with movements, bounded by the precepts of science. Thankfully, there seem to be only a few cases today where the movement scholar's objective is to help the state co-opt or suppress movements. Usually there is just a professional, objective fascination that is distanced, unreflexive, and focused on myopic variables or processes. These authors are less interested in understanding the long-term impact of movements on social communities and more interested in conducting research for peer-reviewed journals, academic conferences, and for non-activists. This is all rather strange, since many SM scholars are quite sympathetic to movements (even radical ones), and I have often found that they were, at one point in their lives, personally influenced by and even participants in SMs. This is understandable when one considers that intellectual curiosities are often driven by personal experience (thus, people with criminal backgrounds or associations with criminals may want to get "criminal justice" degrees, and so forth).

To use the aforementioned theories, even in a fragmented fashion and where theories do not acknowledge their interactions with each other, one must focus on the phenomenon that increases movement participation, internal democracy, and further radicalization. Such elements are most well-suited to describing and explaining anarchist movements. For example, if one is trying to organize a rally, it makes sense to consider the available resources, which the planning organization or local allies possess. Not only does this imply that anarchist organizations and projects should pursue the acquisition of resources (although not all are equally helpful and some may be detrimental, as discussed here), but it also suggests that anarchists should think about the best ways to mobilize the most appropriate resources when needed. Thus, anarchists ought to consider the resources they possess or have access to, and think about how awareness of these resources transforms collective potential and action.

Or, if there is interest in finding new anarchists (akin to recruiting), it makes sense to consider the nature of people's relative deprivation. Where is this deprivation the strongest or most seriously felt? It is illogical to look for anarchist recruits among Wall Street stockbrokers or top military brass, but more among disaffected adolescents or the exploited industrial and service classes. Are there populations or groups that feel deprived in respect of other more privileged populations or who feel it in an absolute fashion? Do proto-anarchists see others as being "freer" than they, see everyone as dominated or disadvantaged (although to varying degrees), or that there are multiple dimensions to our disadvantages (e.g., class, gender, race; see Williams 2012). Do some people who feel deprivation also possess other traits, experiences, personalities, or conditions that would disable their ability to act on the indignation related to such deprivations?

Then, if anarchists wish to communicate their radical ideas to audiences, they ought to consider frame alignment theory, particularly what frames should they choose to present to others. Should the master frame be one of injustice or empowerment or both? A radical, broad critique of society or an encouragement to revolt? All of these frames may be suitable, but perhaps at the right times, with the right audiences. Framing suggests that activists should think about the best ways to make their messages and actions attractive, by presenting them in the most thoughtfully framed ways. Some frames will not resonate with certain audiences and these should be avoided: for example, when speaking to elderly or conservative people, copious profanity might not be wise, although an appeal to anarchistic morality – without initially labeling it as such – might be a better choice.

If anarchists are attempting to further radicalize a riot or uprising that has taken place, the lessons of the Eros effect are a suitable food for thought. Who will be the likely sectors to encourage and push the revolt further? Which groups are likely to try to apply the brakes on social transformation? What are the best social forms to encourage – like popular assemblies and decentralized community watch-groups? The answers to these questions are suggested by previous research, and even though history never repeats itself exactly, is does provide guidance for those who are aware of previously discovered patterns.

But, it is best to not get too seduced by the promises of theory. Theory is merely an explanation or a model, and not necessarily a guarantee or a "one-size-fits-all" solution. For example, it is not always the most down-trodden who will resist. Sometimes having more resources will push movements in reformist directions that ask less of themselves (see INCITE! 2007; Piven & Cloward 1979). For every "value" added, there may be no discernible move toward collective behavior, but rather, well, nothing. And, uprisings can just as often turn towards reformist partisan politics, usher in dictators, or become ugly racialist conflicts complete with rampant thuggishness, just as often as they radicalize a population and push them toward a communistic, free and utopian society. If we remain cognizant of the benefits that a theory offers, we can more realistically understand its shortcomings and then interpret the many idiosyncratic instances in which theory fails to assist. As the pioneering physicist Richard Feynman (1965) once warned, "It does not make any difference how beautiful your guess [read: theory] is. It does not make any different how smart you are ... if it disagrees with experiment it is wrong" (1965: 156).

Ideally, theory is a way to explain something. However, the majority of social theory is only able to provide partial explanations at best, or is mutually contradictory at worst. This post-modernist understanding of social theory – that multiple possible answers exist and there is no one correct answer – is an appropriate position to take, despite its leading to a non-straightforward analysis. We should be skeptical of explanations that are too tidy and simple, since the real world is messy and complicated. This apparent inability to concretely explain social movements leads many activists to reject social movement theories. Then, combined with the dispassion many movement scholars express, and the esoteric and non-practical concerns pursued in the study of movements, it is no wonder that some activists and organizers write off social movement theory as worthless.

Current social movement theories may or may not be worthless. If we accept the poly-theoretical perspective, we can learn certain things about movements, despite those things being detached from other things. Perhaps taken in concert, all theories offer a more comprehensive, multifaceted appraisal of movements. While this may seem somewhat Pollyanna-ish, it is, I believe, a project worth pursuing if we care about the success of social movements.

Anarchists in particular have a curious mixture of intellectualism and skepticism of experts. Although this may seem contradictory to outside observers, it should not be. In general, anarchists honestly want to understand the world and their own movements, and all sorts of rank-and-file anarchists dip into radical theory and classic-age anarchist authors, perhaps far more than most other movements' participants do for their respective traditions. Also, the anarchist rejection of authority figures includes those with special intellectual knowledge or expertise. As Bakunin famously wrote (1970), he defers to the skill of the boot-maker when he needs a boot made, but he reserves the right to reject that boot-maker's input, their authority over him, or the notion of the boot-maker as the final or only authority on the subject of boot-making. This rejection of authority may seem to be anti-intellectual, but it is not. In terms of social movements, anarchists reject the notion that any one person – especially a dispassionate, outside observer – would know better how movements function. Indeed, anarchists wish to foster a lively internal critique of anarchist movements, in order to understand as many vantage points as possible.

It is not too outlandish to argue that there is some value in exploring social movement theories and their potential to explain anarchist movements in greater depth. This chapter has considered a variety of theories, offering various concerns, observations, and conclusions about anarchist movements. But some of the largest, and most sweeping recent perspectives still remain unaddressed. Chapters 5–7 discuss prominent theories pertinent to social movements that I have intentionally overlooked thus far. Anarchist movements, in particular, are analyzed in light of political opportunity, new social movements, and social capital frameworks. These are major North American, European, and non-social movement frameworks, respectively. Discussed next in Chapter 5, political opportunity – when combined with relative deprivation and mobilizable resources – is an important element of the influential political processes model. Chapter 6 explores the much heralded, but not quite internally consistent new social movement approach. In the process, it is clear that these two theories offer additional insights into anarchism, but that each have deep biases that make them unable to truly understand a radical, varied movement like anarchism. Therefore, I try to adapt these two theories to anarchism's unique characteristics, showing how more anarchistic political opportunity and new social movement theories could be drafted. Finally, although social capital theory is rarely considered relevant to movements, I use it in Chapter 7 to explore the social affiliations, networks, and trust established in anarchist movements.

Notes

1   This is presumably not true for what is called "grand theory"; without addressing the merits of such an approach (see Mills 1959 for a critique), let me simply mention that value-added theory and dynamics of contention described later in this chapter both aspire to be grand theories of a sort.

2   Fuchs and Plass (1999) have argued that there are three points of intersect between sociology and social movements: sociology itself as a social movement, the impact of social movements on sociology, and the sociology of social movements. In this chapter, I focus on the last intersection.

3   I wrote in a 2014 article for *Critical Sociology* about the relationships between these classic sociologists and the anarchists of their time. These relationships were both intellectual and personal, ranging from friendly to hostile. Buechler's (2011) analysis also extends credit for movement theory to closely affiliated individuals, such as Vladimir Lenin with Marx, Gustav LeBon with Durkheim, and Robert Michels with Weber. The connections of these additional individuals to anarchism are interesting: Lenin had anarchists arrested following the Bolshevik Revolution, LeBon expressed fear of anarchists, and Michels (although later in his career he became a fascist) wrote positively about anarchism as serving as a "prophylactic" against the iron law of oligarchy (see Williams 2014).

4   This book – like many focused on the Global North – overlooks the contributions of African, Asian, and Latin American sociology to the study of movements. This deficit is considerable and due to willful ignorance; for an example of the potential theoretical power from the Global South (Connell 2007), consider the contributions of even a single analyst, Uruguayan scholar Raúl Zibechi (2012).

5   Lofland (1988) suggested symbolic interactionism as the most ideal sociological fit for anarchism – he associates conflict theory with Marxism and functionalism with capitalism – and identifies numerous bridges between anarchism and sociology.

6   Lynd and Grubacic (2008) refer to the collaboration of anarchists and Marxists within the radical labor movement (especially in the USA) as the "Haymarket synthesis."

7   In addition to the previous discussion on class in Chapter 2, this question is considered more directly in Chapter 6 with new social movement theories, which are a direct response to class struggle theory's weaknesses.

8   National movements as movements to defend a "nation," while social movements as movements to protect the interests of all sorts of social groups (Wallerstein 2004). Both can be anti-state as well as pro-statist.

9   He claims that no one on the Left has been able to "convince the majority that there was any efficacious alternative route"! (Wallerstein 2003: 235).

10 Davies (1962) attempted to explain revolutions via his "J-curve" model, in which a period of rising expectations is suddenly reversed, leading to shocking deprivation and ultimately revolution. While this is an attractive hypothesis, none of Davies's examples were anarchist revolutions and given the perceptual nature of these theories, they are inordinately difficult to test.

11 Think of the many post-2008 rebellions worldwide, including the Arab Spring, Occupy Wall Street, Indignados, and many others, who sought to control public space for liberatory and anti-authoritarian purposes.

12 It must be noted that many of these (notably, except the CNT) were formed after the Francoist coup, in spontaneous resistance to the fascist takeover.

13 The authors admit as much in a later rejoinder on their work (McAdam & Tarrow 2011), identifying the centrality of state and politics in their model ("A state-centric bias"; 2011: 5).

14 This is what the contentious dynamics theory portends to offer with its notion of mechanisms.

5

Anti-state political opportunities

Anarchism is not a romantic fable but the hardheaded realization, based on five thousand years of experience, that we cannot entrust the management of our lives to kings, priests, politicians, generals, and county commissioners. (Edward Abbey)

States and context

This chapter challenges the assumption that the state is a strategic location of opportunity from the perspective of radical, anti-state movements. Routine social movement behaviors that petition, protest, or lobby governments to change or adopt certain laws or policies are familiar in modern societies, from those run by dictatorships to those with representative democracies. However, these now-regular patterns of movement–state interaction are premised on the assumption that movements want something from the state that states are able to give. Presumably, anarchists have no interest in anything that states are willing to offer, nor do such movements attempt to convince states to quit and dissolve themselves through targeted lobbying efforts. What does movement activity and protest mean for such movements, under these conditions? This chapter addresses this question from a political opportunity (PO) perspective by analyzing existent county-level political opportunities and their relationship to the concentration of anarchist organizations. Surprisingly, we see that countries with more political opportunities also have greater organizational density.

Using historical narratives from present-day anarchist movement literature (recorded in A-Infos), I also note various events and phenomena in the last two centuries and their relevance to the mobilization and demobilization of anarchist movements throughout the world (Bolivia, Czech Republic, Great Britain, Greece, Japan, and Venezuela). Labor movement allies, failing state socialism, and punk subculture have provided conditions conducive to anarchism, while state repression and Bolshevik triumph in the Soviet

Union constrained success. This variation suggests that future work should attend more closely to the role of national context, and the interrelationship of political and non-political factors. Additionally, the key question of what constitutes movement "success" for revolutionary movements that "move forward" – yet do not achieve revolutionary transformation (indeed, who conceive a final, complete transformation to be theoretically impossible) – seems to be a problem faced uniquely by anarchist movements. Instead, thinking of opportunity as global, non-politically based, and unattached to "ultimate objectives" like revolution, help to make these ideas more useful for understanding anarchist mobilization.

Anarchists have never been able to rid society of the state, although not for lack of trying. Anarchism, as a radical ideology, appears to possess an optimistic orientation towards the possibility of social change. Accordingly, resistance and change are not only possible in the darkest moments of human history, but are also potentially present in everyday life. Anarchists tend to advocate seizing the opportunities within these moments and helping to encourage others toward a more liberatory future (Ward 1996). Thus, while acknowledging the power, influence, and limitations of existing political and social structures, anarchists also implicitly emphasize the capacity for human agency.

Politically, anarchists argue that opportunities always exist to resist the present social order and to create a new world. Consequently, "Revolution now!" has been and remains a meaningful anarchist slogan. Anarchism differentiates itself from other revolutionary ideologies such as Marxism by rejecting any delay in revolution. Waiting for "the people" to be ready or to trust that the state will "wither away" eventually are not appropriate excuses for inaction. In fact, state participation in the pursuit of revolution is inherently problematic. For example, the Russian anarchist Mikhail Bakunin wrote: "No state, however democratic – not even the reddest republic – can ever give the people what they really want, i.e., the free self-organization and administration of their own affairs from the bottom upward, without any interference or violence from above" (Dolgoff 1971: 338).

Strategy in the anarchist movement is radical and multifaceted. As a political tradition, anarchism has possessed an antagonism toward authority in a broad sense, rather than the limited, popular understanding: as a broad challenge to all forms of domination, not just that of the state. Anarchism focuses on the web of relationships between not only individuals and society, but also among major institutions, such as the state, capitalism, military, patriarchy, White supremacy, and heterosexism. Within relationships, people may act to create a society less encumbered by hierarchy, domination, and authority. Thus, opportunities always exist to create egalitarian, horizontal, and cooperative relationships. This chapter investigates anarchist movements within these spaces and moments, both past and present. Yet, some opportunities have been more conducive to the anarchist movement and some of these moments have been more fruitfully exploited.

I address the following, interrelated questions. Can the theory of political opportunities be used – or at least re-packaged – to understand anarchist movements? What major opportunities has anarchism recently seized upon (and sometimes unintentionally benefited from) to expand its ranks and advance its goals? Finally, despite their implicitly pro-system nature, are various, standard political opportunities (i.e., political rights, democratic regimes) associated with the presence of anarchist organizations?

Political opportunities: potentials and problems

Political opportunities (PO) constitute conditions conducive for action, thereby helping social movement organizations to achieve goals. McAdam described four central POs that past researchers (Ayres 1999; Goodwin 2002; Schock 1999; Snow *et al.* 2005) have consistently deemed relevant to social movements: (1) increased access to political participation; (2) shifts in the alignments of ruling elites or cleavages among elites that create space for challengers; (3) the enhanced availability and accessibility of influential elite allies; and (4) a decline in the capacity or tendency for the state to repress dissent (McAdam 1996). Yet, most scholarship on PO has focused on reform movements. Do anarchists benefit from or utilize such opportunities that are either available from, or interact with, the state or elites? Although anarchists, almost by definition, are not interested in affecting state reform, they may *indirectly* benefit from state action. For example, a decrease in repression allows for overt anarchist organizing. On the other hand, increased state repression may also have encouraged anarchism by providing groups with the motivation to resist domination. Conversely, a nascent anarchist movement may be crushed by state persecution. This suggests a complex relationship between state action and the growth or decline of anarchism. In addition, increased accessibility to political participation in general can allow anarchists to ride the coat-tails of other movements; thus, during elections, anarchists can point out limitations in representative democracy and the indirectness of voting. Or, voting may channel general discontent into the controllable realm of electoral politics and away from disruptive politics. Cleavages within ruling elites – although often making one faction look "better," nicer, or electable – can create a weakened or unstable power structure that is more susceptible to attack and overthrow.

Anarchists do not utilize political rights in a conventional fashion by lobbying government or electing favorable candidates, although they likely do benefit from press rights and other civil liberties. The correlative relationship I discuss later makes more sense as a general measure of tolerance to the challenge of formal authority in a country; the greater the tolerance of dissent, the more likely a state's strongest critics (e.g., anarchists) will overtly organize in public. Anarchist organizations are likely more willing to list themselves in the AYP – and to be "above ground" generally – when they believe the risk level is acceptable. In this respect, the anarchist organizations listed in the AYP may be the result of a selection effect, and the impact of political opportunities on the underground or clandestine anarchist movements remains unknown.

Even if anarchists *do* benefit from some "standard" POs – albeit indirectly – a number of empirical and theoretical issues prevent us from drawing any concrete conclusions about the appropriateness of a traditional PO view for the anarchist movement. First, Shantz (2003b) argued that social movement research has tended to focus on reform movements and has shied away from analysis of radical movements (such as anarchism) that seek to transform the entire foundation of social relations – especially those whose goals do not include the seizure of the state itself. In such a research milieu, it is a mistake to assume that POs crafted to explain movements with moderate goals (e.g., policy advocacy) can adequately address the objectives of radical movements. Even radical movements like Marxism may be measured using conventional research, as the intended outcomes are clearly articulated and assumed to be linear. Marxism represents a mere adaptation to reform movements, as it aspires to a similar ascension to power as do other movements. But a movement such as anarchism, premised upon deliberate practices that reflect "the means are the ends" and a diffusion of power, cannot be analyzed as easily or rigidly. Thus, anarchist movements are vastly understudied by sociologists, and the theories available to scholars are likely to need some revision, and some may not be applicable (as suggested in Chapter 4).

Second, PO theory generally takes for granted that the state is the target of protest. Yet, van Dyke and her colleagues (2004) found that many movements *do not* just target the state. Only half of the targets in protest events from 1968 to 1975 in the USA were state targets; the remaining protests were aimed at educational institutions, "the public," business, individuals, cultural and religious organizations, unions, and medical institutions. In fact, the government was targeted less than 50 percent of the time by the civil rights, gay and lesbian, and women's movements (van Dyke *et al.* 2004).[1] Although anarchists have most famously targeted the state, anarchism's broad critique of authority and domination is not limited to political actors. Further, this critique is not mere protest, but radical opposition to the *very existence* of hierarchical institutions. Thus, anarchism does not only target the state, but also many other hierarchical institutions, ranging from white supremacy and patriarchy to capitalism and militarism.

Third, although activists' agency to exploit opportunities is implicit in PO theory, anarchists themselves do not actively try to use many of these opportunities. If open windows of opportunity are not actively exploited by anarchists, do they really constitute "opportunities"? For example, unlike other movements, anarchists do not engage in standard political activity: they are not apt to engage in letter-writing campaigns against politicians, to vote for (or against) certain candidates, or even to run for office themselves. Obviously, anarchists do not try to lobby the state or pressure for constitutional amendments that would lead to the elimination of a constitution. Could anarchists actually "utilize" progressive politicians who claim to oppose policies and practices that anarchists also do? Ostensibly, such politicians would be *elite* allies; the presence of such "allies" would not seem to ultimately benefit the anarchist movement if it is opposed to negotiating or working with those allies. Since a central principle of anarchism is direct action, anarchists do not request, or wait for, others to act on their behalf. Instead of relying on representatives, one acts directly – either individually or collectively – to immediately accomplish the desired goal, without the facilitation, approval, or agency of elected elites, officials, or bosses.

Fourth, commonly studied POs might actually be detrimental to anarchist organizing and activism, rather than being helpful. Increased access to elites, political space, or participation might direct activists and the public towards reformism and electoral politics, not radicalism. Rifts between elites (like Democrats and Republicans, or politicians and capitalists) might appear to undermine the anarchist claim that "all elites are similar and serve the same end," and thus lead people to conclude that the system does not need to be overthrown. Therefore, POs could either channel rebellious energy for radical change into reformist, institutional mechanisms or undercut any popular impression that radical change is necessary. Consequently, anarchist movement activity appears paradoxical within the PO framework.

On a strictly theoretical level, there is much to criticize in the standard view of POs. Of central importance is the assumption – and perhaps leap of faith – regarding the ultimate goal of social movements. As witnessed by McAdam's (1996) overview of the literature, many scholars have tended to assume and effectively operationalize "political opportunities" as "state opportunities" useful to influence state-based policy making. As such, movements benefit from actions and conditions in which the state is the key adversary or target. Yet this logic conflates "political" with "state" (and, more narrowly, associates political action with elections and politicians), which is the common interpretation of "politics," generally. Anarchists strongly criticize limiting "politics" to the domain of state officials, elected or otherwise. Instead, anarchism argues that politics is the realm of public decision making and debate, of which the state is only one component, albeit the dominant one. It is entirely possible to engage in "politics" without reliance upon the state.[2] Also, to entrust the state with the ability to serve as final arbitrator for what constitutes human rights (or any other right), is to restrict the universality of such rights. Anarchists argue that rights are not guaranteed by the state, but by birth (see Turner 2009). In this view, to rely upon the state to approve of, and administer, human rights is to reify the state as an essential institution for people's everyday lives. However, many states actively attempt to restrict rights and succeed because states tend to be viewed by many citizens as the proper authority for the distribution of rights in a society.

The distinction between objective and subjective opportunities is particularly important for the anarchist movement. Most movements tend to have occasional victories with concrete, definable successes, while anarchism has rarely had victories and none that have lasted for any substantial length of time. Consequently, discussing useful objective opportunities for the anarchist movement is challenging because it is unclear which "opportunities" have or have not led to the few, short-lived anarchist rebellions (which themselves have had unclear and limited consequences) or anarchist-led campaigns. A more useful approach, and the one developed here, is to consider anarchist mobilization through the eyes of anarchists themselves and their subjective understanding of useful opportunities. Since it is difficult to say with any certainty that a particular "opportunity" did objectively and sufficiently cause a particular outcome, I argue that it is often more appropriate to consider what movement actors themselves conclude.

Most research that considers cross-national differences in protest tends to analyze the differences between countries (Kitschelt 1986), and does not look for commonalities across countries' movements, particularly in how they share common narratives that are not specific to their own society. These "common opportunities" are of major importance to internationalist-oriented movements. For example, della Porta (2008) noted the benefit that unemployed movements in *all* six of her (all European) case study countries received from labor unions and positive popular opinion. Internationalist movements like anarchism seem an ideal subject to use such border-crossing common opportunities, particularly as it relates to resisting the "dominant logic" (Melucci 1996: 7) of all hierarchically organized societies, regardless of whether they are constructed on capitalist, socialist, or some other economic foundation.

Regardless of an opportunity's universality, what do movements try to achieve? Meyer's overview of political opportunity research noted half a dozen different forms of movement outcomes, including policy changes, changes in the level of appropriations for established government programs, policy implementations, running candidates for office, creating alternative institutions, and changing actual practices (Meyer 2004). Creating alternative institutions comes closest to an actual anarchist goal, but Meyer's example of this outcome is Andrews' (2002) study of private segregationist schools in the US South, which helped to subvert school integration for white and Black students – far from an anarchist objective. The applicability of Meyer's outcomes for anarchist movements is questionable. None of these movement outcomes includes the elimination of various hierarchical institutions, a central premise of anarchism. Even "protest," in which anarchists are involved, is usually narrowly defined as attendance at protest events and precludes the idea of *resistance* or *rebellion*.[3]

Despite the apparent shortcomings of PO theory, a major empirical question remains: are there political opportunities that benefit the anarchist movement? I argue that anarchist movement activity has coincided with actual and perceived periods of greater freedoms, and, in times of state repression, anarchist organizing may go underground or disappear altogether. But we can and should also broaden the contextual factors that foster movement activity to include cultural and economic opportunities. Although Goodwin and Jasper (1999) warn against watering down the operationalization of political opportunities to the point where *anything* constitutes such an opportunity, anarchism suggests a unique exception to the rule. Since anarchist movements have a strong *non*-interest in greater political access (of the stereotypical, state-based variety), it is prudent to expand the concept of opportunities to other forms, including those that are cultural and economic in character, and to inquire about the extent to which cultural, economic, and traditionally "political" opportunities have shaped these movements in different contexts. Potentially, these realms are of equal importance to anarchists since they oppose all forms of social domination that exist in a variety of social, economic, and political domains (such as racial, gender, and sexuality-based oppression) and are opposed to capitalism. If there are POs (and other opportunities) that align with anarchist movements, what are they? I argue that we can use anarchist organizations as an indicator of anarchist movement activity and then compare the presence of those organizations to existing opportunities.

Objective opportunities and organizational density

Which countries have formal and actual freedoms of speech and protest, and do they correspond with the concentration of anarchist organizations? Is there a legal right to organize trade unions (since many organizations from the Anarchist Yellow Pages described in Chapter 3 are syndicalist) or engage in strikes? Does a country have broad media freedoms?[4] Which countries were previously, or are currently, in a state of "light repression" or "heavy repression" against political dissenters?

We can assess some of these elements by using a number of measures for the broader political environment of countries with anarchist organization – such as civil liberties, political rights, trade union rights, and media rights (data from Freedom House and International Labour Organization reports), democracy (from Polity IV), and human development (from United Nations reports). Specific country-level political factors were significantly correlated with the presence of particular types of organizations, as listed in the 2005 AYP. Presumably, greater political freedom and democratic governance will be associated with higher levels of anarchist organizing. For example, at the country level, freedom of the press will encourage the development of anarchist media organizations, trade union rights will facilitate class-based organizations, and rights related to political participation will foster anarchist community spaces and social centers. These kinds of logical speculations were used simply to help guide the selection of appropriate variables; I expected contradictory or otherwise unexpected findings to emerge from the analysis.

The first three PO measures I use here come from the international human rights research organization Freedom House,[5] whose data is commonly used in comparative research on countries.[6] These variables include political rights, civil liberties, and press rights. The International Labour Organization has developed a measure for trade union rights, which overlaps somewhat with the civil liberties scale and is separately determined by a content analysis of labor rights reports.[7] Then, another PO operationalization measures how democratic or autocratic the polity itself is. The Polity IV Project (Marshall & Jaggers 2005) describes a *democratic* polity as one where political participation is fully competitive, the recruitment of executive is via elections, and the constraints placed on the chief executive are substantial. Some of the component variables in the measure of democracy are the *regulation of participation* and *competitiveness of participation*.[8] This view of "democracy" is the standard view in the highly advanced capitalist countries of Europe and North America (where the majority of anarchist organizations reside in the AYP) and, more accurately, is synonymous with "representative democracy."[9]

All these measures were tested for association with the rate of anarchist organizations per capita. Countries with fewer than 20 anarchist organizations listed in the AYP 2005 directory were excluded, leaving 21 countries in the analysis.[10] Although this threshold for the number of organizations per country is somewhat arbitrary, countries with 20 or more organizations represent 90 percent of the total organizational count in the AYP. In addition, I believe that a focus on countries with 20 or more anarchist organizations is helpful because these also include some (although surely not all) of the most important (Western) countries in the history of anarchism and because I am trying to minimize the problem of potential under-counting due to biases in the AYP (i.e., countries with few political rights may not be represented in the AYP because the risks may be too high for anarchist organizations to disclose their location or even existence).[11] This examination of a reduced sample from the AYP directory is actually a more conservative test of relationships than an analysis that includes all the countries and the results are arguably less subject to biased reporting in the AYP. Because the number of countries considered is small, the analysis relies on bivariate correlation rather than multiple regression, and thus should be considered exploratory, as it does not control for other presumably important factors. I utilized the categorization of anarchist organization types from Chapter 3 – class-based, physical spaces, media, franchise, general anarchist, and others – in this analysis. The number of organizations in each category was divided by the country's population (in millions), to represent the rate of each type per capita. Table 5.1 presents bivariate correlations between these group categories per population and the different types of rights and democracy measures.

A strong pattern emerges here: anarchist organizations tended to be positively associated with those countries that had a variety of freedoms and democracy characteristics. Thus, instead of supporting a relative deprivation argument (refer back to Chapter 4) which suggests that radical resistance would be strongest in the poorest, most repressed countries, the data presented here demonstrate the opposite, at least for anarchist organizations. Every measure for rights or regime "openness" was significantly related to the per capita level of anarchist organization, at least when all such organizations were combined. This finding supports the hypotheses above that predicted a positive relationship between these opportunity structures and anarchist organization density. However, the association between anarchist organization categories and the Human Development Index[12] (not shown) were all non-significant. In other words, a country's level of human development does not indicate the density of its anarchist movement; thus, anarchist movements are not merely the result of advanced human and economic development, typically associated with societal affluence.

Among the grouped types of organizations, results were somewhat mixed in terms of what one would expect from political opportunity theory. For example, press rights were significantly correlated with the degree of media organizations, while trade union rights were not significantly related to class-based organizations – this latter non-association indicates that anarcho-syndicalists and radical worker organizations are not more likely to be found in places with greater worker rights. Competitiveness of participation (the right to express and pursue alternatives) was significantly and logically correlated with physical spaces and media organizations, both of which are organizational categories premised on the ability to formulate and create alternative ways of doing and thinking. For some types of organizations, such as franchise and anarchist organizations, there were no

Table 5.1 Correlations between rights and categories of anarchist organizations per capita

Category/population	Political rights	Civil liberties	Trade union rights	Press rights	Democracy	Participation regulation	Participation competitiveness
Group rate/million	0.523*	0.493*	0.566**	0.545*	0.528*	0.526*	0.516*
Other orgs/million	0.345	0.409†	0.345	0.452*	0.325	0.391†	0.369†
Class orgs/million	0.243	0.159	0.211	0.196	0.194	0.241	0.240
Spaces/million	0.442*	0.331	0.532*	0.315	0.496*	0.469*	0.455*
Media orgs/million	0.403†	0.506*	0.406†	0.540*	0.478*	0.435*	0.402†
Franchise orgs/million	0.254	0.417†	0.335	0.438*	0.286	0.239	0.243
Anarchist org/million	0.405†	0.217	0.456*	0.371†	0.349	0.275	0.315

Note: Two-tailed Pearson's correlation coefficients;
** $p < .01$
* $p < .05$
† $p < .10$

apparent meaningful patterns. But there were a great many significant relationships between organization types and rights. This lends support to the idea that political opportunities may at least partly shape the development of some types of anarchist organizations.[13] The consistency in outcomes across these two very different datasets suggests that biases within a particular data set do not overshadow the fundamental finding that some types of anarchist organizations do, in fact, benefit from political opportunities within particular kinds of states. This finding, although not uniform across all types of anarchist organizations, is somewhat ironic given the assumptions that anarchists tend to have about the undesirable nature of the state itself. Clearly, some types of anarchist organizations are thriving within certain states, relative to others.

The basic rights and democracy measures used in the correlation analysis were still limited in scope; wider conceptions of rights are overlooked (such as the right to education, housing, medical care, etc.).[14] But it should be remembered that political opportunities as described by McAdam (1996) include increased access to political decision making, not broader economic and social rights. The Freedom House measures are still robustly correlated to the presence of anarchist organizations. Thus, regardless of how narrowly Freedom House's conception of rights may be defined, this pattern still holds. Even the antithetical inclusion of "property rights" could facilitate some, albeit limited, access to space to conduct political organizing. Having a physical building in which to hold meetings, plan protests, run community projects, and other activities can be helpful for social movements generally, and there is cause to suspect that anarchism may often share these needs – despite the greater flexibility and amorphous organizational forms preferred by anarchist movements, who must often pursue other avenues to organizing, owing to their limited access to such resources.

However, the positive correlations listed in Table 5.1 do not suggest that prevailing political arrangements are *ideal* for anarchist organizing, a fact highlighted by the relatively low number of anarchist organizations (compared to other civil society organizations) in most countries. Anarchist organizations seem to exist in far fewer numbers than most types of organizations, such as sports clubs, religious groups, or labor unions.

The very presence of such organizations may indicate a level of tolerance by governments that allow them to exist and appear in the AYP. One can imagine the existence of many anarchist organizations in a country as large as China, but such organizations are unlikely to openly disclose their existence, let alone their location in the political context of a repressive state, particularly as such anarchist organizations would be in conflict with Maoist organizations and Confucian culture. Appearing in the AYP would mean a virtual death sentence for the organization (and possibly its members) in states that do not recognize certain basic rights and democratic mechanisms.[15] As I suggested in my discussion on the strengths and limitations of the AYP earlier in this book, some anarchist organizations have an interest in *not* being listed and this concern is not randomly distributed across geopolitical space. This is precisely why I argue that more attention to political opportunities would increase our understanding of the ecology of anarchism as a social movement.

Additionally, anarchists in poorer countries might prefer or choose to operate within other, non-anarchist movements. For example, past labor and environmental movements in peripheral, former colonies tended to be embedded within movements for national liberation and other struggles that are unifying in nature – and thus less explicitly ideological (Rootes 1999; Sturmthal 1972), although counter-examples for anarchist movements are easy enough to generate (see Fernández 2001; Hirsch & van der Walt 2010). A more complete picture of anarchism throughout the world – especially in places without greater rights and democracy, or international communication networks – requires labor-intensive studies (perhaps participant observation) on the ground in those countries.

Do these brief findings mean that anarchists – who want to drastically re-order the existing social order – are actually benefiting from state-based characteristics? Perhaps. Yet it would be misleading to claim that, for example, civil liberties are only offered by the laws of the state, and not by the social norms that everyday people expect and reinforce in their daily lives. It would be equally naive to ignore that greater freedoms and rights weaken the centralized authority of the state. A state with a diminished capacity to enforce the will of its executives and elites may not be an anarchist society, but one could argue that it is closer than one in which a dictator rules. This is to propose that the social order of a society may be a spectrum upon which liberty and despotism are but two extremes, as Proudhon once wrote.[16] The state's internally repressive capacity strengthens itself as it approaches dictatorship, while it weakens itself as it approaches political libertarianism.

Even though past waves of anarchism – such as during the Russian and Spanish revolutions – may have been different, present-day anarchist movements seem largest and most overt in those places where formal and informal political rights, as well as democracy, exist. The opportunities offered in these societies have apparently fostered, if not at least tolerated, the insurgency of a collection of radical organizations with the goal of overthrowing the very institutions that have uncomfortably and temporarily permitted them. The ironic presence of avowedly anti-capitalist and anti-state movements in some of the most capitalist and stable states in the world raises intriguing and important questions with which future research and anarchist activism will have to grapple.

Assessing case studies

I seek to assess two loose, competing hypotheses regarding anarchist political opportunities.[17] First, *country-specific opportunities* may have assisted some anarchist movements but hindered others, with local context being the decisive factor. In this case, what explains the variations in anarchist activity by country (for example, the varied concentrations of anarchist organizations listed in the Anarchist Yellow Pages)? Opportunities that have shaped a particular movement's development, success, and survival ought to be apparent in any analysis. Second, as an international movement – especially one intent on eliminating state borders and global capitalism – *common opportunities* may be larger in scale than the country level. Opportunities may be more general than any one country and instead may be shared across national borders. This possibility suggests that country-specific opportunities are less important.

Opportunities must be perceived as real to insiders in order to be useful in the analysis of historical, subjective narratives, either in the present or in retrospect. Subjectivity is important in analyzing opportunity, especially in the case of movements that persist despite few or no major victories (i.e., most anarchist movements). Insider narratives about perceived opportunities can help to explain the actions of movement participants. Therefore, I next examine country-level movement case studies that are built on the arguments and analyses of anarchists themselves discussing opportunities that each movement encountered. This approach is based on a *verstehen* epistemology; while one might assume that anarchist authors would insert propagandistic claims into such histories, we see that this is not the case – the histories appear to be realistic representations from insider perspectives.[18]

Information on country-specific anarchist movement histories was collected from A-Infos (www.ainfos.ca). Billing itself as "a multi-lingual news service by, for, and about anarchists," A-Infos has provided news articles about anarchist politics, ideas, and movement events for many years. Initially started as a print-based news source, it went online in 1995 and by 2008 the A-Infos archives boasted over 60,000 news items in more than a dozen languages (A-Infos 2008).[19] A-Infos is administered by people who identify with a pro-organizational, class-struggle anarchist tradition. This "capital-A" anarchist identity eschews egocentric individualist, primitivist, and armchair anarchisms, as well as statist anti-capitalism, liberalism, and so-called "anarcho-capitalism."[20] This positioning places A-Infos squarely within the major Left wing of the anarchist movement, often loosely identified as "anarcho-communist," although that term is sometimes seen as exclusionary and inaccurate. A-Infos includes many items that address anarchist organizations and movement strategy, thus making it highly appropriate for the purposes of this analysis. The authors of A-Infos items are usually themselves anarchists, writing either on behalf of a particular organization or in a personal capacity.[21] The intended audience of A-Infos news items are anarchists who participate in anarchist movements around the world. Items focus both on matters internal to anarchist movements, as well as issues of wider social interest to anarchists. Thus, the case studies included here are sampled from a universe representing what is arguably the philosophical center of the anarchist movement.

In order to discover factors contributing to the success of country-level anarchist movements, I sought anarchist-written histories indicating perceived opportunities and barriers within a given country, especially those that were longitudinal in character. I searched the A-Infos archives for English-language articles presenting analyses and histories of country-level anarchist movements. Since I sought mention of factors that indicated positive or negative changes, I had to discard some country-level histories that did not discuss any discernible opportunities afforded to the movements (including histories about Argentina, Serbia, and Turkey). These countries are unlikely to be devoid of opportunities and barriers – authors merely neglected to note such factors. Also of interest to this analysis was any description of conditions external to a country's anarchist movement that the author perceived as having an impact on that movement. Specifically, "positive" opportunities are those factors that enhanced or aided the anarchist movement's mobilization, while "negative" barriers to opportunity are factors which stymied or prevented the anarchist movement's activities, leading to some form of decline. Opportunities were located by the grammar and context that indicated a perceived impact on the anarchist movement. For example, phrases like "success," "influence," "source of," "effect," "created," "led to," and "a real chance to" were a few of the textual indicators for mobilizing opportunities. Negative opportunities and decline were marked by phrases like "displaced," "anarchists were a rarity," "the government then retained control," or "was the end of the classical anarchist movement." More of these phrases are presented in the examples that follow. The opportunities and barriers were categorized organically, based on how the particular phenomena or events were described.[22]

Six movement histories from A-Infos included discussion of opportunities and these countries – Bolivia (IBM 2002), Czech Republic (Slaèálek 2002), Great Britain (Heath 2006), Greece (Fragos & Sotros 2005), Japan (WSM 2008), and Venezuela (Nachie 2006) – compose the data for analysis. With this data, I can compare opportunities that differ by location (see Chapter 1 for discussion of doing movement comparisons), as well as some comparison of locations that differ by time. Next, I present a textual analysis based on the content of these A-Infos articles. I use the histories to construct a picture of which factors have been perceived to help or hurt anarchist movements over time.[23] In addition, secondary materials consisting of peer-reviewed journal articles and books (some of which are also authored by anarchist or "anarcho-friendly" authors) were used to supplement and further contextualize the country-based histories found in A-Infos.

While these countries derive from a convenience sample and should be considered non-representative of other country-level anarchist movements, they represent highly diverse political, economic, and cultural systems and therefore make excellent sites for theoretical comparison. For example, some countries have long-established parliamentary traditions (Great Britain), while others were dictatorships in the recent past (Greece). Wealthy (Japan) and poor (Venezuela) countries are included, as well as those with a sizable indigenous population (Bolivia) and a recent history of state communism (Czech Republic). This sample of countries represents a varied range of political opportunities and anarchist movement histories. This variation will allow for fruitful comparisons and case studies.

Anarchist movement mobilization and decline

As an internationalist movement opposed to borders, we should expect localized anarchist movements to articulate their opportunity structure in global terms. Many of the opportunities mentioned by the case study histories concerned opportunities that either happened outside their country or experiences that were shared across multiple countries. Consequently, there was less evidence for individual country-specific opportunities, but rather common opportunities available to many countries' movements. This does not mean that all countries experienced these global opportunities in the same way, as discussed here. See Table 5.2 for details regarding what phenomena or events were cited for each country, whether the phenomena were considered to lead to mobilization or decline for the movements, and a categorization of the opportunity as political, cultural, or economic.[24]

The A-Infos histories of many countries reflected common themes, particularly the importance of poverty, the political Left and Bolshevism, international interaction, and punk. Repetition of these themes indicates a shared, cross-national narrative of opportunity for anarchist movements. While each country-based movement developed in interaction with global phenomena and local factors, most opportunities were not wholly derived from domestic conditions. Instead, modern anarchists seem to be describing global opportunities that are said to have benefited many countries' anarchist movements concurrently. This finding is particularly striking given the enormous diversity of the countries that comprised the sample.

One of the first opportunities noted in the A-Infos histories is something not often considered to be a movement "opportunity": poverty.[25] The A-Infos histories for Greece and Japan indicate that poor socio-economic conditions in countries were factors influencing the growth and influence

Table 5.2 Mention of political opportunities in A-Infos histories by country

Opportunity	Type	Bolivia	UK	Czech	Greece	Japan	Venezuela
International interaction	C	+		+		+	+
Punk	C		+	+			+
Poverty, anti-capitalism	E	+			+	+	
Radicalized labor unions	E	+					
War	P					+	
Propaganda by the deed	P			−			
Bolshevism	P	−		−	−		
State repression	P			+	+	−	
Democracy	P				+	+	
Hungary 1956/ disappointment with old Left	P		+				
Totals		4	2	5	4	5	2

Note: Movement mobilization (+), movement decline (−); cultural (C), economic (E), Political (P).

of anarchism, particularly in early anarchist history. With many Left movements, poverty and social injustice are framed as a barrier for movements to overcome. But for anarchism, these ills are defined as systemic problems derived from hierarchical institutions, such as capitalism, the state, patriarchy, and the like, so that anarchist analyses frame institutions as creating deprivation, which in turn can give rise to anarchist movements. For example, Fragos and Sotros (2005) assert that "Greek anarchism first appeared during the last quarter of the nineteenth century as a result of the then unfavourable economic and social conditions of poverty, distress and the dependance [*sic*] of the country on European capital." What is deemed "unfavorable" for poor people is actually very favorable for anarchist movement formation, according to these insiders. Likewise, the deprivation affiliated with war was a major factor in fostering anarchist movement development in Japan:

The Russo-Japanese war of 1904–05 was a major event that led to the emergence of the first Japanese anarchists. At the time many Japanese people had converted from Shinto and Buddhism to Christianity, yet they supported the imperialist nature of the war as a way of integrating themselves with the state. It was those who were determined to resist both the state and the war that turned elsewhere for political inspiration, thus laying the foundations for the Japanese anarchist movement. (WSM 2008)

Of particular note in the A-Infos histories is the repeated reference to other Left movements. Anarchism was often largely indistinguishable from the militant labor movement that thrived within industrializing economies throughout the world, but especially in Europe (Levy 2004). Anarcho-syndicalism became a vibrant tendency within organized labor and it was viewed as an alternative to union-led social democratic parties and Marxist vanguardism (Schmidt & van der Walt 2009). As such, anarchism thrived outside the formal realms of political power, taking energy from the masses of working-class laborers. Mobilization opportunities were also provided by active labor and anarchist movements outside each country. For example, Bolivia's anarchist movement was enhanced by cross-border interaction with neighboring countries, specifically Argentina and Brazil (Simon 1946):

The [May 1st Workers Union] probably owes itself, because of its geographic location, to the influence of the anarchist movement in Argentina. The second source of introduction of anarchist ideals in Bolivia stems from the forced emigration of more than 4,000 Bolivian workers to the salt mines in northern Chile, where a strong anarcho-syndicalist movement developed. These workers spread out from the mines into the countryside and the cities carrying newspapers, books and ideas that changed the ideological landscape at the time. This process culminated in 1927 with the appearance of the Local Workers Federation (FOL) which brought together the five most combative, militant unions in La Paz [the Bolivian capital city] ... This experience, with many difficult ups and downs up until 1956, has a key importance in the history of syndicalism. (IBM 2002)

International interaction was also cited as an opportunity in pre-World War I Japan. For example, "In the [United] States, [the exiled anarchist] Kotoku was influenced by many different things, such as his new found correspondence with [the Russian anarchist] Kropotkin. He translated the [book] *Conquest of Bread* into Japanese, which was then distributed clandestinely among [Japanese] workers and students" (WSM 2008). From the 1890s through the 1910s, anarchism spread far and wide, not just throughout Western Europe and North America, but also colonies and former colonies, including Argentina, Cuba, Egypt, and South Africa (Adams 2002). More recently, the Venezuelan newspaper, *El Libertario*, has established international connections helping to grow its national movement (Nachie 2006).

Two major world events in the 1910s halted the further expansion of anarchism: state repression and the Bolshevik victory in Russia. In Japan, state repression all but ended anarchist activity during World War I. Mass imprisonment and even state execution drove remaining anarchists underground or to exile abroad:

> Some unions opted solely for anarchism and grew in number, more journals and newspapers were established and the movement gained huge momentum. Unfortunately, the government then regained control by sentencing more than 7,000 people to life imprisonment for almost any radical involvement. (WSM 2008)

Thus, state repression was experienced as a barrier to opportunity in Japan, while it was a positive opportunity for Greek and Czech anarchists, as reflected in Table 5.2.

The repression in Japan actually began prior to the war with the Japanese state's discovery of an anarchist bombing campaign plan (Crump 1993). Assassination attempts or "propaganda by the deed" may be viewed as radical desperation during the end of a protest cycle (cf. Tarrow 1998). Similarly, in 1919 and 1923 Czech anarchists attempted the assassination of two prominent political figures, including the prime minister. Although neither attempt was successful, the movement faced intense repression, a loss of public legitimacy, and the first Czech fascist organization was founded in response (Slaèálek 2002).[26] The earlier assassination of two capitalists led to harsh repression in Greece (A. Gallery 1982). The repression by the state and by capitalist forces can be interpreted as a response to the increasing victories of anarchist-led labor struggles and the political elite's need to restrict revolutionary change for the preservation of the system.[27]

Contrary to the standard interpretation of PO theory, state repression did not always lead to a decline in anarchism. According to Slaèálek (2002), repression actually *positively* influenced the movement in the Czech Republic:

> A considerable [and important] movement of the nationally and socially radical youth [gathered] around the magazine *Omladina* (*The Youth*). In February 1894, 68 of those were sentenced to a short-term prison. By that, many of them got radicalised and reassured in their anarchistic conviction.

Much later in Greece, the Athens Polytechnic School Uprising in 1973 saw increased participation by anarchists in the struggle against the Greek military junta (Fragos & Sotros 2005). The subsequent crackdown on student protest boomeranged against the regime and led to democratic elections the following year. As a consequence of the state's brutal repression of the uprising, Greek law now prohibits any military or police presence on university property, thus opening up greater opportunities for students (and others, like anarchists) to use universities as staging grounds for political protest and resistance.[28] In fact, the history of the suppressed uprising in 1973 has created a radical "meme" that replicates itself for every generation of youth who have regularly revolted in the same neighborhoods of Athens, thereby providing anarchists with annual opportunities for protest (Karamichas 2009). In this instance, the brutal use of repression by the junta backfired, thus creating opportunities for decades-worth of anarchist mobilization.

According to PO theory, the flip-side to state repression is an expansion of political access and civil liberties. The only country where an increase in political access is noted – outside of the Greeh post-junta years – was Japan. After the state repression early in the century, Japanese anarchism disappeared. According to WSM, "It wasn't until after the Second World War that the anarchists found a real chance to organise. With Japan defeated, humiliated on the world stage and at the mercy of the Americans, the anarchists decided to form a federation in 1946." The fall of imperial rule coincided with the creation of a parliament and an increase in representative democracy. Coupled with the unpopular occupation of the US army, there was both new free space and cause for increased anarchist organizing, the first such opportunity for Japanese anarchist mobilization since the suppression in the 1910s (WSM 2008). This rebirth was, however, circumscribed by the Cold War, as anarchists faced the repressive occupying Supreme Command of the Allied Powers on one side and the more popular Communist Party on the other (Tsuzuki 1970). Thus, greater political opportunities in the form of a more tolerant political climate were balanced by other disadvantageous conditions.

The 1917 October Revolution in Russia – a counter-revolution to the popular revolution of February 1917 – affected anarchists throughout the world. For example, Japanese anarchists in the labor movement found that they had to compete with reformist and pro-Bolshevik elements. By the early 1920s, those forces had squeezed out most of the anarchist influence from Japanese unions (Crump 1993). The Socialist movement split, with anarchists (including Osugi Sakae) refusing to cooperate with the Bolsheviks for multiple reasons – anarchists were unwilling to submit to the Comintern and they considered the political conditions in Russia to be poor (Stanley 1978). Anarchist influence in the Bolivian labor movement was likewise "displaced by the deceptive actions of the Bolshevik parties" (IBM 2002). For the Czechs, the displacement was more formalized:

In 1919, after the end of the war, a meeting of anarchists took place, where despite of [sic] the disagreement of the members, the leaders persuaded them that a [sic] it was necessary that they be united with the national socialists and dismiss the anarchistic organisation. And in fact, that was the end of the classical anarchist movement. (Slaèálek 2002)[29]

According to Fragos and Sotros (2005), after World War I, in Greece "anarchists were a rarity. The main reason for this was the almost complete domination of Marxist-Leninist totalitarianism within the working-class movement as a result of the Bolshevik coup in Russia and also of the successfully [sic] repressive and opportunistic policy of the Communist Party of Greece (KKE)." The Communist Party emerged strong in Greece following World War I and remained dominant in the labor movement until the recent period (A. Gallery 1982). After World War I and the Bolshevik Revolution, anarchism went into a period of demobilization and decline as Communism gained increased legitimacy among the Left as the revolutionary ideology that was perceived to be succeeding in the USSR.

After a long, multi-decade period almost devoid of an anarchist presence, conditions gradually changed as a result of actions by the Soviet Union and its proxies throughout the world. Leftist disapproval of Marxist-Leninism, particularly following the Soviet invasion of Hungary in 1956 and disappointment with the Labour Party created positive conditions for an anarchist resurgence in Great Britain (Heath 2006) and other countries. Soviet premier Khrushchev's acknowledgement of the horrors of Stalinism disillusioned Leftists worldwide, a process that would be completed with the dissolution of the USSR. The rediscovery of anarchist ideas in the 1960s can be attributed to the New Left, although this movement tended to be led more by the middle class and educated than by the working class as during the previous anarchist movement cycle.[30] "This marked a break with the preceding period of 'apathy' used by the old Left to explain lack of movement within the working class ... A revolt, often inchoate and unarticulated, among young people against this complacency meant some were attracted to this new movement" (Heath 2006). During the 1960s, the growth of anarchism ran parallel to intensified social movement struggles, including anti-colonialist movements, civil rights, and anti-war movements (especially with regard to the US war against Vietnam). The British anarchist movement was rejuvenated in the early 1960s through the "ban the bomb" movement, especially the Committee of 100 (Heath 2006). This re-birth of anarchist politics surprised many observers, including esteemed anarchist historian George Woodcock (1962). While 1960s anarchism differed from classical anarchism, Michael Lerner noted certain similarities, including the acceptance of violence, anti-majoritarianism, individual moral responsibility, radical critique of the state, and the longing for a simpler life (Lerner 1970).

Perhaps the most important political opportunity enabling the dramatic mobilization of anarchism in the 1990s was created by the fall of the Soviet

Union. This incredible development affected not only Russia, but former Soviet republics and Eastern Europe. Active social change organizations and movements grew as state repression declined in these countries (Ruff 1991; Tarrow 1998). This decline in repression was coupled with another important, related opportunity that fueled anarchist movements globally: the possible spectrum of radical dissent re-broadened. The demonstrable failure of state-centered socialism freed the political Left from some of its historically accumulated, totalitarian baggage. Marxist vanguardism lost credibility throughout the world's social movements, which allowed for other visions of socialism and Leftism. For radicals, the political and moral failure of Marxism facilitated a greater appreciation and enhanced legitimacy for anarchist ideas and practice. For example, crumbling Communism led Czech anarchists to begin publicly organizing against the army and fascists prior to the fall of the Czech regime. The Czech A-Infos history notes that "[a]fter the fall of Bolshevik in 1989 the [Trotskyists] created a free platform of the autonomous and liberal activities called Lev alternative ('The left alternative'), in which the anarchists also participated" (Slaèálek 2002).

Anarchism seems to have prospered well in the general milieu of the radical working-class movements, but in reverse proportion to the Left, particularly Marxism. The victory of Bolshevism led to anarchist decline, while mid-century disappointment with the USSR and other leftists (e.g., the Hungarian revolt in 1956) increased anarchist mobilization. The record also indicates a dramatic global boom in anarchism in the wake of the USSR's break-up in the late 1980s and early 1990s. This supports Olzak and Uhrig's (2001) argument that similar actors in a social movement field – in this case radical Leftists – compete for scarce resources, including members and popular support.[31] Therefore, in times of one radical tendency's success and legitimacy, others are diminished and vice-versa in other times.

The integration of the East European socialist bloc countries into the world economy intensified global economic integration (commonly called "globalization"). This economic opportunity brought (or, perhaps, forced) social movements from disparate struggles and locations together, compelling dialogue and coordination on a wide variety of issues (Smith 2004). Capitalist integration and hegemony created resistance by those who did not benefit – primarily workers and citizens, but also the indigenous and other disenfranchised minorities. Globalization spurred an increased focus on issues and struggles worldwide about which other activists were previously unaware or unconcerned. Institutions that drove the processes of economic globalization, particularly the World Trade Organization, World Bank, the International Monetary Fund (IMF), and the Group of Eight (G8) became the target of protests in which anarchists played a major role (Epstein 2001; Juris 2008). The protest at these high-profile meetings and summits were popularly represented in the media as events organized and saturated with radicals (especially anarchists) who dramatically faced the state and its repressive forces (namely the police). For example, the 2000 World Bank and IMF meetings were held in Prague, Czech Republic and large protests took place, including multiple marches led by or consisting of anarchists (Juris 2008; Notes From Nowhere 2003). In Bolivia, as in other places, anti-capitalist traditions were merged with a growing awareness of globalized capitalism: "Juventudes Libertarias, a group of anarchist-communists based in La Paz, has risen from a strong history of resistance to capitalism in the country" (IBM 2002).

Finally, a cultural opportunity has been offered by the musical punk subculture of the West since the late 1970s and 1980s. While punk is not explicitly "anarchist," the opportunities offered by punk as a cultural form are undeniable. Punk scenes provided a "safe space" for anti-authoritarian politics, recruiting grounds for future anarchists, and a shared culture that could unite (but also sometimes divide) anarchists. As such, punk is not just a music form, but a subculture grouping and practice that rejuvenated and fed into the broader anarchist movement. In Great Britain – the birthplace of punk – anarcho-punk took a front seat within the anarchist movement:

> The beginning of the 1980s saw another upsurge in anarchism. A number of young people began to refer to themselves as anarchists. This had its origins in the birth of the punk movement in the late 70s and the influence of the Crass group. (Heath 2006)

British punk dovetailed with the Stop the City protests, the confrontational Class War organization, and countless local music scenes throughout Britain (Heath 2006). This chaotic, intense, and confrontational musical form brought with it a strong anti-authoritarian impulse and DIY ("do it yourself") ethic that mirrored the anarchist preference for "direct action." Through these sub-cultural channels, punk rock spread anarchism throughout the world, along with references to historical anarchism, radical left-wing values, and various, relatively new concerns (such as those of the so-called "new social movements"), including anti-racism, feminism, animal liberation, environmental defense, and anti-imperialism (O'Hara 1999). Punk frequently articulated anti-authoritarian politics that were sometimes explicitly anarchist in nature. Influential anarcho-punk bands and organizations inspired punks to become active in radical politics.

Punk soon spread throughout the world, with active "scenes" found throughout Latin America, Europe, and Asia (O'Connor 2004; O'Hara 1999). With the emergence of local or national punk scenes, anarchists mobilized the energies of otherwise non-political punks. For example, punk has been so influential in Venezuela that the national anarchist movement may be separated into two groupings: that which has been fostered by anarcho-punk and that which has not. According to Nachie (2006),

> Although Venezuela has no appreciable history of explicitly-anarchist direct action and the scene is certainly less militant than others in Chile or Brazil for instance, anarcho-punk, organized or unorganized, is undoubtedly the most consolidated and publicly visible source of anarchist ideas in the country.

Punk is also identified as an "important influence" on the re-birth of Czech anarchism (Slaèálek 2002). The influence of anarcho-punk was particularly strong after the 1989–92 "Velvet Revolution" de-sovietized Czechoslovakia and then split Slovakia from the Czech Republic. With over a hundred anarchist groups in the country, many "crystallize[d] around punk and hardrock music groups" (Konvička & Kavan 1994: 175)[32]. The influence of punk on modern anarchism cannot be understated; punk cultural symbols and dress are widely represented among anarchists, almost to the point where the two sometimes appear to merge and become one. Yet, punk may not have had a universal, dominant role in anarchist movements, as indicated by the fact that the Bolivian, Greek, and Japanese narratives did not mention punk.

Comparisons with other countries

This analysis of anarchist movements in six countries indicates a number of common themes. Additional evidence from other non-activist histories (i.e., outside of the A-Infos data) further reinforces the major claims. Here I pose two additional questions. First, are the opportunity themes discovered with Bolivia, Britain, the Czech Republic, Greece, Japan, and Venezuela consistent with those found in more well-known sites of the anarchist movement (e.g., Spain, Russia, and the US)? Thus, can these POs be generalized? Second, are there opportunity themes that were not mentioned in the A-Infos data? In other words, are there "objective" opportunities that anarchist movements could have, or likely took advantage of, that are missing within the activist narratives studied here?

First, let us consider the generalizability of these opportunities. State repression is a common theme throughout the activist and scholarly literatures on anarchism. For example, state response to anarchist opposition of World War I was extreme. Anarchists were (with a few notable exceptions, for example Peter Kropotkin) vocal opponents to World War I itself, viewing it as a war between capitalists and their state agents of some countries against those of another. Public opposition to the war coincided with a crackdown on radicals throughout the world. The Palmer Raids in the USA are an illustrative example: foreign- and native-born anarchists and labor leaders were rounded up, put on trial, and often deported (Renshaw 1968). The anarchist Union of Russian Workers was a target of particular interest, although there was scant evidence of their actual participation in illegality (Coben 1963). Individual US states also passed "criminal anarchy laws" that not only aimed to stop the overthrow of government, but also any criticism of representative government or politicians (Levin 1971). However, efforts at state repression frequently failed to contain anarchist movements – particularly in the case of Italy, Spain and Russia – as the "legal" activities of anarchists turned toward increasingly "spectacular assassinations and terrorist bombings" (Jensen 2014).

The social revolution that seemed imminent within the radical movements of the early 1900s, prior to World War I, did eventually break out. While Marxist theory predicted that revolution would occur in a parliamentarian capitalist society, it instead happened in predominantly feudal and agrarian Russia. The popular revolution in February 1917, as well as the subsequent ascension to power by the Bolsheviks in October 1917, inspired radicals throughout the world. Many anarchists and other radicals were initially drawn towards this successful anti-capitalist revolution, and even if they did not end up converting to communism, they often provided material and propagandistic support for the Bolsheviks (Zimmer 2009). The Soviet Union formed a Third Internationalism which co-opted the radicalism that had grown in opposition to World War I (Levy 2004). Initially, Lenin employed key anarchist concepts in his speeches, thereby supporting the very causes Russian anarchists had pioneered and advocated, including the soviets and worker self-management. However, once in power, the Bolsheviks imprisoned anarchist critics, took control of the worker soviets, attacked and then dissolved the anarchist Mahknovist army in the Ukraine, and laid siege to disgruntled sailors during the Kronstadt Uprising (Avrich 1967). It took years (decades in some cases) for anarchists outside Russia to conclude that the true aims of Lenin and the Bolsheviks were anti-anarchist and "counter-revolutionary" at heart. As Joll (1964) writes:

> The Marxists, by their success in Russia, now appeared to be a far more effective revolutionary force than the anarchists; and it was thus even harder for the anarchists to win and retain the support which would enable them to put into practice their own ideas of what the revolution should be. (1964: 192)

The impact of Bolshevism seems nearly universal, not just within the A-Infos countries and in Russia, but throughout the world. The secondary literature verifies the narratives told within A-Infos. In particular, Communist parties channeled much of the world's radical left into pro-state activities and suppressed alternative "socialisms"; Marxism and anarchism defined themselves "against the other," a dichotomy that did not dissipate until Communist decline (Franks 2012).

The major exception to the movement abeyance that began during the interwar years was in Spain. Revolutionary syndicalism had been widely adopted by large sectors of the Spanish working classes and unlike anarchists in other countries, the movement was large and ideologically driven enough – under the organization of the Confederación Nacional del Trabajo (CNT) anarcho-syndicalist union and later the Federación Anarquista Ibérica – to retain its anarchist character long after Bolshevik repression began in Russia and peaked with the Kronstadt Uprising in 1921 (Bookchin 1998). Anarchists also played a prominent role in facilitating the defense against the attempted, and eventually successful, fascist coup by General Francisco Franco during the Spanish Revolution (1936–39). During this period, the CNT infamously aligned itself with the socialist Republic forces fighting against the fascist army. Having this elite ally (the socialist Republican government) undoubtedly some created pockets of freedom for anarchists to pursue their goals in land and factory collectivization, although many anarchist critics argued that the coalition with the Republican government restrained and ultimately hurt anarchist efforts during these years. The Spanish Left remained divided and was repressed by the Stalinist forces, who were ostensibly aiding the Partido Obrero de Unificación Marxista (POUM: non-Stalinist Marxists) who were part of a Leftist coalition with anarchists and others fighting against Franco. After the Stalinist suppression of the POUM and Stalinist attacks on the anarchist militias (which were predominantly organized by the CNT), Franco easily conquered the remaining outposts of anarchist resistance, thus leading to a decades-long dictatorship. Anarchism, while not dead, then went into a period of dormancy, kept together by scattered newspapers and authors, waiting for a new resurgence. Spanish anarchists who escaped prison or death went underground or into exile abroad (Beevor 2006).

Anarchism's late-twentieth century reappearance would look radically different from the early twentieth-century anarchism that died in Spain. Consequently, the activity of anarchist movements around the world has been bi-modal. First, the "golden age" of anarchism was heavily involved in the labor movement and nearly died away in the early decades of the twentieth century. Second, a re-birth – largely not directly connected to the first wave – mobilized in the second half of the 1960s New Left and counterculture that diffused into many popular movements. The barriers to opportunities noted in Table 5.2 indicate demobilization associated with the repression around the time of World War I and the positive opportunities in the 1960s indicate a new mobilization period, although the data indicate that the specific triggers of anarchist organizing varied by country during this period of generally increased mobilization.

Although the New Left was, "post-Old Left," particularly unaffiliated to the Communist Party, this does not mean it was able to completely break free of the Old Left. For example, the major New Left organization in the USA was Students for a Democratic Society, which by the late 1960s cannibalized itself into a smattering of various Leftist, non-anarchist sects (Balser 1997; Bookchin 2004; Sale 1973). However, the anti-authoritarian impulse of the New Left remained and found a place within other burgeoning movements outside the student movement, especially the feminist, anti-nuclear, and environmental movements, such as the organization called Movement for a New Society (Cornell 2011; Epstein 1991).

The continued evolution of the New Left throughout the 1960s provided opportunities for anarchism to re-emerge. In fact, the current wave of anarchism can be traced back to the New Left's insistence on "participatory democracy," as opposed to "democratic centralism" (as offered by the Soviet bloc) or "representative democracy" (in the West). The New Left's eventual rejection of formal leadership was not an immediate one, but emerged most clearly with the rise of the anti-nuclear and radical feminist movements (Epstein 1991). Here, the tactical emphasis upon cooperation, consensus decision making, and direct action are key anarchist contributions (with other influences originating with radical Quakers and certain Native American deliberative traditions). Many of the key ideas and structures that emerged within this radical milieu would come to represent the anarchist movement of the 1990s, namely grassroots, community-based direct action, through the use of direct democracy and affinity groups (Polletta 2002).

Finally, regarding absent narrative-based opportunities, I expected the A-Infos narratives to identify the advent of the internet as a recent, technological opportunity for mobilization, but none mentioned the internet in this fashion. This is a particularly noteworthy absence, given that this data source is itself based on the internet; I expected anarchists to be reflective of the new chances for organizing being offered by technology. Although unremarked upon, the increasingly widespread use of the internet as a popular tool for communication (the online version of A-Infos being a prime example) seems to have created an incredible set of cultural opportunities. Demands for free speech rights and information exchange have spread throughout the world. The internet facilitated collaboration and networking between movement allies, even where separated by large geographic distances. The ease in coordinating protests also amplified activist voices and allowed for the wider dissemination of demands, as seen by the anti-capitalist protests organized by the decentralized Peoples' Global Action network. It is difficult to miss the uniquely anarchistic nature of the internet, which functions as a decentralized network of information channels, allowing easy voluntary association and the relatively inexpensive ability to provide mutual aid, such as in setting up websites, email accounts, and mailing listserves (Wall 2007). Anarchists were not only early adopters of the World Wide Web for propaganda purposes, but they have also created their own organizational infrastructure to avoid the influence of corporations and the state. Thus, autonomous collectives have spread throughout the world to provide these internet services to anarchists and other activists (Shantz 2003a). Although the case studies did not provide evidence for the self-described utility of the internet to these movements, this does not discount the possibility that it was truly beneficial in an objective sense.

The past and future of anarchist opportunity

This chapter has affirmed established claims that opportunities are a consistent factor necessary for movement success – and anarchism is no exception. However, the conventional view of "political opportunities" makes less sense for an avowedly anti-state movement, since such opportunities are typically oriented towards engaging *with* the state, not disengaging *from* it – to say nothing of dismantling and abolishing the state. Nonetheless, opportunities have been seized by anarchist movements, as demonstrated by a review of the histories of a sample of country's movements. I found evidence of both country-specific and common opportunities in the subjective narratives in the sample, as well as the broader literature, with the common opportunities perhaps being the most decisive in shaping the anarchist movement around the world. One key pattern shows the antagonistic, yet symbiotic, relationship of anarchism to Marxism. Bolshevism all but silenced anarchism in the 1920s, draining it of political appeal for many, as it seemed that the Bolsheviks were "winning" and were a more viable anti-capitalist alternative. Still, each loss of face suffered by the Soviet Union enhanced anarchist movements. The New Left in mid-century benefited from disillusionment with Stalinism, and then the fall of the Berlin Wall and the Soviet Union gave rise to even more anarchist organizing in the 1990s. As Schmidt (2013) notes, the Soviet Union's "collapse" encouraged "the underground anarchist movement in those countries" to reveal itself in Eastern European and former Soviet republics, and contributed to a general resurgence worldwide (2013: 111–112). This pattern clearly illustrates the importance of non-state-based, but still political, opportunities (in this case, the nature of global Marxist regimes or domestic Left movements) in affecting the chances of anarchist movement mobilization.

Another observed pattern is anarchism's parallel development with other anti-mainstream movements, particularly labor during the classical period and punk in recent years. A fruitful, cultural synergy developed between anarchism and both of these, which were sources of new members and inspirational frames for anarchist movements, and thus should not just be considered mere "allies" to anarchism. Such patterns were common opportunities in many countries, not just one or two.

These shared narratives indicate a number of possible conclusions, which point in divergent directions. First, there have been real, empirical opportunities that have facilitated anarchist movement growth and an equally real closing of opportunities that have stymied anarchist movements. In other words, anarchist movements have experienced opportunities that are structurally comparable to other movements, albeit more anti- and non-state in character.

Second, modern anarchists have generalized certain anarchist "opportunities" to many local contexts based on universal narratives that are widely exchanged within the global movement. Thus, present-day anarchists may be articulating claims about opportunities that circulate within the intellectual milieu of anarchist culture, although such claims may be an inaccurate or inappropriate extrapolation of opportunities from one societal context to another. Activist interpretations may also be derived from scholarly sources, thus indicating a feedback loop wherein activist conclusions are based on scholarly perceptions of activist actions. Of course, nothing is "wrong" with this, per se, as most movements tell stories about themselves that may have embellishments or mythology.

Or, a third, combined option may best explain these findings. A combination of substantial and objective opportunities have likely shaped anarchist movement success over time, while modern anarchists may also be selectively framing their analysis to generalize those histories and unite disparate local factions of the movement in a common, internationalist narrative. But, for the moment, consider the *internationalist* character of anarchism. Individuals regularly travel throughout their countries and the world, exchanging ideas with other like-minded people, and fostering a shared identity that transcends national borders (see Owens *et al.* 2013 for a study on a similar process resulting from activist travels throughout Europe via squat networks).

These findings appear to be reliable, in light of other secondary evidence. The anarchist movement narratives from A-Infos were overwhelmingly supported by additional anarchist history sources, not just from the same case study countries under investigation, but also for prominent countries outside the data sample. This congruency confirms the strength of movement narratives as reflective of external scholarly opinion. It also indicates that the opportunities noted in the A-Infos histories were, in fact, major opportunities broadly shared globally – but not universally by all countries – and that the A-Infos authors were astute observers of that history.

Contrary to the main finding about the generalized importance of political opportunities – anarchism in some countries (e.g., Venezuela) has not directly benefited from political opportunities at all, but is rather the result of cultural forces. In other countries, factors related to economics (Greece), culture (Britain, Czech Republic, Japan) – or both (Bolivia) – combined with the "political" to shape the movement. So we should expect the relative importance of political opportunities to vary across countries, even though they are also shaped by common opportunities that transcend state boundaries. "Objective" research could further explore and refine these findings from these subjective accounts. Extreme state repression has historically limited anarchist mobilization, so some minimal level of political freedom is required for the movement to exist. But once this minimal threshold is reached, state repression may advance rather than hinder the movement (as with Greece and the Czech Republic). Further research should explore the conditions that transform state repression into a positive political opportunity beyond the tentative data presented here. Finally, anarchist mobilization has been reduced by the existence of other strong, Left political movements (e.g., Bolshevism), as well by a decline in distrust of the state associated with increased freedom and rights. These ironies, at least for anarchism, of ostensibly positive social change should be more fully explored.

As hinted in the methods section above, these findings raise cautions about how to measure and evaluate the usage of POs. Not all movements take advantage of opportunities in the ways typically expected. Anarchism possesses extra-legislative goals that aim to achieve the overthrow of major social institutions like the state, capitalism, or patriarchy. Consequently, there have been no pure, explicit victories for the anarchist movement (perhaps with the exception of the short-lived Shinmin Revolution in Korea, 1929–32 or the Spanish Revolution, 1936–39). The case study narratives instead had to focus on the perception of movement "growth" or "decline" as opposed to legislative victories. Measuring movement activity in this fashion is out of sync not only with most other scholarship, but also prevailing theoretical assumptions about how movements operate. Some movements do not seek to influence or alter the state, but to abolish it altogether – as well as other hierarchical institutions.

This chapter's analysis does not suggest that PO theories are of no use, but rather require a serious re-working and reflexivity to appreciate the radical, anti-state character of movements like anarchism. Although anarchism has not enjoyed the same level of "success" as other comparable radical movements (such as Bolshevism and Maoism), there have clearly been periods of increased anarchist activity, mobilization, and short-term goal achievement. Obviously, ultimate anarchist goals – the dissolution of all forms of economic, political, and social hierarchies – would be difficult to achieve, and the state would be an unlikely partner in such a mission. Consequently, the notion of "opportunity" is still important to the study of anarchist movements, but it needs to be re-operationalized in order to remain relevant. This re-operationalization would seem to require a focus on the subjective opportunities perceived and sought by movement participants themselves, a de-emphasis on strictly political (and especially state-based) opportunities, and a broadened appreciation of other forms of opportunity (e.g., economic and cultural) that may assist in the social revolution that anarchist movements hope to inspire.

Owing to certain methodological limitations – a small number of countries and only one central narrative per country – this is not necessarily a definitive analysis on anarchism. Instead, I consider this analysis to be an important step towards a new approach in considering opportunities, especially among anti-state movements. Future attempts to consider supposedly "political" opportunities should be sure to distinguish what sorts of opportunities movements seize upon, even though the typical understanding of such opportunities rely on the state for fulfillment. The radical character of the anarchist movement illustrates the need to consider non-state-based opportunities and, potentially, opportunities that are more economic or cultural. In addition, as other research has shown, movements may have multiple, non-state targets. For anarchism, these targets of critique and attack are many, including all forms of domination and authority. How these claims find resonance with different audiences is poorly understood. Where do anarchist movements make their demands (if we may construe anarchists as making "demands" an extension with some problems): to the polity, the state, specific groups of disadvantaged persons, or society at large? Each will have different levels of appreciation for anarchist critiques and goals. The lack of movement success could be partially due to the strong social control mechanisms and self-interest operating in each aforementioned audience, which in turn circumscribe potential opportunities.

The utility of political opportunities for anarchists

What is the significance of an extra-institutional PO theory for anarchist movements? How could anarchists utilize PO theory to their advantage? First, anarchists could deliberately seize upon existent opportunities, at least those which are perceivable. For example, they could seek out punk communities (or other counter-cultural scenes) and look for anarchist-inclined punks, with the goal of growing the ranks of a local anarchist movement. Or, anarchists could search for international solidarity networks, for the purpose of enhancing the mobilizing potential of a local anarchist movement – or at least to gain access to some additional resources, insights, and inspiration. If and when a statist-Left individual or party "fails" or loses support from the broader Left, it would be a ripe moment to provide a contextual frame to better understand that failure.[33] Last, anarchists could take advantage of the focus or "opportunity" created by a variety of current events; things as diverse as climate change, police violence, rape culture, austerity, poverty, or colonialization can be (and are) easily critiqued by anarchists and supplemented with a focused anarchist analysis.

Second, anarchists could also try to create their own opportunities, when and where recognizable opportunities do not seem to be already present. For example, anarchists could try to establish connections with anarchists abroad, even if they are not known by any local anarchists. Or, they could try to deliberately decrease the reputation of the established Left (especially political parties), such as social democrats and labor parties. This can be accomplished by showing others how parties have "sold out" many people, and applying so much pressure on these parties that they react in predictable ways (maybe even via repression, which would illustrate their true allegiances). Anarchists could also consciously create sub-cultural communities that would foster anarchistic attitudes and thus inspire future, potential anarchists (like free software communities, alternative food networks, DIY communities, etc.)

Third, since opportunities also seem to sometimes be contradictory or are dependent upon other factors, we can't always know how anarchist movements can best "seize" them. For example, the success of Marxist-Leninism and statist-Leftists had an un-definitive effect on anarchist movements, just as did the presence of state repression. This mixed track record suggests Leftism and repression may not be as important as they seem, or that other factors may "tip the scales" for these phenomena to benefit anarchist mobilization or harm it. To the extent to which the pro-statist Left can mobilize popular interest in opposing capitalism, their efforts may be good for anarchist movements, as anarchists can "ride the coat-tails" of their fellow anti-capitalists. But, to the extent that new adherents or new movements (e.g., Occupy, anti-austerity) also adopt authoritarian strategies, these Leftists may inhibit anarchist tendencies from developing (except in reaction). If state repression facilitates outrage – including from implicit anarchists – the movement may be strengthened. The movement's "resolve" to persevere may grow, it may not back down, and it could gain new adherents. But, if repression scares people away from the movement, then it may lose support from "fair-weather" supporters or at-risk populations, who decide the gamble is not worth it (especially by publicly supporting anarchists). Others may then choose to libel anarchists (with the three misperceptions) through the domination network (especially the mass media), which could worry supporters that they will also be targets or have such negative connotations applied to them, too.

Last, existing opportunities may not be seized or people may try to seize opportunities that do not really exist. It seems that the typical anarchist strategy (also shared with many other movements) is to seize opportunities that they perceive or that are there, then try to create better opportunities in the future. In other words: "always act, lay the groundwork for the future, and don't give up." Presumably, anarchist movements – even in the absence of authentic opportunity – frame current events and conditions in ways that bolster anarchist claims and analysis. They commit to actions that critique dominant systems and offer alternatives to those systems. For example, in times of housing crisis, anarchists advocate defending people from forced eviction, helping people squat in abandoned buildings, and creating public encampments that confront the state and capitalism, all while showing the potential for democratic, communal alternatives to bureaucratized statecraft and property rights.

Notes

1 More generally, Melucci (1996) notes that social movements of all stripes in the contemporary era, "no longer [coincide] either with the traditional forms of organization of solidarity or with the conventional channels of political representation." He suggests moving beyond simple dichotomies such as "state" versus "civil society," or "public" versus "private," as well as the "reductionism" inherent in exclusively "political" analyses, in order to more fully comprehend the interrelationships among different sectors of society (1996: 3–6).

2 Communes and popular assemblies are frequently cited examples of this understanding of politics (McKay 2008).

3 See Martin (2007) for the anarchist principles behind the anti-globalization movement's resistance and alternatives-creation.

4 The problem with this theory is that many of the above questions must be subjectively answered by considering what exactly constitutes "repression" or "democracy."

5 Some have alleged a pro-Western bias by Freedom House, which may less critically evaluate official US allies and more critically evaluate official US enemies (Barahona 2007). Many well-known neo-conservatives sit on the board of trustees and much of its funding comes from the US State Department. This possible bias should be considered for all interpretations.

6 Also available at www.freedomhouse.org. *Political rights* afforded citizens are the right to participate freely in the political process, vote freely in legitimate elections, and have representatives that are accountable to them. *Civil liberties* include the right to exercise freedoms of expression and belief, to be able to freely assemble and associate, to have access to an established and equitable system of rule of law, and to have social and economic freedoms, including equal access to economic opportunities and the right to hold private property (Piano & Puddington 2004). *Press rights* include three sub-measures. The legal environment considers laws and regulations that could influence media content and the government's desire to use such laws to restrict media. The political environment encompasses the degree of political control over news media content. The economic environment

consists of the structure, transparency, and concentration of media ownership, as well as other costs associated with the establishment and functioning of media (Karlekar 2005).

7   The most commonly observed violations measured in this index are arrests or other punishments for union activities, interference with union rights, dismissal or suspension for union activities, the inability to elect representatives freely, intervention of authorities in collective bargaining, and exclusion of economic sectors from the right to strike (Kucera 2005). It is important to emphasize that "rights" are not necessarily contingent upon state-backing, but also broad social norms, as some anarchist critics have pointed out (e.g., Turner 2009).

8   The regulation of participation is the extent to which there are binding rules for when, whether, and how political preferences are expressed. Competitiveness of participation is the extent to which alternative policies and leadership can be sought in the political arena (Marshall & Jaggers 2005).

9   A more anarchist view of "democracy" would refer to either "direct democracy" or "participatory democracy," where decisions are not filtered through elected or appointed official representatives. Anarchists instead prioritize the ability to make decisions through collective participation with others in either a consensus-based or direct-voting process. Future research on anarchist organizations should seek measures that are able to evaluate these types of conditions. See Held (1987) and Pateman (1970) for these distinctions.

10   Countries include: Australia, Austria, Belgium, Canada, Denmark, Finland, France, Germany, Great Britain, Greece, Italy, Mexico, Netherlands, Norway, Poland, Russia, Spain, Sweden, Switzerland, Turkey, and the USA.

11   I have analyses for the full sample (available on request), and when all countries are included all of the same variables are significant and additional variables attain significance as well.

12   The United Nations' "human development index" (HDI) measured life expectancy, adult literacy and education enrollment, and gross domestic product per capita (at purchasing power parity). Note that the recent HDI is measured somewhat differently now.

13   Correlation analyses ought to be interpreted as non-directional; thus, it is technically fallacious to assume that one variable *causes* the other. However, it is more reasonable to suggest that POs help to shape conditions advantageous for anarchist organizations, than it is to assume that the presence of anarchist organizations modifies the available POs of society. The latter would be an impressive effect, but probably wishful thinking on the part of anarchist movements.

14   Thank you to Daniel Egan for pointing out the restrictiveness of this conception of rights, as well as the right-wing bias of Freedom House as a source of data.

15   Arguably, the issue may be broader than "rights," per se, but rather a whole array of orientations, norms, and values, as well as the level of tolerance, respect, or inclusion that dissent is afforded. In this critique, "rights" are a myopic, legalistic limiting of these other important factors.

16 Proudhon (2011).

17 As I do not aim to generalize these findings, nor argue that such a goal is possible using this research design, the "hypotheses" may be better considered as general expectations, given past research. I am not interested in testing or proving either, but merely expressing what was suspected to find at the outset of this research.

18 Apart from monumental but short-lived events – like the Paris Commune (1871), Russian Revolution (February 1917), and Barcelona uprising during the Spanish Revolution (1936) – anarchism has had few concrete successes that scholars can reference as outcomes of open opportunity structures. Consequently, narratives offered by anarchists about themselves and their movement's history can serve as an appropriate guide to understanding anarchist movement-specific mobilization and decline. While it is still difficult to determine what "success" looks like for anarchism, we can analyze the factors that participants think has helped or hurt their movement.

19 Languages include: Chinese, Dutch, English, Finnish, French, German, Greek, Italian, Polish, Portuguese, Russian, Spanish, Swedish, and Turkish.

20 A-Infos may not be as strict in its promotion of certain ideological presentations of anarchism as it claims to be. For example, the archives include materials that discuss (and sometimes promote) primitivism as well as purely philosophical anarchist analysis.

21 Although there are presumably fewer A-Infos authors than readers, I believe it is fair to build an understanding of anarchist movement opportunities using these authors because: (1) they influence the perceptions of other anarchists, especially A-Infos readers; (2) they themselves are anarchists and active participants in the movement; and (3) they are likely more reflective participants in the movement and are good sources for well-read, well-reasoned reflection. Of course, this is simply one dataset and the narratives should not be taken to represent the consensus views of the anarchist movement as a whole, since these views are quite variable (as this chapter demonstrates).

22 I acknowledge that one weakness of this analysis is the broad inclusion of any form of success present in the narratives. Other PO studies have had to clearly define what constitutes a successful outcome acquired via a political opportunity. Unfortunately, it is difficult to operationalize outcomes such as "abolition of an oppressive institution" because complete abolition is rarely achieved and some movement participants focus on the use of non-hierarchical means rather than the achievement of specific ends. Historically, anarchists have almost never been able to achieve such victories on anything but a micro-scale or short-lived basis. Opportunities are still real, though, even if the ultimate goal has never been concretely reached. Consequently, this analysis aims to consider the more abstract, progressive gains of anarchist movements, often manifested as a growth in participating membership, campaign victories, or increased conflict with elites. Some may decide that this stretches political opportunity too thinly or results in a still-born definition of "success"; I consider this approach a necessary adaptation to the nature and statuses of anarchist movements historically.

23   When referencing a history published via A-Infos, I cite the author of the essay, not A-Infos itself.

24   I coded specific opportunities that were seen as causal in a temporal sense rather than contextual/historical. For example, discussion of patterns in a country's literature or art across centuries may have played a role in shaping the anarchist movement, but this does not represent a specific "opportunity" in the same sense that the emergence of the punk movement in music did. The punk movement occurred at a specific point in time, which according to Heath (2006), led to an "upsurge in anarchism" in the 1980s at which point "A number of young people began to refer themselves as anarchists." This is a specific opportunity with a defined outcome occurring at an identifiable point in time. I operationalized this example as an opportunity. In contrast, the discussion by Slaèálek (2002) of "revolts against authorities" during "the Czech Middle Ages" may be important for the context in which anarchism developed there in the twentieth century, but I did not operationalize it as an "opportunity" because such background conditions always exist and are neither necessary nor sufficient for movement growth at a particular time.

25   As Giugni (2008) has suggested, the discursive context in which movements exist can be important for movement success. If movement actors collectively define something to be beneficial for them (even post-hoc, decades later), it may be interpreted as having a motivational influence on later movement activity and success. (For example, Christiansen's 2009 study of the contemporary Industrial Workers of the World (IWW) found that members told themselves decades-old stories about the IWW and established a direct connection with anarchism that mutually stimulated growth for both the IWW and the anarchist movement.) Thus, subjective opportunities can include dynamics that would not otherwise be considered "open" opportunities, such as grievances or deprivation.

26   Dictators elsewhere did not require attempted assassinations to justify anarchist repression. For example, the Gómez dictatorship in Venezuela did not tolerate unions or anarchists during its twenty-seven year reign from 1908 to 1935 (Simon 1946).

27   Sabatini (1996) argues – somewhat unconvincingly – that repression is "not very tenable as a main causal factor" in anarchist movement decline (1996: 175). This "decline" occurs earlier (1900) in Sabatini's estimation and the evidence offered earlier does not operationalize how "decline" or "repression" is measured. "Repression" is only considered in a narrow number of countries and the massive red scare of the late 1910s and early 1920s is not considered.

28   Evidence for the importance of this protection has been shown in many instances, including the late-2008 protests following the police murder of a 15-year-old Greek (Karamichas 2009).

29   "National socialism" here is not comparable to fascism, but rather refers to the country-based socialist parties.

30   Incidentally, Breines (1982) argues that anarchists and pacifists had a substantial influence on the New Left, too, including Murray Bookchin, Paul Goodman, and C. Wright Mills. Also, for more on class differences in modern anarchism, see Williams (2009c).

31 Franks (2012) puts this well: "Throughout the 1980s and 1990s, the continuing totemic influence of state-socialism was so great that anarchists still felt they needed to dedicate significant resources to distinguishing their politics from those of the orthodox Marxist left" (2012: 215)

32 Recall Table 3.6's organizational count in the Czech Republic in 1997: only seven. This low figure shows how focused analyses like Konvička & Kavan (1994) can compensate for the AYP's tacit undercounting.

33 For example, "the statist-Left does not always have 'bad ideas' (anarchists share the Left's insistence upon justice, opposition to war, etc.), but they poorly execute their ideas due to the reliance upon charismatic personalities and others who have acquired corrupting power."

6

Anarchism as a "new social movement"?

The conception of society just sketched, and the tendency which is its dynamic expression, have always existed in mankind, in opposition to the governing hierarchic conception and tendency – now the one and now the other taking the upper hand at different periods of history. (Peter Kropotkin)

The new?

Few sociological perspectives excel at summarizing the character of current anarchist movements, with the exception of those grouped under the moniker of "new social movement" (NSM) theories. This chapter presents the essential dimensions of these theories (Sutton & Vertigans 2006), paying close attention to how each dimension may be applied. I interrogate examples and characteristics drawn from present-day anarchist movements – including ideology, organizations, and strategy – with the NSM framework. Although not totally identical, it will be clear that modern anarchism greatly exemplifies the ideal typology created by NSM theories. Finally, I delineate differences between the contemporary anarchist movement and other NSMs. Anarchism suggests the need to modify and extend the NSM typology to include revolutionary anti-statism, radical practicality, anti-capitalism, and a clear connection to classical-era anarchism (late 1800s) – all qualities that distinguish the anarchist movement from other well-studied NSMs. The anarchism of today is different than in the past, and anarchism has affixed itself, often creatively, to the unique conditions of the modern world.

NSM theories challenged other dominant theories in the contemporary study of social movements. The earliest threads of these ideas originate in the late 1960s (with Touraine's reaction to the political turmoil of 1968), but most were presented to English-speaking audiences during the 1980s. Although often used to refer to *current* social movements, the NSM framework goes beyond a mere label for chronologically new social movements.

The ideas may be best described as a collection of *theories*, rather than a concrete *theory* (Buechler 1995).

To understand the perspectives offered by NSM theories we must consider the contributions of various social thinkers (cf. Buechler 1995), including Alain Touraine, Jürgen Habermas, and Alberto Melucci. Touraine (1981) categorized contemporary society in affluent, Northern countries as post-industrial. Every type of society is centered around one primary modality of conflict; industrial society centered conflict around material production and the workers' movement, while struggle in post-industrial society is within the cultural realm. Touraine claims that modern societies must deal with the privatization of social problems, conflict with consumers and clients against managers and technocrats, and struggle over the issue of who will be able to dictate the basis and capacity for self-management. Habermas (1987) further argues that NSMs reside at the seams between "the system" and "lifeworld" (which is the lived realm of informal, culturally grounded understandings). Thus, movements have a largely defensive character that attempts to prevent colonization of the lifeworld by the forces of rationalization and bureaucracy. Such movements are more likely to engage in conflict over matters of cultural reproduction than material production. Finally, Melucci (1989, 1993) interprets NSMs as ongoing social constructions rather than empirical objects. These movements attempt to create identities, resist social control and conformity, and engage in collective action through networked groups. These contemporary social movements represent a break from previous eras due to the changed nature of our complex society (Melucci 1989), while certain continuity may persist. Production is less industrial, conflict is waged less at the economic level, and struggle involves new actors as opposed to the poor and working classes. Post-industrial society (also according to Touraine 1981, 1984) results in conflict at the cultural and symbolic levels, primarily with elements of the "new middle class". Power is in the process of decentralizing and thus power has become more autonomous from the state (see Katsiaficas 2006).

This story – told of NSM theories' development – is disputed (Cox & Fominaya 2013). The aforementioned theorists may also be viewed as a heterodox collection of generally unrelated scholars, rather than observers with compatible ideas. The NSM framework is more of a European response to Marxist theories of social movements than to North American theories, such as relative deprivation and resource mobilization theories. There have also been multiple waves of NSM work and theorizing.

NSM theories have detractors, in part based upon confused and incompatible understandings. Bagguley (1992) was critical of the NSM theory, because the aforementioned movements and organizational traits existed before the 1960s and the rise of post-industrialism, thus making a clear delineation difficult. Traits of NSMs, even in American movements during the early 1800s, are readily observed by Calhoun (1993; and also argued by Olofsson 1988; Tucker 1991), thereby suggesting the inaccuracy of the word "new" in the theory's name. Owing to the far-too-common academic practice of placing "new" before an established phenomenon, NSM theories have been sorely misunderstood and misused. For example, Day (2005) referred to the recent anarchistic tendencies within the global justice movement as the "newest new social movements." His application of a NSM framework to global justice movements is appropriate, but compounds the problems associated with using "new." As something "new" will invariably one day become "old," it would have been preferable for NSM theorists and Day to avoid the label "new." Other perpetrators of this chronologically blasphemous problem include new institutionalism, new Left, new racism, and even new anarchism.[1]

Pichardo (1997) also criticized NSM perspectives for various reasons. First, he points out that NSM theory focuses solely on left-wing movements (such as the labor movement), to the neglect of right-wing movements (such as those initially explored by Lo 1982). NSM ideas frequently lack solid empirical evidence and, as such, tend to be more anecdotal. Finally, Pichardo claims that NSM theory is less a brand new theory than just an addition of new academic concerns to the social movement theory canon. For example, some of these NSM concerns have found their way into North American scholarship as emotional theories and the "cultural turn" in social movement theorizing (see Goodwin & Jasper 2004).

Despite some conceptual shortcomings, NSM theories offered a formidable challenge and contribution to prior social movement theories, including relative deprivation, Marxism, resource mobilization, and others. According to della Porta and Rucht (1995), NSMs possess a strong left-libertarian nature, an orientation consistent with anarchism. Recent postmodern movements present a variety of "ways that oppositional, anti-establishment, anti-hegemonic, and liberationist identities may be linked with pressing, everyday grievances and translated into concerted, collective action against the state" (Johnston & Lio 1998: 468) and anarchism may be an exemplar of these patterns. Thus, it is appropriate to see how well NSM theories address the characteristics of contemporary, burgeoning anarchist movements.

Methodology for assessing anarchism with NSM theories

In their summary of NSM ideas, Sutton and Vertigans (2006) suggested six key features, which I apply to modern anarchist movements:

1   Post-industrial and post-material politics: new politics displace class-based social movements with post-materialist values that are concerned with the quality rather than the quantity of life.[2]

2   New social constituencies: NSMs tend to defy a simple class analysis and movement participants are presumed to come from a "new middle class."

3   Organizations are anti-hierarchical: NSM organizations are based on loose networks, horizontal structures, and participatory approaches to decision making.

4   Symbolic direct actions rely on mass media attention to bring new issues before the public: NSM actions directly target problems at their source and aim to bring about cultural change rather than attempting to take political power.

5   A self-limiting radicalism: NSMs have limited political ambitions, eschew grand schemes, and focus on the defense of civil society against state encroachment.

6   New identities: a principal concern is with creating new identities via an expressive politics that promote self-realization and the right to autonomy.

NSMs value living out lifestyle changes and acting on expressive identity politics. I expect that current anarchist movements are strongly akin to NSMs and that – in many ways – anarchism is an excellent example of the ideal type NSM. Later, I further develop an extension to Sutton and Vertigans' typology that is more applicable to radical, anti-state movements like anarchism.

I apply the NSM framework to the secondary literature on anarchism. Specifically, I utilize the scholarly and activist literature in English that focuses on anarchism. As my sampling frame, I select the time period since the late-1960s, but more thoroughly focus on anarchism from the 1990s on. Since anarchism is an international – and internationalist – movement, I include examples from activity around the world, although most examples are based in Western, English-speaking countries.

NSMs and anarchism

As discussed, Sutton and Vertigans (2006) noted six general characteristics of NSMs, but applied these NSM dimensions to fundamentalist Islamic organizations, like Al-Qa'ida. Although anarchists are located on the opposite end of the socio-political spectrum (left-wing and secular, as opposed to right-wing and religious), anarchism is also a movement that includes strong values and radical ideology, distinct counter-cultural practices, disruptive action, and has recently experienced high media visibility. Thus, the application of this typology is not inappropriate for anarchism and much of its practiced behaviour, though clearly the two movements' values and desired goals are incompatible. In the following, I argue that anarchism closely follows Sutton and Vertigans' six NSM characteristics and I describe these connections in detail, noting important areas of divergence from their NSM typology.

Post-industrial politics

The early non-social psychological view of social movements was often Marxist: class conflict led to social movements, revolutions, and social change. NSM theories took issue with the Marxist interpretation of social movements, particularly the emphasis on struggle at the point of capitalist production. First, anarchists are not aligned with authoritarian Marxists and likewise consider the exclusive emphasis that political Marxists put upon class exploitation as a perpetual blind-spot of Marx (see Bookchin 1991). Indeed, Marx *believed* the industrial proletariat were *the* revolutionary class – a view rejected by Marx's anarchist contemporaries who also saw revolutionary potential in peasants and the lumpenproletariat. Ironically, the first society to undergo a left-wing or "Marxist" revolution was feudal Russia, which had a very small urban proletariat. The rural anarchists of the Ukraine, led by Nestor Makhno, were a serious countervailing force and threat to Bolshevik domination in the Russian empire. But, Marx (and his contemporaries and present-day followers have) tended to ignore or marginalize the many other forms of non-class-based inequality – such as privilege, status, and power (as well as domination by gender, race, and sexuality, etc.) – that exist in society, particularly political inequality manifested in the state. Although not all Marxists have prioritized an analysis of industrial capitalism and class exploitation, this is more common than not.

Unlike Marxist analyses, NSM theories argue that modern social conflict in advanced capitalist countries is post-industrial or non-class based. For example, Touraine (1981) principally observed cultural and political conflict, a sensible claim considering the dramatic rise of the peace, feminist, environmental, and gay rights movements since the late 1960s. Superficially, these movements were not inherently concerned with class or economics (although wings of each were). But, are modern anarchist movements equally dismissive of class matters as these "new social movements"? While many anarchists are not engaged directly in class-struggle efforts, other strands of anarchism are still intimately concerned with class and capitalism (e.g., Robinson 2009). Not only does class still figure prominently in the anarchist critique of modern society, but anarchists are also explicit anti-capitalists.

Anarcho-syndicalism and anarcho-communism are two ideological variants that not only advocate anti-capitalism, but emphasize activism around class issues. The anarcho-syndicalist unions of France and Spain (the UGT and CNT), the Industrial Workers of the World in Anglo countries, and others view class struggle in the workplace between bosses and workers as an important struggle. Anarcho-syndicalists advocate cross-industry solidarity, direct action tactics, and worker self-management (Rocker 2004). The International Workers Association (IWA) is a global anarcho-syndicalist federation with over 200 member organizations, including some of the above unions (Williams & Lee 2008). While not explicitly anarcho-syndicalist, the British Class War organization also highlighted the role the working class plays in community struggles, external to unions, and argued that the working class has a central role in revolution.

Anarcho-communists are similar to their anarcho-syndicalist counterparts, but advocate a more community-oriented version of anti-capitalist class-struggle. They envision a future communist society that is different from the Bolshevik version – a collective society without a central party, vanguard, or "dictatorship of the proletariat." Anarcho-communist federations exist, including anarchists referred to as "Platformists" who adhere to a general platform of beliefs and action (see Skirda 2002). One such US-Canadian grouping was the Northeastern Federation of Anarchist Communists (NEFAC), while globally, the International of Anarchist Federations linked together over 80 anarcho-communists organizations (Williams & Lee 2008).

Even more broadly than anarcho-syndicalism or anarcho-communism ideological subvariants, anarchism is *itself* anti-capitalist. This means that all anarchists – not just those who self-identify with the two aforementioned tendencies – advocate the elimination of capitalism, so-called "free markets," and the modern business corporation.[3] This attention to class conflict has been around since the origins of anarchism in the mid-nineteenth century, when anarchists argued that capitalism destroys communities, the human spirit, and the earth. The recent global justice movement, which has featured prominent anarchist participation, has been propelled by a strong anti-capitalist streak (Epstein 2001). For example, the Direct Action Network (Graeber 2009; Polletta 2002) and Peoples' Global Action (Maiba 2005; Wood 2005), which are laden with anarchist values and have anarchistic organizational structures, played a pivotal role in planning cross-national "days of action" to challenge capitalism at international economic forums and meetings.[4]

The anarchist movements of the late nineteenth and early twentieth centuries were almost indistinguishable from the labor movement (individualist tendencies in North America aside) – or the general swell of activity we associate with the resistance to industrial capitalism. Nevertheless, anarchism less exclusively focuses on class and class struggle today. Some anarchists have actually emphasized the *decreasing* importance of industrial capitalism and class in modern movements. Why might this be? Sheppard (2002) has suggested that divergent values, lifestyles, and occupational patterns have kept anarchists and labor unions apart in recent decades. More importantly, anarchists and other radicals have long been critical of hierarchical business unionism that conducts professional labor negotiations in which rank-and-file union members take little, if any, role in decision making and planning. Often, collective bargaining is favored in place of strikes. Conflict is kept to a bare minimum as workers are essentially bought off by corporations in a supposed "capital-labor truce" (Aronowitz 1973; Brecher 1997). Anarchists like Zerzan (1974) and Black (1997), and others have criticized anarchist participation in labor unions, concluding that labor unions – and their industrial-age structures and strategies – should not be considered viable revolutionary organizations in the struggle against modern capitalism.

A new strand of anarchism termed "post-left anarchism" has arisen in the wake of such critiques of Leftism. Post-leftists reject large federations – like the IWA and IAF – as old, sloth-like super-organizations, that simply build organizations for the sake of organization. As such, post-leftists are more apt to characterize "organizationalists" as the "Stalinists of anarchism" than to admire their revolutionary gumption. Post-leftist criticisms implicitly replicate many similar concerns and observations raised by NSM theories, while still asserting that people are exploited in terms of class and they remain anti-capitalist in orientation.

Another recent, vaguely anarchist philosophy called "primitivism" challenges not only unions and capitalism for their hierarchical and destructive capacities, but industrial society itself. It is debatable whether or not primitivism's concern over the near-apocalyptic destruction of the environment by "civilization" and primitivism's advocacy for a return to a less-destructive hunter-gatherer existence can be considered to be "post-industrial." This desire for a future mirroring the past could be considered both "post-" and "pre-industrial." However, a non-genocidal strategy for activists to achieve these ends is unclear from much primitivist literature. Despite primitivist critiques of anarchist activity within the industrialized world, some anarchists *do* consider union syndicalism to be well-suited to the task of re-charting a more environmentally sustainable course via labor-environmental coalitions, "green-bans," and other strategies (see Purchase 1994; Shantz 2002a; Shantz & Adam 1999).

Touraine's (1981) observation of increased *cultural*-conflict (in place of industrial conflict) finds support since most modern anarchists reject a narrow emphasis on only class conflict. Post-class conflict now includes engagement with gender and race domination. Anarchists have been active, and in some respects, major actors in radical feminist and anti-racist movements. Radicals in feminism's second wave included anarcha-feminists who demanded not only a rejection of sexism and patriarchy, but also an end to capitalism and the state; they argued all such institutions oppress women (C. Ehrlich 1977; Kornegger 2002). Anarcha-feminists in the USA came to play an influential role in the activities of the anti-nuclear movement of the late 1970s (Epstein 1991). Anarchism today also clearly incorporates a rejection of white supremacy. Some Black radicals in the USA, who were militants in the Black Panther Party and Black Liberation Army, have become relatively widely read theorists, injecting critical race theory into anarchism (see Williams 2015). Anarchists have participated in anti-racist struggles throughout Europe, North America, and South America, in organizations such as Anti-Fascist Action (or "Antifa"), Anti-Racist Action (ARA), Red and Anarchist Skinheads (RASH) since the time of, and even before, the fall of Communism and the reappearance of so-called "white power" activism (neo-Nazi and other fascist organizing). New identities based on these distinctions will be explored more in Section 6 below. While these new forms of conflict have added on to the original anarchist critique of the state and capitalism, they have not displaced such concerns.

New social constituencies

Both NSM theories and resource mobilization emphasize the "middle class." In both theories, the middle-class has a central role in movement struggles. Yet, this emphasis is derived from different premises. For resource mobilization, the middle class is the logical agent of movements since they are more likely to belong to organizations with greater resources than the working class (cf. McCarthy & Zald 1977). NSM theories emphasize middle-class participation due to the shift of societal struggle from industrial/economic to cultural/political. (Note that both perspectives presume and best describe highly advanced capitalist societies.)

While anarchism has historically been a working-class movement (Guérin 2005), NSM theorists suggest that modern movements include greater participation and leadership by middle-class members. Williams (2009c) notes a similar, NSM-like trend for contemporary anarchists: only 31 percent of respondents to the Infoshop web survey self-identified as "working class" (also see Chapter 2). Although still a sizable minority, this could represent a change from classical anarchism. Also, only 24 percent were members of an economic, class-based organization: the labor union (Williams 2009c). The presence of a self-identified working class – as well as one apt to belong to labor unions – indicates a certain discontinuity with NSM arguments about the "classlessness" or middle-class character of contemporary movements.

Instead of working class-led movements, NSMs supposedly consist of a "new middle class" that includes non-managerial professionals, such as artists, students and academics, and social service workers. Many well-known anarchists work in such occupations, although this presence is clearly not sufficient evidence for accepting NSM arguments. Numerous anarchist artists and organizations exist, including Clifford Harper, Gee

Vaucher, Josh MacPhee, Eric Drooker, Seth Tobocman, Art & Revolution, Black Mask/Up Against the Wall, Just Seeds, and many small art collectives (see MacPhee & Reuland 2007). Anarchists have been at the forefront of alternative education projects since the turn of the last century. Francisco Ferrer's "modern schools" were early attempts to steer children away from the indoctrination by both state nationalism and capitalism's workforce obedience (Avrich 1980; Spring 1998). Free schools have also received consistent support from anarchists (see Ehrlich 1991), although the extent to which these projects are exclusively anarchist is debatable, as is the association between those who may "work" at such schools (likely without pay) and their subsequent class status. Famous anarchist intellectuals like Noam Chomsky, Paul Goodman, Howard Zinn, David Graeber, and others have occupied academic positions, even at elite universities, while maintaining anarchist identities. The brief re-birth in the mid-2000s of Students for a Democratic Society in the USA in a more anarchistic (and less Marxist) form was another example of this constituency. Finally, social work is an active, action-oriented profession/practice, aimed at directly helping people. Yet, there are few openly anarchist social workers, perhaps because the occupation tends to be subsumed within the bureaucratic confines of state welfare systems (Gilbert 2004).

Ultimately, contemporary anarchists (and likely classical anarchists, too) may not be distilled down neatly into just the middle class (and its professional occupations) or the working class; anarchist movement composition is too nuanced and complex for the typical reductionism NSM theories have previously offered. It could be that middle-class anarchists have higher than average visibility in these movements, perhaps owing to their human capital (multi-language fluency or sophisticated communication skills) or other resources (such as flexible work schedules).

Anarchism pulls from an ideological – rather than ethnic, religious, or class-based – community. All anarchists are linked by their ideology, not socio-economic-cultural background. In most anarchist organizations – outside of organizations founded to create safe spaces for traditionally oppressed groups, like anarcha-feminist or anarchist people of color (APOC) collectives – the uniting factor is belief in anarchism. Thus, young and old, educated and under-educated, or middle class and working class, work together for common goals. Unlike old movements where unity might have come from common class background or ethnic status, NSMs like modern anarchism are founded on a shared radical vision and praxis. Yet, this unity based on ideology is not inherently new – anti-authoritarianism was also the uniting factor in classical anarchism, too. Thus, contemporary anarchism cannot easily be categorized as a NSM if its adherents share the same commonalities as in an earlier era.[5]

Youth are one final "new constituency," in particular students. This constituency presents unique problems for movements in the long term: younger participants grow older. Anarchist movements share other commonalities with the standard NSMs usually noted (i.e., student, environmental, anti-war) in that its ranks are incredibly young.[6] Unlike other movements – such as the anti-war movement – anarchism seems to have been less able to retain its membership cohorts over the past few decades. The extent to which this pattern will continue is presently unclear. During anarchism's "golden age" in the late 1800s and early 1900s, anarchists included all ages, as they were socialized to be anarchists during childhood in working-class families and communities, or were radicalized through industrial experience. Today, anarchism is associated in the media with "youth rebellion" against society, thus implying that anarchism is a side-effect of immaturity. To the extent that this is true, once youthfulness recedes such rebellious tendencies may also pass. Older anarchists may appear as aging rebels or immature, as they have not discarded the radicalism of youth. Instead of socialization into responsible positions in mainstream society, older anarchists flaunt expectations and ignore convention – behavior unacceptable for people of their age.

Anti-hierarchical organization

New social movements allegedly use more horizontally distributed organizational forms than hierarchically centralized ones, aiming to be highly participatory and democratic. But according to popular perception, anarchists are opposed to any and all organization and order. As with the other misperceptions regarding anarchism, this is clearly incorrect. Anarchists are usually very much in favor of organization and order, although of a particular variety. They oppose bureaucratic, authoritarian, and hierarchical organization, whether in the economic, political, or cultural spheres of society (Ehrlich 1996). Instead, anarchists envision anti-hierarchical forms of organization that are more organic, small-scale, directly democratic, and often temporary. As Bookchin (1989) observes, "the new social movements share a libertarian ambience," as well as the tendency for decentralization, affinity groups, confederation, and "anti-hierarchicalism" (1989: 270). Thus, anarchism has emphasized participatory democracy, self-help groups, and cooperative styles of organization (Ward 1996).[7] Unlike other NSMs, these organizational forms are not "new" to anarchism as they were widely employed during anarchism's classical period. Indeed, anti-hierarchical structures are a founding characteristic of anarchism.

Anti-hierarchical organization requires conscious choice, since it results from the adoption of anarchist values such as self-determination, solidarity, cooperation, and mutual aid. Instead of planning for an idealistic, perfect future, anarchists aim to create a new society in the shell of the old society by expressing and living their values in the present.[8] If that future society is to be non-hierarchical, then people who wish to nurture that future society ought to act without hierarchy now. Thus, values are not merely abstractions to be debated; for anarchists values must be lived on a daily basis. To avoid living these values would mean having to avoid being an anarchist. As such, there are no mere "philosophical anarchists" in anarchist movements, who only think about and debate anarchist ideas. Anarchism is practiced and created in the continual deliberation, and activities of anarchist lives and organizations.

Anarchist politics may be viewed as a particular strain of "anti-politics" that oppose the typical forms of political activity, such as participation through political parties. Instead, principal anarchist organizational forms include affinity groups, cells, collectives, cooperatives, networks, and federations (see Day 2005; Ehrlich 1996; Gordon 2008; Ward 1996). These forms constitute "looser" and more fluid organizational structures than those found in standard bureaucratic and top-down organizations.

Affinity groups are "closed" organizations composed of people who have intimate relations with each other – trust, companionship, and common interest are prerequisites – and are utilized in specific situations, such as protests. Affinity groups, which were made famous during the Spanish Civil War for their decentralized defense of the Republic against fascist forces (Bookchin 1998), have since been deployed during anti-war, environmental, anti-nuclear, feminist, and global justice movement protests (e.g., Epstein 1991; Finnegan 2003; Solnit & Solnit 2009). These groups provide a small-scale, flexible alternative to bureaucratic or command-and-control style organizations that are common at many conventional protests. Members of affinity groups are in a constant process of evaluating their goals for present and future situations, as well as their levels of commitment and appreciation for specific tactics (Bookchin 2004).

The most decentralized organizational form that anarchists utilize is that of the autonomous cell. Although some have argued that cells are not anarchist, the Earth Liberation Front (ELF) and Animal Liberation Front (ALF) take seriously the anarchist concepts of decentralization and direct action against authority. Anyone who takes an action – illegal or legal – either to stop the destruction of the environment or the exploitation of animals, or to curb the potential for such abuses, may claim to be a member of these "organizations." So successful were ELF and ALF cells at their goals of disruption and property destruction of symbols of capitalist America, that in 1999 the FBI called them the top "domestic terrorist threat" in the USA (Federal Bureau of Investigation 1999) – despite both groups' denunciation of violence and physical harm to human or animal life.[9] In a practical sense, such "organizations" are not really organizations at all, but rather loose collections of associates or even single individuals who assume and operate under the auspice of the "ELF" or "ALF" labels (Beck 2007). In the case of the ELF, a "front press office" (run by an unaffiliated but sympathetic individual) received press releases from such groupings announcing an action, often calling themselves a unit, cell, faction, or wing of the ELF based in a particular location. In this capacity, the press office was merely a central location to distribute information about the actions of pro-ELF people, while the office had no control over what any particular ELF cell did. Other anarchistic groupings also take on a relatively clandestine approach, also implied in their self-labels, notably the Biotic Baking Brigade (described in the next section).[10] CrimethInc is also well known for encouraging various groupings of people and individuals – who may not know each other – to publish propaganda under its moniker.

Collectives are designed to serve an above-ground and longer-lasting purpose. Anarchist collectives have flat organizational structures, particular goals, and an established (although not always formalized) decision-making process. These organizations may do many different things: run a social center or "infoshop," print an activist newspaper or manage a guerrilla radio station, provide women's health care and advice, organize a community garden, offer legal aid, or wage non-electoral political campaigns. Atton's (1999) research on the British tabloid, *Green Anarchist*, demonstrates how NSM organizational characteristics drawn from Melucci (1996) can be seen in many aspects of the paper's collective, including self-management of writing and distribution among many geographically dispersed people, and decentralized editing.

Some collectives could also be considered cooperatives – designed to either manufacture or provide a good or service, or to purchase or acquire such things, respectively. Anarchists have been active members for decades of housing, food, bike, child care, and even punk rock record store cooperatives. Cooperative members pool their economic resources and physical labor in order to create the best possible, equal outcome for all involved. Rothschild-Whitt (1979) has argued that cooperatives possess a collectivist-democratic nature, which appears largely analogous to anarchist values (another relationship yet to be seriously explored by sociologists). There are no elite owners of worker cooperatives, only members. Consequently, many cooperatives have a staunchly anti-hierarchical structure that empowers equal participation.[11]

While most anarchists emphasize the need for localized organization, they also acknowledge that larger, more complex forms are also sometimes necessary. Yet, instead of creating centralized bodies that coordinate policy, anarchists advocate network or federation structures. Networks are flexible, informal mechanisms for interaction. Both individuals and organizations may participate in the coordination of campaigns, events, or other projects. According to Day (2005), these anarchistic organizational structures rely upon a "logic of affinity" as opposed to a "logic of hegemony." Sometimes networks exist merely for the exchange of information and communication (Juris 2008). Federations, on the other hand, are a more structured way of linking formal organizations and sympathetic, supporter organizations to each other. Unlike many federation systems, however, anarchist federations are horizontal relationships: no central committee exists and no member organization has any more power than any other. The anarcho-communist NEFAC, for example, made decisions at yearly conferences via direct democracy of all members. In-between meetings, a federation council – consisting of recallable spokespersons from each member organization – dealt with administrative and executive functions (NEFAC n.d.).[12] By mandating recallable positions, NEFAC collectives aimed to control wayward spokespersons.

If there is an enduring quality to all of these organizational forms, it is their impermanence. Anarchists emphasize the appropriate means almost as much as the goal itself, assuming that it is impractical for anarchist organizations to use hierarchical and rigid means, even to achieve supposedly liberatory ends. As such, Welsh (1997) finds disdain in Melucci's assumption that

> new social movements have to transform themselves into durable organisations in order to achieve [success] remain problematic in terms of anarchist and libertarian approaches ... SMOs [social movement organizations] reproduce hierarchies and bureaucratic structures which are antithetical to grassroots movements. (1997: 167)

Another common thread in all the above organizations is that no one person or small group of persons can control these groups. Theoretically, everyone in each organization has equal input in how the organization is run. Leadership is usually informal and decentralized, and, if it exists at all, it resides in rotating positions with little power. Positions like "facilitator" or "note-taker" exist not to direct the trajectory of an organization, but to allow the group to realize its collective goals. Anarchist organizations operate on the basis of either direct democracy or consensus decision making (or some modification of either). Unlike in representative democracy, where people elect others who will then supposedly vote in their best interests, anarchists advocate direct democracy, where everyone votes on each individual issue to be considered. Members vote on proposals without channeling their "voices" through other individuals presumably chosen to represent them, as in most "representative democracy" systems.[13] Consensus decision making may be considered even more radical; an organization must try to reach a common decision that everyone involved can live with. With consensus, even small minorities must be respected and organizations must find ways to reach common ground where all participants are satisfied with a decision and its foreseeable outcome (Gelderloos 2006a).

These are not "new" characteristics as NSM theories imply, but values and practices that have driven anarchist movements since their origins (although the practices around formal consensus decision making were introduced in the 1960s). These organizational forms and decision-making processes are not seen by anarchists as approaches to be selectively implemented, but are appropriate (or necessary) elements of everyday society. Presently, they represent a minority of approaches in society and operate in a "sub-political" world, but anarchists view them as potentially the major political forms in a future, more-anarchist society.

Symbolic direct actions

New social movements enact highly dramatic forms of demonstration, laden with symbolic representation. Anarchists and anarchistic organizations employ direct action tactics both within and apart from regular protest. The former type of direct action exists in an oppositional and confrontational setting, aligned against hierarchical authority figures. The latter type of direct action persist within a counter-cultural milieu where anarchists prefigure and create alternatives to hierarchical forms of social organization.

Anarchists favor protest tactics that are novel and unconventional – that is, not a standard rally with a slate of formal speakers, followed by a legally permitted march (a common practice in many Western societies). Instead, anarchist actions are deliberately designed to confront authority and provoke a response, demonstrate how to live differently, or to involve otherwise non-political people in a participatory, political event. Mass media attention often focuses upon these efforts, thus conveying anarchist values and practices to a wider public audience. (Of course, even something as straightforward and consciously packaged as symbolic direct actions often get distorted by mass media.) Such anarchist actions are also distinct from many conventional NSMs because these actions have a practical component that allow participants to directly target a particular problem and solve that problem immediately, without resorting to requests to authority figures.

Dramatic and symbolic protest may be seen most clearly by the black bloc tactic. Originally developed by autonomists from Germany in the 1980s, and calling themselves Autonomen, the black bloc is a solidaritious direct action in street protests,[14] where all participants wear black (thus the name, "black bloc"), covered their faces for security and anonymity, and operated in affinity groups to challenge police lines (Dupuis-Déri 2014; Geronimo 2012; Knutter 1995).[15] These black blocs serve to disrupt the repetition of typical protest as well as the appearance of police authority at protests (Katsiaficas 2006; Thompson 2010). Indeed, black blocs are fundamentally "ungovernable" since they are not interested in negotiation with authority (Paris 2003). According to Starr (2006), what is commonly perceived and presented as black bloc "violence" is in fact an amalgam of theater and practical self-defense. Black bloc activities often include masking one's face, throwing tear-gas canisters *back* to police, destruction of corporate property, mobile defense, un-arresting fellow demonstrators from police custody, and the use of makeshift weapons – usually objects found on the street – as projectiles for defensive purposes.[16]

The explosive engagements between Autonomen and police were transported to other countries during the 1990s. The first appearance of the black bloc in the USA resulted from an initiative by the Love and Rage Network during anti-Persian Gulf War protests (Ickibob 2003). Symbolic visual theater occurs when police wearing indistinguishable riot gear engage with all-black-clad (but still uniquely adorned) activists in the street. Black bloc actions also demonstrated that some activists were willing to defend themselves during demonstrations when attacked by police, which has, in turn, instigated rounds of inter-movement debate around issues of pacifism, self-defense, and violence.[17] Although there is a practical utility to covering one's face with a bandanna – to deter police profiling of people who potentially break laws – there is also an echo of the Zapatistas in the regular use of masks by anarchists. The poor Mayans of Southern Mexico, who form the base of support for the Zapatistas, were continuously ignored by the national Mexican political institutions and they thus chose something dramatic, almost illicit-seeming, to cause the state to pay attention. As a Zapatista leader poetically said, they had to hide their faces in order to be seen (Marcos 2001).

Actions by black blocs are also highly symbolic. During the 1999 WTO protests, black bloc participants smashed the windows of chain stores and multinational corporations. In a communiqué released later, this vandalism was explained as an effort to "smash the thin veneer of legitimacy that surrounds private property rights … Broken windows can be boarded up (with yet more waste of our forests) and eventually replaced, but the shattering of assumptions will hopefully persist for some time to come" (ACME Collective 1999).

A similar phenomenon in Europe emerged, loosely identified as "disobedients," who engage in essentially nonviolent direct action during protests where they are confronted by police lines with protective gear such as shields, helmets, and lots of personal padding. Organizations like Ya Basta (Spanish for "enough is enough") and WOMBLES, have had numerous successes since the mid-1990s, breaking through police lines in efforts to reach protest goals, with the eventual goal usually being the shutdown of a target's functionality. The WOMBLES – or White Overalls Movement Building Libertarian Effective Struggles – and their counterparts creatively and dramatically provoked media coverage in ways that protest with standard signs and speeches would be unable to achieve.[18] In London, on May Day 2001, WOMBLES helped to turn central London into a large-scale Monopoly game-board, encouraging others to participate in a "lived critique" of modern capitalism during the protests scheduled for that day.

"Players" engaged in protests and direct actions at symbolic sites throughout London to articulate and illustrate the ill of capitalism, to "subvert the game" itself (Uitermark 2004). Such anarchist methods are highly confrontational, which is a symbol that anarchists are radicals committed to revolution.

Some protest-based activities combine even more playfulness and humor. The Clandestine Insurgent Rebel Clown Army (CIRCA) in Britain served the same role as that played by clowns in rodeos – to distract charging bulls (or police officers). CIRCA aimed to not only de-escalate potentially violent street confrontations between demonstrators and law enforcement, but also to mock authority and its supposedly well-established grip on civil order. "Radical cheerleaders," on the other hand, present their performances for protesters. Instead of trying to ridicule the authority of the police in protest situations, radical cheerleaders provide an alternative "pep rally" at radical protests. Anarchist women (and some men) dress up in homemade "cheerleader outfits" and shake "pom-poms" made from shredded garbage bags. They present radical "cheers" to assembled demonstrators or onlookers like: "hey all you anarchy fans / let me hear you clap your hands / if you think yer freedom's sweet / let me see you stomp yer feet."[19]

Anarchists were behind the highly symbolic actions of the Biotic Baking Brigade, who took a decentralized approach to humiliating authority figures. Autonomous groups of activists throughout the world have used the "BBB" moniker to claim "pie attacks" upon hundreds of corporate CEOs, politicians, financial figures, and even former radicals and liberals. By smearing a pie in someone's face – especially when a video camera is conveniently present to record the target's surprise or outrage – the BBB attempts to show that otherwise untouchable authority figures may be publicly "brought down a notch." The BBB also uses clever play-on-words and puns in their press releases to further symbolize their radical dissent: "pie any means necessary," "let slip the pies of war," "some people need their just desserts," "speaking pie to power," and "pies for your lies" (Apple 2004). These actions reflect Melucci's observation that NSMs challenge symbolic codes by unmasking obscured technocratic and bureaucratic power.

Another phenomenon – spread globally, like political pieing – occurs on the last Friday of most months in cities where cyclists gather for a rush-hour traffic bike ride. Critical Mass (CM) attempts to create "pockets of freedom" for individual and collective expression, safety, and community on streets that are otherwise monopolized by cars, which in turn seal drivers off from each other. Such "organized coincidences" are coordinated in an anarchistic fashion – no one is in charge of the rides, anyone can promote and help organize the rides, all participants "police themselves," and spontaneous direct action creates temporary autonomous zones for people to be free of car culture, if only briefly (Blickstein & Hanson 2001; Carlsson 2002). Anarchists often use CM as a tool to allow others to "experience anarchy," and to spread the word about other anarchist projects and events happening in the local area.

Other anarchist direct action strategies assume a less confrontational, and more pro-active and creative orientation. While these approaches are still "protest" of a certain kind, they are less likely to be labeled as such and to emerge during protest events. Two anarchist organizations are not just symbolic in terms of the values their names imply, but also in the consequences their actions suggest. Food Not Bombs (FNB) and Homes Not Jails (HNJ) indicate specific anarchist values about the world within their organizational names, but also utilize direct action to offer examples of potential ways to reorganize social relationships and societal priorities. FNB collects food that would otherwise be thrown out, cooks meals using the food, and then shares the meals with anyone who would like to eat them – often homeless people. The organization opposes militarism and corporate profiteering, and instead suggests a symbolic reorientation of priorities towards human needs, such as housing, food, education, and health care (Butler & McHenry 2000; Gelderloos 2006b). HNJ targets the need for adequate housing more specifically; activists squat abandoned buildings, fix the buildings, and provide the space to homeless families to live in (Roy 2003). This direct action suggests that homelessness and unemployment often lead to downward spirals into desperation, crime, and violence. HNJ represents how basic human needs like housing are essential to stem the tide of rising crime rates and imprisonment – which they argue unfairly harms the poor and people of color. There are many other examples of radical political squatting throughout Europe (van der Steen *et al.* 2014) and Latin America.

Perhaps the most dramatic forms of non-street direct action is organized by radical environmentalists, such as Earth First! (EF!). In order to protect old-growth forests from being logged, EF! activists engage in creative forms of civil disobedience, including road blockading and tree-sitting. By occupying stands built high in trees, EF!ers prevent loggers from chopping trees in large areas unless they wish to be responsible for putting tree-sitter lives in danger. This photogenic tactic has been highly successful in many EF! campaigns in North America (Ingalsbee 1996; London 1998). In the UK, EF! groups have been active in the anti-roads movement where they attempted to prevent new roads from being built (Welsh & McLeish 1996). EF! originally employed a strategy more reliant upon sabotage, but today it focuses on civil disobedience (Balser 1997), still emphasizing the intensity of resistance to environmental destruction in its slogan: "no compromise in defense of Mother Earth." EF! sympathizers who wish to engage in eco-sabotage and property destruction are encouraged to do so under the banner of the ELF, and keep EF! actions within the realm of civil disobedience (Molland 2006). (CM, EF!, and FNB are discussed in greater detail in Chapter 8.)

Direct action is an integral part of the anarchist praxis. Such actions embody polemical symbolism, often illustrating polar opposites: hierarchy and domination of elites on the one hand, freedom and egalitarianism of anarchists on the other. However, unlike other movements where symbolism is enough to motivate others (e.g., politicians) to respond, symbolic anarchist actions actually aim to immediately further the goal of a less authoritarian future. Consequently, while usually symbolic, anarchist direct action is also substantive, not merely illustrative. Many of the aforementioned examples of anarchist groupings, including FNB, HNJ, and EF! involve practical and often material resistance, thus differentiating these anarchist tendencies from the more theatrical. "Direct action" is an important anarchist quality (Rocker 2004) and, symbolic or not, anarchism is thus a radical *and* practical movement. Anarchist direct action does not only aim to avoid taking political power in the course of acquiring self-determination, but actively seeks to usurp political power itself. Thus, instead of relying on representatives to act in one's favor, anarchists diminish such representative influence by accomplishing goals without external assistance. Anarchism aims to empower people, but not through the means of conventional politics.

Self-limiting radicalism

NSMs eschew grand attempts to seize the state apparatus, whether through dramatic revolution or elections. Efforts to shape society – within the parameters of NSM ideologies – take place in civil society, not within the state. Radical goals are pursued, but often through reformist strategies. Likewise, anarchists have no interest in acquiring representation in, or control of, the state. They do not seek to work with the state or in it, but rather seek the state's abolition. Unlike Leninists and Maoists, anarchists do not wish to seize the reins of the state in revolution to allegedly turn it over to workers or peasants. Anarchists argue that to simply replace a right-wing or capitalist government with a left-wing or socialist one does not solve the problem of what the state itself is (i.e., an institution of domination). Nor do anarchist movements aim to achieve their anti-authoritarian goals through electoralism. Thus, anarchist movements pursue a radical agenda limited to realms that can be democratized and liberated.

Habermas – by no means an anarchist[20] – argues that NSMs resist the "occupation of the lifeworld" by the state (Habermas 1987). NSMs are "new" since their potential to transform society is not within established politics, but within the socio-cultural sphere. In fact, movements aim to re-appropriate society from the state, which has not only repressed people through violence but also undercut their potential by fostering reliance on the state for social welfare. According to anarchist theory, it is counter-intuitive to expect liberation from various systems of domination deriving from the state. The state props up and feeds upon these very systems, and thus the anarchist solution comes from action outside the state. Power is pursued to regain control over one's own life, not to acquire a position within the established halls of power. Anarchists believe that a new world will not be built with the seized apparatus of the state, but by disengaging from all systems of domination and creating alternative institutions that serve human needs and are in-sync with the natural world. But, rather than protecting an abstract "lifeworld" or civil society from state encroachment, anarchists explicitly advocate defense of individuals and their collectivities. This may be seen as another example of radical practicality.

Anarchists seek self-determination, the ability for ordinary people to have control over their daily lives. According to anarchists, the state does not offer this control to all, but only to a select few officials who claim to act on behalf of all. To anarchists, allowing others to make decisions for you, even if the decision makers are benevolent and you agree with the decisions, is to relinquish one's natural right to self-determination.

Unlike nearly all others on the Left, anarchist organizations do not run or support candidates for political office. The slogans "our dreams do not fit in their ballot boxes" and "don't just vote, get political" have been used by anarchists during recent elections. Anarchism does not suggest a complete disavowal of politics – or the political matters that people make decisions about – but rather a rejection of the notion that politics is best done via the election of candidates or via the state. Thus, modern anarchism distinguishes between self-determined political activity and the mechanisms of the state (including elections). Anarchism argues that elections and statecraft are only one part of politics.[21]

If specific policy changes are demanded by anarchists, the goal is not simply a change in policy. Anarchists use changes in policy as launching pads for greater changes, ones that strike even deeper into ruling institutions. Albert (2002) advocates anarchist support for what he calls "nonreformist reforms"; or, in other words, reforms which are not ends in themselves (i.e., "reformism"). Some anarchists have advocated participation in campaigns that involve electoral participation as a means of coalition-building – particularly across race and class boundaries, in order to defeat oppressive laws which would further restrict liberties – instead of advocating voting as a means to an end (Crass 2004). In these examples, the engagement in mainstream politics is to critique the state, oppose its long-term goals, and advocate and support immediate, self-directed reforms.

Self-limiting radicalism should not be read as implying "limited radicalism." Revolution is the ultimate goal of all anarchists, yet anarchists do not desire or aim to be the coordinators of a mass revolution. Instead, anarchists believe that people as individuals and collectives need to reclaim control over their lives – in a radical fashion – and anarchists do not presume to speak for how others should do this. Or, as Malatesta wrote (Turcato 2014),

"We anarchists do not want to *emancipate* the people; we want the people to *emancipate themselves*" (2014: 243, emphasis in original). Mumm (1998) argues that it is much more important and desirable for movements to act anarchistically than to merely have a movement of anarchists. By millions of small-scale transformations and revolts, society will undergo a process of revolution that is undirected and undirectable.

Some anarchists do advocate immediate revolution, including via spontaneous uprising of oppressed peoples, which is not limited radicalism. However, even "insurrectionist anarchists" do not think that mass, revolutionary action should be aimed at seizing state power or that a party should direct the insurrection (see Bonanno 1988). Insurrections should topple centralized power, and those immediately engaged in the insurrection should help to disperse and democratize control of society. Thus, anarchists do not have limited ambitions; their "limitedness" refers only to the use of non-state means to accomplish revolution.

New identities

New social movements are formed out of unique, fresh identities. Like other NSMs, anarchists adhere to specific value- and action-based identities. Many anarchists place themselves in social categories linked to particular ideologically rooted anarchisms. New identities have emerged within the anarchist movement, in part replacing old ones that were more closely tied to economic ideologies. Mutualism and collectivism, for example, are older anarchist strains that many present-day anarchists are no longer identified with. While identities such as anarcho-communism are still around, Tucker's anarcho-individualism is rarely identified with today. Even during Tucker's time (late 1800s), anarchist strains were points of contention (Nettlau 2001). Voltairine de Cleyre's "anarchism without adjectives" – the rejection of specific labels or strains, and a general adherence to the liberatory trajectory of a self-directed future – can be witnessed within the current movement (de Cleyre 2004), yet her label is infrequently used. Other developments have occurred. De Cleyre's orientation towards gender is now labeled anarcha-feminism, an identity that many anarchists since the 1970s – particularly women – share. It can be argued that today the major schism between anarchist identities, particularly in North America, is not simply between communists and individualists, but between "reds" and "greens," or "organizationalists" and "anti-organizationalists." Stark geographic patterns in the USA exist: red anarchists (those with an economic, working-class focus) tend to reside in the Northeast region while green anarchists (those with an environmental focus) tend to be found in the West.[22] This dispersion can be partly explained by certain historical structural and organizational factors (Williams 2009b).

Anarchism today is arguably even more multifaceted and potentially contentious than during its classical period, as many of the preceding NSM components have indicated. Recent times have also witnessed an explosion of other hyphenated anarchism strains: eco-anarchists, anarcho-primitivists, anarcho-punks, practical-anarchists, post-left-anarchists, anarcho-situationists, queer-anarchists, and anarchist-people-of-color. All of these identities are new amalgams created by the anarchistization of pre-existing identities and the extension of other concerns into anarchist theory. In the case of anarcha-feminists, queer-anarchists, and anarchist-people of color, not only do these categories define an identity that links together some anarchists – usually in such a way as to create smaller caucuses within the movement to discuss internal democracy and tolerance issues – but also indicate the broad character of cultural conflict in society (that extends beyond mere industrial conflict, as discussed earlier).[23]

NSM theories imply that participants resist conventional lifestyles. Modern anarchism includes practices aimed at sustaining anarchist life-styles, whether as ends themselves or as a way of building alternative culture for the "long haul" toward revolution. Even though some mainstream social movement scholars have only recently begun to acknowledge it, all movements have their own cultures and anarchists are no exception. Cultural lifestyles permit movement participants the opportunity to practice their alternative views and choices, particularly when such alternatives are strongly at odds with mainstream society.[24] As with second-wave feminists, the anarchists consider the "personal to be political"; the way people live their lives is a reflection of their dedication to anarchism. Thus, it would be controversial, within anarchist culture, for a self-professed anarchist to own a corporation and employ multiple workers, or to use aggressive violence against others. Vegetarianism, residing in cooperative housing situations, solidarity with oppressed groups, rejecting partisan politics, or permaculture gardening are all practices that anarchists may include in their daily repertoires that allow them to live anarchy.[25]

Anarchists have a lifestyle heavily influenced by certain alternative subcultures, such as "do it yourself" (DIY) culture, which includes many things, from the printing of zines (short for "magazines") to planning local events. Punk culture is a major influence on DIY and has had a strong influence over – or at least interaction with – much of the anarchist movement since the late 1970s (O'Connor 1999, 2003a). This synergy may be witnessed in the exchange of punk fashion among anarchists and anarchist politics among many punk banks. Hundreds of anarcho-punk bands have performed throughout the world, seeing punk's revolt against authority and DIY practice as essentially anarchist in nature (O'Hara 1999). Famous anarchist bands like Crass, Chumbawamba, The Ex, Dead Kennedys, Propagandhi, Against Me!, and others are not only mainstays of punk history, but also serve as artistic inspiration to many anarchists. Punk constitutes an anti-establishment lifestyle and identity, which is often both anti-capitalist and anarchistic, and is created in the crucible of local conflict with social control agents (Johnston & Lio 1998).

Cultural anarchy, perhaps best represented by early Crimethinc, promotes an anarchist way of life, personal freedom, and lifestyle choices. Crimethinc's unique combination of situationism, primitivism, punk culture, and insurrectionism is visible within sectors of the North American anarchist movement, and was particularly noteworthy for its advocacy of hitch-hiking and train hopping, "dumpster-diving," and scamming or stealing from corporations. In the advocacy and practice of such activities, Crimethinc drew on a long tradition of survival techniques developed by hobos, as practiced during the Great Depression, and by Beats and hippies. This identity is sometimes derogatorily referred to as "lifestyle anarchism," which prioritizes the individual, or romanticizes "chaos" and spontaneity at the expense of a more serious social anarchism (cf. Bookchin 1995). Instead, many Crimethinkers feel it is more important to remove oneself from a destructive and hierarchical society than try to organize within it, such as class-struggle anarchism often advocates (CrimethInc 2001). Thus, Crimethinc advocates the abandonment of identity politics, stating that it is more important to practice anarchy than to be an anarchist.

Beyond "new": the future of, and uses for, new social movement theories

Modern anarchism overlaps with many features of the NSM framework. I have argued – and this chapter provides suggestive evidence – that NSM theories' observations about modern movements *parallel* contemporary anarchism and greater anarchist movements. Still, certain themes relevant to anarchist movements indicate either contradiction or the need for extension to the NSM typology offered by Sutton and Vertigans (2006). The tension between anarchism and NSM theory has important implications that have so far not been addressed by scholarly research. I suggest that anarchism differs from standard NSMs in its revolutionary anti-statism, radical practicality, anti-capitalism, and apparent connection to an earlier wave of nineteenth-century anarchism.

Although most NSMs do not aim to seize state power, they do tend to prefer or tolerate coexistence with the state. Anarchists, on the other hand, seek not only to overthrow the state, but to dissolve its centralized power so it may not be utilized by any elite group. Thus, anarchist ambitions are not limited to *non*-state goals, but rather *anti*-state goals are pursued via non-state means. Movement strategies and tactics aim to usurp power through direct action that is designed to empower people – not political representatives. The typical approach of NSMs to utilize the state to achieve its goals finds little support with the anarchist movement.

The anarchist movement shares the same symbolic character as its NSM cousins, but refuses to neglect what it views as the more important goal of providing for people's everyday needs. This radical practicality is present in all forms of anarchism activity, where symbolic direct actions are not merely symbolic, but also pragmatic, demonstrable, and functional. Whether Food Not Bombs providing food to the hungry, Anti-Racist Action protecting against fascist attacks, Earth First!'s blockading forest clearing or oil pipeline routes, or the black bloc disrupting "business as usual" during large demonstrations, anarchists aim not only to demonstrate, but also to *prefigure* a different world. Such practicality is both radical in how it addresses fundamental needs, but also directly targets the perceived source of social problems. Anarchists' practicality does not merely seek to defend "civil society" from state encroachment, but also from capitalism, patriarchy, white supremacy, and bureaucracy.

Whereas the NSMs have allegedly – but debatably – transcended the working class and industrial concerns, anarchism has only partially grown in a post-industrial direction. Instead, there is still a sizable participation by self-identified working-class anarchists in the movement, and the movement itself cannot be reduced to either purely working-class or middle-class interests (refer back to Chapter 2's survey results). Instead, capitalism remains a central (although not the only) enemy of anarchism. Capitalism has not been dropped by anarchists as a concern, nor do anarchists believe capitalism can be reformed or partnered with, as with other NSMs. All anarchist tendencies – and not merely the still-active anarcho-syndicalists and anarcho-communists that have the most obvious ideological orientation in this direction – are by definition anti-capitalist. Class is not a "dead issue," but remains a major form of inequality and domination in all societies, whether industrializing or "post-industrial."

Last, many of Sutton and Vertigans characteristics were present during early periods of anarchism. As van der Walt and Hirsch (2010) have argued, these "NSM" tactics and repertoires, symbolic direct action, and anti-hierarchical organizational forms were evidenced throughout the early global anarchism (2010: 399). Classic-era anarchism also involved radically democratic means, middle-class and even upper-class constituents (although it was dominated by working-class members), a denouncement of political ambition within states, and the creation of alternative identities. Anarchists have always been united, not by ethnicity, disability, gender, or even class, but rather by common ideology. The rejection of authority (even if it is sometimes limited in earlier definitions) has been a central value for anarchists in the First International and the Paris Commune until today. The horizontal and anti-authoritarian organizational forms chosen by anarchists are not recent characteristics, but qualities that pre-date the 1960s New

Left. Affinity groups, federations, and cooperatives have been the main form of anarchist organization for nearly – and, in some cases, over – a century. Anti-"political" politics are not new to anarchists, but rather were founding principles considered necessary for the construction of a new social order. Consequently, like observations made by other critics of the NSM theories' "new" label, anarchist movements seem to have been "new" even when they were decidedly old.

Thus, NSM theories help to categorize contemporary anarchism, although not perfectly. NSM arguments are somewhat over-extended (particularly in regards to class and capitalism) and the revolutionary quality of anarchist goals is overlooked by NSM theories. Future research on NSM theory and contemporary movements should consider the prominent role that anarchism has begun to play in global movements and how its presence offers particular challenges to the received understanding of movements to date. Anarchists' critique is radical, as is their solution to social problems. NSM theories have begun to appreciate these noteworthy characteristics, but have yet to consider their depth and their respective consequences. Potentially, with a deeper appreciation of the relationship between anarchism and social movement theory, this scholarship may move closer to the development of a unique "anarchist-sociology," which in turn could provide a new, critical framework for interpreting society and radical social movements.

Notes

1 A similar linguistic problem results from the tendencies to deploy the prefix "post-" in front of terms and phrases, instead of specifically identifying the new phenomenon. Numerous examples here: post-modernism, post-industrial, post-racial, and even "post-anarchism."

2 See Inglehart (1990) for an empirical and quantitative analysis of post-material politics. According to Inglehart, advanced capitalist societies do not simply value material well-being, but also independence, self-expression, personal choice, multiculturalism, anti-authoritarianism, and quality of life.

3 Anti-capitalist anarchists participate in typical movement behavior: they engage in protest, extra-electoral political activity, and conflictual social discourse. Still, as described earlier, some people with free-market orientations do identify as anarchists, while lacking social movement qualities. "Anarcho-capitalists" or "Big-L Libertarians," in the view of the anarchist *movement*, are not anarchists, but are rather pro-capitalist individualists or propertarians (McKay 2008).

4 On the micro-level, a case study of a small Midwest US town found strong class-based themes throughout its local movement, including a broad critique of corporate capitalism and participation in anarchist unionism (Robinson 2009).

5   NSM theory's temporal ambiguity is also the target of Calhoun (1993) and
    Tucker (1991).

6   Williams's (2009c) study shows an average age of 26 years old. However, as
    this figure is based on an internet survey, it may be dramatically
    undercounting older anarchists.

7   Western (2014) refers to these preferences as "autonomist leadership"; when
    labeled as such, activists understand better how the organization functions in
    the absence of authority.

8   According to Gordon (2007) this is a central tenet of modern anarchism
    – an open-ended experimentation that supplants the Marxist-Leninist
    practice of "Five Year Plans" and other pre-determined visions of Utopia.
    The IWW inserted "the structure of the new society within the shell of
    the old" in their Constitution. See: www.iww.org/culture/official/
    preamble.shtml

9   Compare to numerous examples of actually violent right-wing organizations
    (e.g., anti-choice, militia/patriot, and fascists).

10 ALF, BBB, and ELF can also be referred to as AFOs (anarchistic franchise
    organizations or occurrences). See Chapter 8 for more details.

11 Intensive debates rage about whether worker cooperative businesses – even
    those staffed wholly by anarchists – can be effectively anti-capitalist in
    thoroughly capitalist societies.

12 This emphasis that associations should use delegates and not representatives
    – and that coordinating bodies should be purely administrative not
    deliberative – dates back to the origins of the modern anarchist movement in
    the First International (Graham 2015).

13 See Skirda (2002: 80–93) and Graham (2015) for historical accounts of
    anarchist direct democracy voting at international anarchist gatherings.

14 For more on autonomist Marxists, see Katsiaficas (2006).

15 Ryan (2006) suggests that the black bloc got its name from the black
    hooded sweatshirts that were the unofficial uniform of Central European
    squatters – the color black could confidently conceal stains (2006: 50).

16 Graeber (2009) even argues that the use of Molotov cocktails is "defensive"
    as it keeps violent police away from citizens.

17 See One Off Press (2001) for such debates – and an enthusiastic defense of
    confrontational protest – centered around the 2001 anti-G8 protests in
    Genoa, Italy.

18 However, mass media may explain direct action in a misleading or obscuring
    way; thus, a simple, radical banner helps to convey an anarchist message,
    regardless of media actions.

19 See CIRCA's website at: www.clownarmy.org. See more on the Radical
    Cheerleaders (and their cheers) at: http://radcheers.tripod.com/.

20 He briefly mentions having conflicts with anarchists in his interview book
    Autonomy and Solidarity (1992).

21 Here, we can see the myopic definition of "political" among some NSM
    theorists, thus limiting the imagination of a horizontal, direct, and liberatory
    politics.

22 These red and green identities are also tied to organizational preferences
    (more formal organizations versus looser collectives and networks) and

tactical preferences (community and workplace organizing versus covert action, sabotage, and property destruction, respectively).

23 Arguably these identities also indicate the inclusion of new social constituencies.

24 "Dual power" is a particular anarchist strategy – since re-appropriated from Lenin – that extends these counter-cultural efforts, aiming to create alternative institutions that could eventually overtake and make mainstream, hierarchical institutions obsolete.

25 Historically, some anarchists have also participated in theater, Esperanto advocacy, and nudism.

7

Social capital in anarchist movements

Those who build walls are their own prisoners. I'm going to go fulfill my proper function in the social organism. I'm going to go unbuild walls. (Ursula K. Le Guin, *The Dispossessed*)

Social capital and Bourdieu

"Anarchists of the world … unite!"

This tongue-in-cheek joke reflects the commonly held belief that anarchists do not work well with others. Most people assume that anarchists are extreme individualists, unwilling to compromise, or collaborate in groups (i.e., every person is "an island," completely independent of others). In reality, this is far from true. Anarchists prefer to work on projects, in groups, or within relationships where their participation (and everyone else's) is voluntary, not coerced, and where the power relations are equally balanced and power is not monopolized by a small group of people (Ehrlich 1996; Graeber 2009; Milstein 2010; Shantz 2010; Ward 1996). This is not only possible, but is the standard operating procedure in anarchist movements. The social phenomenon at the crux of this conception of organization is social capital.

Social capital theory has not typically held a central place within the sociological study of social movements. For many movement scholars, social capital is a theory of peripheral significance, subordinate to the popular theories discussed in Chapters 4–6, a few exceptions aside (see Diani 1997). However, I seek to prioritize social capital theory here for three reasons: (1) movement scholarship has typically overlooked things that keep inner-movement solidarity alive; (2) social capital is highly relevant to radical actors like anarchists (as I argue in this chapter); and (3) a closer interrogation of the multiple targets of "trust" demonstrate highly anarchist (and non-anarchist) orientations, which makes trust (a key component of social capital theory) relevant to the study of movements. Social capital – the valuable and exchangeable social connections individuals have with others – is one way of approximating people's relationships to each other. Movements both require social capital in order to form and succeed, but movements also create social capital through their organizing efforts.

This chapter explores ideas from major social capital theorists, including Pierre Bourdieu, James Coleman, and Robert Putnam, and considers the value of social capital (which is infrequently utilized in movement analysis) for anarchist movements. Important attributes of social capital, such as trust, information channels, norms, and others receive particular focus. A closer inspection suggests that the dense networks of anarchist association serve as a bulwark against state repression, but also alienates the movement from wider audiences, unless efforts are made to popularize discursive frames and organizing methods. Finally, I use the World Values Survey to explore the extent to which anarchist-inclined people – who trust in others, but lack confidence in government – are more apt to protest and advocate revolution.

Defining social capital can be challenging, but the French sociologist Pierre Bourdieu's (1986) conception may be the best. Capital can take on a variety of forms, including economic, human, social, and symbolic.[1] Social capital consists of social obligations or connections, which can be converted into economic capital. It is "the aggregate of the actual or potential resources which are linked to possession of a durable network of more or less institutionalized relationships of mutual acquisition and recognition" (1986: 248–249). By being members of a group, people have a degree of access to a group's "collectively owned capital." According to Bourdieu, capital of any form "takes time to accumulate" (1986: 241).

The possession of social capital depends on the size and complexity of the network that people can mobilize, as well as the quality and quantity of capital that people in that network have available to them. This network is a series of relationships premised upon efforts to socially invest in each other (whether consciously or not), in ways that help to grow and sustain these relationships for future use. Consequently, anarchist movements have greater capital to the extent that anarchist networks possess complex, diverse, and strong social connections. Bourdieu writes: "The reproduction of social capital presupposes an unceasing effort of sociability, a continuous series of exchanges in which recognition is endlessly affirmed and reaffirmed" 1986: 250).

Organizations are arguably one of the more important units of analysis when studying social movements (McCarthy & Zald 1977). Some scholars have applied social capital theory to social movement organizations (SMOs), with intriguing results (Diani 1997; Mayer 2003; Paxton 2002; Smith 1998). Thus, the breadth of social capital theory offers great opportunities to explain social movements and SMOs. In addition, anarchist movements ought to seriously consider how to improve their social capital in order to benefit their chances of goal-achievement, especially within the context of anarchist organizational forms (e.g., affinity groups, collectives, syndicalist unions, federations, or other projects).

Forms of social capital for anarchist movements

The various forms of social capital theorized by James S. Coleman can help to clearly define the important factors that contribute to such social capital. For those lacking economic and financial capital, social capital is a key means to not only individual agency, but also *social* change, particularly within SMOs. Social capital theory applied to social movements suggests that the common denominator of any movement is usually its raw, collective people power – both bodies and minds.[2] I describe the significance of Coleman's forms for anarchist movements below.

Sociologists and activists alike have long debated the contradictory degree to which social action is facilitated by agency and restricted by social structure.[3] For Coleman (1988), social capital is one immediate means of agency and it is created by people within the relationships they share. "[S]ocial capital is productive making possible the achievement of certain ends that in its absence would not be possible... Unlike other forms of capital, social capital is inherent in the structure or relations between" (1988: S98). Coleman (1988) describes three important forms social capital can take: (1) trust, (2) information channels, and (3) norms and sanctions.[4] Seen through these varieties, it is clear that social capital is an important "thing" created within social movements. Coleman's conception of social capital may be seen as akin to a particular operationalization of social resources, as described by resource mobilization theory (Edwards & McCarthy 2004); the very strength of movements themselves may derive from the accumulation and application of *social* capital. In other words, movements build social capital as a resource and then mobilize it when appropriate. According to Coleman (1988), individually useful resources like human capital (e.g., knowledge, skills, credentials) necessitate the acquisition and deployment of social capital in order to make an impact. Thus, people need each other in order to pursue social goals as well as their own private ends. Taken to its logical conclusion, social capital helps people working in movement organizations, groups, and networks to acquire the collective power that they would not possess as mere individuals.

The first form of Coleman's (1988) social capital is trust, which facilitates the exchange of expectation and obligation. The ties between individuals are stronger when there is greater expectation – people know they can rely on others to follow through on important or necessary tasks. Stronger ties foster a more intense sense of obligation, as friends, comrades, fellow participants, and activists feel they have to support each other. This obligation may be rooted in common values, shared experiences, or promises.[5] This form of social capital is clearly an unspoken component of the anarchist theory and practice of "mutual aid": the free exchange of physical, monetary, or political support with the expectation that others will in turn feel obliged to support them if and when necessary (cf., Kropotkin 1972). This activity feels very "natural" to most people and they seek out relationships in which they can practice mutual aid with others. Movements that encourage the practice of mutual aid are likely to have greater social capital and people are more likely to trust one another. Anarchists also place trust in others in ways that are contingent upon a person's position in a hierarchy. Thus, it is generally assumed that most "average" people are worthy of a degree of trust, while those in positions of authority are not worthy of such trust.

Trust is particularly useful in revolutionary movements where the risk of state repression is highest. Part of this deep trust is represented in the willingness to plan possibly illegal actions (e.g., property destruction against corporate property, blockading military depots, sabotaging logging equipment, supporting wildcat strikes, or unpermitted marches) with each other and the ability to assume that sensitive information will not be conveyed to anyone else, whether loose-lipped associates or police. Sharing secrets in a safe manner is an important practice in radical movements and anti-authoritarian direct action plans tend to be kept strictly within the immediate social circles that are involved in the planning. A key example of such trust is that found within the SMO called an "affinity group": small groupings composed exclusively of people who know, trust, and share common identities with each other. Affinity groups are similar to families, but deliberately built around political commitments. They may engage in contentious politics and challenging activities – such as militant protest or other direct action – that require strong trust and support from the affinity group.

Coleman's (1988) second form of social capital – information channels – can also lead to the empowerment of social movements. By personally knowing people who have valuable information, one has less need to independently gather information. Thus, there is "information potential" in our relationships with others. Social capital is fostered and accumulated when activists create and regularly exercise communication through radical information channels. As the networks of communication broaden within movements, it is easier for those movements to understand the obstacles they face. Even within geographically diffuse networks, people may remain in contact through telecommunication and internet technologies, such as cell phones, email listserves, and groupware (software that facilitates organizational decision making via democratic and collective methods).[6] Activists rely on each other to gather important information, such as on-the-ground observations about the layout of a city's downtown area, which is useful for planning a protest, civil disobedience, and a variety of direct actions. If one's comrades know whom to contact in other communities, this would provide valuable information when seeking allies and broader solidarity. Most importantly, anarchist networks are premised upon free access to information, whether it is mere data, facts, analysis, ideas, or theory. Consequently, anarchists place an emphasis on lowering the cost – economic and social – to information (via free 'zines, leaflets, internet essay archives, or guerrilla radio programs), the democratic creation of movement analyses (such as with the Independent Media Center model), and mass distribution of news (for example, the A-Infos News Service and its accompanying free radio project). To the extent that these information channels permeate every sector of anarchist movements, the more likely participants will be highly engaged in important movement debates and theorizing, will have up-to-date understanding of current events and movement activity, and will feel a sense of unity with each other (even if sometimes nuanced or contingent). The quality of information people can acquire in these networks determines the level of social capital and thus influence the potential of movement personnel's ability to achieve their goals. Movements can aspire to accomplish their goals by wielding information as a tool to combat ignorance, confusion, censorship, and seclusion.

Coleman's third and final social capital form manifests in social norms, which facilitate certain actions while constraining others. If a movement norm exists that calls on participants to help each other out, even in extreme situations, then the movement will be stronger. Norms can facilitate social capital in all manner of situations. For example, if police attempt to place a fellow demonstrator under arrest during a physically confrontational protest, a common anarchist norm encourages other demonstrators to assist the person facing arrest. The norm of "de-arresting" exists especially when using "black bloc" tactics, which involves demonstrators physically pulling such an arrestee away from police officers, removing that demonstrator from police "custody." If the de-arresting is successful, the targeted person is pulled deeper into the bloc's ranks and helped to disappear from observing or pursuing police. This anarchist norm contributes to the social capital of all participants, as they understand that others will "have their back."

The norms – and potential sanctions – lobbied against those who deviate from these expectations within SMOs help to create and sustain a radical culture of both internal and external criticism. For instance, acting in the interest of the collective is often a SMO norm. Therefore, meetings and events are managed collectively, open-endedly, or with popular input. This fosters greater social trust. Also, as mentioned, if illegal activities (civil disobedience, direct action, property destruction, etc.) are potentialities for the anarchist movement, participants tend to make broad, general statements in support of such actions, but withhold relevant details from individuals not within one's own affinity group. This norm of "security culture" prevents law enforcement from gaining accurate or useful information about an organization or action (Robinson 2008). Violating this norm would result in informal sanctions from other anarchists. A "loose-lipped" individual: (1) will be educated and pressured by others to understand the accompanying risks of sharing private information, (2) is unlikely to be trusted as much in the future and (3) may perhaps be asked to leave the organization. A regular violation of such a norm (especially by multiple individuals) is apt to harm the social relations on which social capital rests. For example, intervention by government and corporate actors (in the form of subversion, spying, and disruption) is more successful when the security culture norm is weak or non-existent. In such instances, agent provocateurs may be used to disrupt, frame, or set up activists (see Boykoff 2007). Thus, movement sanctions are key methods for improving adherence to important movement norms. Strong social trust in an organization may seem to enable the state's use of agent provocateurs, as people may unwisely place trust in a new member who is actually interested in spying or subversion. But, equally strong social norms against dangerous SMO behaviors can serve as a bulwark against misplaced trust, too.

Social capital benefits can also be generalizable. Arguably, a key objective of a *social* movement is to achieve changes that benefit a group of people larger than the movement's immediate participants. Thus, the social capital acquired by a particular movement can benefit members within an entire social category. For example, feminist movements create benefits for all women and female-identified people in society, not just participants in that movement. Anti-racist movements benefit the members of all disadvantaged groups (such as racial, ethnic, or religious minorities), not just those who populate anti-racist organizations.[7] Gains by anarchist movements – to expand the domains of freedom, to challenge the legitimacy of hierarchical institutions, to create alternative institutions founded on radical values – indirectly benefit others in a society who can use such accomplishments for themselves (this extension may or may not actually enhance social capital itself, for everyone, though, but may just extend its immediate benefits). Thus, social capital's democratizing benefits are different from economic capital where usually only those who invest in such capital forms enjoy benefits.[8]

The dualities and disappearance of social capital

Perhaps the most famous work on social capital has been Robert Putnam's *Bowling Alone* (2000), which describes – in incredible detail – the long decline of social capital, community, and participation in American society.[9] His work describes a number of dualities that are highly relevant to the analysis of anarchist movements.

A first crucial duality concerns what a social capital effort actually attempts to accomplish. Sometimes people seek to improve the strength of their existing social relationships and in other moments the goal is to expand those relationships out to new groups. Both these efforts are crucial for the long-term vitality of social capital and human communities. Putnam (2000) describes these two efforts as bonding and bridging, respectively. Social capital bonding aims to improve the capital among those who already share relationships, enhancing their ties to each other. Bonding is an internally focused social capital effort. For anarchists, bonding helps to create intra-movement solidarity. By introducing and bringing more closely together those who identify as anarchists, a movement enhances the connections among individuals and the trust within that movement. This bonding is crucial, since without internal social capital, coordination is difficult – if not impossible. Various groups within a poorly bonded movement will not feel a sense of solidarity for each other, or extend mutual aid when needed.

Social capital bridging attempts to create connections between otherwise unconnected people and groups. Bridging crosses divides that may exist and bring diverse groups into closer contact and affinity. It is an outwardly focused effort to enhance social capital. For example, anarchists may seek to improve relations between anarchists with divergent ideological orientations, such as anarcho-syndicalists and anti-civilization anarchists. In addition, anarchist movements regularly pursue bridging whenever speaking to or working with non-anarchists. Thus, any broader organizing effort involves social capital bridging. For example, the 1999 demonstrations in Seattle against the World Trade Organization brought diverse people together, uniting them under a radical critique of corporate-led globalization. By connecting anarchists to non-anarchists, the connections multiply and trust grows across movements and in relation to the general population. For any movement to grow and spread its ideas, bridging is a crucial prerequisite. It thrusts movements into contact with those who have different ideas or those who are not yet "converted" and hopes to gain new adherents, allies, sympathetic audiences, or at least to not make new enemies.

While bonding and bridging accomplish separate goals, both are necessary for movement strength, flexibility, and potency. Bonding and bridging functions operate in different spheres of movement activities, yet can easily coexist. As movements are networks of individuals and organizations – who sometimes acquire allies outside the ideological borders of that movement – bridging happens across movement borders, while bonding happens within. Recall the network diagram of the North American anarchist movement in the 1990s and 2000s (Figure 1.1): outside of the dotted lines of the anarchist movement borders, anarchists occasionally collaborate with left-ists, mainstream unions, certain non-profit organizations, the Catholic Worker, alternative spaces, and the punk scene. Internal to the movement itself, the different organizations, factions, projects, structures, and press work to discuss matters of strategy, tactic, and ideology, to share news, and to facilitate and maintain solidarity.

A second duality that Putnam (2000) explores is between those who either choose to do formal or informal social organizing. He identifies "machers" as those who invest lots of time in formal organizations. These people are the heart and soul of community groups and the driving forces that make things happen. As such, machers are more organized and purposeful in their actions. Many anarchists engage in macher activity: doing community organizing with diverse non-anarchist populations (homeless rights organizations, immigrant populations, pro-choice clinics, militant trade unions and workers, and others). Other machers consciously form organizations – explicitly "anarchist" or not – through which further activities and campaigns can occur. Transparency, outreach, and formality are key efforts of anarchist machers. When acting openly, machers are displaying values to others, clearly declaring their intentions, and are making themselves accountable to others. In the extent to which macher anarchists speak and act reliably, they will likely incur trust from others.

Another population, those called "schmoozers," spends much of its time engaged in informal conversation and communion, eschewing efforts to wade through formal organizations. Schmoozers are more spontaneous and flexible in their schedules and efforts, and more willing to relate to people individually as opposed to groups of people in formal settings. Many anarchists, of course, pursue these activities, too. Anarchists often hang out with each other and meet people in informal scenes, socializing at parties, squats and social centers, in cultural settings, after political rallies, or at other meeting places. The anarchist schmoozer may give intense attention to a small number of people or maybe even just one person; this creates a strong bond, although typically fewer overall connections. Schmoozers create more spaces for private trust to emerge, independent of formal decisions made in organizations and public coalitions. Schmoozers exchange political analysis, ideas, and values in intimate settings, especially when such information is of a private nature. The sharing accomplished in these informal environments enhances individual trust. Both the machers and schmoozers seem to reflect qualities of Etzioni's (1965) categories of instrumental and expressive leaders, respectively – the first contributes in practical and clearly defined ways, while the second contributes to the overall mental well-being and motivation of groups.[10] Machers are much more likely to be represented in the projects cataloged by the Anarchist Yellow Pages (see Chapter 3) than the schmoozers who work within more informal relationships that are less likely to be recorded.

A key concern for Putnam (2000) is the comprehensive decline in social capital in the USA (changes elsewhere in the world have not been investigated as thoroughly). He considers this decline in social capital to be detrimental for civil society and for representative democracy. For American anarchists, other severe consequences result from declining social capital, which does not bode well for revolutionary social transformation.

According to Putnam, there are various, general sources of this decline in social capital. With each source, it is worth considering how they affect anarchist movements and such movements' capacities to pursue a revolutionary agenda. First, pressures of time and money have forced people to work more, work longer, and have less time for community and social activities. This is particularly true for middle-class women who have traditionally had more opportunity to pursue these activities because male-breadwinners' salaries allowed them to stay out of the labor market. There is a seemingly endless drive and economic imperative for work in order to pay bills, consume products, and build individual careers; all of this detracts from the ability (and desire) of people to focus on others and, thus, foster transformative social capital.

If the anarchist movement still had a strong anarcho-syndicalist orientation, this increased focus on work might serve as an entry point into radical workplace and union politics. However, this ideological subvariant within anarchism (especially in the USA) is about as weak as the overall labor movement's community organizing efforts. Consequently, everyone – including many anarchists – spends more time doing things that do not directly result in greater political awareness, class-consciousness, or radicalism.[11] A possible counter-balance to the destructive results of this social capital-decreasing factor is simple: work less. Instead of spending so much time engaged in wage labor, an anarchist could – indeed, many already are – find alternative ways to have their economic needs met. Whether through house cooperatives, food-sharing networks, and other mutual aid projects, people could further extract themselves from labor markets and capitalist enterprise. To do so would require developing economic survival mechanisms that transcend anarchist subcultures. The benefit for social capital would be two-fold: people would have more non-employed time available for community and social capital building, and the necessities of alternative survival would themselves reinforce stronger social ties with people.

A second source of decreased American social capital is mobility and sprawl. For decades, urban dwellers have been uprooted (willingly and unwillingly) from their traditional, more-or-less organically created neighborhoods. The clearest indicator of this is the dramatic growth of suburbs, which are generally more affluent, white, and inaccessible to other groups. This suburbanization – as well as the block-busting, red-lining, white-flight, and other racial dynamics that helped drive it – has created relatively homogeneous neighborhoods, in terms of both class and race. But, as a permaculturalist would argue, monocultures are not only devastating for nature and food systems, but also for human communities. Impoverished people and people of color residing in the centers of major cities lack the economic and cultural capital that affluent individuals took with them to the suburbs. People in the wealthier suburbs lose contact with people different from them, develop callousness towards the problems of "others," and simply do not understand what is going on a few miles from where they live. Since many Americans move regularly (even every year), there is little chance for people to develop long-term, stable relationships with neighbors or to feel responsible for their community. The sprawling nature of suburbs makes it more difficult for residents to reach other areas they seek to go to, thus requiring long periods of travel, usually solitary in cars. None of these factors bode well for maintaining social capital.

The solution to this problem is relatively simple to state, but harder to accomplish. Anarchists argue that there is no easy way to create community – it is hard work, which requires establishing long-term trust. To do this, people must be brought into closer contact. Classic community organizing approaches do this: bringing together diverse people who share common interests and allowing them to see each other's human worth, figure out how to trust each other, and articulate a shared vision and course of future action. This is, unfortunately, easier said than done. But anarchists often advocate clustering together in communities.

During the early 2000s, after the protests against the Republican National Convention, I heard rumors that there were entire anarchist neighborhoods in Philadelphia. And other cities have communities like this: the Exarchia neighborhood of Athens, Greece has a strong anarchist presence, as do many areas with squatted social centers in cities like Barcelona and Rome. In the city I lived once lived, the Catholic Worker (which was not necessarily anarchist) owned four houses on a single city block, which allowed residents and volunteers to share resources, do communal activities, and maintain strong face-to-face communication. Living in community does not require living communally, of course, although group-houses, squats, intentional communities, and other co-living options help. Close proximity is itself a partial solution to the malaise that long distance inflicts upon social capital.

Third, Putnam observes that technology and mass media have helped to destroy social capital. A key culprit is television. There are numerous reasons why TV has had a detrimental impact upon social ties, but two bear repeating. The first is that even though people may watch TV in groups, it is usually viewed alone. Moreover, although TV can be viewed collectively, it does not mean that it is a collective activity, since the focus is upon the TV, not each other. It is difficult to communicate, share, and focus on anything else except the TV program. Since TV watching has been shown (Kubey & Csikszentmihalyi 2004) to induce a cognitive state comparable to sleep, TV viewing numbs our emotional and social abilities to interact with others. A second reason why TV is detrimental pertains to the portrayals typical to TV. Deviance, law-breaking, extreme personalities and behaviors, violence, individualism, and other programming themes suggest to viewers that people in the outside world cannot be trusted.[12] The more TV people watch, the less they believe others can be trusted.

The anarchist solution to the scourge of hierarchical TV programming is not for the insertion of anarchist TV programming on mainstream channels. Instead, most anarchists have advocated a solution similar to that for overworking: turn off the TV! It is impressive how much extra time can be liberated in a person's day when it is not wasted away with idle TV viewing. While this is a hard sell to audiences who are seduced by highly sophisticated and well-funded programming (the purpose of which is to deliver advertisements to audiences), it is still an important goal. Instead of relying on stupefying TV news to convey information, anarchists ought to pursue and expand on the strategies already used by many anarchist newspapers (and within other medium), like the UK's *Freedom*, which engages directly with ongoing events, adding a subtle anarchist spin, analytical perspective, and aesthetic. The key is engagement: one of the benefits of Indymedia was that people could participate in the creation and propagation of media, but do so directly with each other and discuss it without proxy (something that TV has never allowed for).[13] By communicating with people about things that matter – during days when there is far more time and less propaganda – there is a greater likelihood of growing social capital. Then, in lieu of individualized activities (like TV-watching), collective activities deserve encouragement: neighborhood sports, potluck meals, festivals, collective work projects, and participatory entertainment.

Lastly, one of the most serious sources of declining social capital, according to Putnam, is an inter-generational one. From generation to generation, ever since those who came of age during the Great Depression and World War II, people have had less and less involvement in community. Newer generations have been more severely affected by this phenomenon and have not had the same crucial community-building opportunities that earlier generations had. Baby Boomers were considered highly individualistic by their parents, as was the so-called "me generation" of those growing up in the 1980s. Current cohorts will likely be even more individualistic, as they rely upon personal consumption and technology to differentiate them (often remotely) from each other.[14]

Radical socialization was one of the main ways that classical age anarchists kept inter-generational ideas and values strong (see Williams 2011b). Anarchist families and communities kept anarchism alive in order to pass it along to youth. A strong, adversarial-to-capitalism working-class culture enabled this. However, with the deliberate destruction of working-class culture, the buying-off of class allegiances, and the elimination of whole sectors of the economy that employed working-class people, these cultures of resistance disappeared. Combined with political repression with the Palmer Raids and the McCarthy era, new radicals often had to re-discover older traditions for themselves, independent of an older generation who would otherwise have taught them directly (see Cornell's [2016] study of anarchism in between the classical and contemporary periods). By focusing on inter-generational anarchist socialization, the ideas can persist and possibly strengthen over time. But focusing on maintaining anarchism over the life-course, by continual, ongoing socialization and education projects, anarchist movements can keep adherents connected as they age and change their roles in society (especially in becoming parents). Making sure that anarchism does not remain the domain of a youthful age group is key. Designing movement activities supportive of people's familial obligations by providing childcare and having safe, family friendly events, will further this end (Law & Martens 2012). Also, giving older people a role in anarchist movements will keep people around for longer; thus, a static movement that exclusively emphasizes militant street protest is unwise, as it will exclude people with reduced physical capacities, whether due to ability or age. Taken together, these strategies suggest methods for reinvigorating social capital, especially for anarchist movements.

The remainder of this chapter focuses on a number of issues and questions pertaining to trust. First, how did classic age anarchists speak of and write about social trust? What do contemporary anarchists do that consciously bonds and bridges social capital? And, who are the likely recruits for anarchist movements? In other words, who has a positive orientation toward generalized social trust, but does not have political trust in authority figures? Existing survey data is used to explore the extent to which certain types of people are horizontalists or hierarchicalists when it comes to trust. First, I turn to classic era anarchists' words regarding trust.

Classic Age anarchists and trust

While seemingly off-topic in a book on contemporary anarchist movements, classic age anarchists illustrate the long-term consistencies in anarchist movements' attitudes regarding trust. The following is a completely non-probabilistic sampling of classical anarchists' words – and, although these words come from well-known anarchists, there is no reason to suspect that rank-and-file anarchists did not agree with and hold views similar to these. An obvious, initial observation is that anarchists used the word "trust" in two different ways, one of which has slightly gone out of fashion in English. First, they refer to relationships between people, and second, to an economic structure (i.e., huge, monopolistic, economic entities). The latter meaning can be excluded here as largely irrelevant to the topic of this chapter.

Anarchists focused on a variety of themes when discussing trust, ranging from what happens when trust is put in certain people and how trust is demanded from some, to the need to withdraw trust from elites and placing trust in social equals. For example, Malatesta (1974) argued that placing trust in governments generally, but state socialist managers in particular, would "[lead] to the exploitation and oppression of the masses by the few" (1974: 47). According to Kropotkin (2006), when trust is placed in the powerful, especially the state, people will end up not trusting themselves and each other: "By too much trusting to government, they had ceased to trust to themselves; they were unable to open new issues. The State had only to step in and to crush down their last liberties" (2006: 182). Additionally, elites demand trust from their subordinates. Thus, Bakunin (cited in Maximoff 1953) argued that no one with power should be trusted, as "anyone invested with authority must ... become an oppressor and exploiter of society" (1953: 249). He also argued (Dolgoff 1971) that even revolutionaries would abuse people's trust, "try to squelch the popular passions," and "in the name of the Revolution, seized and legalize ... their own dictatorial powers" (1971: 180).

Classic age anarchists thus believed there was no need to trust elites. Goldman (1969) wrote: "Time and time again the people were foolish enough to trust, believe, and support with their last farthing aspiring politicians, only to find themselves betrayed and cheated" (1969: 64). Indeed, anarchists argued for withdrawing their trust from elites. Berkman (2003) claimed that the elite's power was illusory if people withdrew their support: "Now, what makes governments exist? The armies and navies? Yes, but only apparently so. What supports the armies and navies? It is the belief of the people, of the masses, that government is necessary; it is the generally accepted idea of the need of government. That is its real and solid foundation. Take that idea or belief away, and no government could last another day" (2003: 177). Peter Kropotkin (2006) hypothesized that social trust is a *natural* thing: "The sophisms of the brain cannot resist the mutual-aid feeling, because this feeling has been nurtured by thousands of years of human social life and hundreds of thousands of years of pre-human life in societies" (2006: 228). Further, Kropotkin suggested that the state supersedes and supplants people's ability to trust each other.[15] Later in this chapter, I quantify these anarchist assumptions by illustrating who may be the best candidates for recruitment to anarchist movements and where the biggest challenges to anarchist organizing reside.

In Kropotkin's famous *Encyclopedia Britannica* entry on anarchism, he wrote: "since the foundation of the International Working Men's Association in 1864–1866, they have endeavoured to promote their ideas directly amongst the labour organizations and to induce those unions to a direct struggle against capital, without placing their faith in parliamentary legislation" (cited in McKay 2014: 165). The IWPA itself wrote in its "Pittsburgh

Declaration" that "Whoever agrees with this ideal, let him grasp our out-stretched brother hands! Proletarians of all countries, unite! Fellow-workingmen, all we need for the achievement of this great end is ORGANIZATION and UNITY!" The later International Workers' Association also advocated for worker solidarity and trust, in "The international bond of struggle and solidarity that unites the revolutionary unionist organizations of the world." Of course, anarchist organizations are not strictly labor-based anymore, but the same sentiments continue in contemporary anarchist movements.

Contemporary anarchist movements bonding and bridging social capital

Among contemporary anarchist movements, social capital bonding and bridging takes a variety of forms, including some described here. Movements possess both an inward and outward focus and anarchism is not remarkably different in this regard. There is a need to maintain current participants while also attracting new ones in order to further transform society. These can be split into internal movement discussions and activities that bond capital among current anarchists, while also organizing and building coalitions with non-anarchists (or not yet anarchists). For example, anarchists spend a great deal of time together debating current events, and trying to determine and position an anarchist analysis in relation to those events, as well as working with other movements, participating in revolts and engaging in propaganda efforts. Bonding can be seen as more personal, cathartic, and joyful, while bridging seems to be more political, practical, and instrumental. But, bridges can be built between anarchists and those who are not yet involved with anarchist movements by attracting people by portraying anarchism as cathartic and joyous.

Consider anarchist book fairs as an example of social capital dualism. Book fairs are free, public events where anarchists, as well as those sympathetic to or interested in anarchism, convene, to give away, trade, and sell anarchist literature, socialize and network, and listen to anarchist speakers. Book fairs serve both bonding and bridging functions. In the festive environment of book fairs, many diverse people mingle and socialize, which encourages dialogue and the formation and reinforcement of rough consensus among anarchists. But, book fairs also serve to bring in those curious with the *spectacle* of an anarchist gathering as well as to invite non-anarchist allies to enter into dialogue and engagement with a local area's anarchist movement. The bonding and bridging impact of these book fairs has yet to be thoroughly analyzed, but the impacts are likely considerable as well as geographically widespread. A 2017 list compiling anarchist book fairs throughout the world counted 65 in total, in countries as diverse as the Czech Republic, South Africa, Portugal, Sweden, Russia, and Brazil.

Formal and informal anarchist social events, such as those held at squatted social centers in Europe, help to bond social capital among participants and attendees. Social centers and the social events sponsored by them serve as epicenters for anarchist organizing and they create and nurture strong affinities between movement activists. More formal social events – like music concerts, art shows, and festivals, bring in people who are interested in or attracted to alternative culture. In doing so, non-anarchist attendees get to visit anarchist-organized spaces, meet anarchists, and experience events that are structured in an anarchistic fashion.

Anarchist media and propaganda have dual purposes, too. Movement reporting takes place via A-Infos and Indymedia, and critique of that reporting and other discussions occur within the comments sections among the latter (as well as many other forum, including anarchist newspapers and websites). These media enable anarchists to address and debate internal disagreements, adjust ideological boundaries, and collaboratively plan movement strategy. Some of these media also exist as propaganda and thus have an external orientation, serving to bridge social capital with non-anarchists. "Agit-prop" (or agitation propaganda) is often more general and is values-based (e.g., the CrimethInc collective's materials "Fighting For Our Lives" and "To Change Everything"). Bridging via propaganda is meant to attract people who have anarchistic orientations (unidentified as such or even unconscious) into a more formal relationship with anarchist movements.

Finally, anarchists movements have also long pursued a "mass strategy" that mirrors the bonding/bridging dichotomy. Schmidt (2013) identifies the mass strategy as a two-pronged effort that anarchists have practiced for many decades. First, anarchists tend to form officially anarchist organizations (as shown vividly in Chapter 3), which allow for solidly anarchist politics and practice, getting all participating anarchists "on the same page," perhaps via conscious or subtle support for the tenets of The Platform. Second, anarchists participate in popular, non-anarchist organizations. This serves to link anarchists to not-explicitly anarchist struggles and organizations; but through such relationships and participation, anarchists infuse these struggles with anarchist content (i.e., anarchist ideas, strategies, organizational values, and goals).

Social and political trust: measuring potential pro-anarchist sentiments

While it is theoretically possible (although practically difficult) to empirically measure trust within anarchist movements, I wish to take a different approach to applying the above sociological insights. We can approximate the level of potential pro-anarchist sentiment within societies and, thus, estimate the "chances" for anarchistic movements to emerge. This also implies discovering the factors working against this potential for anarchist movements (i.e., people who are hierarchical in orientation).

The German social theorist Niklas Luhmann (1979) once wrote that "one who goes unarmed among [others] puts trust in them" (1979: 25). We can interpret Luhmann in a variety of ways useful to the study of anarchist movements. We may not need weapons, since everyone can be trusted. Or, we may need lots of weapons because *no one* can be trusted. Or instead of simple dichotomies, it may be important to have weapons trained upon our fellow equals, since other people cannot be trusted. Finally, weapons might be needed to be trained on those in power, since the state cannot be trusted. Each of these positions exemplifies a set of attitudes people may have about others who are their social equals and those who are in power (e.g., parliaments, the police, militaries, courts, etc.). Following Luhmann, we may need (or not need) weapons because of our perceptions of the threats posed by different social actors. Anarchists exemplify the position that other people can be (more or less) trusted, but that those with power are not to be trusted. Of course, people who are social equals can still harm us in a variety of ways, but anarchists generally believe in the potential goodness of ordinary people who are untainted by hierarchical power.

Thus, it is fair to argue that anarchism generally assumes that other people can be trusted to do what is right (and thus warrant social trust). Additionally, anarchists also caution to not trust those with power (and thus withhold political trust from state actors and other hierarchical institutions). While this combination of trust and distrust may superficially appear to be contradictory or confused, from the vantage point of anarchist movements, it is very sensible and compatible with anarchist values and history. Therefore, these two sentiments are combined in the following exploration of those who possess (or lack) social and political trust.

To combine these sentiments begs the question: "How do people tend to trust most other people and how do they trust authority figures?" Do people extend trust similarly to both groups, or does a negative relationship exist (i.e., as one form of trust increases, the other decreases)? The introduction of hierarchy creates problems: people are infinitely more trustworthy when they do not seek or possess power over others. An example of graffiti summarizes well the anarchist impulse about this dilemma: "Stop believing in authority and start believing in each other."

At the heart of anarchist's social assumptions are simple ideas about human nature. People have the potential to work well with others and to accomplish socially meaningful goals, and to do so without government. While not everyone can be trusted, the average person can be trusted far more than government agents (or others with hierarchical power). Thus, the typical anarchist social orientation extends social capital among social equals, but limits social capital among non-equals (those in possession of power). The varied nature of the targets of an individual's social capital is a useful way of thinking about not only who anarchists are (and what kinds of other social characteristics they possess), but also how non-anarchists are different from this pro-anarchist social capital.

Here I propose a way to quantify (although not without flaws) the anarchistic orientations towards socio-political trust possessed by people throughout the world. I utilize a large, cross-national survey called the World Values Survey (WVS) to determine the varied levels of social trust and political trust for people in dozens of countries. The WVS asks questions pertaining to: (1) "generalized social trust" (the extent to which people believe that others can be trusted, or that one "cannot be too careful"); and (2) political trust (the level of confidence people have in a variety of political institutions). These two types of variables clearly address fundamental anarchist values, first of mutual aid and social solidarity (in the case of social trust) and anti-authoritarianism (in the case of political trust). These variables can be combined to establish a socio-political trust measure, suitable for estimating individuals' anarchistic tendencies.

I use the single measure of social trust from the WVS, but combine (into an index) two different political confidence measures to estimate political trust. The WVS asks about confidence in all sorts of hierarchical institutions, including churches, militaries, government, political parties, and major companies (to name a few). However, I use questions pertaining to just two institutions: parliaments and police. I do this for two reasons, one theoretical, one pragmatic. First, I argue that parliaments are each country's top law-making bodies, while police are the law-enforcing agents. Thus, combining these two institutions joins the law-makers with the law-enforcers. Second, the WVS did not ask about each of the many possible institutions listed above for every country sampled by the WVS. Also, there is a universality to these two selected institutions that is not possessed by other institutions; for example, armed forces are sometimes very popular expressions of national pride, just as they are often the brutal enforcers of statecraft (if not the actual power-brokers themselves, in the cases of military juntas).

Most cross-national research in the past (Levi & Stoker 2000; Nannestad 2008) has found a weak, positive correlation between social trust and political trust – so, if people possess social trust, they often also possess political trust. Vice-versa, those who lack social trust, often lack political trust. However, this overlooks two key groups (that should be immediately obvious to readers): people who lack social trust, but possess political trust, and people who possess social trust, but lack political trust. In other words, assuming social and political trust are correlated minimizes the observation of those with hierarchical, stratified orientations towards trust (the first alternative above), and those who have a horizontalist orientation toward trust, that appears distinctly anarchist (the second alternative). Table 7.1 shows a typology of these orientations towards social and political trust.

As it turns out, very few countries have a substantial anarchist-orientation toward trust. Of 46 countries analyzed in the WVS, the average "horizontalist" percentage of the respondent population was 7.5 percent (Table 7.2). In other words, fewer than one out of ten people in these countries trusted each other while simultaneously distrusted the state. This fact indicates the formidable hurdles for anarchist movements to overcome. If anarchist movements necessitate social trust *and* an opposition to state power, then very few people would seem to be even open to joining such movements, let alone likely to do so.

Of the countries that were one standard deviation above the world mean for horizontalism (countries with a 12.7 percent horizontalist population), most do not have many – if any – representation in the organizational databases described in Chapter 3. Only the Netherlands (15.8 percent

Table 7.1 Typology of socio-political trust

	Confidence in hierarchical institutions	No confidence in hierarchical institutions
Don't trust others	Hierarchicalists/ authoritarians	Distrusters/paranoid
Trust others	Trusters/gullible	Horizontalists/social anarchists

Table 7.2 International distribution of anarchist potential, percent of socio-political trust categories

Category	Country with the highest percentage of category	Overall average percentage of category	Country closest to overall average
Hierarchicalist	Uzbekistan (81.8)	41.2	Estonia
Distruster	Peru (70.3)	34.5	Uruguay
Truster	Sweden (54.5)	16.8	Russia
Horizontalist	Yemen (27.2)	7.5	Sweden
Total		*100.0*	

Note: Data from World Values Survey, Wave 6 (2010–13); 46 countries horizontalists) had a considerable number of anarchist organizations and Russia has seen considerable growth since the fall of the USSR. However, Kyrgyzstan, Pakistan, Ukraine, and Yemen have virtually no above-ground anarchist organizations on record. Thus, it is worth noting that even the existence of socially trusting anti-state people does not indicate pro-anarchist individuals – they could be right-wing, religious fundamentalist, or simply apolitical. Also, respondents' opposition to state authorities may be reflective of just *who* those authorities are (e.g., not the respondent's favored political party) than a systemic opposition to those authorities in principle.

While there surely are weaknesses to survey data in general and this data in particular, this sort of analysis is illustrative. It suggests that there are vastly different orientations toward socio-political trust throughout the world. Still, caution is warranted at the preliminary stage of such research; just as with all surveys there is the potential for conscious and unconscious biases. First, respondents may be unwilling to honestly assess their trust, perhaps because they are living under a dictatorial regime. Second, respondents may be incapable of accurately assessing their trust – they may not understand what trust is or may have false consciousness about the trust they claim to have. Regardless, this general strategy of contrasting social trust with political trust may bear promising fruit for future analysis of anarchistic individuals and societies.

To be clear, the above data does not indicate the presence of *actual* anarchists. But, if we could compare anarchists' social capital across space, we would likely find some interesting patterns. For example, people who reside in a geographic area with a strong movement, especially within an anarchist scene, likely experience stronger social capital and get more opportunities to live anarchistically. These anarchists probably "get it" (i.e., understand and internalize anarchism) more than others who discovered anarchism independently of an active movement or scene. Independently socialized anarchists may have to "guess" and "interpolate" more than others when it comes to anarchist ideas and practice, likely having to draw upon anarchist literature opposed to direct experience.

Conversely, it is also worth considering if it is possible for a community to possess *too* much social capital, particularly if heightened social capital comes with social compulsion. It is possible that too much social capital could dampen individual freedom and autonomy. Thus, tight-knit communities may seem more empowered, but may be less free in an anarchist sense. Durkheim's insights here are potentially helpful: the strength of mechanical solidarity derives, in part, from commonality and similarity (Durkheim 1964). Presumably stable and free anarchist communities would need to strike a balance between under-regulation and over-regulation. Durkheim (1951) noted that under-regulation results in anomic indecision and chaos, while over-regulation results in fatalistic limits and strictures. If indeed "anarchy is order," anarchist social relationships with too much "strong" social capital may foster conditions contrary to anarchy.[16]

The significance of social capital for anarchist movements

Anarchist movements that focus on their access to, caring for, and deployment of social capital, will likely be more successful than those that ignore such concerns. This is particularly true to the extent that social capital is linked to movement strength. Anarchist movements would benefit from enhancing participants' social trust, expanding information channels with others, and solidifying norms and propagating expectations.

Specifically, by seizing opportunities for social bonding and bridging, anarchists can, and will, likely increase their social trust. Bonding necessitates growing trust inside of a movement or scene; this does not require every movement participant to be alike or to agree on every issue, but it *could* mean that. Strategies for fostering social capital bonding include creating more opportunities for social activities that take place outside of pure political action, sharing perspectives and engaging in sympathetic discussions, and trying to enhance the respect and tolerance that participants have for each other. Social capital bridging requires the establishment and nurturing of connections between anarchists and non-anarchists. These connections are most easily made between overt anarchists and implicitly anarchistic people, but connections to other potential allies are clearly important. Similar strategies as with social capital bonding could be beneficial with these anarchist-to-non-anarchist bridging efforts. Most obviously, this could include creating spaces and setting aside time to socialize and debate with liberals, community groups, and statist-Leftists, but pains must be taken to not subordinate anarchism and anarchist SMOs to the will of such erstwhile attitudes, which sometimes have lukewarm or even hostile sympathies toward anarchists and horizontal organizing. However, traditional outreach, propaganda, and organizing efforts with heretofore "unorganized" or apolitical people may be the most efficacious use of anarchist social capital bridging energy.

In terms of the latent anarchist potential found in others – understood via my proposed socio-political trust typology – many opportunities exist to appeal to the existing orientations of others, as well as to encourage the development into a more complete anarchist orientation. For example, anarchists could seek out individuals who "ought to be" more open to horizontalist values, since they would already be the most sympathetic to an anarchist world-view and practice. More deliberate strategies would have to be used to reach out to distrusters, to help them move toward a horizontalist perspective; this would require fostering greater social trust, perhaps via opportunities to see that strangers are not necessarily to be feared, that other people have decent intentions, and that people can help each other out when need be. Trusters would seem to be a bit too naive regarding political trust toward state elites, so anarchists ought to target them with arguments and experiences that illustrate just how untrustworthy such elites are. Hierarchicalists are clearly the furthest from an anarchist position. Here, two choices could be pursued by anarchists: attempt to keep such people as apolitical or un-active as possible (by various strategies of discouragement?), or attempt the equally challenging task of reversing their non-anarchist orientations (improving their social trust, while depressing their political trust). Given how pro-state (or, cast differently, pro-fascist or authoritarian) this position is, efforts may be better allocated toward encouraging distrusters and trusters toward anarchist positions.

Notes

1 The forms of capital present are dependent on the "field" in which they function (Bourdieu 1986).
2 Charles Tilly notes the importance of mass participation; he emphasizes the importance of WUNC (worthiness, unity, *numbers*, and commitment; Tilly 2004); see Chapter 4.
3 Anthony Giddens (1984) proposes a solution to this supposed dichotomy, through his theory of structuration.
4 Later, in his magisterial – albeit dense and abstract – work *The Foundations of Social Theory* (1990), Coleman ruminates upon three additional elements of social capital, the first two of which are far less relevant here; these include authority relations, appropriable social organization, and intentional organization.
5 See Graeber's (2011a) work on the importance of "debt" in social relationships.
6 The Riseup Collective's "CrabGrass" software project is a prime example.
7 Additionally, feminist and anti-racist movements also indirectly benefit privileged people (e.g., men and whites), as the elimination of domination facilitates egalitarian social relations, happiness, and greater social trust (Williams 2012).
8 This, of course, introduces the problems of free-riding (see Olson 1965), which may be overcome by value-driven action as opposed to purely "rational" action, social pressures to participate, small-sized groups, and a fair and even distribution of collectives goods in society.
9 Many of Putnam's results are clearly generalizable to other societies, too.
10 Leadership should be interpreted critically. Anarchists have varying definitions for "leader," but all indicate that no person should have the ultimate control over the actions of individuals or groups. Social capital clearly plays a role in the construction of leaders and allegiance to

leadership. But, Nepstad and Bob (2006) describe how such "leadership capital" is at odds with anarchist values and practice.

11   Indeed, more work just leads to alienation, social injustice, and environmental devastation (Crimethinc 2011).

12   This is particularly true for some TV programming, but less true for other programming (Lee *et al.* 2003). Additionally, TV viewing with non-strangers (e.g., family members) further reduces social trust (Patulny 2011).

13   Of course, another reason for high rates of activist participation with Indymedia, pertains to its organizational structure which imitates desired anarchist social relations.

14   Recent American generations have become more narcissistic and less empathetic (Konrath *et al.* 2011; Twenge & Foster 2010).

15   Durkheim, who was sixteen years younger than Kropotkin, argues similarly that a pre-contractual solidarity exists among members of a society. Thus, they do not need to meet and discuss ground rules before they know what to expect from each other – they simply engage in accepted behaviors from the beginning of their relationship (Durkheim 1964).

16   Niman (2011) describes how Rainbow Family self-policing strategies rely on trust, respect, and social capital, thus facilitating strong social order, far more than external efforts by state authorities. There is also the possibility for latently coercive groupthink in small or tightly knit anarchist movements.

Part III

Interaction

8
Radical isomorphism and the anti-authoritarian diffusion of leaderless organizations

Once you begin to look at human society from an anarchist point of view you discover that the alternatives are already there, in the interstices of the dominant power structure. If you want to build a free society, the parts are all at hand. (Colin Ward)

Nothing better than a good idea

Anarchists are commonly depicted as selfish iconoclasts who could not cooperate with others even if their lives depended on it. Owing to this perception, the idea of an anarchist movement, which coordinates among large numbers of self-identified anarchists, seems impossible. This chapter addresses how such coordination is possible, by focusing on anti-authoritarian approaches to the spreading of anarchist ideas and organizational strategies. I apply research on diffusion and institutional isomorphism to the organizational forms and tactics often chosen by contemporary anarchist movements. In particular, I investigate a number of organizational templates that have spread globally in recent decades, which are not only replete with active anarchist participation, but also infused with anarchistic values, objectives, and organizational strategies. The different processes at work in these popular anarchistic projects are described, showing the numerous pathways for the diffusion of ideas and organizational strategies. The decentralized resilience of these organizations and the continued diffusion of common approaches indicates that anarchists tend to consider these to be favorable strategies.

In general, copying a failed idea is not a great strategy. For example, anti-authoritarian socialists – who criticized the Soviet Union – often argued that the Bolsheviks tried to pursue a social revolution via the same institution that all other countries used to enforce their capitalist economic systems: the state. Although Marx and Engels claimed the state would eventually "wither away" with time to become truly "communist" (Engels 1966), the "revolutionary" Soviet state took on a persistent inertia that lasted decades, replicating a state that was as totalitarian and repressive as under the Czar. From its beginnings in 1917 to its fall in the late 1980s, the Soviet Union served as a principal example of what dissident libertarian socialists consider to be the inappropriate use of hierarchical structures to achieve social equality.[1] Other post-Lenin Marxists – from Mao to Castro – followed the same Marxian prescription: seize military dominance, establish party supremacy, and silence non-Marxist critics. Predictably, these "state communist" societies are highly similar to state capitalist systems. For example, the Soviet Union and many Eastern European countries copied the bourgeois state-form and were not able to run the economy very differently than capitalists had, even after they seized power. The one difference was that the state owned the means of production instead of a capitalist class.

On a more strategic level, the same criticisms are leveled by anarchists at the mainstream Left's tendency to utilize the same organizational structures as mainstream politics: political parties. Thus, many Left-statist political parties, including the Communist Party, Greens, Labor Party, and Socialist Workers Party advocate following the same route as mainstream parties (for example, in the USA, the Democratic and Republican parties, or Christian democrat and social democrat parties in Europe), by gaining a large membership base, using elections to get their candidates elected, and then taking over the governing apparatus of the state.[2] Anarchists have argued that this is a fundamentally flawed approach for Leftists interested in changing the world, since it leaves intact the major institution that protects modern capitalism. As anarchist Mikhail Bakunin famously wrote: "Take the most radical of revolutionaries and place him on the throne of all the Russias or give his dictatorial powers ... and before the year is out he will be worse than the Czar himself" (quoted in Guérin 1970: 25–26). This concern over the replication of institutional features – in this case, hierarchy – is the starting point for the subject of this chapter: where do anarchists get their tactics and organizational forms from?

There are very few examples of anarchists in the popular culture for aspiring or established anarchists to copy. In fact, the small number of examples available to most people are rife with the three misperceptions discussed earlier. These poor examples are funneled through the lens of the domination network, which benefits from portraying anarchists as violent, chaotic, and naive. These characteristics are not only undesirable ones to replicate, but also rather ineffective or difficult. Indeed, the lack of positive, accurate examples of anarchists in the mainstream of most societies means that anarchists have had to seek out organizational and tactical ideas by discovering and reading about historical examples, or locating rare subcultural scenes where practicing anarchists operate. Consequently, anarchists face numerous challenges for their behavioral and practical operation that are not faced by other movements, let alone the general, non-anarchist population.

There is also an absence of scholarly research on non-hierarchical diffusion, as well as a theoretical explanation for how such diffusion occurs. Whereas most sociological research on diffusion and isomorphism has focused on mainstream organizations (like corporations) or reformist social movements, anarchist movements pose a particular challenge to earlier findings focused on these non-anarchists. Unlike the reliance upon central coordination and leaders, anarchists eschew hierarchical strategies of movement growth in favor of decentralized, leaderless networking. Anarchists presume that using principled means will help ensure the best possible ends, an approach opposite that of Left-statists who theorize that a free society can be created via the hierarchical state.

I focus on four specific leaderless organizations that I term "anarchistic franchise organizations" (AFOs). These organizations include Anti-Racist Action (ARA), Critical Mass (CM), Earth First! (EF!), and Food Not Bombs (FNB). These AFOs possess anarchistic values, aesthetics, and strategies. Here, "anarchistic" means they do not necessarily claim anarchist identity, but possesses anarchist qualities (refer to "implicitly anarchists" in Chapter 1). I call them AFOs to highlight their value-anchored orientations, and that there is an organizational quality to each (even if only loosely expressed). They imitate the general style of "franchises" that are set up in different geographic locations – independently operated, but similar in many ways to each other. Unlike other franchises (e.g., sports teams, fast food restaurants), AFOs are not *forced* to behave in a certain way, no central authority regulates their behaviors or interactions with each other, and no authorization occurs to approve of their founding and operation. With the exception of CM,[3] these AFOs are also formal organizations. This means they self-identify with a name, have internal norms and rules, and are fairly permanent in nature. All four of these AFOs appear in the Anarchist Yellow Pages introduced in Chapter 3 – although only a very small percentage of the existing local collectives of each are listed. Even though these four AFOs are the main focus here, there are many other things that anarchists call "projects" that are relevant as leaderless, decentralized initiatives, such as ''zine "distros," affinity groups, reading circles, graffiti crews, prisoner-writing groups, book fairs, and many more. Although some of the above lack the trappings of formal organizations (i.e., official names, positions, decision-making structures, etc.), the following analysis still applies to them, too.

Inventing the wheel

Movements generally and social movement organizations (SMOs) specifically have life-cycles. This means that there is typically a discernible beginning and end to their existence, even though those points may be debatable or only perceived in hindsight. At the beginning of movements and SMOs' formation, we ought to ask: why this type of movement or organization, and not another? In other words, sociologists continue to grapple with the issue of movement formation. And, why do some movements or organizations end? Does the demobilization of movements or the folding of an organization indicate that it was a less-attractive option compared to other alternatives, or was it ended through external pressures? Or other reasons?

SMOs may have a variety of origins. Some are complete innovations: they are unique to their time and place, and do not resemble any other comparable SMO. This may be very rare as movements are constantly evolving from earlier movements, learning from the past and copying from contemporaries. Thus, many SMOs are likely "mash-ups" or combinations of new and old ideas. For example, FNB is acknowledged to have diverse influences (ranging from the anti-nuclear movement to the San Francisco Diggers and the Black Panther Party).[4] Finally, an SMO may be a simple copy of an already existing model, just applied in a new situation. Thus, the black bloc protest tactic is an application of tactics used by the German Autonomen in the 1980s (see Geronimo 2012).

The intentionality of those adopting examples is a key concern. Some SMOs intend to fill a void, niche, or need. For example, anarchists may choose to create a radical reading group if they perceive a lack of "intellectualism" around their local anarchist scene. Thus, anarchists are often very rational about their organizational choices, seeking practical solutions to perceived problems. Or, SMOs may be founded independent of such voids, niches, or needs. Such organizations may be more a consequence of participants' own purposes and desires. Anarchists may start a squatting group, even if a lot of relatively cheap and affordable housing is available. If there is adequate vacant housing that makes it easier to squat, such efforts may or may not be a pressing political or organizing need.

The conscious replication of other models can serve various purposes. Surely adopters hope to accomplish what other like-SMOs have achieved in other places. The success (whether empirical or simply perceived) of a FNB collective in a city like San Francisco may increase its attractiveness to people in other places. Replication seeks to capitalize on the innovations of an SMO, particularly its anarchistic qualities, as well as its anti-anti-anarchist qualities (i.e., resistance to internal-hierarchy formation). Black bloc strategies, for example, seem to be able to avoid police surveillance, so local anarchists may adopt those practices in a protest even if a black bloc has never been locally used. This easy replication reduces the necessary mobilizing time and the need to strategize more about local conditions. People can quickly read or talk about a mass bike ride (e.g., Critical Mass), and just go out and do it, without requiring much effort or planning.

Diffusion and isomorphism

The practices of borrowing from other times and places are referred to differently by various scholars. Social movement scholars speak of diffusion, while organizational sociologists analyze institutional isomorphism. While related, these phenomenon – and the adjoining research literatures about them – are distinct. Movements and SMOs diffuse by spreading geographically, often (in organizational terms) by adopting the same structural features as other similar organizations. According to Snow and Soule (2010), diffusion is "the spread or flow of some innovation through direct or indirect channels, across actors in a social system" (2010: 193). Consequently, diffusion occurs through both direct (i.e., personal networks and communication) and indirect (e.g., media) channels. Diffusion is what SMOs sometimes do, while isomorphism is the occasional nature of that diffusion. Often isomorphism refers to any replicated organization or organizational attribute, not just those within social movements. Thus, isomorphism involves diffusion, but the kind of diffusion that is patterned and "similar."

Soule (2007) has defined four elements of social movement diffusion. These elements work together to accomplish tactical and organizational diffusion. The first element of diffusion is a transmitter or source, often people or organizations that have already done something. For example, experienced anarchists and early innovators (such as FNB founder Keith McHenry) are key transmitters. The second element is a corresponding adopter (or target) who begins employing the already established practices. The adopters are those who are interested in acting (consciously, at least), but don't yet know what to do. These could be younger people who are interested in anarchist ideas, but have not encountered fellow anarchists. The third element of diffusion is the innovation being diffused. An innovated "object" could be a name, idea, strategies, or set of practices, which are possessed by a transmitter and are attractive to an adopter. In the case of EF!, the name "Earth First!," an idea like "no compromise in defense of Mother Earth," and strategies like tree-sitting may be attractive innovations. Finally, a channel or medium is needed along which the innovation may be transmitted. In some cases, diffusion for anarchist movements happen via the anarchist press (magazines, books, websites), while in others the channel is face-to-face communication, such as in local anarchist scenes.

Depending on the actors involved in diffusion, different processes can result (Snow & Benford 1999). The transmitters and adopters can be either active or passive, and the combinations of these orientations cause varied outcomes. For example, *reciprocation* is a process in which an active transmitter interacts with an active adopter. Many anarchist collectives do this in respect to each other, especially those involved in a federation, wherein they mutually influence other collectives. The same could be said for anarcho-syndicalist unions, who reciprocate in the context of their international union. Social movement scholars are in agreement that diffusion does not occur when a "transmitter" and "adopter" are both passive (thus the skeptical quote marks). However, it is conceivable that some movement actors may be active, while others are passive. *Adaptation* is a process in which an active adopter gleans from a passive transmitter. The originator of an idea, organization, or tactic is not actively involved in diffusion – the adopter is the one borrowing. Here, many AFOs are "taken" by adopters – and sometimes modified – with little participation from the actual innovators. While *accommodation* is another conceivable diffusion process, where the transmitter is active and the adopter passive (Snow & Benford refer to a proselytizing religious movement as an example of this), this is far less likely with anarchists. Thus, of the various combinations of active and passive diffusive processes, reciprocation and adaptation are most likely for anarchist movements – wherein the adopters have an active role in the process. Consequently, the anarchist models of diffusion lean toward a proximal practice, as opposed to a hierarchical one (see Soule 2007). A hierarchical model of diffusion involves top-down interactions from high-status to low-status actors. It is unlikely that influential anarchists (to the extent to which such people exist) would be able to get others to adopt strategies, except via moral or rational appeals. Instead, a proximal model is more relevant: actors mimic others who are spatially or culturally relevant to them. Thus, witness the diffusion of plaza encampments in the early 2010s or anarchist book fairs.

Soule (2007) argues there are two primary ways to conceive of tactical diffusion. First is Tilly's (1978) "repertoires of contention" – sets of tactics that are available to people at a certain time. A flexible repertoire allows people to observe others' tactics and adopt them when deemed effective (e.g., street protest repertoires). Second is Tarrow's (1998) notion of "modularity," which assumes that tactics are understood and used by people, who can readily deploy them within movements in any situation. Thus, there are no mandatory, direct linkages to unite movements together. It is conceivable that many AFOs are easily selected "solutions" to local issues and struggles – the AFO is the module that can be fitted into the local context.

The pathways of diffusion along relationships can be relational, non-relational, or mediated (Tarrow 2010). Relational pathways work through pre-existing relationships where there is the presence of trust, intimacy, or regular communication between transmitters and adopters. For anarchists, "travelers" may move from place to place, spreading ideas through their contacts in different locations. Or, an older generation of activists can pass along ideas to younger generations of activists. Non-relational pathways require an adopter to learn through impersonal means (e.g., media). Mainstream or movement-controlled media sometimes mentions (sometimes inaccurately or with bias) ideas, organizational forms, or tactics, or even constructs "how-tos" for readers to follow. Finally, mediated pathways require adopters to learn from third-parties who know both the adopters and initiators. These third-parties are not themselves initiators. Thus, someone who once saw an AFO "in action" could be inspired by that experience and pass it along to someone who eventually adopts it.

The second research literature relevant to understanding AFOs focuses on institutional isomorphism. DiMaggio and Powell (1983) refer to isomorphism as the process of homogenization. The processes that make many organizations very similar can be categorized by three different operating mechanisms: coercive, mimetic, and normative. These mechanisms lead organizations like universities, churches, sports teams, government agencies, hospitals, military units, corporations, and many other organizations to have very similar structures to other organizations of the same category, even though there appears to be little rationale for those similarities. Anarchist movements in general – and AFOs in particular – are surely influenced by these three mechanisms, although in ways very different from most mainstream organizations. There is likely less influence of coercive isomorphism, while mimetic processes and normative pressures are surely more responsible for similarities among anarchist organizations.

Coercive isomorphism stems from political influence and the need for legitimacy. Since government organizations do not "oversee," regulate, endorse, or certify anarchist projects, the influence of this mechanism is less direct. Sometimes this mechanism leads to change as a direct response from government mandates or other actions. Thus, law enforcement infiltration and informants have led activists to behave differently, such as in Earth First! It is common practice in EF! for activists to adopt "activist names," which are distinct from their legal names. These alternative identities allow for a separation between activists' personal and political lives, preventing police from connecting the activists they spy on (e.g., doing "forest defense") and their private identity (perhaps as tax-paying citizens who have "straight" jobs). But, this practice (across EF! chapters) is more of a negative *reaction* to government action than an effort to acquire legitimacy from that institution. Inter-movement pressures may result in certain common traits, which may be adopted to garner legitimacy from fellow anarchists.

Mimetic processes are undoubtedly more influential on AFOs. This mechanism is a standard response to uncertainty. By copying or duplicating (i.e., mimicking) an existing practice, the likelihood of a predictable response or success increases. Thus, if anarchists do not readily know what kind of project they want to do (or if they have ambiguous goals), there are pre-existing templates ready for adoption that streamline the work needed to "get active." While DiMaggio and Powell (1983) refer to trade associations or consulting firms as agents that diffuse practices, anarchist conferences or book fairs are events that bring anarchists into close contact, thus facilitating the diffusion of ideas from transmitter to adopter. If activists perceive some groups to be fairly legitimate and successful (e.g., established AFOs), they may pattern their own actions after those very models.

Normative pressures are typically associated with professionalization. While there are no true "anarchist" professions or institutions to regulate anarchism, it is not difficult to see how a loose, albeit unofficial "professionalization" occurs with anarchists. Professionalization often encourages similar orientations and dispositions (in addition to policies and skills). For anarchists, such orientations and dispositions are transmitted through anarchist subcultures. The socialization in local anarchist scenes encourages participants to have common expectations (e.g., regarding dress, personal behavior, vocabulary, methods of speaking and operating). Anarchist subcultures exists within these local scenes, in larger gatherings, and is also transmitted via anarchist media (the equivalent of "trade magazines" in anarchist movements).

Some glaring shortcomings exist with the organizational studies which constituted the early elaboration of institutional isomorphism. Powell's (1990) influential article called "The Transformation of Organizational Forms" is symptomatic of the general trend in organizational literature: it starts with lofty, admirable, and broad purposes, yet cascades into dry, uncreative analysis of capitalist businesses. The whole range of organizational forms is reduced to a narrow band of profit-seeking social groupings, discounting the countless non-profit, voluntary associations that exist in society. If "organization" refers to a formalized collection of individuals, Powell and his many colleagues in organizational studies have been misusing, or at least narrowing, the term "organization" for a long time.[5]

Although these for-profit corporations and workplace organizations are dominant and ubiquitous, they do not represent all organizations, thus this field overlooks voluntary, non-profit, and democratic organizations (a category in which anarchist organizations would be included). So, what about organizations that are disinterested or even opposed to the "profit motive" of corporations? If other "motives" are driving the activities of anarchists, how well can isomorphism scholarship explain these radical movements?

Organizations that exist for non-monetary profit reasons, such as the majority of activist-oriented groups are also left out of this implicitly pro-corporate interpretation of "organization." Although many activist organizations are run as if they were businesses – having experienced "professionalization" pressures, often to meet grant requirements, to gain legitimacy, and to Taylorize their "outreach" – many others are not. Some activist organizations have boards of directors, presidents, and layers of bureaucracy, while others have none of the above, and have been strident in their resistance to such pressures (see INCITE 2007). How can we explain the existence, functioning, and change of voluntary, non-professionalized organizations, using the otherwise very good, general ideas of institutional isomorphism expressed by DiMaggio and Powell (1983)?

Of course, there are all sorts of *wrong* things to copy, from the vantage point of anarchists. Destructive characteristics that lead to internal implosion – long before the usefulness of an organization has come to fruition – is not ideal. Organizations that self-sabotage or do not last long enough, are not ideal to copy. Strong leadership dynamics are even more repugnant for anarchists, wherein the organization is either run by or dominated by a single person or a small, unaccountable cabal. Organizational characteristics that compromise anarchistic principles and nature for the sake of expediency or convenience are unhelpful; since a relatively unique characteristic of anarchist movements is the emphasis on pre-figuration and the alignment of means and ends, shortcuts to social transformation are not only contrary to values, but also to success. Finally, an organization that does things that are detrimental to the wider movement (e.g., attract police violence upon everyone else) or stymies moves towards revolutionary transformation are not desirable models to copy.

Isomorphism does not need to be only organizational in nature. Tactics can be isomorphic – the use of zines for communication, consensus decision-making inside groups, and black bloc-like protest formations are all tactical adaptations, not merely organizational. Issues may also be isomorphically transmitted; the things that attract the attention and inspire the reaction of anarchists can spread from location to location, such as the emphasis on anti-fascism, anti-militarism, or squatting. Finally, individual personalities or personas can be found from place to place. Anarchists often have comparable dispositions, interests, personality types, knowledge, practical skills, and more. It is debatable whether or not these individual characteristics are spread via anarchist subculture, or if anarchist movements attract people who already have certain dispositions or personalities. If the former case, then isomorphism is occurring, if the latter, it is not.

It is possible to determine if organizational (or tactical, issue, etc.) isomorphism is occurring. In the case of anarchist movements, we can see when entire categories of SMOs are created around the same time period. For example, ARA was founded in Minneapolis in 1987 (Snyders 2008), but by 1997 (according to the AYP; see Chapter 3), 46 ARA groups existed across Canada and the USA.[6] When many similarly titled organizations throughout anarchist movements exist in different locales, it is inconceivable that they were all independently founded in isolation of each other. Similarly titled SMOs that do the same kinds of things, regardless of location or personnel is another indication that isomorphism has occurred. The fact that all FNB collectives share non-meat food, that many of them "cater" at social justice protest events, or that they are outspoken on issues of war and homelessness is hardly a coincidence. Finally, isomorphism is likely occurring when we find evidence of the deliberate circulation of ideas, plans, and stories about these SMOs. Thus, if activist media are regularly discussing an AFO (even in one specific place), it is likely that information sharing is leading to isomorphism in the present moment or at some indeterminate point in the future.

An iron cage resisted

Numerous activist-scholar authors have also described aspects of this phenomenon, including some of the various anarchistic projects that I am labeling AFOs here. In each case, the following authors are emphasizing the benefits of a good example, the suggestion, but not mandate, of such examples, and the utility of copying labels and identifiers from context to context. While the examples and terms discussed here can be applied to many other anarchist or anarchistic projects, I stick to the four primarily under investigation in this chapter.

ARA and FNB are spread through "molecular dissemination" as they are "just an idea" (Graeber 2009: 236). Organizations like FNB constitute "decentralized service groups" (2009: 35); it is, along with other organizations, a "non-branded tactic" that tends "to spread in a viral way, with no one taking ownership or attempting to exercise control over how they are implemented" (Day 2005: 19). The *Recipes for Disaster* collection (CrimethInc 2012b) features a number of chapters (from different authors) that point indirectly to various AFOs. For example, "bike parades" (i.e., CM) are a "format" (2012b: 71),[7] ARA (as well as other anti-racist or anti-fascist actions) constitute "models" (2012b: 30), and FNB is "something between a strategy and an organization" (2012b: 165). Holtzman *et al.* (2007) suggest that both CM and FNB arise from DIY culture. Finally, Gordon (2008) argues that organizations like ARA, EF!, and FNB are "banners," essentially

> umbrellas under which certain parts of the anarchist movement act in a particular area. A banner, in this sense, is a convenient label for a certain goal or type of political activity, which can also – though not always – be accompanied by a concrete network, in the sense that people operating under the same banner in different locations have a significant level of communication tools (meetings, email lists, websites, a newsletter). (Gordon 2008: 15)

Thus, while these nouns – idea, non-branded tactic, format, model, banner – are different, they all suggest a similar set of processes and diffusion strategies. Here, I refer to these leaderless organizations as anarchistic franchise organizations, which I believe embody a set of overlapping agreements with the above authors' terms.

The AFOs I chose to review here are part of the most recent wave (from the 1990s on) of anarchist movement activity. All four are found in the

Anarchist Yellow Pages (although only a handful of local collectives for each). They are found across many countries, but they all appear to be strongest and most centrally located in the USA (an unfortunate, but curious, circumstance) likely due to their US origins. The local versions of each AFO possess the same name, style, program, and general efforts of most other local AFOs that share the same name. While insight into the processes of AFO diffusion could be gained by conducting interviews or gathering surveys on current and former local AFO founders, this strategy is not pursued here (mainly due to the difficulty of tracking down the initial founders of each local AFO). Instead, I rely on a more indirect method, which, although not as powerful, is still informative. I use existing research literature and popular writings on these AFOs, documents published by radical movements and the AFOs themselves (e.g., newspaper articles or self-published directories), and other sources.

The four AFOs have their own niche, issues, and practices. Anti-Racist Action is a direct action organization that confronts racism and fascism, sexism, and homophobia in its respective community. Critical Mass is a leaderless, monthly event where bicyclists take to the streets en masse to draw attention to issues of sprawl, oil consumption/auto-culture, and alternative transportation. Earth First! is commonly engaged in eco-defense, usually of old-growth forests, road construction, or mineral extraction by the techniques of blockades, tree-sits, and other tactics. Food Not Bombs is a vegetarian food-sharing organization that commonly aligns itself with the homeless and anti-militarism.

There is no centralized authority to determine which local AFO qualifies or gets "approved" as an official organization; new groupings of individuals simply declare themselves to be a new, local version of an organization which already exists elsewhere. Even though legitimacy is immediately claimed without the need for external verification, each AFO possesses principles that are generally accepted for all new local meme organizations. Although each organizations is autonomous, many interact and share information, ideas, and resources with each other, and provide solidarity in campaigns. People more central to the founding circles of a certain AFO may investigate a new AFO in order to determine if it is truly living up to its normative expectations. Regional, national, and sometimes international gatherings of group members helps to spread ideas and sometimes leads to the creation of more formal links, such as networks and federations.

None of these AFOs have anything even remotely approaching a centralizing structure (except a "federation" in the case of ARA), although they appear in large directories (like the AYP). Such listings suggest autonomy and erstwhile coordination, as opposed to centralization. Given the decentralized nature of these relationships, no true "official" databases or directories exists for AFOs. Various individuals or organizations take it upon themselves to catalog other active organizations, and trust that they are "legitimate" versions of the same AFO.

All these AFOs are founded on strong anarchist principles, a main component being direct action: providing for and addressing a very specific need or creating visible protest of current societal problems. Not all AFOs, nor their membership, would likely identify their organization as "anarchist," although many would. However, there is a clear affinity with anarchist ideals, not to mention the active participation of many self-identified anarchists within AFOs.[8]

It is impossible to know how many chapters or collectives of any of these groups are active throughout the world, let alone have existed in the past. Numbers will vary based upon access to first-hand accounts, duration of the group's existence, a group's definition of itself, and so forth. In fact, all that can be said about existing groups is that they must at least take to heart the general values of the group or movement. By identifying as a Food Not Bombs collective or an Earth First! group, people within the organization are defining their own involvement and organizational mission – much like Mead's (1964) "I" is what determines which "me," a group will collectively show at any given moment. New organization members adopt the general values they perceive in other organizations and internalize them as their own. By staking a claim to an organization that has a national or international presence, activists are placing themselves in a large movement that is greater than just their own local organization. Being part of a movement justifies their own actions as legitimate and part of something that others have already given meaning to.

Reviewing the main English-language webpages for the four AFOs under study suggests that the internet is an excellent conduit for mimetic isomorphism. Central webpages for all four of the AFOs include information regarding starting new organizations. Each has lists of suggestions to help people start a local collective in the spirit of organizations bearing the same name. Anti-Racist Action and Food Not Bombs even go so far as to number the recommended steps. All pages use authoritative language that range from soft suggestions ("To start an Earth First! group in your area, consider the following elements ...") to discourse that sounds like a direct order ("All ARA members and chapters MUST agree with everything we say in the Points of Unity"). The various recommendations appear to be crafted to help new locals get started as quickly and painlessly as possible. The past experiences of other local AFOs are used to show that the advice given to new groups is based on tried-and-trusted methods and practice.

All websites recommended some form of mass communication: email addresses, webpages, post-office mailboxes, telephone numbers and voice mail, fliers, and things similar to "xerocracy" (photocopier manifestos for distribution). The ability to communicate with each other, as well as making it easy for interested, prospective participants to find the AFOs is incredibly important. Since AFOs have political messages that are often usually well outside of mainstream discourse, corporate media and establishment political officials are unlikely to advocate on behalf of an AFO's actions or ideologies. Thus, finding ways to communicate their own message is of central importance for these organizations. In the following discussion, each of the four AFOs are described in light of this problem.

Anti-Racist Action

Anti-Racist Action (ARA) is a militant anti-racist organization that confronts white supremacist organizations and individuals, often neo-Nazis or the Ku Klux Klan. ARA often attempts to prevent rallies, marches, or other events organized by the aforementioned groups from taking place, arguing for zero tolerance of racist and fascist speech. ARA organizations and their members are united behind four general principles ("Points of Unity").

1 We go where they go: Whenever fascists are organizing or active in public, we're there. We don't believe in ignoring them or staying away from them. Never let the Nazis have the street!
2 We don't rely on the cops or courts to do our work for us: This doesn't mean we never go to court. But we must rely on ourselves to protect ourselves and stop the fascists.
3 Non-Sectarian defense of other Anti-Fascists: In ARA, we have lots of different groups and individuals. We don't agree about everything and we have a right to differ openly. But in this movement an attack on one is an attack on us all. We stand behind each other.
4 We support abortion rights and reproductive freedom. ARA intends to do the hard work necessary to build a broad, strong movement against racism, sexism, anti-Semitism, homophobia, discrimination against the disabled, the oldest, the youngest and the most oppressed people. We want a classless society. WE INTEND TO WIN!
(ARA Network webpage, "About")

These principles display a clear preference for direct action (also avoiding police and courts) and solidarity across political differences. Even though the organization is mainly oriented toward opposing racism and fascism, it also prioritizes an opposition to other forms of domination (e.g., poverty, patriarchy, homophobia). For these reasons, ARA may be considered an AFO.

ARA differentiates itself from other anti-racist organizations in terms of its analysis, strategies, and rhetoric. ARA can be compared with the People's Institute for Survival and Beyond (PI), another predominantly white anti-racist organization in the USA. O'Brien (2001) sees significant differences in how these two groups (one anarchistic, the other not) frame and define racism. ARA and PI can be presented as stark opposites:

> ARA seems more focused on raising the sheer numbers of ARA members and is not as concerned about educating them into any particular framework, provided that they agree to the four principles ... ARA members tends to be *selectively* race cognizant ... [which means] ARA members recognize how "racists" use race as a way of dispensing power and privilege but strive not to notice race in their own interactions ... For ARA members, colorblindness is a desired goal for all ... [and] prejudice in any form is the target, and the race of the perpetrator is of no concern ... ARA members challenge institutions such as the police force which they explicitly advocate in their principles should not be considered *allies*, much less should ARA members consider *being* police officers ... ARA members point to high attendance at protest events as a success. (2001: 136–139, all emphasis in the original)[9]

How has ARA grown over time? McGowan (2003) describes the spread of ARA from Minneapolis to other Midwest US cities during the late 1980s. ARA began as a response to fascist organizing within skinhead punk subculture. Anti-racists united together under the auspice of ARA in order to confront fascist organizers in their Minneapolis subcultural scene and to drive those people out of that community. Racist skinheads ended up in next-door St. Paul, Minnesota (McGowan 2003). The newly formed ARA took their name from the British Anti-Fascist Action (AFA) which had formed only two years earlier (Snyders 2008).[10]

After beginning in Minneapolis, ARA spread through the Midwest to Toronto, Columbus, and Chicago, and started to create an anti-authoritarian identity within skinhead subculture, attempting to oppose internal sexism but also banning American flags and other patriotic displays on jackets. As this anti-authoritarianism was nurtured, ARA began to interact with the existent anarchist movement of the 1980s and 1990s. In Minneapolis, relationships were formed between ARA and the Revolutionary Anarchist Bowling League (RABL). By the 1990s, RABL was instrumental in helping to found a cross-continental anarchist federation called Love & Rage, which also promoted and spread information about ARA in its newspaper. Anarcho-punks also circulated information about ARA, especially through the punk press, such as *Profane Existence* and *maximumrocknroll*. An ARA network was created in 1995, using the Points of Unity to hold together the many different groups. The Points of Unity also served to keep consistent values during a time of increased right-wing activity in the USA and a growing anti-racist response – which involved sectarian Left-statist groups who struggled for power within various ARA chapters. The peak activity of ARA was during this period in the mid-1990s, partially spurred on by anti-Klan activity throughout the country.[11] The experiences of ARA groups cross-fertilized with anarchists who began using black bloc tactics with greater frequency (McGowan 2003). ARA chapters also began to create CopWatch projects and spread that project throughout ARA social networks. First-hand and activist press were the main avenues for distributing information and news. For example, the South Chicago ARA chapter created a dense zine in 1999 that included information on how to form an ARA chapter, how to fight racism, a collection of writings and news from different ARA chapters, and a long directory of ARA chapters in North America (totaling 110).

Today, ARA websites advertise their message and methods. One main ARA website includes instructions called "How To Start An ARA Chapter." These directions implore interested persons to follow a number of steps in order to claim the name "ARA." First, the Points of Unity are implied to be mandatory: "All ARA members and chapters MUST agree with everything we say in the Points of Unity." Next, finding another ARA chapter is recommended. It is not entirely clear why making this contact is necessary, although it seems that existing ARA groups will provide assistance in starting new groups. Third, having various forms of communication channels available, such as an email address, a post-office box, and a voice mail, is encouraged. Again, the reason for this is not clear, although one can easily assume that it is to help manage the new organizations' growth and facilitating contact with new interested members. Fourth is publicizing the new group via pre-made fliers from the ARA network website (with local contact information) that can be hung up in a variety of local areas. The website also encourages other forms of advertising: T-shirts, buttons, patches, cultural events, and a website; for these, no template is offered and considerable autonomy seems to be implied. Fifth, as with any activist organization, the website recommends creating an email list of interested people and having regular meetings. Finally, direct action ought to flow from a local, community concern. The website suggests issues of police brutality, anti-choice harassment of clinics, or anti-immigrant activities as worthy targets of opposition and protest. The website's suggested steps sign off with a final attempt at inspiration, including a common rallying cry for ARA (and motivational framing): "Be Young, Have Fun, Smash Fascism!"

Critical Mass

Critical Mass (CM) began in 1992 as a norm-violating event in San Francisco that broadly targeted car culture. Cyclists gather together in a large group to travel on city roads. Owing to the number of cyclists, CM tends to take over the entire street thereby temporarily creating a car-free zone where cyclists can enjoy a safer form of travel, leisure, community, and engagement. CM is a form of direct action that many are able to participate in and that allows for community building, while incorporating recreation with an anti-authoritarian ethos.

CM's only real credo is the saying: "We're not blocking traffic, we are traffic!" This slogan reflects the semi-legalistic nature of the event, while trying to assert the inclusion of diverse transportation forms into a society dominated by the automobile. Blickstein and Hanson (2001) explain that CM has been

> referred to as a protest, a form of street theater, a method of commuting, a party, and a social space. Difficult to pin down, CM is often easier to define by what it is not than by what it is. It is not, for example, a formal bicycle advocacy organization. It has no dues-paying members, provides no particular services, and has no stated mission ... most Critical Mass groups share a number of common elements, including a decentralized network of organizers and the use of both traditional and cyber-facilitated methods of communication. Critical Mass' open form allows movement issues to be framed in ways that encompass multiple geographic scales and that mobilize supporters with a wide range of motivations for participating in the monthly rides. (2001: 352)

CM may be the most "formless" of the AFOs discussed in this chapter, as they lack membership, solid decision-making structures, or even official objectives. Anyone can help organize a CM ride; the routes are often either spontaneous or contingent upon rider votes, and many people bring diverse (and even conflicting) views and messages to a ride. In fact, while CM is ostensibly a rejection of car culture and an advocacy of the bicycle, many rides lack any direct messages to that effect – except by the mere presence of many bikes together. However, many riders likely share similar attitudes and the many possible messages related to CM can be spread among riders, such as "anti-oil wars," ecological protection, anti-climate change, sustainable communities, and others (see Carlsson 2002).

One of the most profound recruiting and diffusion methods for CM seems to be word-of-mouth communication. People who have first-hand experiences with CM – particularly those who attend rides that go well, in low-risk situations – are strong advocates for others to do the same. Experienced CM riders encourage people to attend rides and talk to people in other areas about CM. People then may seek out opportunities for rides elsewhere, or possibly start their own small ride. I have personally ridden with CM in five separate cities, across three US states. In each location, I have witnessed first-time riders experience joy from being on large, collective bike rides, and to subsequently speak favorably about attending again, inviting others to attend with them, or hoping to start their own ride elsewhere. We can call this the "meme of a good time," premised on spreading a joyful occurrence. That positive experience may be simply attached to pleasure (see Shepard 2011), but also may be political (liking CM's message) or practical (having group protection on a bike ride).

Today, numerous websites advertise CM bike rides. At least three large directories have existed in the last decade that list specific information for CM rides throughout the world, including starting times and locations, contacts, and other ride details. While these details can quickly go out of date if a ride dies out or changes its plans, it can also provide inspiration and indirect assistance in planning a new ride. People can easily triangulate the necessary details for their own new ride by viewing other locations' details.

Earth First!

According to Earth First!'s website, EF! "is not an organization, but a movement. There are no 'members' of EF!, only Earth First!ers." EF! identifies as a response to "an increasingly corporate, compromising and ineffective environmental community." By physically, legally, and politically stopping the destruction of the Earth, EF! aims to "[draw] attention to the crises facing the natural world, and it saves lives." Founded in 1979 and influenced by deep ecology philosophy, EF! rejects "human-centered" worldviews, in favor of an a view of humans as part (but not the most important part) of a densely interconnected web of life on Earth.

Typical EF! actions focus on raising awareness about threats to the local ecosystems, organizing with others to oppose those threats, and attempting to stymie threats. Most dramatically, EF! engages in photogenic civil disobedience (e.g., tree-sitting in forests apportioned to be cleared or blocking the office doors of corporations benefiting from resource extraction) and other symbolic direct actions. EF! groups adhere to their well-known slogan "No Compromise in Defense of Mother Earth!," and do not have paid professional staff or formal leadership. Instead, activists are encouraged to start an EF! group via a set of recommendations found online and in their newspaper.

EF! is the only AFO focused on here that has its own widely read magazine (which can be purchased in many mainstream locations). The *Earth First! Journal* has spread the concerns and practices of EF! far and wide. Since the journal has a directory in each issue, people can network easily with existing EF! chapters, and there is information about EF! in each issue that helps to explain EF!'s structure and how to replicate it.

A fair number of scholarly articles have been written about the activities of EF!, likely because of their prominence and the increased focus on environmental movements generally.[12] According to Ingalsbee (1996), EF! can best be understood through a symbolic interactionist lens. He argues that

EF! activists seek to mobilize symbolic resources that "represent socially constructed cognitive frameworks that help to psychologically and physically organize, unify, and empower actors for collective action" (1996: 264). This is done through a biocentric philosophy that identifies Earth First!ers with an "ecological self" and "the wild within." These symbolic resources aid in activist identification and mobilization. As such, "EF! symbolic actions are both means and ends of subverting the dominant technocratic worldview and constructing alternative ecotopian worldviews" (1996: 273), as well as functioning to create and utilize "dual power."

Shantz discusses what he calls "green syndicalism"[13] (2002a, 2012) and the attempts made by EF! to unite with exploited lumber workers in Northern California. Activist Judi Bari helped to create the IWW/Earth First! Local 1, to help organize these workers, who were often without union representation (or those in the International Woodworkers of America #73 who often found their union making concessions to management). Bari argued that workers themselves were in the best position to be environmentalists, but they first had to be approached in the context of their own workplace-based disputes and issues (Shantz 2002b). Interestingly, this red-green coalition in California was the only one of its kind. The failure of this strategy to disperse among other EF! collectivities could represent a growing aversion to creating coalitions with organized labor, perceived repression meted out to Bari and a colleague who was injured by a bomb planted in a car they were driving, or a lack of success with the IWW/EF! campaign.

There is undoubtedly an "ebb and flow" towards AFOs, as participation levels and activity changes, as does the number of active AFOs. This latter phenomenon is well illustrated by the fluctuation in the EF! chapter population over two decades (from 1990 to 2009), as shown in Figure 8.1. The 1990s was a high point for EF! activism, as the number of American EF! groups dramatically dropped after 2001. Across these two decades, the number of EF! groups was cut in half.

EF! in the USA changed at one point, thus the recruitment of new EF!ers also changed. A major transition occurred around 1990 as the original "redneck" constituency, which was more social conservative and interesting in monkey-wrenching, was slowly replaced by a social justice constituency (see Balser 1997; Scarce 2006). This change involved the incorporation of traditional "Left" concerns, such as union organizing, gender and race equality, and anti-authoritarianism. Ultimately, the "old guard" found itself in opposition to an insurgent anarchist constituency (Scarce 2006, especially pp. 87–90). The USA and UK have had active EF! chapters, but their foci have been somewhat different. In the USA, EF! may be best known for its forest defense, while activists in the UK have been strongly associated with anti-roads campaigns. Both countries have also had loose, but never official, affiliations with the Earth Liberation Front (ELF). Practically and officially,

8.1 Earth First! groups in the USA, 1990–2009. Source: EF!-labeled groups in the USA from the *Earth First! Journal* directory

monkey-wrenching actions (especially property destruction) today generally happen under the banner of the ELF, even though there is surely cross-fertilization between EF! and ELF participants.[14] The *Earth First! Journal* also provides thorough coverage of news pertaining to the ELF. The rationale and logic of AFOs can be easily applied to the ELF, too, as the ELF qualifies as both anarchistic and franchising.

Food Not Bombs

FNB collectives usually proclaim three or four general principles that include: (1) nonviolence, (2) consensus decision making, and (3) vegetarianism – and sometimes (4) food-recycling. The core practice for all groups is their efforts to cook and share food for free. Typically, food ingredients are either donated from local stores or individuals, gleaned from "waste-streams" (a fancy term to describe "dumpster-diving"), or grown in gardens. The people who usually eat FNB meals are homeless or other indigent groups, and thus food sharing happens in public spaces (e.g., parks or plazas) where such folks typically must congregate. Consequently, FNB is a strong advocate on the rights of homeless and poor people, associating the class inequality experienced by these people with a society's misplaced priorities. In the USA, where FNB originates, the plight of poor people is connected to the country's substantial military budget (approximately half of all federal government spending). Regardless of location, FNB's message remains the same: society is awash with food, and thus hunger is an illogical and avoidable phenomenon.

FNB is an easy organization to start, like many of the AFOs mentioned. Like CM, some of FNB's founders have also published a "how-to" book on their organizational creation (Butler & McHenry 2000). An entire chapter is dedicated to strategies for starting a FNB local, featuring "Seven Steps to Organizing a Local Food Not Bombs." These seven steps include: creating ways to contact the group; promoting it; figuring out transportation needs for FNB participants and the food; finding food sources; delivering food to other charities (initially); once established, skimming some of the collected food to give away for free; and then starting regular meal distribution as FNB. These suggestions reflect a classic organizing model, as well as an incremental approach to the task of saving and distributing food, with the ultimate goal of transitioning into a full-time FNB operation.

Different eras in FNB's early diffusion are discernible: when it first started in Cambridge, Massachusetts (1981–82); an "affinity group era" (especially FNB's presence in Nevada and at peace camps during mid-1980s); and its spread to San Francisco and Washington, DC. Then, following the news of the dramatic Labor Day arrests in 1988 in San Francisco,

FNB spread around the world, initiating an "international organizing era (1992–99).

Many things have circulated the *idea* of FNB throughout the world. Radical media has not only reported on FNB, but also actively promoted its efforts. For example, the Berkeley, California-based Slingshot collective featured a "How To Start a Food Not Bombs" entry in its 2009 calendar ("Organizer").[15] Many activists discover FNB through its presence at various peace, justice, and radical events. Local FNB groups often "cater" at Left activist events, providing food for attendees (thereby fulfilling a core anarchist value of direct action, to satisfy needs without the state or capitalist market). Activists who witness FNB in action at such catered events can carry the idea of FNB elsewhere. Some anarchists start FNB locals simply because of its affiliation with anarchist politics and subculture.[16] People who may wish to start a FNB group can also attend FNB "gatherings" which happen irregularly throughout the USA and the rest of the world. Regional and international gatherings have been held in various US cities, but also abroad, such as in the Ukraine in 2007. One of FNB's original founders in Cambridge, Keith McHenry, was responsible for transporting FNB to San Francisco and has since also spoken widely around the world, advocating for FNB values and various local FNB campaigns. However, beyond McHenry's own advocacy, there is little evidence of any central efforts to coordinate FNB's diffusion – FNB's diffusion happens horizontally by people discovering it somewhere and then transplanting the idea.

Spreading the message

As described, there are multiple pathways for the formation of AFOs – they are diffused through various mechanisms and distributed from various sources. What cannot be said with certainty are how each local AFO *generally* discovers an AFO template and decides to replicate it for themselves. To make that determination would require an in-depth survey of the founders of all the different, local AFOs under examination here – something that I have not attempted. Instead, I have mapped out idiosyncratic and probable connections. Surely some AFOs have established relationships with people in other comparable AFOs. In these cases, communication has flowed from those sources to the adopters. In other cases, though, there may be no connections – or at least any direct, personal connection. Here, people may have heard rumors of an AFO, seen the AFO presented in the media (whether activist or mainstream), or other source. Today, most of this indirect diffusion is occurring, at least in part, via the internet. Figure 8.2 visually diagrams some of these likely connections.

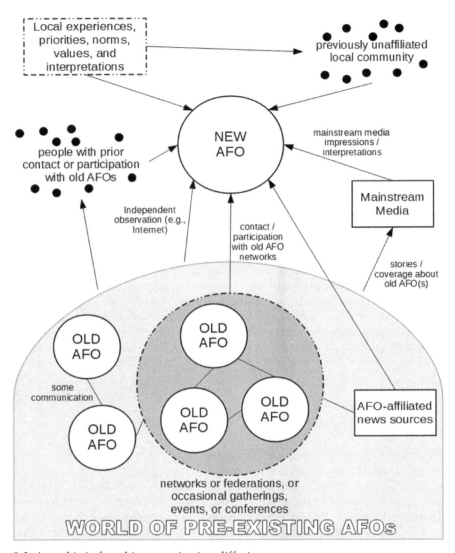

8.2 Anarchistic franchise organization diffusion

Finally, the role of mainstream media in AFO diffusion is not discussed here. However, there is not only that potential, but also indirect evidence for mainstream media as a diffusion channel. Established media channels may spread the name and ideas of an AFO to wide and diverse audiences. Even if no personal communication exists, indirect transmission through mainstream media can be potent, although the ideas of the AFO are filtered through the distorting lens of media and not conveyed (unfiltered) by actual AFO participants elsewhere. We can approximate how some of this may have happened with the AFOs under study here, by investigating mentions in major media, such as the prominent *New York Times*. The *NYT* has an incredible reach, wide readership, and inclusion suggests legitimacy.[17] While ARA has never been mentioned in the pages of the *NYT*, the other three AFOs have. CM was first mentioned on July 27, 1997 in a short story describing a mass arrest of more than 250 riders in San Francisco. This article appeared five years after the initial founding of CM and the bike ride would receive more mentions in the *NYT* after this.

EF! was included in an article from August 21, 1983 (during EF!'s "redneck" period), in which EF! critiqued mainstream environmentalists' relenting to the construction of high-voltage power lines across Montana. However, media hits of EF! in the *NYT* rapidly increased in 1990 when activists Judi Bari and Darryl Cherney were injured in a car bomb – as this occurred during "Redwood Summer" (named to reflect the famous civil rights movement era "Freedom Summer" of 1964). Media coverage also picked up on this campaign. Mainstream media relayed police accusations that EF! was transporting a bomb that exploded, thus allowing the anti-anarchist network to play up a key misperception: terrorism and violence. These charges were eventually revealed to be false, indicating that Bari and Cherney were the *targets* of terrorism, not the perpetrators.[18] Finally, FNB first appeared in the pages of the *NYT* on August 30, 1988 when 29 people were arrested in San Francisco for distributing free food in Golden Gate Park. FNB's advocacy for the homeless during this period and their continual arrests for food distribution led to even more media coverage.[19]

We can learn something of the diffusion pathways experienced by anarchists from consulting the Big Anarchist Survey (BAS) discussed in Chapter 2. The survey asked where respondents had "first heard about anarchism." While some respondents gave more than one answer, the results are telling. Online contact was the top answer (33 percent gave this answer), followed closely by "through friends" (30 percent), reading about it (25 percent), song lyrics (18 percent), and school or university (10 percent). Two percent stated that they first heard about anarchism from parents or family. We can see the general points of connection for AFOs, as described above, represented in these responses to the BAS. Also, the entry points for anarchism are radically different from in the past.

It should be noted that just because many AFOs have structures or rules that are "written down" somewhere, does not mean that those practices work well, are followed, or even reflect the intentions of those who originally made them. There are surely characteristics of these AFOs that are counterproductive, although many other characteristics have been "time-tested." It is highly unlikely that all local AFOs follow the general consensus held by all their fellow AFO relatives perfectly. Surely, some ARA chapters have been less militant, even reformist, just as some CM rides have negotiated routes with police. The complicated histories of all four AFOs means that they are not the product of just one person's "great idea," but a complicated result of hundreds or maybe thousands of early innovators who used trial and error, or even made random decisions.

Ultimately, most anarchist projects are not simple duplicates of others. Much innovation occurs alongside copying. Additional "tweaks" or customization is typically done to accommodate local conditions, and the personalities and preferences of participants. This is not only reasonable, but completely predictable. Thus, lesser or greater variation may be encountered when traveling between ARA actions, CM rides, EF! encampments, FNB food sharing events, and others.

In addition, a generalizable "anarchist culture" exists, permitting ideas – such as the design or components of AFOs – to flow from location to location, without requiring any direct or even indirect contact between fellow anarchists. Consequently, this anarchist culture allows anarchists to rely on their movement's basic values and history in order to construct meaningful and effective projects without requiring communication. Still, it is unlikely that such an anarchist culture would randomly result in similarly named and structured projects in the absence of the actual cross-fertilization of specific ideas about them. It is more likely that anarchist culture would lead to anarchist projects with different (although sometimes similar) names that have comparable structures, across space.

The significance of AFOs

Many conclusions can be drawn from AFOs. AFOs constitute relatively easy-to-copy previous anarchist strategies, tactics, and organizational forms. With little effort, a relatively recognizable anarchistic project can be initiated. Whereas much of the information and metadata on AFOs used to be transmitted through "old media" and personal contact, the internet has facilitated the wide proliferation of such ideas, thus creating vast potential for AFO diffusion and adoption. But, as with the internet generally, there is a risk of overload and confusion. Consequently, finding a usable model may be challenging for interested parties, and the information may be unhelpful or diluted, thereby resulting in an inappropriately applied AFO model.

A downside to readily adoptable templates are that the strategies for disruption are also easily transmitted, and readily adopted by law enforcement and the domination network generally. Common strategies for dealing with black bloc formations (the use of infiltrators and agent provocateurs), FNB (food sharing bans and enticement with "legal," indoors spaces), CM (over-policing and the deliberate division of biking subcultures), Earth

Liberation Front (informants, agent provocateurs), and even Occupy (nationally coordinated police raids on public encampments) have all had negative consequences for local AFOs. The modularity of activist actions can be matched with the modularity of suppression.

It may work best to mix and match characteristics. Borrowing some ideas, but adapting them to specific conditions in one's local context will make them more effective and resilient. The extent to which anarchists share analyses of how AFO strategies are working, the more capable local AFOs will be to adapt to changing circumstances, domination network suppression efforts, and the like. Speeding up the rate of innovation is crucial to outsmarting and out-pacing anarchist movement enemies.

AFOs are not always, or even often, explicitly anarchist; in some instances this is appropriate, whereas in other it might be good to formalize a project's politics. Formalized anarchist politics have certain benefits. The organization may be able to unambiguously take principled positions and actions if anarchist politics are open and transparent. This orientation may deter prospective members with authoritarian tendencies and plans, while also introducing interested people to anarchist ideas and practices. However, there are possible downsides to formalizing anarchist politics (in some cases). To identify as "anarchist" too early on may attract the state's wrath far sooner than the organization is able to defend itself. The label "anarchist" may turn some people off, owing to misperceptions of what that means, even among those who might otherwise be interested in participating. Likewise, it may discourage people who agree with the AFO's mission, but do not identify as anarchists and thus think they cannot, or should not, join.

Ultimately, AFOs are likely more helpful to those who reside in geographically isolated areas that have a low concentration of anarchists, and for people who lack experience starting an independently labeled project. They may be less useful for places where there are many experienced anarchists. In bigger cities, these models may be unnecessary, except for recruiting anarchistic people who are not-yet-anarchist identified.

Notes

1   Not coincidentally, post-USSR Russia has been plagued by similar problems of crony capitalism, mob–state collusion, and brutal violence against citizens (Cheloukhine 2008; Kneen 2000).
2   Can a movement be successful if it just repeats all previously failed efforts? Left-statist parties have decided to follow in Marx's footsteps, as this approach was advocated by Marx and the General Council of the First International in the 1860s and 1870s (Graham 2015).
3   CM may be more appropriately called an "occurrence" than an organization, since no real organizational structure tends to exist among its organizers and

participants. Many CM participants have called CM an "organized coincidence." We can still refer to CM as an AFO (anarchistic franchise occurrence).

4　See more on the connections between FNB and the Black Panthers in Williams (2015).

5　This is part of a more general criticism of organizational sociology which primarily focuses on workplace (i.e., capitalist) organizations (see H. J. Ehrlich 1977).

6　Record-keeping for AFOs and other anarchist organizations is highly challenging, as discussed in Chapter 3. Point in fact: McGowan (2003) describes the period 1995–96 as the high point for ARA, although the AYP's count in 1997 of ARA chapters is dwarfed by ARA's own tabulation in 1999, of 110 chapters in the USA and Canada (South Chicago ARA 1999). Incidentally, only 25 of these groups from 1997 and 1999 are the same (i.e., overlap on the two lists), indicating that the total count would be 131 unique groups in North America.

7　The "bike parade" chapter also suggests that "Critical Mass [is] the Food Not Bombs of bike parades" (Crimethinc 2012b: 71).

8　Of course, some local AFOs may be dominated by non-anarchists, non-radicals, or even non-activists. ARA may include Marxists or "apolitical" people; CM may involve large numbers of bicycle-mainstreamers; EF! can include liberal environmentalists; FNB may consist of students, Greens, and the highly religious. In such situations, there may be additional conflict between pro-anarchist factions and non-anarchists about how to execute the AFO's expected behaviors or how to interpret its traditional values.

9　This 1990s analysis of ARA is somewhat out of date and is not as accurate regarding ARA in the 2000s and 2010s.

10　AFA and ARA are generally categorized as "antifa" (short for antifascist) organizations. The word "racism" was likely chosen in the US due to a narrower experience with fascism, as compared to Europe. Antifacist has become a more important framing after the election of Donald Trump in 2016 and the resultant increase in fascist, alt-right, and far-right organizing in the US.

11　Interestingly, centrist Democrat presidencies seem to provoke the worst racist, right-wing activism, first with Bill Clinton and then Barack Obama, which quietened down considerably during George W. Bush's administration.

12　Far less scholarship has focused on ARA, CM, or FNB. Other anarchistic organizations do not receive much publicity (in either academic journals or the mainstream press), which results in few things written about them.

13　"Green syndicalism" may be yet another philosophy to create a more environmentally sound world, perhaps complementing other "eco-city" philosophies cited by Roseland (1997), that include two anarchist-influenced theories: social ecology and bioregionalism.

14　Molland (2006) describes the foundation of EF! in the USA, its diffusion to the UK, then the development of the ELF in the UK (mirroring the Animal Liberation Front or ALF), then the importation of ELF back to North America.

15 The 2009 Slingshot Organizer also featured a "how to" guide for CM, entitled "Ride Slow Talk Fast."

16 Curiously, many non-anarchists join FNB collectives, seeing it as a humanitarian or social justice organization, not necessarily an anarchist(ic) one. As such, FNB has been called a "gateway drug to activism" (Crimethinc 2012b: 165).

17 Social movement scholars have often used the *NYT* as a data source for protest events, although this is not a practice without controversy (McCarthy *et al.* 1996).

18 Various suspects of the bombing have been suggested since, including law enforcement, right-wing fundamentalists, and the timber industry. For more on Bari, Redwood Summer, and the car bombing, see Bari (1994) and Widick (2009).

19 Although I do not wish to dwell on the observation, it is worth noting that the coverage of these three AFOs centers on the San Francisco Bay Area and Northern California. Also, only political suppression and a bombing concretely broke these AFOs into the mainstream media first, not their practical politics or anarchistic values (the political equivalent of "if it bleeds, it leads").

9

Conclusion: Revisiting the epistemology of anarchist movements

Universities have consistently overlooked anarchism. Despite some remarkable but scattered studies in various fields, academics have never tried to form a school of thought based on anarchist paradigms ... Most research on anarchism – and the best – is done outside academia. (Ronald Creagh)

In summary

So, what have the previous chapters demonstrated? First, despite subtle, contrarian grumbling, anarchist movements *really are* social movements. Anarchist movements meet every requirement of every definition one cares to use for "social movements" – unless, of course, one presumes that movements must always seek state power, be large, win regularly, and so forth. Those obtuse criteria are not employed for any other movement, thus to hold anarchism to that standard is absurd. Social movement scholars' consistent avoidance of anarchist movement analyses illustrates both a preference for state-oriented subject matter and a confusion and frustration with explaining anti-state movements via typical frameworks. Like other movements, anarchist movements are composed of individuals and organizations that are embedded in dense and diffused networks, who share collective identities, who are definitely involved in extra-institutional actions. Additionally, even though a large, active domination counter-network exists that opposes anarchist efforts, the regular, popular framings of anarchism is flagrantly and undeniably incorrect. Anarchists are misperceived to be violent and chaotic, or – perhaps in a presumably more "positive" light – as naive utopians. Quite the contrary, we have seen how these labels combine both libel and hypocrisy leveled by those who routinely possess comparable characteristics.

Second, we have analyzed multiple data sources that describe who and where anarchists are. Primarily, anarchists are somewhat different from past generations of anarchists, but really not that different. Today, anarchist movements tend to pull participants from all class backgrounds, and have a range of ideological orientations, while some still belong to labor unions – just as in the Golden Age of anarchist movements in the late 1800s and early 1900s. Hundreds of thousands (and likely millions) of individuals work within thousands of anarchist organizations that are found in major cities in many countries throughout the world – especially in Europe and North America. There is a broad range of organizational types, but certain forms are central to these anarchist organizations: media-oriented groups, physical spaces like infoshops and bookstores, syndicalist unions, and generalist anarchist organizations. Just as with many other movements – especially those with many small, decentralized organizations – there is little carry-over from previous waves of anarchist movement activity, indicating a movement populated by rather impermanent organizational structures. Still, the repeated consistency in location from an early generation suggests local, structural factors that contribute to the routine creation of both organizational forms and the socialization of new anarchists.

Third, a variety of sociological movement theories can be deployed to explain the prevalence and activities of anarchist movements. In truth, many existing social movement theories contribute to understanding anarchist movements, although often imperfectly. For example, political opportunity theory, while centrally concerned with state-based opportunities, is still moderately relevant to anti-state movements, although anarchists use these opportunities in different ways and for different purposes in their mobilization efforts. Countries with greater opportunities and rights have more anarchist organizations. More specifically, anarchists' fortunes tended to swing opposite of the Marxist-Leninist left's fortunes, anarchists are helped by the presence of outside allies as diverse as labor unions and punk rock scenes, and state repression has had a mixed effect – either smashing movements or inspiring greater resistance. However, political opportunity theory as classically framed is biased toward a statist interpretation of social movement processes and prefers state-oriented movement subject matter. Current anarchist movements differ from classic age anarchists, but even classical era anarchism may qualify as a "new social movement." Throughout anarchism's history, it has tended to involve revolutionary anti-statism, anti-capitalism, radical practicality, and a general compatibility across movement waves (i.e., a lack of "newness"). Given the risks faced by anarchists, social capital has great importance. Social trust in particular allows for outward and inward orientations appropriate for these movements. People who possess social trust but lack political trust may be ideal, potential anarchists, whether explicitly or implicitly defined.

Finally, given anarchist movements relatively small sizes in contrast to many "mainstream movements," anarchists often form a variety of relationships with and within other movements. Anarchist ideas notably permeate many other movements, with personnel, tactics, and ideological influence. For example, anarchistic organizational styles are easily copied from location to location. Anarchistic franchise organizations, such as Anti-Racist Action, Critical Mass, Earth First!, and Food Not Bombs, are spread by personal contacts, informal stories, movement and mainstream press, and (most importantly today) the internet. Finally, anarchists regularly collaborate with non-anarchists, especially with those who share the same goals, such as stopping an imperialist war. Coalitions may lead to differing results, depending on who anarchists collaborate with and their mutual intentions. For example, progressives often have both strategic and tactical critiques and discomforts with anarchist methods, while Marxist-Leninists are apt to be in direct competition. Students share some commonalities, although may not be the most reliable partners. The importation of anarchist ideas – whether leaderless organizations or "diversity of tactics" preferences – indicate anarchist participation in non-anarchist movements, but also some of the compromises and disagreements generated by such coalitions.

Problems with research on radical movements

There is an ethical dimension to this book's epistemology: whether knowing "things" about an anarchist movement can be bad for that movement. If states, corporations, and other authority figures can use knowledge about anarchist movements against those movements, does that not make research that acquired knowledge problematic? If such research appears in externally accessible sources (like books or academic journals), this likely makes movements easier to understand. While knowledge is often universally viewed as a good thing, it depends for whom. States rarely believe that citizens or other states should know state secrets – the same is true for radical social movements. Anarchists do not want militaristic states, corporations, and other enemies to know their secrets – how they organize, who and where they are, what their plans are, and how best to stop them. Movement outsiders, such as state officials, possess values contrary to anarchism that will impair their comprehension of anarchist movements. Predictably, this is a good thing for anarchists. But, should there be more information explaining how to interpret these movements – especially from those with insider knowledge who have a better, more accurate understanding of them – then the distribution of such knowledge is decidedly bad for anarchists.

It is safer for new anarchists to be socialized in anarchist circles first, where anarchist information can be protected and distributed strategically; this would prevent general templates or "organizing manuals" from being released, which could fall into the hands of authorities, who could use this information in their social control efforts against radical movements. Since experience helps people to understand things, only undercover cops know much about current anarchist movements. If strong research exists, it might help state agencies to understand – and thus be able to suppress – movements without the need for costly informants or undercover police. Right now, law enforcement agencies and states have only incomplete information about anarchist movements. Yes, they know many facts and bits of information, but do they have the insight to interpret that information properly? Witness the "research" conducted by Borum & Tilby (2005), which presents some rather exotic and amusing conclusions (at least from the vantage point of experienced anarchists). Clearly, law enforcement officials (and academics in this case, too), don't seem to have all the tools or keys to make sense of the limited information they do have. This incompleteness and opaqueness aids anarchist movements, but reliable and accurate research may weaken such an advantage.

One last dimension to this epistemological problem pertains to authorities' efforts to map social networks within society generally and movements specifically (Greenwald 2014). Whether by local law enforcement, the National Security Agency, the Egyptian government, or anybody with the interest in knowing how movements *work*, such mapping efforts may help to suppress movements far more effectively than any informant, spy, tapped phone line, or agent provocateur could. For example, phone metadata – who was called, called from where, and length of call – can be compiled en masse and analyzed to find patterns. Which radicals communicate with other radicals? Has there been an increase in frequency of communication, perhaps signaling an upcoming collaboration? How do these movements seem to function? This information can be used – and *is* used – by authority figures to disrupt movements and plan future social control.

Thus, any information that could aid these mapping efforts needs to be seriously considered by those who share such information, especially if specific relationships are explicated. Even within radical movements, there is a troubling duality that is probably unresolvable: the need to operate openly and freely to build movement power, contrasted against the needs of a movement to protect its interests and participant safety from enemies. In other words, should anarchist movements pursue transparency, which may help them to attract new participants, or maintain a security culture that keeps information from as many people as possible?[1] Neither effort is always best. A movement that (metaphorically) hands over its keys to the state, is simply asking to be crushed. But, on the other hand, as CrimethInc wrote, regarding their new "anarchist cookbook," which detailed dozens of "recipes" for anarchist strategy, projects, and organizations: "Why give away our secrets? Because if they stay secrets, we're fucked" (CrimethInc 2012b). I have endeavored here to work with either publicly accessible data or to withhold crucial identifying information. Even when describing the patterns and processes of anarchist movements – surely of interest to the domination network – I have done so in the spirit of providing those movements with helpful clarity to beat back social control efforts.

The purpose of study

Finally, I wish to humbly propose a set of goals and objectives for scholars of anarchist movements and (most importantly) anarchist movements' scholars. While these goals would extend the general orientation proposed here, I know full well that other approaches have their own unique value and potential contributions to offer.

It seems to be key to de-emphasize nomothetic analysis or efforts to extrapolate hard-and-fixed theories, and instead to emphasize understanding situational nuance. Also, to use knowledge in a flexible fashion, from instance to instance. Therefore, while I use seemingly all-encompassing datasets in this volume (e.g., Chapter 2's Infoshop.org survey or Chapter 3's Anarchist Yellow Pages organizational directory), I do so with appropriate nuance. I recognize that each are samples – and unrepresentative and thus ungeneralizable samples at that – which only identify certain snapshots in time, with biases that over-emphasize the presence of anarchists and their organizations in more affluent societies. Still, while I downplay the impulse to pursue a nomothetic course, this book has not been strictly ideographic either, since I have tried to extract lessons that may have broader importance beyond their idiosyncratic circumstances.

Lofland (1993) advocated trying to improve our answers to important questions, feeling that this was a more important orientation to bring to the study of social movements. I have tried to address many of those important questions, such as: who participates, where do anarchist exist, what external factors influence anarchist mobilization, how new are anarchist movements in social movement history, how do anarchists build trust within movements, how do anarchist project proliferate horizontally, how does organizational structure prefigure the kind of values that anarchists think are important to live by, how do anarchists collaborate with non-anarchists, and how do people with different ideological orientations discover anarchism? Yes, some of these questions can be addressed with theories (e.g., political opportunity, NSM, or social capital), but my goal has not been to merely bash theories.

Instead of just trying to test the popular academic theories of the day (which I, admittedly, do), students of anarchist movements ought to focus on delivering critical and thoughtful movement analysis. These contributions ought to be focused upon helping activists reflect on their practices and to improve their outcomes.[2] This necessitates a social justice and activist impulse among movement students. While some sociologists find movements personally fascinating and may privately cheer for their successes, it is imperative to realize that the world that anarchist-sociologists wish to live in will not be created in the absence of committed, improving, radical, and participatory social movements (anarchist or otherwise). The movement student-as-partisan may also seek to involve movement participants themselves in such scholarship (see Martin 1998b). In fact, numerous "militant research" collectives exist within the radical milieux of many countries. These collectives synchronize their participation, research, and dialogue in movements. Others, such as the former Research Group One in the USA (headed by sociologists such as Howard Ehrlich) turned over their skills and resources to movements themselves (Williams & Shantz 2016).

As I have stated before (Williams 2009a), it is absurd to assume that anarchist movements can face-off (successfully, anyway) against some of the most powerful, deliberate, malicious, and resource-rich institutions human history has ever seen – ranging from imperialism, patriarchy, White supremacy, fundamentalist religion, capitalism, and nation-states – alone. These hierarchical institutions all employ a variety of means to achieve their ends, including social research. The RAND Corporation, Cato Institute, World Bank, Focus on the Family, and National Security Agency (just to name a few based in the USA), all work tirelessly to promote their nationalistic, pro-capitalist, and patriarchal agendas – and they do so with some of the deepest pockets imaginable. Do anarchists – and other radicals – honestly expect to be able to accurately understand the horrifying world they occupy, let alone understand the best strategies towards change, in the face of these foes? Hopefully not. This does *not* mean all anarchists should go get PhDs, take advanced statistics courses, and hang up their bandannas for computer keyboards. But, there is unmeasurable value in a dual power strategy to create a better world that accomplishes our needs, without resorting to hierarchy, substitutionism or representation, or indiscriminate violence. We need to know that "we" means those of us who want a progressive social revolution that levels hierarchies and empowers everyday people. And that it's okay to stand on that side of the barricade, even if you *do* have a PhD. Let us understand anarchist movements (and every other movement) as best we can, from any and every possible angle. In doing so, we can build the best possible collectivities and networks for fighting back and winning the better world we want, one victorious day at a time.

Notes

1   It is important to note that "security culture" is itself a form of resistance to the label of "terrorist" that the anti-anarchist network places on anarchist movements (Robinson 2008).
2   To be clear, much of the US-based anarchist press does this already – *Slingshot*, *Rolling Thunder*, *Fifth Estate*, and many others, as well as the more scholarly *Upping the Anti* and *Perspectives*.

Appendix: Sources of knowledge and error

Every analysis ought to acknowledge the shortcomings of its epistemology. Knowledge comes from a variety of sources. Some sources are secondary, while other knowledge is gathered at first hand. All pre-existing data and datasets will be incomplete, and thus the sampling error will be unknown (and thus all conclusions will be ungeneralizable). Therefore, generalizable (i.e., nomothetic) knowledge may be impossible for movements (and perhaps undesirable).

One undesirable result of any conclusion-drawing enterprise affects activists, scholars, and authority figures: the issue of error. People are often simply wrong. Yes, there is the possibility for multiple truths, including different subjective interpretations of the same thing, but there is also such a thing as inaccuracy.

There are a few different types of error that are relevant when observing movements. First, sampling error occurs when one makes generalizations based on an incomplete collection of cases, thus misrepresenting how generalizable the analysis is. Second, observational error happens either when one does not accurately understand what is being observed or when inaccurately reflecting on what one witnesses (direct or indirect observational error). Finally, analysis error occurs when one draws a faulty conclusion from the available data. Anyone can make these errors, whether intentionally or unintentionally – and both outcomes are bad. Activists can, of course, cause errors in their analyses or representations, but more often scholars are likely to squeeze findings into pre-existing frameworks. And authorities are less apt to sugar-coat things than to exaggerate problems for propagandistic purposes. Many types of things could be erroneous: observations, datasets, data analysis (including statistics), interpretations, conclusions, and so on.

The most interesting thing to consider is *why* people make errors. Let us divide these errors according to who makes them (activists, scholars, and authorities) and by the nature of error (either intentional or unintentional). Activists are the most immediate people to movements – since they generally *are* the movement – but this does not preclude the potential to produce errors in their analyses of their activities. Intentionally, activists may erroneously represent their behaviors for propaganda purposes; in so doing they may idealize the processes they use or pursue ("consensus decision making works perfectly in our collective!") or exaggerate their successes ("our protest was amazing and we were successful in our goals!"). Unintentionally, activists may introduce erroneous conclusions, too. They may speculate about things or use conjecture to extend conclusions beyond what they can confidently argue. In other words, some activists do not have enough observations or information to make certain claims. More critically, activists may not understand the methodological limitations of science well; they may draw faulty conclusions because they misunderstand what is needed to make certain claims (i.e., was it really "the entire local anarchist scene" that supports Campaign X?). The types of potential error about anarchist movements are listed in Table A.1.

Scholars can commit numerous errors intentionally. Principally, scholars regularly squeeze their "findings" into pre-existing frameworks (which can have little significance or bearing on the movement in question). Put differently, scholars may not have the ability or language to understand or describe a movement, but they try anyway. Other scholars may wish to make a "name" for themselves as experts on a "hot topic" (e.g., anarchist movements). These scholars are more concerned with "buzz" than accuracy and are willing to misconstrue any number of facts to create excitement, controversy, or enhance the significance of their "scholarship." Scholars are also capable of unintentionally generating errors when observing movements. Since many are not on "the inside" of the movements they study, they do not thoroughly understand the nature of those movements. Their concluding research is superficial and it lacks "ground truth" that would resonate with a more immediate observer. The structural constraints on scholars also causes problems. The pressures of tenure (e.g., "publish or perish") can spur faulty research, as scholars cut corners or generate shoddy scholarship in a rush to crank out research papers. Scholars may be capable of overcoming errors, but the institutions they are embedded within structurally – although unintentionally – encourage error-making.

I would place myself within these first two camps – activist and scholar. I am certainly subject to the risks mentioned and I have tried my best to reduce and be transparent about potential errors in the book you have read. But, one final category of "interested persons" analyze movements, and this group I have no affinity with: authorities. Whoever they may be (politicians, police, intelligence officials or spies), authorities have vested interests in controlling movements – this may involve redirecting movements' trajectories or repressing them. Thus, authorities often consciously and intentionally act to hide the success of movements, as they worry that others will wish to join the movements if they appear too attractive to others. Even though they are interested in vocally minimizing the significance of

Table A.1 Who makes erroneous observations about movements and why?

Who	Intentional error	Unintentional error
Activists	Propaganda purposes (idealizing process, successes) Throw off surveillance of authorities (attempt to be deceptive because they are under surveillance)	Do not understand methodological limitations or science well (draw faulty conclusions because they misunderstand what is needed to make certain claims) Speculation, conjecture (do not have enough experience or information)
Scholars	Squeeze findings into pre-existing frameworks (do not have ability to understand movement but they try anyway) Wish to make a "name" for themselves as experts on "hot topic" (concerned with "buzz" more than accuracy)	Pressures of "tenure" (publish or perish) generate faulty research Are not on the "inside" of movements and thus do not thoroughly understand their natures (research is superficial, lacks "ground truth")
Authorities	Wish to hide the success of movements (worried others will wish to join it if it appears too attractive) Wish to exaggerate the "threat" of movements for bureaucratically-useful reasons (more funding for policing, spying)	Are unable to "get inside" movement's "heads" (the movement is confusing) Ideology prevents them from understanding (can't "get" how movements work since it is a different paradigm and set of values)

movements (especially radical ones), they also, somewhat paradoxically, seek to exaggerate a movement's "threat," too. Presenting a movement as a threat serves bureaucratically useful ends: it helps to justify the existence of authorities ("we're here to keep everyone safe from the trouble-makers/terrorists/radicals"), generate endless funding sources for more policing of, and spying upon, radical movements, and to legitimate their current efforts at social control. Although the hierarchical positions of authorities is motivation enough for the blatant, intentional misrepresentation of movements, authorities also introduce unintentional error, too. Since authorities are rarely able to "get inside" a movement's "head" and understand it, the movement usually appears confusing or seems to be something it is not. Thus, the distance authorities have from movements stymie their ability to accurately see them for what they are. Authority figures' ideologies are additional impediments that prevent them from understanding movements. Authorities often can't "get" how movements work since they operate on completely different paradigms (i.e., democratically, collectively) and with contrary values (i.e., mutual aid, solidarity). The belief many authorities have in the weaknesses of "human nature" or that people do everything based on cold, calculating self-interest will make movements and their participants look like aliens from another planet, doing strange things for even stranger reasons.

Although not listed in Table A.1, another actor within the domination network (see Chapter 1), the media, makes erroneous observations, too. I do not describe them in detail here, except to note that they make many of the same errors that scholars and authorities make, often for similar reasons.

BIBLIOGRAPHY

Ackelsberg, Martha A. 1991. *Free Women of Spain: Anarchism and the Struggle for the Emancipation of Women*. Bloomington: Indiana University Press.

ACME Collective. 1999. "N30 Black Bloc Communique." www.infoshop.org/octo/wto_blackbloc.html.

Adams, Jason. 2002. *Nonwestern Anarchisms: Rethinking the Global Context*. Johannesburg: Zabalaza Books.

A. Gallery. 1982. *A Brief History of Anarchism in Greece*. Athens: A. Gallery.

A-Infos. 2008. *A-Infos Information – History*. Retrieved May 1, 2007 (www.ainfos.ca/org/history-en.html).

Albert, Michael. 2002. *Trajectory of Change: Activist Strategies for Social Transformation*. Cambridge, MA: South End Press.

Albert, Michael and Robin Hahnel. 1991. *The Political Economy of Participatory Economics*. Princeton, NJ: Princeton University Press.

Alexander, Robert. 1998. *The Anarchists in the Spanish Civil War*. London: Janus Publishing.

Alinsky, Saul. 1971. *Rules for Radicals: A Practical Primer for Realistic Radicals*. New York: Random House.

Amster, Randall. 2003. "Restoring (Dis)order: Sanctions, Resolutions, and "Social Control" in Anarchist Communities." *Contemporary Justice Review*, 6 (1): 9–24.

Anarchy FAQ. 2004. An Anarchist FAQ, Version 10.0. www.anarchyfaq.org.

Andrews, Kenneth T. 2002. "Movement-Countermovement Dynamics and the Emergence of New Institutions: The Case of "White Flight" Schools in Mississippi." *Social Forces*, 80 (3): 911–936.

Apple, Agent. 2004. *Pie Any Means Necessary: The Biotic Baking Brigade Cookbook*. Oakland, CA: AK Press.

Aronowitz, Stanley. 1973. *False Promises: The Shaping of American Working Class Consciousness*. New York: McGraw-Hill.

Aronowitz, Stanley. 2005. "On the Future of American Labor." *Working USA: The Journal of Labor and Society*, 8: 271–291.

Asal, Victor and R. Karl Rethemeyer. 2008. "Dilettantes, Ideologues, and the Weak: Terrorists Who Don't Kill." *Conflict Management and Peace Science*, 25: 244–263.

Atkinson, Joshua. 2009. "Analyzing Resistance Narratives at the North American Anarchist Gathering: A Method for Analyzing Social Justice Alternative Media." *Journal of Communication Inquiry*, 30 (3): 251–272.

Atton, Chris. 1999. "*Green Anarchist*: A Case Study of Collective Action in the Radical Media." *Anarchist Studies*, 7 (1): 25–49.

Atton, Chris. 2003. "Reshaping Social Movement Media for a New Millennium." *Social Movement Studies*, 2 (1): 3–15.

Avrich, Paul. 1967. *The Russian Anarchists*. Princeton, NJ: Princeton University Press.

Avrich, Paul. 1980. *The Modern School Movement: Anarchism and Education in the United States*. Princeton, NJ: Princeton University Press.

Ayres, Jeffrey M. 1999. "From the Streets to the Internet: The Cyber-Diffusion of Contention." *Annals of the American Academy of Political & Social Science*, 566, November: 132–143.

Babbie, Earl. 2010. *The Practice of Social Research*, 12th edition. Belmont, CA: Wadsworth.

Bagguley, Paul. 1992. "Social Change, the Middle Class and the Emergence of 'New Social Movements': A Critical Analysis." *The Sociological Review*, 40 (1): 26–48.

Bakunin, Michael. 1970. *God and the State*. New York: Dover.

Balser, Deborah. 1997. "The Impact of Environmental Factors on Factionalism and Schism in Social Movement Organizations." *Social Forces*, 76 (1), September: 199–228.

Bamyeh, Mohammed. 2013. "Anarchist Method, Liberal Intention, Authoritarian Lesson: The Arab Spring between Three Enlightenments." *Constellations: An International Journal of Critical & Democratic Theory*, 20 (2), June: 188–202.

Barahona, Diana. 2007. "The Freedom House Files." *Monthly Review Zine*, January 3. http://mrzine.monthlyreview.org/barahona030107.html.

Bari, Judi. 1994. *Timber Wars*. Monroe, ME: Common Courage Press.

Beallor, Angela. 2000. "Sexism and the Anarchist Movement." *Onward*, 1 (1).

Beck, Colin J. 2007. "On the Radical Cusp: Ecoterrorism in the United States, 1998–2005." *Mobilization: An International Quarterly Review*, 12 (2): 161–176.

Beevor, Antony. 2006. *The Battle for Spain: The Spanish Civil War 1936–1939*. New York: Penguin.

Bender, Frederic L. 1983. "Taoism and Western Anarchism." *Journal of Chinese Philosophy* 10: 5–26.

Berkman, Alexander. 2003. *What is Anarchism?* Edinburgh: AK Press.

Black, Bob. 1997. *Anarchy After Leftism*. Columbia, MO: C.A.L. Press.

Blackstone, Lee Robert. 2005. "A New Kind of English: Cultural Variance, Citizenship and DiY Politics Amongst the Exodus Collective in England." *Social Forces*, 84 (2): 803–820.

Blickstein, Susan and Susan Hanson. 2001. "Critical Mass: Forging a Politics of Sustainable Mobility in the Information Age." *Transportation*, 28: 347–362.

Boehrer, Fred. 2000. "The Principle of Subsidiarity as the Basis for a Just Community." *Contemporary Justice Review*, 3 (2): 213–224.

Boehrer, Fred. 2003. "Anarchism and Downward Mobility: Is Finishing Last the Least We Can Do?" *Contemporary Justice Review*, 6 (1): 37–45.

Bonanno, A. 1988. *From Riot to Insurrection: An Analysis for an Anarchist Perspective Against Post Industrial Capitalism*. London: Elephant.

Bookchin, Murray. 1977. *The Spanish Anarchists: The Heroic Years, 1868–1936*. New York: Free Life.

Bookchin, Murray. 1989. "New Social Movements: The Anarchic Dimension," in *For Anarchism: History, Theory, and Practice*, pp. 259–274, edited by D. Goodway. London: Routledge.

Bookchin, Murray. 1991. *The Ecology of Freedom: The Emergence and Dissolution of Hierarchy*. Montreal: Black Rose.

Bookchin, Murray. 1995. *Social Anarchism of Lifestyle Anarchism: An Unbridgeable Chasm*. Edinburgh: AK Press.

Bookchin, Murray. 1996. *The Third Revolution: Popular Movements in the Revolutionary Era, Volume One*. London: Cassell.

Bookchin, Murray. 1998. *The Spanish Anarchists: The Heroic Years, 1868–1936*. Edinburgh: AK Press.

Bookchin, Murray. 2004. *Post-Scarcity Anarchism*. Edinburgh: AK Press.

Bookchin, Murray. 2005. *The Ecology of Freedom: The Emergence and Dissolution of Hierarchy*. Oakland, CA: AK Press.

Borum, Randy and Chuck Tilby. 2005. "Anarchist Direct Actions: A Challenge for Law Enforcement." *Studies in Conflict & Terrorism*, 28 (3): 201–223.

Bourdieu, Pierre. 1986. "The Forms of Capital," in *Handbook of Theory and Research for the Sociology of Education*, pp. 241–258, edited by J. G. Richardson. New York: Greenwood.

Boykoff, Jules. 2007. *Beyond Bullets: The Suppression of Dissent in the United States*. Oakland, CA: AK Press.

Brannen, Julia. 2005. "Mixing Methods: The Entry of Qualitative and Quantitative Approaches into the Research Process." *International Journal of Social Research Methodology*, 8 (3), July: 173–184.

Bray, Mark. 2013. *Translating Anarchy: The Anarchism of Occupy Wall Street*. Winchester, UK: Zero Books.

Brecher, Jeremy. 1997. *Strike!* Cambridge, MA: South End Press.

Breines, Wini. 1982. *Community and Organization in the New Left, 1962–1968: The Great Refusal*. New York: Praeger.

Brinton, Maurice. 2004. *For Workers' Power: the Selected Writings of Maurice Brinton*, edited by David Goodway, Oakland: AK Press.

Buechler, Steven M. 1995. "New Social Movement Theories." *The Sociological Quarterly*, 36 (3), Summer: 441–464.

Buechler, Steven M. 2000. *Social Movements in Advanced Capitalism: The Political Economy and Cultural Construction of Social Activism*. New York: Oxford University Press.

Buechler, Steven M. 2011. *Understanding Social Movements: Theories from the Classical Era to the Present*. Boulder, CO: Paradigm.

Burawoy, Michael. 1982. "Introduction: The Resurgence of Marxism in American Sociology." *American Journal of Sociology*, 88: S1–S30.

Burawoy, Michael. 2005. "For Public Sociology." *American Sociological Review*, 70: 4–28.

Bureau of Labor Statistics. 2004. *Union Members in 2003*, Press release, January 21. www.bls.gov/news.release/pdf/union2.pdf.

Burns, Danny. 1992. *Poll Tax Rebellion*. Stirling, Scotland: AK Press.

Butler, C.T. and Keith McHenry. 2000. *Food Not Bombs*. Tucson, AZ: See Sharp Press.

Calhoun, Craig. 1993. 'New Social Movements' of the Early Nineteenth Century. *Social Science History*, 17 (3), Fall: 385–427.

Carlsson, Chris. 2002. *Critical Mass: Bicycling's Defiant Celebration*. Oakland, CA: AK Press.

Cheloukhine, Serguei. 2008. "The Roots of Russian Organized Crime: From Old-fashioned Professionals to the Organized Criminal Groups of Today." *Crime, Law, & Social Change*, 50 (4–5): 353–364.

Chirot, Daniel. 1986. *Social Change in the Modern Era*. San Diego: Harcourt Brace Jovanovich.

Chomsky, Noam. 1973. *For Reasons of State*. New York: Pantheon.

Christiansen, Jonathan. 2009. "'We Are All Leaders': Anarchism and the Narrative of the Industrial Workers of the World." *Working USA: The Journal of Labor & Society*, 12 (3), September: 387–401.

Christie, Stuart. 2008. *We, The Anarchists: A Study of the Iberian Anarchist Federation (FAI), 1927–1937*. Edinburgh: AK Press.

Class War Federation. 1992. *Unfinished Business: The Politics of Class War*. Edinburgh: AK Press.

Clawson, Dan. 2003. *The Next Upsurge: Labor and New Social Movements*. Ithaca, NY: ILR/Cornell University Press.

Clawson, Dan and Mary Ann Clawson. 1999. "What Has Happened to the US Labor Movement? Union Decline and Renewal." *Annual Review of Sociology*, 25: 95–119.

Cobb-Reiley, Linda. 1988. "Aliens and Alien Ideas: The Suppression of Anarchists and the Anarchist Press in America, 1901–1914." *Journalism History* 15 (2–3), Summer/Autumn: 50–59.

Coben, Stanley. 1963. *A. Mitchell Palmer: Politician*. New York: Columbia University Press.

Cogan, Brian. 2007. "'Do They Owe Us a Living? Of Course They Do!' Crass, Throbbing Gristle, and Anarchy and Radicalism in Early English Punk Rock." *Journal for the Study of Radicalism*, 1 (2): 77–90.

Cohen, Jean L. 1985. "Strategy or Identity: New Theoretical Paradigms and Contemporary Social Movements." *Social Research*, 52 (4): 663–716.

Cohn-Bendit, Daniel and Gabriel Cohn-Bendit. 2000. *Obsolete Communism: The Left-Wing Alternative*. Edinburgh: AK Press.

Coleman, James. 1988. "Social Capital in the Creation of Human Capital." *American Journal of Sociology*, 94: S95–S120.

Coleman, James S. 1990. *Foundations of Social Theory*. Cambridge, MA: Belknap Press.

Collins, Patricia Hill. 2009. *Another Kind of Public Education: Race, Schools, the Media, and Democratic Possibilities*. Boston: Beacon Press.

Connell, Raewyn. 2007. *Southern Theory: The Global Dynamics of Knowledge in Social Science*. Cambridge, MA: Polity.

Cornell, Andrew. 2011. *Oppose and Propose! Lessons From Movement for a New Society*. Oakland, CA: AK Press.

Cornell, Andrew. 2016. *Unruly Equality: U.S. Anarchism in the 20th Century*. Berkeley, CA: University of California Press.

Cox, Laurence and Cristina Flesher Fominaya. 2013. "European Social Movements and Social Theory: A Richer Narrative?" in *Understanding European Movements: New Social Movements, Global Justice Struggles, and Anti-austerity Protest*, pp. 7–29, edited by C. F. Fominaya and L. Cox. London: Routledge.

Crass, Chris. 2001. *Collective Liberation on My Mind*. Montreal: Kersplebedeb.

Crass, Chris. 2004. *Beyond Voting: Anarchist Organizing, Electoral Politics and Developing Strategy for Liberation*. Clamor Communique #42.

CrimethInc. 2001. *Days of War, Nights of Love: Crimethink for Beginners*. Atlanta, GA: CrimethInc.

CrimethInc. 2005. *Recipes for Disaster: An Anarchist Cookbook*. Olympia, WA: CrimethInc Workers Collective.

CrimethInc. 2006. *Recipes for Disaster: An Anarchist Cookbook*. Salem, OR: CrimethInc Workers Collective.

CrimethInc. 2011. *Work: Capitalism. Economics. Resistance*. Salem, OR: CrimethInc.

CrimethInc. 2012a. "Nightmares of Capitalism, Pipe Dreams of Democracy: The World Struggles to Wake, 2010–2011." *Rolling Thunder*, 10: 18–34.

CrimethInc. 2012b. *Recipes for Disaster: An Anarchist Cookbook*. Olympia, WA: CrimethInc Workers' Collective.

CrimethInc. 2014. "After The Crest: What To Do While the Dust is Settling." *Rolling Thunder*, 11: 13–18.

Crossley, Nick. 2002. *Making Sense of Social Movements*. Buckingham: Open University Press.

Crump, John. 1993. *Hatta Shūzō and Pure Anarchism in Interwar Japan*. New York: St. Martin's Press.

Damier, Vadim. 2009. *Anarcho-Syndicalism in the 20th Century*. Edmonton: Black Cat Press.

Davies, James C. 1962. "Toward a Theory of Revolution." *American Sociological Review*, 27 (1), February: 5–19.

Day, Richard J. F. 2004. "From Hegemony to Affinity: The Political Logic of the Newest Social Movements." *Cultural Studies* 18 (5), September: 716–748.

Day, Richard J. F. 2005. *Gramsci is Dead: Anarchist Currents in the Newest Social Movements*. London: Pluto Press.

De Cleyre, Voltairine. 2004. *The Voltairine de Cleyre Reader*. Oakland, CA: AK Press.

DeLeon, David. 1996. "For Democracy Where We Work: A Rationale for Social Self-Management." In *Reinventing Anarchy, Again*, edited by Howard J. Ehrlich, 192–210. Edinburgh: AK Press.

della Porta, Donatella. 2008. "Protest on Unemployment: Forms and Opportunities." *Mobilization: An International Journal*, 13 (3): 277–295.

della Porta, Donatella and Mario Diani. 2006. *Social Movements: An Introduction*, Second Edition. Malden, MA: Blackwell.

della Porta, Donatella and Dieter Rucht. 1995. "Left-Libertarian Movements in Context: A Comparison of Italy and West Germany, 1965–1990." In *The Politics of Social Protest: Comparative Perspectives of States and Social Movements*, pp. 229–272, edited by J. C. Jenkins and B. Klandermans. Minneapolis: University of Minnesota Press.

de Marcellus, Olivier. 2000. "Peoples' Global Action: A Brief History." *Race & Class*, 41 (4): 92–99.

Diani, Mario. 1992. "The Concept of Social Movement." *Sociological Review*, 40 (1), February: 1–25.

Diani, Marco. 1997. "Social Movements and Social Capital: A Network Perspective on Movement Outcomes." *Mobilization*, 2 (2), September: 129–148.

DiMaggio, Paul J. and Walter W. Powell. 1983. "The Iron Cage Revisited: Institutional Isomorphism and Collective Rationality in Organizational Fields." *American Sociological Review*, 48: 147–160.

Dirlik, Arif. 1993. *Anarchism in the Chinese Revolution*. Berkeley, CA: University of California Press.

Dixon, Chris. 2012. "Building 'Another Politics': The Contemporary Anti-Authoritarian Current in the US and Canada." *Anarchist Studies*, 20 (1): 32–60.

Dolgoff, Sam. 1971. *Bakunin on Anarchy: Selected Works by the Activist-Founder of World Anarchism*. New York: Alfred A. Knopf.

Dolgoff, Sam. 1977. *The Relevance of Anarchism to Modern Society*. Minneapolis: Soil of Liberty.

Dupuis-Déri, Francis. 2010. "Anarchism and the Politics of Affinity Groups." *Anarchist Studies*, 18 (1): 40–61.

Dupuis-Déri, Francis. 2014. *Who's Afraid of the Black Blocs? Anarchy in Action Around the World*. Oakland, CA: PM Press.

Durkheim, Émile. 1951. *Suicide: A Study in Sociology*. New York: Free Press.

Durkheim, Émile. 1964. *The Division of Labor in Society*. Glencoe, IL: Free Press.

Edwards, Bob and John D. McCarthy. 2004. "Resources and Social Movement Mobilization," in *The Blackwell Companion to Social Movements*, pp. 116–152, edited by D. A. Snow, S. A. Soule, and H. Kriesi. Malden, MA: Blackwell.

Ehrlich, Carol. 1977. *Socialism, Anarchism, and Feminism*. Baltimore: Research Group One.

Ehrlich, Howard J. 1977. "Anarchism and Formal Organizations," in *Research Group One Report Number 23*, pp. 1–2. Baltimore: Vacant Lots Press.

Ehrlich, Howard. 1991. "Notes from an Anarchist Sociologist: May 1989," in *Radical Sociologists and the Movement: Experiences, Lessons, and Legacies*, pp. 233–248, edited by M. Oppenheimer, M. J. Murray, and R. F. Levine. Philadelphia: Temple University Press.

Ehrlich, Howard J. 1996. *Reinventing Anarchy, Again*. Edinburgh: AK Press.

Engels, Friedrich. 1966. *Herr Eugen Dühring's Revolution in Science*. New York: International Publishers.

Epstein, Barbara. 1991. *Political Protest and Cultural Revolution: Nonviolent Direct Action in the 1970s and 1980s*. Berkeley, CA: University of California Press.

Epstein, Barbara. 2001. "Anarchism and the Anti-Globalization Movement." *Monthly Review*, 53 (4), September: 1–14.

Etzioni, Amitai. 1965. "Dual Leadership in Complex Organizations." *American Sociological Review*, 30 (5): 688–698.

Farrow, Lynne. 2012. "Feminism as Anarchism," in *Quiet Rumours: An Anarcha-Feminist Reader*, pp. 19–24, edited by Dark Star. Oakland, CA: AK Press.

Federal Bureau of Investigation. 1999. *Terrorism in the United States*. Washington, DC: Department of Justice.

Federal Bureau of Investigation. 2011. "Anarchist Extremism Overview." Domestic Terrorism Operations Unit.

Ferguson, Kathy E. 2011. *Emma Goldman: Political Thinking in the Streets*. Lanham, MD: Rowman & Littlefield.

Fernández, Frank. 2001. *Cuban Anarchism: The History of a Movement*. Tucson, AZ: See Sharp Press.

Feynman, Richard. 1965. *The Character of Physical Law*. Cambridge, MA: MIT Press.

Finnegan, William. 2003. "Affinity Groups and the Movements Against Corporate Globalization," in *The Social Movements Reader: Cases and Concepts*, pp. 210–218, edited by J. Goodwin & J. M. Jasper. Malden, MA: Blackwell.

Fischler, Steven and Joel Sucher. 2006. *Anarchism in America DVD*. Oakland, CA: AK Press.

Fitzgerald, Kathleen J. and Diane Rodgers. 2000. "Radical Social Movement Organizations: A Theoretical Model." *Sociological Quarterly*, 41 (4), Fall: 573–592.

Flacks, Richard. 2003. "Review." *Social Movement Studies*, 2 (1): 99–102.

Foreman, Dave and Bookchin, Murray. 2001. *Defending the Earth: A Dialogue Between Murray Bookchin & Dave Foreman*. Cambridge, MA: South End Press.

Foster, Thomas W. 1987. "The Taoists and the Amish: Kindred Expressions of Eco-Anarchism." *The Ecologist*, 17: 9–14.

Fragos, Spyros and James Sotros. 2005. "The General Social, Political and Economic Situation in Greece and the Greek Anarchist Movement." Retrieved May 1, 2007. www.ainfos.ca/05/apr/ainfos00252.html.

Franks, Benjamin. 2012. "Between Anarchism and Marxism: The Beginnings and Ends of the Schism …" *Journal of Political Ideologies*, 17 (2): 207–227.

Friedland, Roger and Robert R. Alford. 1991. "Bringing Society Back In: Symbols, Practices, and Institutional Contradictions," in *The New Institutionalism in Organizational Analysis*, pp. 232–263, edited by W. Powell and P. DiMaggio. Chicago: University of Chicago Press.

Fuchs, Stephan and Peggy S. Plass. 1999. "Sociology and Social Movements." *Contemporary Sociology*, 28 (3), May: 271–277.

Gambone, Larry. 1997. *Saint Che: The Truth Behind the Legend of the Heroic Guerrilla, Ernesto Che Guevara*. Montreal: Red Lion Press.

Garner, Jason. 2016. *Goals and Means: Anarchism, Syndicalism, and Internationalism in the Origins of the Federación Anarquista Ibérica*. Oakland, CA: AK Press.

Gelderloos, Peter. 2006a. *Consensus: A New Handbook for Grassroots Social, Political, and Environmental Groups*. Tucson, AZ: See Sharp Press.

Gelderloos, Peter. 2006b. "A Critical History of Harrisonburg Food Not Bombs: Culture, Communication, and Organization in an Anarchist Soup Kitchen." *Social Anarchism*, 39: 64–70.

Geronimo. 2012. *Fire and Flames: A History of the German Autonomist Movement*. Oakland, CA: PM Press.

Giddens, Anthony. 1984. *The Constitution of Society: Outline of the Theory of Structuration*. Cambridge: Polity.

Gilbert, Martin S. 2004. *Anarchists in Social Work: Known to the Authorities*. Self-published.

Giugni, Marco. 2008. "Welfare States, Political Opportunities, and the Mobilization of the Unemployed: A Cross-National Analysis." *Mobilization: An International Journal*, 13 (3): 297–310.

Goffman, Erving. 1974. *Frame Analysis: An Essay on the Organization of Experience*. New York: Harper & Row.

Goldman, Emma. 1969. *Anarchism and Other Essays*. New York: Dover.

Goldman, Emma. 1970. *Living My Life*. New York: Dover.

Goodwin, Jeff. 2002. "Are Protesters Opportunists? Political Opportunities and the Emergence of Political Contention." Working paper, Department of Sociology, New York University.

Goodwin, Jeff and James M. Jasper. 1999. "Caught in a Winding, Snarling Vine: The Structural Bias of Political Process Theory." *Sociological Forum*, 14 (1): 27–54.

Goodwin, Jeff and James M. Jasper. 2004. *Rethinking Social Movements: Structure, Meaning, and Emotion*. Lanham, MD: Rowman & Littlefield.

Gordon, Uri. 2006. "Research Note: Αναρχια – What Did the Greeks Actually Say?." *Anarchist Studies*, 14 (1): 84–91.

Gordon, Uri. 2007. "Anarchism Reloaded." *Journal of Political Ideologies*, 12 (1), February: 29–48.

Gordon, Uri. 2008. *Anarchy Alive! Anti-Authoritarian Politics From Practice to Theory*. London: Pluto Press.

Graeber, David. 2002. "The New Anarchists." *New Left Review* 13, Jan/Feb: 61–73.

Graeber, David. 2009. *Direct Action: An Ethnography*. Oakland, CA: AK Press.

Graeber, David. 2011a. *Debt: The First 5,000 Years*. New York: Melville House.

Graeber, David. 2011b. "Interview with David Graeber." *The White Review*, published December 7. www.thewhitereview.org/interviews/interview-with-david-graeber/

Graham, Robert. 2015. *We Do Not Fear Anarchy–We Invoke It: The First International and the Origins of the Anarchist Movement*. Oakland, CA: AK Press.

Greenwald, Glenn. 2014. *No Place To Hide: Edward Snowden, the NSA, and the U.S. Surveillance State*. New York, NY: Metropolitan.

Grubacic, Andrej and David Graeber. 2004. "Anarchism, Or the Revolutionary Movement of the Twenty-First Century." Z-Net.

Guérin, Daniel. 1970. *Anarchism: From Theory to Practice*. New York: Monthly Review Press.

Guérin, Daniel. 2005. *No Gods, No Masters: An Anthology of Anarchism*. Oakland: AK Press.

Guillamón, Augustín. 2014. *Ready for Revolution: The CNT Defense Committees in Barcelona, 1933–1938*. Oakland, CA: AK Press.

Gurney, Joan Neff and Kathleen J. Tierney. 1982. "Relative Deprivation and Social Movements: A Critical Look at Twenty Years of Theory and Research." *The Sociological Quarterly*, 23 (1): 33–47.

Gurr, Ted. 1970. *Why Men Rebel*. Princeton, NJ: Princeton University Press.

Habermas, Jürgen. 1987. *The Theory of Communicative Action. Lifeworld and System: A Critique of Functionalist Reason*. Boston: Beacon Press.

Habermas, Jürgen. 1992. *Autonomy and Solidarity: Interviews with Jürgen Habermas*. London: Verso.

Hannan, Michael T. and John Freeman. 1989. *Organizational Ecology*. Cambridge, MA: Harvard University Press.

Heath, Nick. 2006. "40 Years of British Anarchism." Retrieved May 1, 2007. www.ainfos.ca/06/nov/ainfos00272.html.

Held, David. 1987. "Models of Democracy." Stanford, CA: Stanford University Press.

Hirsch, Steven and Lucien van der Walt (eds). 2010. *Anarchism and Syndicalism in the Colonial and Postcolonial World, 1870–1940: The Praxis of National Liberation, Internationalism, and Social Revolution*. Leiden: Brill.

Hodges, Donald C. 1986. *Intellectual Foundations of the Nicaraguan Revolution.* Austin, TX: University of Texas Press.

Hodges, Donald C. 1992. *Sandino's Communism: Spiritual Politics for the Twenty-first Century.* Austin, TX: University of Texas Press.

Holtzman, Ben, Craig Hughes, Kevin Van Meter. 2007. "Do It Yourself … and the Movement Beyond Capitalism," in *Constituent Imagination: Militant Investigations // Collective Theorization,* pp. 44–61, edited by S. Shukaitis and D. Graeber. Oakland, CA: AK Press.

Hong, Nathaniel. 1992. "Constructing the Anarchist Beast in American Periodical Literature, 1880–1903." *Critical Studies in Mass Communication,* 9: 110–130.

hooks, bell. 2000. *Feminism is For Everybody: Passionate Politics.* Cambridge, MA: South End Press.

Hurwitz, Heather McKee and Verta Taylor. 2012. "Women's Cultures and Social Movements in Global Contexts." *Sociology Compass,* 6 (10): 808–822.

IBM. 2002. "Discussions With Bolivia's Libertarian Youth." Retrieved May 1, 2007. www.ainfos.ca/02/oct/ainfos00382.html.

Ickibob. 2003. "On the Black Bloc," in *A New World in Our Hearts: Eight Years of Writings from the Love and Rage Revolutionary Anarchist Federation,* pp. 39–40, edited by R. San Filippo. Oakland, CA: AK Press.

INCITE! 2007. *The Revolution Will Not Be Funded: Beyond the Non-profit Industrial Complex.* Cambridge, MA: South End Press.

Ingalsbee, Timothy. 1996. "Earth First! Activism: Ecological Postmodern Praxis in Radical Environmentalist Identities." *Sociological Perspectives* 39 (2): 263–276.

Inglehart, Ronald. 1990. *Culture Shift in Advanced Industrial Society.* Princeton, NJ: Princeton University Press.

International Blacklist. 1983. *International Blacklist: An Anti-Authoritarian Directory.* Berkeley, CA: Anti-Authoritarian Studies.

Jaworski, Gary Dean. 1993. "Pitirim A. Sorokin's Sociological Anarchism." *History of the Human Sciences,* 6 (3): 61–77.

Jensen, Richard Bach. 1981. "The International Anti-Anarchist Conference of 1898 and the Origins of Interpol." *Journal of Contemporary History,* 16 (2): 323–347.

Jensen, Richard Bach. 2014. *The Battle Against Anarchism Terrorism: An International History.* New York: Cambridge University Press.

Jeppesen, Sandra, Anna Kruzynski, Rachel Sarrasin, and Émilie Breton. 2014. "The Anarchist Commons." *Ephemera: Theory & Politics in Organization,* 14 (4): 879–900.

Johnston, H. and Lio, S. 1998. "Collective Behavior and Social Movements in the Postmodern Age: Looking Backward to Look Forward." *Sociological Perspectives,* 41 (3): 453–472.

Joll, James. 1964. *The Anarchists.* Boston: Atlantic Monthly Press.

Juris, Jeffrey S. 2008. *Networking Futures: The Movements Against Corporate Globalization.* Durham, NC: Duke University Press.

Kahn, Joseph. 2000. "Anarchism, the Creed That Won't Stay Dead." *New York Times,* August 5.

Kanaan, Ramsey. 2004. "How One Small Scottish Anarchist Group Toppled the Thatcher Government," in *Globalize Liberation: How to Uproot the System and Build a Better World,* pp. 397–410, edited by D. Solnit. San Francisco, CA: City Lights Books.

Karamichas, John. 2009. "The December 2008 Riots in Greece." *Social Movement Studies*, 8 (3), August: 289–293.

Karlekar, Karin Deutsch. 2005. *Freedom of the Press 2005: A Global Survey of Media Independence*. New York: Freedom House.

Katsiaficas, George. 1987. *The Imagination of the New Left: A Global Analysis of 1968*. Boston: South End Press.

Katsiaficas, George. 1997. *The Subversion of Politics: European Autonomous Social Movements and the Decolonization of Everyday Life*. Atlantic Highlands, NJ: Humanities Press.

Katsiaficas, Georgy. 2006. *The Subversion of Politics: European Autonomous Social Movements And The Decolonization Of Everyday Life*. Oakland, CA: AK Press.

Katsiaficas, George. 2013. *Unknown Asian Uprisings: People Power in the Philippines, Burma, Tibet, China, Taiwan, Bangladesh, Nepal, Thailand, and Indonesia, 1947–2009*. Oakland, CA: PM Press.

Katz, Neil H. and David C. List. 1981. "Seabrook: A Profile of Anti-Nuclear Activists, June 1978." *Peace and Change*, 7 (3), Spring: 59–70.

Kellerman, Aharon. 2004. "Internet Access and Penetration: An International Urban Comparison." *Journal of Urban Technology*, 11 (3): 63–85.

Kitschelt, Herbert. 1986. "Political Opportunity Structures and Political Protest: Anti-Nuclear Movements in Four Democracies." *British Journal of Political Science*, 16 (1): 57–85.

Klandermans, Bert and Jackie Smith. 2002. "Survey Research: A Case for Comparative Designs," in *Methods of Social Movement Research*, pp. 3–31, edited by B. Klandermans and S. Staggenborg. Minneapolis, MN: University of Minnesota Press.

Klein, Naomi. 1999. *No Logo: No Space, No Jobs, No Choice*. New York: Picador.

Kneen, Peter. 2000. "Political Corruption in Russia and the Soviet Legacy." *Crime, Law, & Social Change*, 34 (4): 349–367.

Knoll, Stefanie and Aragorn Eloff. 2010. *2010 Anarchist Survey Report*. Self-published.

Knutter, Hans-Helmuth. 1995. "The 'Antifascism' of 'Autonomen' and Anarchists." *Telos*, 105, Fall: 36–42.

Koch, Nadine S. and Jolly A. Emrey. 2001. "The Internet and Opinion Measurement: Surveying Marginalized Populations." *Social Science Quarterly*, 82 (1), March: 131–138.

Konrath, Sara H., Edward H. O'Brien, and Courtney Hsing. 2011. "Changes in Dispositional Empathy in American College Students Over Time: A Meta-Analysis." *Personality and Social Psychology Review*, 15: 180–198.

Konvička, Libor and Jan Kavan. 1994. "Youth Movements and the Velvet Revolution." *Communist and Post-Communist Studies*, 27 (2): 160–176.

Kornbluh, Joyce. 1998. *Rebel Voices: An IWW Anthology*. Chicago: Charles H Kerr Publishing.

Kornegger, Peggy. 2002. "Anarchism: The Feminist Connection," in *Quiet Rumours: An Anarcha-Feminist Reader*, pp. 21–31, edited by Dark Star. Edinburgh: AK Press.

Kropotkin, Peter. 1972. *Mutual Aid: A Factor in Evolution*. London: Allen Lane.

Kropotkin, Peter. 2006. *Mutual Aid: A Factor in Evolution*. Mineola, NY: Dover.

Kubey, Robert and Mihaly Csikszentmihalyi. 2004. "Television Addiction is No Mere Metaphor." *Scientific American*, 14 (1): 48–55.

Kucera, David. 2005. "Measuring Trade Union Rights: A Country-Level Indicator Constructed from Coding Violations Recorded in Textual Sources." Geneva: International Labour Organization.

Lacey, Anita. 2005. "Spaces of Justice: The Social Divine of Global Anti-Capital Activists' Sites of Resistance." *Canadian Review of Sociology & Anthropology*, 42 (4): 403–420.

Law, Victoria and China Martens. 2012. *Don't Leave Your Friends Behind: Concrete Ways to Support Families in Social Justice Movements and Communities.* Oakland, CA: PM Press.

Lee, GangHeong, Joseph N. Cappella, and Brian Southwell. 2003. "The Effects of News and Entertainment on Interpersonal Trust: Political Talk Radio, Newspapers, and Television." *Mass Communication & Society*, 6 (4): 413–434.

Le Guin, Ursula K. 1975. *The Dispossessed*. New York: Avon Books.

Lerner, Michael. 1970. "Anarchism and the American Counter-Culture." *Government and Opposition*, 5 (4), August: 430–455.

Levi, Margaret and Laura Stoker. 2000. "Political Trust and Trustworthiness." *Annual Review of Political Science*, 3: 475–507.

Levin, Murray. 1971. *Political Hysteria in America: The Democratic Capacity for Repression*. New York: Basic Books.

Levy, Carl. 2004. "Anarchism, Internationalism and Nationalism in Europe, 1860–1939." *Australian Journal of Politics and History*, 50 (3): 330–342.

Lo, Clarence Y.H. 1982. "Countermovements and Conservative Movements in the Contemporary U.S.." *Annual Review of Sociology*, 8: 107–134.

Lofland, John. 1988. "Interactionism as Anarchism." *SSSI Notes*, 14 (3), March: 5–6.

Lofland, John. 1993. "Theory-bashing and Answer-Improving in the Study of Social Movements." *American Sociologist*, 24 (2), Summer: 37–58.

Lofland, John. 1996. "Students' Case Studies of Social Movements: Experiences with an Undergraduate Seminar." *Teaching Sociology*, 24 (4): 389–394.

London, Jonathan K. 1998. "Common Roots and Entangled Limbs: Earth First! And the Growth of Post-Wilderness Environmentalism on California's North Coast." *Antipode*, 30 (2): 155–176.

Luhmann, Niklas. 1979. *Trust and Power: Two Works*. Chichester: John Wiley & Sons.

Luke, Timothy W. 1994. "Ecological Politics and Local Struggles: Earth First! As An Environmental Resistance Movement." *Current Perspectives in Social Theory* 14: 241–267.

Lynd, Staughton and Andrej Grubacic. 2008. *Wobblies & Zapatistas: Conversations on Anarchism, Marxism and Radical History*. Oakland, PM Press.

MacPhee, Josh and Erik Reuland. 2007. *Realizing the Impossible: Art Against Authority*. Oakland, CA: AK Press.

Maiba, Hermann. 2005. "Grassroots Transnational Social Movement Activism: The Case of Peoples' Global Action." *Sociological Focus*, 38 (1), February: 41–63.

Makrygianni, Vaso and Haris Tsavdaroglou. 2011. "Urban Planning and Revolt: A Spatial Analysis of the December 2008 Uprising in Athens," in *Revolt and Crisis in Greece: Between a Present Yet to Pass a Future Still to Come*, pp. 29–57, edited by A. Vradis and D. Dalakoglou. Oakland, CA: AK Press.

Malatesta, Erricco. 1974. *Anarchy*. London: Freedom Press.

Marcos, Subcommandante. 2001. *Our Word is Our Weapon: Selected Writings*. New York: Seven Stories Press.

Marshall, Monty G. and Keith Jaggers. 2005. *POLITY IV Project: Political Regime Characteristics and Transitions, 1800–2004*. Arlington, VA: Center for Global Policy, George Mason University.

Marshall, Peter. 2010. *Demanding the Impossible: A History of Anarchism*. Oakland, CA: PM Press.

Martin, Brian. 1990. "Democracy Without Elections." *Social Alternatives*, 8 (4), January: 13–18.

Martin, Brian. 1998a. *Tied Knowledge: Power in Higher Education*. www.bmartin.cc/pubs/98tk/.

Martin, Brian. 1998b. *Information Liberation*. London: Freedom.

Martin, Carolina. 2007. "Creating Another World, One Bit At a Time: Understanding Anti-Globalization Resistance." Conference presentation at the American Sociological Association Annual Meetings, New York.

Martin, Greg. 2004. "New Social Movements and Democracy." In *Democracy and Participation: Popular Protest and New Social Movements*, edited by M. J. Todd and G. Taylor, 29–54. London: Marlin Press.

Martínez, Miguel. 2007. "The Squatters' Movement: Urban Counter-Culture and Alter-Globalization Dynamics." *South European Society & Politics*, 12 (3), September: 379–398.

Maximoff, G. P. 1953. *The Political Philosophy of Bakunin: Scientific Anarchism*. Glencoe, IL: The Free Press.

Mayer, Gerald. 2004. *Union Membership Trends in the United States*. Washington, DC: Congressional Research Service. http://digitalcommons.ilr.cornell.edu/cgi/viewcontent.cgi?article=1176&context=key_workplace.

Mayer, Margit. 2003. "The Onward Sweep of Social Capital: Causes and Consequences for Understanding Cities, Communities, and Urban Movements." *International Journal of Urban and Regional Research*, 27 (1): 110–132.

Mbah, Sam and I. E. Igariwey. 1997. *African Anarchism: The History of a Movement*. Tucson, AZ: See Sharp Press.

McAdam, Doug. 1982. *Political Process and the Development of Black Insurgency, 1930–1970*. Chicago: University of Chicago Press.

McAdam, Doug. 1996. "Conceptual Origins, Current Problems, Future Directions," in *Comparative Perspectives on Social Movements: Political Opportunities, Mobilizing Structures, and Cultural Framings*, pp. 23–40, edited by D. McAdam, J. D. McCarthy, and M. N. Zald. Cambridge: Cambridge University Press.

McAdam, Doug and Sidney Tarrow. 2011. "Introduction: *Dynamics of Contention* Ten Years On." *Mobilization*, 16 (1): 1–10.

McAdam, Doug, Sidney Tarrow, and Charles Tilly. 2001. *Dynamics of Contention*. Cambridge: Cambridge University Press.

McCarthy, John D. and Mayer N. Zald. 1977. "Resource Mobilization and Social Movements: A Partial Theory." *American Journal of Sociology*, 82 (6), May: 1212–1241.

McCarthy, John D., Clark McPhail, and Jackie Smith. 1996. "Images of Protest: Dimensions of Selection Bias in Media Coverage of Washington Demonstrations, 1982 and 1991." *American Sociological Review*, 61 (3): 478–499.

McGowan, Rory. 2003. "Claim No Easy Victories: Anarchist Analysis of ARA and its Contributions to the Building of a Radical Anti-Racist Movement." *Northeastern Anarchist*, 7, Summer.

McKay, Iain. 2008. *An Anarchist FAQ: Volume 1*. Edinburgh: AK Press.

McKay, Iain (ed.). 2014. *Direct Struggle Against Capital: A Peter Kropotkin Anthology*. Edinburgh: AK Press.

McLeod, Douglas M. and Benjamin H. Detenber. 1999. "Framing Effects of Television News Coverage of Social Protest." *Journal of Communication*, 49 (3): 3–23.

McLeod, Douglas M. and James K. Hertog. 1992. "The Manufacture of 'Public Opinion' by Reporters: Informal Cues for Public Perceptions of Protest Groups." *Discourse & Society*, 3 (3): 259–275.

Mead, George Herbert. 1964. *George Herbert Mead on Social Psychology*. Chicago: University of Chicago Press.

Meltzer, Albert. 1996. *Anarchism: Arguments For and Against*. Edinburgh: AK Press.

Melucci, Alberto. 1989. *Nomads of the Presents: Social Movements and Individual Needs in Contemporary Society*. Philadelphia: Temple University Press.

Melucci, Alberto. 1993. "Paradoxes of Post-Industrial Democracy: Everyday Life and Social Movements." *Berkeley Journal of Sociology*, 38: 185–192.

Melucci, Alberto. 1996. *Challenging Codes: Collective Action in the Information Age*. Cambridge: Cambridge University Press.

Meyer, David S. 2004. "Protest and Political Opportunities." *Annual Review of Sociology*, 30: 125–145.

Michels, Robert. 1949. *Political Parties: A Sociological Study of the Oligarchical Tendencies of Modern Democracy*. Glencoe, IL: Free Press.

Mills, C. Wright. 1959. *The Sociological Imagination*. Oxford: Oxford University Press.

Mills, Kathryn and Pamela Mills. 2001. *C. Wright Mills: Letters and Autobiographical Writings*. Berkeley, CA: University of California Press.

Milstein, Cindy. 2010. *Anarchism and Its Aspirations*. Oakland, CA: AK Press.

Mintz, Frank. 2013. *Anarchism and Workers' Self-Management in Revolutionary Spain*. Oakland, CA: AK Press.

Molland, Noel. 2006. "A Spark That Ignited a Flame: The Evolution of the Earth Liberation Front," *Igniting a Revolution: Voices in Defense of the Earth*, pp. 47–58, in edited by S. Best and A. J. Nocella. Oakland, CA: AK Press.

Monaghan, Jeffrey and Kevin Walby. 2012. "'They Attacked the City': Security Intelligence, the Sociology of Protest Policing and the Anarchist Threat at the 2010 Toronto G20 Summit." *Current Sociology*, 60 (5): 653–671.

Moore, Barrington. 1972. *Reflections on the Causes of Human Misery and Upon Certain Proposals to Eliminate Them*. Boston: Beacon Press.

Morrison, Denton E. 1971. "Some Notes Toward Theory on Relative Deprivation, Social Movements, and Social Change." *American Behavioral Scientist*, 14 (5), May: 675–690.

Mudu, Pierpaolo. 2004. "Resisting and Challenging Neoliberalism: The Development of Italian Social Centers." *Antipode*, 36 (5): 917–941.

Mumm, James. 1998. *Active Revolution*. http://www.infoshop.org/texts/active_revolution.html

Nachie. 2006. "Notes on the Anarchist Movement in Caracas." Retrieved May 1, 2007. www.ainfos.ca/06/jul/ainfos00085.html.

Nannestad, Peter. 2008. "What Have We Learned About Generalized Trust, If Anything?." *Annual Review of Political Science*, 11: 413–436.

NEFAC. n.d. "The Constitution of the Northeastern Federation of Anarcho-Communists (NEFAC)." Available online: www.nefac.net/node/105.

Nepstad, Sharon Erickson and Clifford Bob. 2006. "When Do Leaders Matter? Hypotheses on Leadership in Social Movements." *Mobilization*, 11 (1), March: 1–22.

Nettlau, Max. 1996. *A Short History of Anarchism*. London: Freedom Press.

Nettlau, Max. 2001. "Anarchism: Communist or Individualist? – Both." In *Anarchy! An Anthology of Emma Goldman's Mother Earth*, edited by Peter Glassnold, 79–83. Washington, DC: Counterpoint.

Niman, Michael I. 2011. "Rainbow Family Peacekeeping Strategies." *Contemporary Justice Review*, 14 (1), March: 65–76.

Northeast Ohio Radical Action Network (NEO-RAN) electronic mailing list. Yahoo!Groups.

Notes From Nowhere. 2003. *We Are Everywhere: The Irresistible Rise of Global Anti-Capitalism*. London: Verso.

O'Brien, Eileen. 1999. "Mind, Heart and Action: Understanding the Dimensions of Antiracism." *Research in Politics and Society*, 6: 305–321.

O'Brien, Eileen. 2001. *Whites Confront Racism: Antiracists and Their Paths to Action*. Lanham, MD: Rowman & Littlefield.

O'Connor, Alan. 1999. "Whos Emma and the Limits of Cultural Studies." *Cultural Studies*, 13 (4): 691–702.

O'Connor, Alan. 2003a. "Anarcho-Punk: Local Scenes and International Networks." *Anarchist Studies*, 11 (2): 111–121.

O'Connor, Alan. 2003b. "Punk Subculture in Mexico and the Anti-globalization Movement: A Report from the Front." *New Political Science*, 25 (1): 43–53.

O'Connor, Alan. 2004. "Punk and Globalization: Spain and Mexico." *International Journal of Cultural Studies*, 7 (2): 175–195.

O'Hara, Craig. 1999. *The Philosophy of Punk: More Than Noise*. San Francisco: AK Press.

Oliver, Pamela E. and Hank Johnston. 2000. "What a Good Idea! Ideologies and Frames in Social Movement Research." *Mobilization*, 5 (1): 37–54.

Olofsson, Gunnar. 1988. "After the Working-class Movement? An Essay on What's 'New' and What's 'Social' in the New Social Movements." *Acta Sociologica*, 31 (1): 15–34.

Olson, Mancur. 1965. *The Logic of Collective Action: Public Goods and the Theory of Groups*. Cambridge, MA: Harvard University Press.

Olzak, Susan and S. C. Noah Uhrig. 2001. "The Ecology of Tactical Overlap." *American Sociological Review*, 66 (5), October: 694–717.

One Off. 2001. *On Fire: The Battle of Genoa and the Anti-capitalist Movement*. Edinburgh: One Off Press.

Owens, Lynn and L. Kendall Palmer. 2003. "Making the News: Anarchist Counter-Public Relations on the World Wide Web." *Critical Studies in Media Communication* 20 (4), December: 335–361.

Owens, Linus, Ask Katseff, Baptiste Colin, and Elisabeth Lorenzi. 2013. "At Home in the Movement: Constructing an Oppositional Identity through Activist Travel across European Squats," in *Understanding European Movements: New Social Movements, Global Justice Struggles, Anti-Austerity Protest*, pp. 172–186, edited by C. F. Fominaya and L. Cox. London: Routledge.

Pallister-Wilkins, Polly. 2009. "Radical Ground: Israeli and Palestinian Activists and Joint Protest Against the Wall." *Social Movement Studies*, 8 (4), November: 393–407.

Pannekoek, Anton. 2003. *Workers' Councils*. Oakland: AK Press.

Paris, Jeffrey. 2003. "The Black Bloc's Ungovernable Protest." *Peace Review*, 15 (3), September: 317–322.

Pateman, Carole. 1970. *Participation and Democratic Theory*. London: Cambridge University Press.

Patulny, Roger. 2011. "Social Trust, Social Partner Time and Television Time." *Social Indicators Research*, 101: 289–293.

Paxton, Pamela. 2002. "Social Capital and Democracy: An Interdependent Relationship." *American Sociological Review*, 67 (2): 254–277.

Paz, Abel. 2007. *Durruti in the Spanish Revolution*. Oakland, CA: AK Press.

Paz, Abel. 2011. *The Story of the Iron Column: Militant Anarchism in the Spanish Civil War*. London: Kate Sharpley Library.

Peirats, José. 2011. *The CNT in the Spanish Revolution*. Oakland, CA: PM Press.

Perrow, Charles. 1986. *Complex Organizations: A Critical Essay 3/e*. NY: McGraw-Hill.

Peytchev, Andy, Mick P. Couper, Sean Esteban McCabe, and Scott D. Crawford. 2006. Web Survey Design: Paging Versus Scrolling. *Public Opinion Quarterly* 70 (4), Winter: 596–607.

Piano, Aili and Arch Puddington. 2004. *Freedom in the World 2004: The Annual Survey of Political Rights & Civil Liberties*. New York: Freedom House.

Pichardo, Nelson A. 1997. "New Social Movements: A Critical Review." *Annual Review of Sociology*, 23 (1): 411–430.

Pickles, John. 1995. *Ground Truth: The Social Implications of Geographic Information Systems*. New York: Guilford Press.

Piven, Frances Fox and Richard A. Cloward. 1979. *Poor People's Movements: Why They Succeed, How They Fail*. New York: Vintage.

Polletta, Francesca. 1999. "'Free Spaces' in Collective Action." *Theory & Society*, 28 (1): 1–38.

Polletta, Francesca. 2002. *Freedom is an Endless Meeting: Democracy in American Social Movement*. Chicago: University of Chicago Press.

Powell, Water W. 1990. "The Transformation of Organizational Forms: How Useful is Organization Theory in Accounting for Social Change," in *Beyond the Marketplace: Rethinking Economy and Society*, pp. 301–329, edited by R. Friedland and A. F. Robertson. New York: Aldine de Gruyter.

Proudhon, Joseph-Pierre. 2011. *Property is Theft! A Pierre-Joseph Proudhon Anthology*. Oakland, CA: AK Press.

Purchase, Graham. 1994. *Anarchism & Environmental Survival*. Tucson, AZ: Sharp Press.

Purchase, Graham. 1997. *Anarchism and Ecology*. Montreal: Black Rose Books.

Purkis, Jonathan. 2004. "Towards an Anarchist Sociology," in *Changing Anarchism: Anarchist Theory and Practice in a Global Age*, pp. 39–54, edited by J. Purkis and J. Bowen. Manchester: Manchester University Press.

Putnam, Robert D. 2000. *Bowling Alone: The Collapse and Revival of American Community*. New York: Simon & Schuster.

Ramnath, Maia. 2011. *Decolonizing Anarchism*. Oakland, CA: AK Press.

Renshaw, Patrick. 1968. "The IWW and the Red Scare 1917–24." *Journal of Contemporary History*, 3 (4): 63–72.

Renz, Katie. 2005. "A Tradition of Resistance." *clamor*, 32: 14–16.

Rothbard, Murray N. 2007. *The Betrayal of the American Right*. Auburn, AL: Ludwig von Mises Institute.

Robinson, Christine M. 2008. "Order in Chaos: Security Culture as Anarchist Resistance to the Terrorist Label." *Deviant Behavior*, 29: 225–252.

Robinson, Christine. 2009. "The Continuing Significance of Class: Confronting Capitalism in an Anarchist Community." *Working USA: The Journal of Labor & Society*, 12 (3), September: 355–370.

Robinson, J. Gregg. 1988. American Unions in Decline: Problems and Prospects. *Critical Sociology* 15: 33–56.

Rocker, Rudolf. 1990. *Anarcho-Syndicalism*. London: Phoenix Press.

Rocker, Rudolf. 2004. *Anarcho-Syndicalism: Theory and Practice*. Edinburgh: AK Press.

Rootes, Christopher. 1999. "Environmental Movements: From the Local to the Global." *Environmental Politics*, 8 (1), Spring: 1–12.

Roseland, Mark. 1997. *Eco-City Dimensions: Healthy Communities, Healthy Planet*. Gabriola Island, BC: New Society Publishers.

Rosemont, Franklin. 2005. "The Legacy of the Hoboes: What Rebel Workers Today Can Learn From the Footloose Wobblies of Yesteryear." *Working USA: The Journal of Labor and Society*, 8, September: 593–610.

Rosie, Michael and Hugo Gorringe. 2009. "'The Anarchists' World Cup': Respectable Protest and Media Panics." *Social Movement Studies*, 8 (1), January: 35–53.

Rothschild-Whitt, Joyce. 1979. "The Collectivist Organization: An Alternative to Rational-Bureaucratic Models." *American Sociological Review*, 44, August: 509–527.

Routledge, Paul. 2003. "Convergence Spaces: Process Geographies of Grassroots Globalization Networks." *Transactions of the Institute of British Geographers*, 28 (3): 333–349.

Roy, Ananya. 2003. "Paradigms of Propertied Citizenship: Transnational Techniques of Analysis." *Urban Affairs Review*, 38 (4), March: 463–491.

Ruff, Philip. 1991. *Anarchy in the USSR*. London: ASP.

Ruggiero, Vincenzo. 2000. "New Social Movements and the 'Centri Sociali' in Milan." *Sociological Review*, 48 (2), May: 167–185.

Ruggiero, Vincenzo and Nicola Montagna. 2008. *Social Movements: A Reader*. London: Routledge.

Ryan, Ramor. 2006. *Clandestines: The Pirate Journals of an Irish Exile*. Oakland, CA: AK Press.

Sabatini, Peter Joseph. 1996. *The Marginalization of Anarchism*. Unpublished dissertation. University of California, Irvine.

Sale, Kirkatrick. 1973. *SDS*. New York: Random House.

Sanderson, Stephen K. 2005. *Revolutions: A Worldwide Introduction to Political and Social Change*. Boulder, CO: Paradigm.

Scarce, Rik. 2006. *Eco-Warriors: Understanding the Radical Environmental Movement*. Walnut Creek, CA: Left Coast Press.

Schlembach, Raphael. 2013. "The 'Autonomous Nationalists': New Developments and Contradictions in the German Neo-Nazi Movement." *Interface: A Journal For and About Social Movements*, 5 (2): 295–318.

Schlosser, Eric. 2002. *Fast Food Nation: The Dark Side of the All-American Meal*. New York: Perennial.

Schmidt, Michael. 2013. *Cartography of Revolutionary Anarchism*. Oakland, CA: AK Press.

Schmidt, Michael and Lucien van der Walt. 2009. *Black Flame: The Revolutionary Class Politics of Anarchism and Syndicalism*. Oakland: AK Press.

Schneider, Nathan. 2013. *Thank You, Anarchy: Notes From the Occupy Apocalypse*. Berkeley, CA: University of California Press.

Schock, Kurt. 1999. "People Power and Political Opportunities: Social Movement Mobilization and Outcomes in the Philippines and Burma." *Social Problems*, 46 (3): 355–375.

Shantz, Jeff. 2002a. "Green Syndicalism: An Alternative Red-Green Vision." *Environmental Politics*, 11 (4), Winter: 21–41.

Shantz, Jeffrey. 2002b. "Judi Bari and 'the Feminization of Earth First!': The Convergence of Class, Gender and Radical Environmentalism." *Feminist Review* 70: 105–122.

Shantz, Jeff. 2003a. "Seize the Switches: TAO Communications, Media, and Anarchy," in *Representing Resistance: Media, Civil Disobedience, and the Global Justice Movement*, pp. 209–223, edited by A. Opel and D. Pompper. Westport, CT: Praeger.

Shantz, Jeff. 2003b. "Beyond the State: The Return to Anarchy." *disClosure: A Journal of Social Theory*, 12: 87–103.

Shantz, Jeff. 2010. *Constructive Anarchy: Building Infrastructures of Resistance*. Burlington, VT: Ashgate.

Shantz, Jeff. 2012. *Green Syndicalism: An Alternative Red/Green Vision*. Syracuse, NY: Syracuse University Press.

Shantz, Jeffrey A. and Barry D. Adam. 1999. "Ecology and Class: The Green Syndicalism of IWW/Earth First Local 1." *International Journal of Sociology and Social Policy*, 19 (7/8): 43–72.

Shantz, Jeff and Dana M. Williams. 2013. *Anarchy and Society: Reflections on Anarchist-Sociology*. Leiden, Netherlands: Brill.

Sheppard, Brian Oliver. 2002. "Anarchism and the Labor Movement." Retrieved: August 20, 2004. www.zmag.org/content/showarticle.cfm?SectionID=41& ItemID=2188.

Shepard, Benjamin. 2011. *Play, Creativity, and Social Movements: If I Can't Dance, It's Not My Revolution*. New York: Routledge.

Simon, S. Fanny. 1946. "Anarchism and Anarcho-Syndicalism in South America." *The Hispanic American Historical Review*, 26 (1), February: 38–59.

Skirda, Alexandre. 2002. *Facing the Enemy: A History of Anarchist Organization from Proudhon to May 1968*. Edinburgh: AK Press.

Skocpol, Theda. 1979. *States and Social Revolutions: A Comparative Analysis of France, Russia, and China*. Cambridge: Cambridge University Press.

Slaèálek, Ondøej. 2002. "Brief History of the Czech Anarchism." Retrieved May 1, 2007. www.ainfos.ca/02/nov/ainfos00698.html.

Smith, Jackie. 1998. "Global Civil Society?: Transnational Social Movement Organizations and Social Capital." *American Behavioral Scientist*, 42 (1): 93–107.

Smith, Jackie. 2004. "Exploring Connections Between Global Integration and Political Mobilization." *Journal of World-Systems Research*, 10 (1): 255–285.

Smith, Jackie. 2008. *Social Movements for Global Democracy*. Baltimore, MD: The Johns Hopkins University Press.

Smelser, Neil. 1963. *Theory of Collective Behavior*. Glencoe, IL: Free Press.

Snow, David A., E. Burke Rochford, Steven K. Worden, and Robert D. Benford. 1986. "Frame Alignment Processes, Micromobilization, and Movement Participation." *American Sociological Review*, 51 (4): 464–481.

Snow, David A. and Robert D. Benford. 1988. "Ideology, Frame Resonance, and Participant Mobilization." *International Social Movement Research*, 1: 197–217.

Snow, David A. and Robert D. Benford 1999. "Alternative Types of Cross-National Diffusion in the Social Movement Arena., in *Social Movements in a Globalizing World*, pp. 23–39, edited by D. della Porta, H. Kriesi, and D. Rucht. New York: Palgrave Macmillan.

Snow, David A. and Sarah A. Soule. 2010. *A Primer on Social Movements*. New York: Norton.

Snow, David A., Sarah A. Soule, and Daniel M. Cress. 2005. "Identifying the Precipitants of Homeless Protest Across 17 U.S. Cities, 1980 to 1990." *Social Forces*, 83 (3): 1183–1210.

Snyders, Matt. 2008. "Skinheads at Forty." *City Pages*, February 20. www.citypages.com/news/skinheads-at-forty-6745568.

Solnit, David and Rebecca Solnit. 2009. *The Battle of the Story of the Battle of Seattle*. Oakland, CA: AK Press.

Sorokin, Pitirim. 1967. *The Sociology of Revolution*. New York: H. Fertig.

Soule, Sarah A. 2007. "Diffusion Processes Within and Across Movements," in *The Blackwell Companion to Social Movements*, pp. 294–310, edited by D. A. Snow, S. A. Soule, and H. Kriesi. Malden, MA: Blackwell.

South Chicago ARA. 1999. *Anti-Racist Action Primer*. Self-published.

Spring, Joel. 1998. *A Primer of Libertarian Education*. Montreal: Black Rose Books.

Stanbridge, Karen. 2006. "Charles Tilly and Sidney Tarrow. Contentious Politics." *Canadian Journal of Sociology Online*, December.

Stanley, Thomas A. 1978. *A Japanese Anarchist's Rejection of Marxism-Leninism: Õsugi Sakae and the Russian Revolution*. Western Conference of the Association for Asian Studies.

Starr, Amory. 2006. "'Excepting Barricades Erected to Prevent Us From Peacefully Assembling': So-Called 'Violence' in the Global North Alterglobalization Movement." *Social Movement Studies*, 5 (1), May: 61–81.

St. John, Graham. 2008. "Protestival: Global Days of Action and Carnivalized Politics in the Present." *Social Movement Studies*, 7 (2), September: 167–190.

Sturmthal, Adolf. 1972. *Comparative Labor Movement: Ideological Roots and Institutional Development*. Belmont, CA: Wadsworth.

Sunshine, Spencer. 2008. "Rebranding Fascism: National-Anarchists." *The Public Eye*, 23 (4): 1, 12–19.

Sunshine, Spencer. 2013. *Post-1960 U.S. Anarchism and Social Theory*. New York: CUNY Graduate Center. Unpublished dissertation.

Sutton, Philip W. and Stephen Vertigans. 2006. "Islamic 'New Social Movements'? Radical Islam, Al-Qa'ida and Social Movement Theory." *Mobilization: An International Journal*, 11 (1), March: 101–115.

Tarrow, Sidney. 1998. *Power in Movement: Social Movements and Contentious Politics*. Cambridge: Cambridge University Press.

Tarrow, Sidney. 2010. "Dynamics of Diffusion: Mechanisms, Institutions, and Scale Shift," in *The Diffusion of Social Movements: Actors, Mechanisms, and Political Effects*, pp. 204–219, edited by R. K. Givan, K. M. Roberts, and S. A. Soule. Cambridge: Cambridge University Press.

Thompson, AK. 2010. *Black Bloc, White Riot: Anti-Globalization and the Genealogy of Dissent*. Oakland, CA: AK Press.

Threat, Alphabet. n.d. "What It Is Like To Be a Girl in an Anarchist Boys Club." www.spunk.org/texts/anarcfem/sp000168.html

Tilly, Charles. 1978. *From Mobilization to Revolution*. Reading, MA: Addison-Wesley.

Tilly, Charles. 2004. *Social Movements: 1768–2004*. Boulder, CO: Paradigm.

Tilly, Charles and Lesley J. Wood. 2009. *Social Movements, 1768–2008*, 2nd edition. Boulder, CO: Paradigm.

Touraine, Alain. 1981. *The Voice and the Eye: An Analysis of Social Movements*. Cambridge: Cambridge University Press.

Touraine, Alain. 1984. "Social Movements: Special Area or Central Problem in Sociological Analysis?." *Thesis Eleven*, 9, July: 5–15.

Tsuzuki, Chushichi. 1970. "Anarchism in Japan." *Government and Opposition*, 5 (4), Autumn: 501–522.

Tucker, Kenneth H. 1991. "How New are the New Social Movements?" *Theory, Culture & Society*, 8: 75–98.

Turcato, Davide. 2014. *The Method of Freedom: An Errico Malatesta Reader*. Oakland, CA: AK Press.

Turner, Scott. 2009. "Anarchist Theory and Human Rights," in *New Perspectives on Anarchism*, pp. 133–146, edited by N. J. Jun and S. Wahl. Lanham, MD: Lexington.

Twenge, Jean M. and Joshua D. Foster. 2010. "Birth Cohort Increases in Narcissistic Personality Traits Among American College Students, 1982–2009" *Social Psychological and Personality Science*, 1: 99–106.

Uitermark, J. 2004. "Looking Forward by Looking Back: May Day Protests in London and the Strategic Significance of the Urban." *Antipode*, 36 (4), September: 706–727.

van der Steen, Bart, Ask Katzeff, and Leendert van Hoogenhuijze. 2014. *The City Is Ours: Squatting and Autonomous Movements in Europe From the 1970s to the Present*. Oakland, CA: PM Press.

van der Walt, Lucien and Michael Schmidt. 2009. *Black Flame: The Revolutionary Class Politics of Anarchism and Syndicalism*. Edinburgh: AK Press.

van Dyke, Nella, Sarah A. Soule, and Verta A. Taylor. 2004. "The Targets of Social Movements: Beyond a Focus on the State." *Research in Social Movements, Conflicts and Change*, 25: 27–51.

Wagner, David G. and Joseph Berger. 1985. "Do Sociological Theories Grow?" *American Journal of Sociology*, 90 (4): 697–728.

Wall, Melissa A. 2007. "Social Movements and Email: Expressions of Online Identity in the Globalization Protests." *New Media & Society*, 9 (2): 258–277.

Wallerstein, Immanuel. 1974. *The Modern World-System I: Capitalist Agriculture and the Origins of the European World-Economy in the Sixteenth Century.* New York: Academic Press.

Wallerstein, Immanuel. 1980. *The Modern World System II: Mercantilism and the Consolidation of the European World-Economy, 1600–1750.* New York: Academic Press.

Wallerstein, Immanuel. 1989. *The Modern World-System III: The Second Era of Great Expansion of the Capitalist World-Economy, 1730s-1840s.* San Diego: Academic Press.

Wallerstein, Immanuel. 2003. *The Decline of American Power.* New York: New Press.

Wallerstein, Immanuel. 2004. *World-Systems Analysis: An Introduction.* Durham, NC: Duke University Press.

Ward, Colin. 1996. *Anarchy in Action.* London: Freedom Press.

Weber, Max. 2011. *Methodology of Social Sciences.* New Brunswick, NJ: Transaction.

Welsh, Ian. 1997. "Anarchism, Social Movements, and Sociology." *Anarchist Studies*, 5 (2), October: 162–168.

Welsh, Ian and Phil McLeish. 1996. "The European Road to Nowhere: Anarchism and Direct Action Against the UK Roads Programme." *Anarchist Studies*, 4: 27–44.

Western, Simon. 2014. "Autonomist Leadership in Leaderless Movements: Anarchists Leading the Way." *Ephemera: Theory & Politics in Organization*, 14 (4): 673–698.

Widick, Richard. 2009. *Trouble in the Forest: California's Redwood Timber Wars.* Minneapolis, MN: University of Minnesota Press.

Williams, Dana M. 2009a. "An Anarchist-Sociologist Research Program: Fertile Areas for Theoretical and Empirical Research," in *New Perspectives on Anarchism*, pp. 243–266, edited by Nathan J. Jun and Shane Wahl. Lanham, MD: Lexington Books.

Williams, Dana M. 2009b. "Red vs. Green: Regional Variation of Anarchist Ideology in the United States." *Journal of Political Ideologies*, 14 (2), June: 189–210.

Williams, Dana M. 2009c. "Anarchists and Labor Unions: An Analysis Using New Social Movement Theories." *Working USA: The Journal of Labor and Society*, 12 (3), September: 337–354.

Williams, Dana M. 2011a. "The Anarchist DNA of Occupy." *Contexts*, 11 (2), Spring: 19–20.

Williams, Dana M. 2011b. "Why Revolution Ain't Easy: Violating Norms, Resocializing Society." *Contemporary Justice Review*, 14 (2), June: 167–187.

Williams, Dana M. 2012. "From Top to Bottom, a Thoroughly Stratified World: An Anarchist View of Inequality and Domination." *Race, Gender & Class*, 19 (3–4): 9–34.

Williams, Dana M. 2014. "A Society in Revolt or Under Analysis? Investigating the Dialogue Between Nineteenth Century Anarchists and Sociologists." *Critical Sociology*, 40 (3), May: 469–492.

Williams, Dana M. 2015. "Black Panther Radical Factionalization and the Development of Black Anarchism." *Journal of Black Studies*, 46 (7), October: 678–703.

Williams, Dana M. and Matthew T. Lee. 2008. "'We Are Everywhere': An Ecological
Analysis of Organizations in the Anarchist Yellow Pages." *Humanity & Society*,
32 (1), February: 45–70.

Williams, Dana M. and Jeff Shantz. 2011. "Defining an Anarchist-Sociology: A
Long-Anticipated Marriage." *Theory in Action*, 4 (4), October: 9–30.

Williams, Dana and Jeffrey Shantz. 2016. "An Anarchist in the Academy, a Sociologist in the Movement: The Life, Activism, and Ideas of Howard J. Ehrlich."
Journal for the Study of Radicalism, 10 (2): 101–122.

Wollstonecraft, Mary. 1999. *Vindication of the Rights of Woman, Vindication of
the Rights of Man*. Oxford: Oxford University Press.

Wood, Lesley J. 2005. "Bridging the Chasm: The Case of Peoples' Global Action," in
Coalitions Across Borders: Transnational Protest and the Neoliberal Order, pp.
95–117, edited by J. Brandy and J. Smith. Lanham, MD: Rowman & Littlefield.

Wood, Lesley J. 2007. "Breaking the Wave: Repression, Identity, and Seattle Tactics."
Mobilization, 12 (4), December: 377–388.

Woodcock, George. 1962. *Anarchism: A History of Libertarian Ideas and Movements*. Cleveland: Meridian.

World Bank. 2006. *2006 Information & Communications for Development: Global
Trends and Policies*. Washington, DC: The World Bank. www.worldbank.org/
ic4d.

Wright, Erik Olin. 1997. *Class Counts: Comparative Studies in Class Analysis*. New
York: Cambridge University Press.

Wright, Nathan. 2003. "Chaos, Organization, and Imagined Community: An Ethnography of an Anarchist Collective." American Sociological Association annual
meetings.

WSM. 2008. "WSM Talk On the history of Japanese Anarchism." Retrieved May
1, 2007. www.ainfos.ca/en/ainfos20822.html.

Zerzan, John. 1974. "Organized Labor Versus 'The Revolt Against Work': The Critical Contest." *Telos*, 21, Fall: 194–206.

Zibechi, Raúl. 2012. *Territories in Resistance: A Cartography of Latin American
Social Movements*. Oakland, CA: AK Press.

Zimmer, Kenyon. 2009. "Premature Anti-Communists?: American Anarchism, the
Russian Revolution, and Left-Wing Libertarian Anti-Communism, 1917–1939."
Labor: Studies in Working Class History of the Americas, 6 (2): 45–71.

Zinn, Howard. 1995. *A Peoples' History of the United States 1492–Present*. New
York: HarperPerennial.

Zinn, Howard. 1997. "Anarchism," in *The Zinn Reader: Writings on Disobedience
and Democracy*, pp. 644–655, edited by H. Zinn. New York: Seven Stories.

Zipp, John F. and Rudy Fenwick. 2007. "Is the Academy a Liberal Hegemony? The
Political Orientations and Educational Values of Professors." *Public Opinion
Quarterly*, 70 (3): 304–326.

INDEX